WORLD WAR 2: THE CALL OF DUTY

A Complete Timeline

LIAM DALE

AUTHOR'S NOTE

If you complete your way entirely through almost 150,000 words, then you will have my gratitude and respect. It's been the biggest book of my life; a roller coaster of emotions to work through while trying my very best to accurately reflect the period of history recorded here.

We now live in times of different conflicts, the global threat of suicide bombers and terrorism at its worse. Limited military activity appears mostly to be afflicted by non-manned drones and missiles. War by remote control. I do hope that the history of WW2 is never repeated and there is never the threat of nuclear bombing again. There are however, a lot of these particularly devastating weapons in the world's arsenal and it takes the action of just a few unstable minds to press a few buttons.

In the alleged words of Mark Twain:

History never repeats itself but sometimes it rhymes.

Liam Dale, September 3rd, 2019 – 80 years to the day after the start of WW2.

Would you please consider leaving a review? Even just a few words would help others decide if the book is right for them.

I've made it super simple: just visit **LiamDale.net/WW2review** and you'll travel to the Amazon review page for this book where you can leave your review.

Best regards and thank you in advance,

Liam

INTRODUCTION

It's easy to look back at the past, study the history of war and uncover dramatic reports of heroic exploits, daring deeds, evil megalomaniacs and vicious dictators, and all too soon you'll find yourself completely detached from such events. The turbulent wars that took place so long ago seem to have little connection with reality, and will in fact often be, the stuff of legend.

Whether you consider the conflicts of the Ancient Greeks, the battles for Troy, or Alexander the Great's conquest for world domination, what we now know often owes more to movie makers of the more recent past's interpretations. War is about heroes, glory and a rip-roaring story, and invariably the true horrors of human conflict are lost in the telling. What's more the adage that history is only ever written by the victors is extremely accurate, or it was, until the wider use of photography and film developed through the course of the 20th Century, painting a very different picture indeed.

So, to really understand the concept of war, on a global scale, the World War II years of 1939 to 1945 provide perhaps the first complete overview of man's inhumanity to man, alongside the bravery and heroism that show the very worst and the very best facets of human nature. Incredibly there are archive images from every stage of this conflict, and as we consider the events of the Second World War chronologically, this book will build into the complete timeline.

THE ROAD TO WAR

September – December 1939

I t's easy to look back at the past, study the history of war and uncover dramatic reports of heroic exploits, daring deeds, evil megalomaniacs and vicious dictators, and all too soon you'll find yourself completely detached from such events. The turbulent wars that took place so long ago seem to have little connection with reality, and will in fact often be, the stuff of legend.

Whether you consider the conflicts of the Ancient Greeks, the battles for Troy, or Alexander the Great's conquest for world domination, what we now know often owes more to movie makers of the more recent past's interpretations. War is about heroes, glory and a rip-roaring story, and invariably the true horrors of human conflict are lost in the telling. What's more the adage that history is only ever written by the victors is extremely accurate, or it was, until the wider use of photography and film developed through the course of the 20th Century, painting a very different picture indeed.

So, to really understand the concept of war, on a global scale, the World War II years of 1939 to 1945 provide perhaps the first complete overview of man's inhumanity to man, alongside the bravery and heroism that show the very worst and the very best facets of human nature. Incredibly there are archive images from every stage of this conflict, and as we consider the events of the Second World War chronologically, this book will build into the complete timeline.

This is our past that we can truly connect with, revealing a history littered with living, breathing survivors who can still tell stories of the comradeship, hardship, suffering and sadly, on occasion, the futility of battle.

However, we are already racing rather ahead of ourselves, because by the very fact of this being a Second World War, the events of the First World War are key to unravelling the whys and wherefores of everything from Adolf Hitler's rise to power in Germany, right through to America's President Truman giving the order to bomb Hiroshima.

The First World War, spanning the years of 1914 to 1918, is often referred to as The Great War, although there was little that was 'great' about it. It was also called the war to end all wars, which is rather a tragic misnomer with the benefit of hindsight. The figures for the casualties are staggering with approximately 40 million people suffering injury on a very personal level, and at least half of these casualties proved to be fatal.

This so-called "Great" War ended with an armistice, at 11am on the eleventh of November, (the eleventh month) 1918, after which the defeated German Empire had its own internal revolution, leading to the end of the monarchy and the setting up of Germany as a republic. Even after the armistice was signed, the victorious forces kept up their blockades around the country. This led to imports and exports being severely reduced, which did little to help Germany to rebuild itself.

In 1919 delegates from all over the world met in Paris to restore a sense of world order, harmony and unity. The main objective was to prevent another War on this scale ever happening again and The League of Nations was formed.

The official treaty that marked the ending of the First World War came a little while after the Paris Peace Conference and formed the backbone of The League of Nations.

The Treaty of Versailles was drawn up by the victorious Allies and signed by all parties on June 28th 1919. But many historians believe that this well-intentioned treaty did more to cause a Second World War, rather than prevent it. Signed in Versailles's magnificent Hall of Mirrors, the only country not allowed to take part in the process, was Germany. The repercussions and heavy penalties imposed were therefore unworkable and would create a national feeling of resentment and revenge. It was this lack of foresight that eventually would allow the extremist views of Adolf Hitler to not only be listened to, but also acted upon.

And it wasn't only Germany that was dissatisfied with the outcome. Italy felt they should have done better, and Imperial Japan was unhappy about its failure to gain parts of China. We now know of course that these three countries would form a dangerous alliance, with Germany, Italy and Japan joining an axis coalition to demand territory and respect, which they felt the Treaty of Versailles had robbed them of.

Matters were made much worse because Germany was also forced to accept sole responsibility for the conflict, pay huge sums of money to the Allied nations for the damage that the War had caused and relinquish land to specific ethnic groups to form new countries. Part of the deal also required Germany to disband the military, and the manufacture of any armaments was prohibited.

For a proud nation with a distinguished tradition of empire building, the Treaty added insult to injury and as the history books tell, an agreement of any kind will only ever hold if all parties involved have something to gain from adhering to it and feel that whether victor or loser, justice has been done.

At the end of the First World War, most nations who had been involved, and their citizens, developed a pacifist mentality, never wanting to experience the horrors of conflict again. However, there were those, sadly, who had been inspired by the experience and two of the most famous of these men were Adolf Hitler and Benito Mussolini. With equally distorted views and a distinct fondness for fascism, they posed a danger to the much longed for idea of world peace and neither of them would waste any time rising to power.

In 1919, it was generally assumed that all European states would in future be democratic in structure and therefore sufficiently like-minded and peace-loving to make the machinery of the League of Nations work effectively, but this was to prove far more of a dream than a reality.

Nevertheless, Europe did rebuild and within a decade had regained the same productivity levels as it had enjoyed in 1913, before the First World War started. But this prosperity was to be short lived and after the Wall Street Crash of 1929, the whole world faced a period of history that has come to be known as The Great Depression.

For the people of Germany, already hard hit by the huge war debt they had incurred because of the Treaty of Versailles, this was a terrible blow for their already crumbling economy.

However, what was bad news for the ordinary German in the street proved very advantageous to Adolf Hitler, and he was quick to seize the chance to rise to power.

This chapter is entitled *The Road to War* and there was nobody keener to follow this path than Adolf Hitler, who ironically was an Austrian by birth. Born on April 20th 1889, the son of Alois and Klara Hitler, in the small town of Braunau am Inn, Adolf rarely excelled at school and having lost both his parents while still a youth, found himself alone in Vienna, struggling to make his way in the world as an artist.

Already blaming others for his troubles, along with the group of anti-Semitic

Austrians he fell in with, the Jews became a target for his hatred. Hitler despised the Austrian authorities for allowing the Jews to occupy positions of power and as his fortunes went from bad to worse, until he was living on the streets having failed miserably as an artist, his dislike of Austria and the Jews became more deeply entrenched than ever.

At the first opportunity Hitler left Austria and in 1913 he headed for Germany, moving to Munich. When WW1 was declared the following year, he requested permission to fight with the German Army and he fast became a fierce patriot. After service in the trenches, Hitler along with many of his German comrades was disgusted when the German government surrendered in 1918 and after the war, joined with them to fight for a restoration of his adopted homeland to a position of power.

It was not so long after the Treaty of Versailles was ratified that Hitler started his political career, speaking at a German Worker's Party meeting and his oratory skills were soon noticed.

He quickly took charge of the party, which became more widely known as the National Socialist German Workers Party and the Nazis were on their way. Nevertheless by 1923 Hitler felt political means were too slow and he attempted a military coup in a Munich Beer Hall which was a disaster.

Hitler was sentenced to five years in prison, but his popularity was already well established, and he only served 13 months, during which time he wrote *Mein Kampf,* laying out all his plans for a new Germany. And of course, this put him in the perfect position to offer Germany salvation in the early 1930s as the terrible hardships of the Depression really began to bite, and rational people who would otherwise have dismissed Adolf Hitler as a fanatic, started to believe what he was saying. This was very much the case when it came to re-building the German Military, providing much needed jobs, but was strictly forbidden by the Treaty of Versailles.

. . .

After the Reichstag Fire of 1933, Hitler blamed the Communists for attempting to destroy the seat of German government, and soon afterwards Hitler stormed to power. His position was further secured when President Hindenburg died in 1934, and at this point in time Hitler's power became absolute. The German Führer now held the titles of Head of State, Commander in Chief of German military forces, Chancellor and Chief of the Nazi Party. There was no question; Hitler reigned supreme, and he began building his empire with alarming speed.

By 1935 the ranks of the army had swelled to over 500,000 and production of arms and ammunition had resumed. Also, the Rhineland, a region in the west bordering France, was re-occupied by military units.

This region had been demilitarized after World War One, but despite the violation of treaty after treaty, little was done by the rest of the world to control the new German military regime.

Despite the threat that Hitler was now posing, the British and the French failed to take any action. In fact, Hitler was quite vulnerable at this point, had the Allies all but realized it. Evidently, gaining in confidence, Hitler started to accelerate the process, and before there was a chance for anyone to do anything further, the Nazis were on the move through Europe.

When Hitler announced his intentions at a Nazi Congress in Berlin to march into Czechoslovakia, the cheers were resounding, and in 1938 the new British Prime Minister Neville Chamberlain was forced to do something about German aggression. But Hitler was able to play for time because Chamberlain was staunchly against war, prepared to pay any price not to fight, and in September he flew to Munich to meet with Hitler, the Italian leader Mussolini and the French Premiere, Edward Daladier.

. . .

For Chamberlain appeasement was the way forward, and as British citizens prepared for war just in case, their Prime Minister agreed a peaceful solution with Hitler. By allowing the German Dictator some land in Czechoslovakia, he would go no further, and when the Munich Treaty was signed, Chamberlain flew home triumphant, claiming he carried a piece of paper that assured peace rather than war.

Chamberlain was cheered as a hero, but fellow politician, Winston Churchill was far from convinced. He claimed that Britain and France had to choose between war and dishonor, and for Churchill, both nations had chosen dishonor and he predicted there would be war.

Then on March 15th 1939, without warning, the Nazis marched into Czechoslovakia, and as Prague fell, Winston Churchill's worst fears were proven to be well founded and Chamberlain had to face the full horror of what lay ahead. With great speed Hitler looked towards Germany's eastern neighbor, Poland, but with a real danger of the Russians attacking his Nazi storm troopers, he had to plan his next move with great care. Although unlikely allies, Hitler agreed a non-aggression pact with the Russian leader Joseph Stalin, and the road to war was laid wide open.

There could be no doubt that the British and the French would have no choice but to come to the aid of Poland if there was a German invasion because of pacts already in place. But Hitler had used his time well, and was ready and waiting to face any consequences, as well as anything the Allied forces could throw at him.

| German army corps marching to Poland

In the early morning hours of September 1st, 1939 an overwhelming German force of more than a million troops, backed by tactical aircraft and speedy Panzer tank divisions on the ground were mobilized and swarmed into Poland using a three-front blitzkrieg.

The term *"blitzkrieg"*, when translated, means quite simply: *Lightning Strike*.

It was a tactical military maneuver developed by an Army officer called Hans

Guderian and championed by Hitler himself, based on surprise and speed. It utilized foot soldiers on the ground and tanks, with planes providing further cover from overhead, and the reason that Hitler took to such a radical new plan was due to his experiences in the First World War, where very little progress was made for months at a time. The opposite was true with the "blitzkrieg", as the whole point was to storm in quickly and create havoc and panic using speed, co-ordination and tactical movement.

Stuka dive-bombers flew in first to cut the place off and isolate a target area. This was done by destroying railway lines and communication centers, which resulted in nobody even being able to think about mounting a defense before the arrival of tanks and the infantry to complete the occupation.

With Hitler's blitzkrieg already underway, Neville Chamberlain issued an ultimatum: Either Germany was to withdraw from Polish soil by 11 O'clock on the morning of September 3rd, or there would be war. When no word was forthcoming from Hitler, just fifteen minutes after the deadline had passed, Chamberlain announced to the nation that war had been declared.

The nations of the Commonwealth, Australia, Canada, New Zealand, South Africa and India were all prepared to stand up and be counted in the fight against Nazi tyranny, and France quickly followed Chamberlain's lead a few hours later, also declaring war on Germany.

Whatever errors of judgement Chamberlain had made failing to prevent the onset of World War II, on this most historic of days he did at least make one of his better decisions. Winston Churchill, who had argued so vigorously against negotiating with Hitler, was asked to return to his post as First Lord of the Admiralty, which he had last held in 1916. Folklore has it that the Admiralty flashed a jubilant message to all its ships, simply announcing, "Winston is Back".

· · ·

Understanding Churchill's role in World War II is crucial, because he was a unique character capable of changing the course of history by the sheer force of his personality. Equally, in these early months of the war he was already at retirement age and had a colorful political background to say the very least.

Born into the British aristocracy in November 1874 at Blenheim Palace in Oxfordshire, Winston was the son of Lord Randolph Churchill and his American wife, the society beauty, Jenny Jerome. When it came to education Winston was far from outstanding, but he was determined to pass the entrance exam for Sandhurst, and when he did, it was the beginning of a military career that would take him as far afield as India and South Africa. Nevertheless, it was his work as a war correspondent rather than a soldier that brought him to public notice.

When he returned to Britain, Winston decided to follow in his father's footsteps and enter politics, which is how he came to be First Lord of the Admiralty during World War I.

Unfortunately though, his outspoken style meant he became the scapegoat for the disaster at Gallipoli where so many soldiers from Britain and the Commonwealth died, forcing Winston to take a back seat in the House of Commons.

Churchill was never one to give up without a fight and by the 1920s he was back in business rising to be Chancellor of the Exchequer. However, again, his outspoken views caused problems, and as the 1930s saw Hitler rise to power, Winston was in his wilderness years.

Even so, there was no silencing Churchill about Hitler, as we've already heard, warning the whole world of what would happen if action wasn't swiftly taken. Consequently, as Winston Churchill took up his post at the Admiralty, the

British people looked to the man who had so resolutely predicted what Hitler would do and expected great things of him.

And never was it more vital for a leader of men to emerge, because on the very same day that Churchill took over commanding the Naval side of the warfare division, a German U-boat torpedoed a British passenger ship that was carrying over a thousand people from Glasgow to Canada, of which about 300 were American. The ship, called the *"Athenia"* was sunk, killing 118 civilians who had been onboard.

The U-Boat's commander, Lieutenant Fritz-Julius Lemp, was undoubtedly aware of the rules of international seafaring convention, which stated that it was illegal to open fire on passenger or cargo ships. Without warning, he shot off two torpedoes, dived and then resurfaced to fire one last torpedo. However, it's likely that he mistook the Athenia for a war ship, and his failure to offer aid, while maintaining radio silence compounded the error as the U-Boat quickly left the scene.

As news of the Athenia's fate flashed around the world, over the next 24 hours all who heard of it were outraged. In fact, the first thing Adolf Hitler did was to deny all knowledge of the incident, as he ordered the submarine's log book to be re-written, while Josef Goebbels, the Nazi Minister of Propaganda, claimed it was a torpedo from a British submarine that had hit the Athenia. Later he added that it was all a publicity stunt by Winston Churchill to discredit Germany and to pull the United States into the war, proving beyond all doubt that the new First Lord of the Admiralty was already making waves.

Meanwhile, as the Battle for supremacy at sea started in deadly earnest, the first British air assault, courtesy of the RAF, was launched on September 4th, but all did not go according to plan. Planes got lost, were shot down, and just like Lemp's U-Boat, attacked the wrong ships, and even worse at one point, the wrong country. Out of 29 bombers scrambled to strike fear and terror into Germany's naval bases, only eight managed to do so.

Two days later, another disaster hit the RAF when a false air raid alert sounded, inciting several Hurricanes and Spitfires to take to the skies only to end up shooting each other down, with no enemy planes anywhere in sight. Nevertheless, as are the fortunes of war, just a week later there was success for the British when the first German ship was destroyed; a U-boat, depth-charged and sunk by a British destroyer.

Any jubilant celebrations were to be sadly cut short though, because on September 17th, HMS Courageous was sunk off the coast of Ireland by a retal-iatory U-boat, claiming the lives of five hundred of the British aircraft carrier's crew.

After the initial shock of the declaration of war, in Britain life went on pretty much as normal. In fact, this lull before the storm is often referred to as the phony war, and many of the children so speedily evacuated to the countryside returned home. A routine of curfews soon became commonplace, and nightly blackouts to prevent German bombers finding their targets should they take to the skies with immediate effect, were strictly adhered to. Street lighting was also blacked out and motorists were not permitted to use headlamps, which resulted in a number of casualties due to road accidents.

However, for the people of Poland it was a very different story and the horror of what the soldiers under Hitler's command were capable of soon became all too evident. There was no escaping the well-ordered German war machine, and while the British and French felt confident the Polish could defend them-selves for the time being at least, they were sadly mistaken. The attack on the Polish people was also blistering, and in *Operation Tannenberg*, mass execu-tions resulted in more than 20,000 ruthless killings, as the atrocities of war took their toll. Despite the odds being so stacked against them, what was left of the Polish Militia and as many civilian volunteers as could be mustered attempted to defend Warsaw.

But worse was still to come, and on September 17th, the Soviet Red Army invaded Poland from the east, with 40 Divisions, adding up to 800,000 men, making any hope of Poland withstanding attacks on both sides, impossible. The Russians had been promised the land as part of Hitler's non-aggression deal and Stalin was determined to claim what he believed Russia was owed.

However, in one piece of good fortune, members of the Polish Cipher Bureau, armed with inside knowledge of the Enigma code, used by the Germans for many of their communications, managed to escape from the clutches of the invading Russians with two of the Enigma machines. When they arrived safely in Paris it was to a rapturous reception on October 1st, and for very good reason. These Enigma Machines were used to encrypt and decrypt secret messages, and although in commercial use during the 1920s, it was during WWII that they were adopted by the German military. Although the true implications of this escape would not be fully realized for some time to come, the intelligence gained through this source, codenamed ULTRA, would prove to be of significant aid to the Allied war effort.

| Enigma machine plugboard

As September drew to a close, the besieged and battered city of Warsaw fell to the Nazis, after being bombed into submission by the low-flying Luftwaffe. There was no respite for Poland as this was already one of the strongest, most advanced, and battle-experienced air forces in the world at the outbreak of war in 1939. Officially unveiled in 1935, in direct violation of the Treaty of Versailles, its purpose was to support Hitler's Blitzkrieg across Europe. The aircraft that were to serve in the Luftwaffe were of a new age and far superior to that of most other nations in the 1930s.

Under such pressure it took just only days for Poland to surrender unconditionally on September 27th.

Just a day later Poland was callously partitioned off by Russia and Germany, with Hitler claiming almost 73,000 square miles of Polish territory, which was tragically home to nearly 2 million Jews, while Russia swallowed up 78,000 square miles. The Baltic States of Lithuania, Latvia and Estonia were also taken by Russia. Of the Polish militia, the majority were taken prisoner by the Germans, while Hitler's military losses during this campaign were minimal, and for the Russians the casualties were even less, due to the fact that by the time they invaded, Poland was already overwhelmed.

During the early days of October, Adolf Hitler's treatment of the vanquished Poles was appalling as his plan to evict or kill as many as possible was put into action. They were in his words an 'alien population' dangerous to the Reich, and even at this early stage the atrocities committed in the name of racial purity were sickening. But the program of extermination, codenamed Aktion T4, did not just apply to Poland, because in Germany what had started much earlier with the enforced euthanasia of the elderly and mentally ill was extended as Hitler's evil master plan for an Arian nation also began to focus on new-borns and very young children.

It was the job of doctors and midwives to register any child born with any kind of deficiency, so Hitler's officials could decide who lived or died.

Questionnaires were also sent out to anyone who didn't have German citizenship or were not of German blood, and as Hitler's regime of terror spread through the territories he conquered, his own people suffered equal horrors.

Experiments using gas chambers at the euthanasia killing centers, whether in Germany or elsewhere, ultimately served as training for the SS. This elite band of Nazis, basically the Führer's Praetorian Guard would implement Hitler's

"Final Solution" of genocide, and under Heinrich Himmler's command, the SS were growing in strength rapidly. It's interesting that although it is the SS's extermination of the Jews that is most widely known, communists, ethnic races, homosexuals and even the freemasons were also targeted equally viscously.

As the war progressed the technical experience gained during the euthanasia program was used in the construction of huge killing centers at Auschwitz, Treblinka and other concentration camps in an attempt to exterminate the entire Jewish population of Europe, and of the approximately six million European Jews murdered during the Holocaust, many, many of them were Polish.

Despite Hitler's actions in Poland resulting in the declaration of war, he still had hopes for a negotiated settlement with the British, but on October 12th, Prime Minister Neville Chamberlain rejected Hitler's insincere peace proposals and told the people of Britain that no promises from Hitler or the present German government should be believed or accepted as fact.

Nevertheless, although the lesson that Hitler was not to be trusted had been learnt from the debacle of the Munich Treaty, which he had so readily agreed to, under Chamberlain's leadership there was no attempt to become proactive against the Nazis.

Consequently, the German Führer wasted no time strengthening his position while the Allies continued to maintain a watching and waiting brief.

Meanwhile in Poland, matters deteriorated further as the Nazis concentrated their efforts to round up the nation's Jewish population and either send them to enforced labour camps or confined them to a localized ghetto in Warsaw, creating endless restrictive and pointless laws for them to adhere to. For example, the wearing of a felt hat would be punishable by death, and it's hard to imagine the terror that this kind of persecution generated.

Despite the already well-oiled German propaganda machine under the watchful command of Joseph Goebbels, by November, news of what was happening to those not considered to be of "pure race", home and abroad, began to spread, and there were those who began to wonder whether Hitler was the savior of Germany he had promised to be. At the very start of the month a folder full of Top-Secret German weapon's research was sent to Norway, with a note attached, which read, *From a German scientist who wishes you all well*.

Then a matter of days later, the first of a number of failed assassination attempts on Adolf Hitler's life was carried out. This was in the same Munich Beer Hall where Hitler had attempted his own military coup so many years earlier, and ironically had been equally disastrous. The bomb that could have brought the Second World War to a halt before it had really had a chance to get started, detonated twenty minutes after the Führer had left, and as eight people were killed in the blast, the odds are that if Hitler hadn't finished his speech earlier than expected, it could well have been his last.

| Munich Beer Hall meeting

The man responsible for the bomb, Georg Elser was actually arrested while attempting to illegally cross the border into Switzerland, as Hitler was still speaking. He appears to have acted alone, outraged by the fact that the German people had lost so much personal freedom, as even the education of children had been taken away from their parents and turned over to such institutions as the Hitler Youth.

The main protagonists in this early part of the war were now beginning to maneuver themselves into position, and having secured their advantage in Poland, the Russians turned their attention to Finland. Joseph Stalin had every reason to distrust Adolf Hitler, as the years of war ahead would prove, and although the non-aggression pact between them enabled the Germans to storm through Europe, Stalin also had his own agenda. Equally Russia was watchful of the Allies, and Finland would give them a tactical buffer, protecting what Stalin saw as the vulnerable city of Leningrad from any army that might target it.

When the battle lines had been drawn between Russia and Finland by the end of November, the Russian Red Army believed that they had an easy task ahead of them. Adopting a similar offensive to the German's blitzkrieg that they'd seen work so effectively in Poland, they were anticipating victory within a matter of weeks, but this was the first of many occasions when other factors, not least the weather would have an important influence on the outcome.

With Finland being a relatively sparsely populated country, they struggled to muster an army large enough to defend against the Russians who had what appeared to be an unlimited supply of soldiers. Even so, the Finnish troops were able to use their hostile terrain to their advantage. They were well accustomed to the forests and snow-covered regions of their homeland, and although outnumbered by the opposition, their determination to defend Finland was fiercely patriotic. The winter of 1939 was one of the worst ever known in Finland, and ironically the Red Army troops had actually been sent from the south of Russia, so the cold weather made them particularly vulnerable.

But the Russian Army had another weakness; commanders in the field couldn't decide without approval from a higher authority, which resulted in significant delays on the battlefield. Therefore, the Russian Army was frequently a slow-moving dinosaur hindered by both the geography of Finland and its rigidity in terms of strategy. Whereas blitzkrieg had been designed to incorporate all aspects of Germany's Army and Air Force, each part of the Russian military acted as separate entities. Also, white camouflage clothing was not issued to the Russians and their vehicles simply could not cope with the freezing conditions.

. . .

Many parts of the 600-mile border were simply impassable, so the Finns could predict the routes the initial stages of the invasion would take.

The Russian air force was also limited in the amount of time it could help the army because the days were so short during the winter months. When they did fly, the Russians took heavy casualties, losing 800 planes, and although it would be into the New Year of 1940 before this particular conflict would be resolved, the Finns were far from intimidated by the Russians.

Back in Great Britain, during December, the age limit for conscription was expanded twice in two weeks, with men aged between 19 and 41 called up to join the armed forces. Women aged between 20 and 30 were accepted for different levels of service. It was also the month that the Royal Navy became embroiled in the first big naval battle of the South Atlantic during World War Two, which has become known as the Battle of the River Plate. It took place off the coast of Argentina and Uruguay where the German warship the Graf Spee, had been successfully attacking merchant shipping in the area. The British Navy had not one but four cruisers in the area, the Ajax, the Exeter, the Cumberland and the Achilles, and the commander of this South American Division set off in hot pursuit of the dangerous German craft.

The Treaty of Versailles had forbidden Germany from building large, classic battleships when the nation had been forced to disarm and cease military production.

Germany therefore built smaller and more compact vessels, and The Graf Spee, commissioned in 1936, was fast enough to outrun many battleships, and because it had also been armed with enough weapons, it was a potent enemy. Nevertheless, in the Battle of the River Plate, the British Navy eventually forced the Graf Spee into the neutral Port of Montevideo.

· · ·

The Exeter in particular was badly damaged, but as there was a time restriction on how long the German ship could remain, the captain of the Graf Spee, Hans Langsdorff, knew he could only put off a confrontation with the British Navy for a short while. It was however, British Intelligence that really won the day on this occasion, having convinced Langsdorff he was completely outclassed, and stood no chance at all of escaping, even though it would be days before the fleet would actually arrive. Determined to save the lives of his crew, the German captain decided to scuttle the ship, and three days later committed suicide to prove that he was no coward. Ironically, all the British sailors captured by Langsdorff claimed they had been treated extremely well by him, and he was without doubt a man of honor, even if some historians have questioned his judgement.

These were still early days in the war, and not all of the action was at battle stations. In the League of Nations, the Russian actions against the Finns meant that they were expelled. The international peacekeeping organization still believed that there was a chance for diplomacy, but with such determined individuals as Stalin and Hitler to try and control, there was little room for maneuver or rationality.

The League of Nations had been the brainchild of American President Woodrow Wilson and although his motivation was laudable, in practice, the concept was fraught with difficulties. While the League was born with the exalted mission of preventing another "Great War", it proved ineffectual, being unable to protect China from a Japanese invasion, or Abyssinia from an Italian one.

The League had also been powerless when it came to reacting to German rearmament, and in the lead up to the outbreak of the Second World War, there was little the League of Nations could do to fulfill the task entrusted to it in the aftermath of WW1, that should by rights, have ended all wars. Germany and Japan voluntarily withdrew from the League in 1933, and Italy left in 1937.

. . .

The true imperial designs of Russia soon became apparent with its occupation of eastern Poland in September of 1939, whilst Lithuania, Latvia, and Estonia had been terrorized into signing a "mutual assistance" pact, which gave Stalin air and naval bases in strategic positions. Even so it was the invasion of Finland, where no provocation or pact could justify the aggression, which resulted in worldwide condemnation.

Interestingly, President Wilson's successor, Franklin D. Roosevelt, who was forced to stay on the side-lines during the opening skirmishes of the war because of American public opinion, spoke out against the invasion, resulting in the Russians withdrawing from the New York World's Fair.

And the next step was for the League of Nations to expel Russia, while as the World faced a global conflict that no group of peacekeepers could hope to pacify, the organization born out of such good intentions faced its own conclusion.

As 1939 drew to a close, with Christmas on the horizon, more British troops were being sent from their families to help the war effort for nations already in direct danger from Adolf Hitler's advancing Nazis. And the Commonwealth added to the number of available men with over seven thousand Canadian troops arriving in Britain, ready to swell the numbers, while soldiers from India were sent to France. The roller coaster ride that had been the Road to War was now poised at its highest point, and although in Britain at least things still appeared little changed, the momentum of the aggression was about to become unstoppable.

As people's thoughts turned to Christmas and the prospect of a New Year, everything that they had feared since Hitler first started to make his presence felt in the early 1930s came sharply into focus.

. . .

Tucking into a festive lunch the threat of rationing was already on the cards, and the full implications of the lethal efficiency of the German U-Boats were about to be revealed. With so much of Britain's food being imported by sea, it was imperative that the Government made sure there was enough to feed both the rich and the poor.

The idea of people growing their own fruit and vegetables, or keeping chickens, even in the most suburban of gardens, would make a huge contribution to the war effort, resulting in front lawns being dug up to make way for the "vegetable patch" and the "hen house".

These few months really were the lull before the storm, and as Neville Chamberlain and his government watched for what Hitler would do next, Winston Churchill was speaking out against Britain's inactivity once again. For the First Lord of the Admiralty the best form of defense was most definitely attack, and Chamberlain was well and truly in the firing line alongside Adolf Hitler.

Churchill was desperately worried that the Germans were about to target Norway, from where Hitler's war machine accessed much of the iron ore needed for production. But it was as if the lessons of 1938 and the Munich Treaty had been forgotten by Chamberlain, as Churchill's grave warnings were once more ignored, and the first few months of 1940 were about to prove very interesting indeed.

2

BATTLE LINES DRAWN

January – March 1940

| U-Boat attack on a merchant ship

In the autumn of 1939, the relative tranquillity that Europe had enjoyed since the end of the First World War was shattered, as the leader of Nazi Germany, Adolf Hitler, ordered the invasion of Poland on September the 1st.

The invasion of the Second Polish Republic was an event which would shape the history of the world, as Germany, a nation embittered by poverty and disgrace born from their defeat in the First Great War, was driven to seize territory that they considered was rightfully theirs. The glory days of the French and British Empires were over, and as Adolf Hitler's forces charged furiously across the continent, it was clear that the devastating power of the Third Reich was now carving out a new and truly terrifying chapter in the pages of history.

While Stalin's Red Army and the German Wehrmacht roamed the terrain of Europe unchecked, it would be some considerable time before the Allies could muster the strength to combat the invaders' relentless advance and the months of January to March 1940 would be marked by cautious moves and maneuvers.

Although this period of the Second World War is generally described as the phony war, the storms now brewing at sea, on land and in the political arena would be of vital significance as hostilities between the European nations escalated. Adolf Hitler believed that for his fatherland to rise once more from the economic abyss, a violent and terrible struggle would be necessary. According to the Nazi Führer, since the French Revolution, the world had been moving steadily towards a new great conflict and it was Germany's duty, to secure her own existence by every means possible. He promised the Germans an improved economy, the reclamation of territory lost after the First World War and justice for the humiliation the country had faced as a result of the Treaty of Versailles.

· · ·

Hitler also harbored many more personal grievances, including a deep routed hatred of Jews and communists, and although his uneasy alliance with the Soviets as he stormed into Poland meant he had to tolerate communism for the time being, he immediately set his plans for exterminating the Jewish race in motion.

With a zealous determination to exact revenge Hitler was ready, willing and able to show the world that any attempt at diplomacy and reasoning would be futile. The events leading up to the declaration of war had proved that Hitler was not to be trusted, and with a seemingly invincible military machine snatching what the Nazis believed to be rightfully theirs, any nation that attempted to stand in their way was destined to be crushed.

Hitler's star was most definitely in the ascendancy, Czechoslovakia had been occupied, Austria forcibly pushed into union with Germany, and as the 1930s had drawn to a close Poland was now the third nation to see Nazi soldiers marching across its borders. Having signed the Anglo-Polish Agreement, Britain allied with France, had no alternative but to go to war with the Third Reich, but just how to tackle the supremacy of Hitler's troops was still to be decided.

While the Allies watched events unfold, as January 1940 heralded the start of a most uncertain New Year, still no action had been taken to intervene in the Nazi and Soviet invasion, and on the war-torn streets of Poland there was little to celebrate.

What's more, following the terror of the initial attack the German occupation was proving to be ever more devastating.

Hitler had no respect for the people of Poland, who he viewed as little more than sub-human, and it was soon evident that it was their country that he wanted. For some time, Hitler had advocated creating more living space for German civilians and he planned to clear all Poland's inhabitants, allowing only a designated number to remain working as slaves.

The crisis now facing Poland was truly appalling. In January plans were drawn up for prison camps, similar to those already existing in Germany, to be built on Polish territory. The most notorious of these was located on the edge of the small village of Auschwitz, and to this day just the mention of its name conjures up all the horrors of the Second World War. Many Poles were systematically sent there to die, among them countless men, women and children of Jewish descent. Hitler's persecution of the Jews was gaining momentum.

But these prototype concentration camps were only the beginning of Hitler's plans for the Polish nation; he wanted all traces of Polish culture to be obliterated. Universities were closed or destroyed, and professors, teachers and intellectuals arrested and executed. Teenage boys and girls were rounded up and sent to Germany to work in factories, while young children with fair hair, blue eyes and other Aryan traits were snatched from the arms of their parents to be brought up as Germans and children of the Third Reich.

There can be no doubt that the war waged by Hitler against Poland was to be one of complete and utter annihilation, and by the end of the war in 1945 around a fifth of the country's citizens would be dead, the highest death rate for any country involved in the Second World War.

Three million of those killed, were Jews and as Nazi forces edged further west, the events in Poland were about to become one of the greatest tragedies in human history. And it wasn't only the Nazis that the beleaguered Poles had to contend with.

· · ·

WORLD WAR 2: THE CALL OF DUTY

While the west of Poland fell beneath the shadow of the German occupation, to the east the terrified citizens were facing the threat of a Russian invasion. Unlike the fierce fighting to the west, Stalin's Red Army had initially been met with little resistance, following the great success of Soviet propaganda fed to the many Ukrainians, Belarusians and pro communists in the country. They were convinced that the Soviets were there for their benefit and welcomed the invaders with open arms. In the confusion many Poles believed that the Russian soldiers planned to fight the Nazis, but it was soon clear that despite their differences, Germany and the Soviet Union were now working together, and the Polish would suffer as much at the hands of the Russians as they did Hitler's commanders.

In August 1939 the Soviet Union had signed a Non-Aggression Pact with Hitler, which ensured that in the face of German belligerence, the Russians would remain on peaceful terms with the Nazis. But there was also a secret protocol only discovered after the end of the war, which revealed that Stalin and Hitler had made plans to carve Eastern Europe up, sharing the spoils between Nazi Germany and the Communist Soviet Union. In return for Stalin's help in the conquest of Poland, Hitler agreed to leave the east to the Soviets.

The Russians would also be allowed to occupy Estonia, Latvia and Lithuania without opposition from Germany, as well as seizing valuable territory in Finland. In the meantime, Hitler would push further west ensuring valuable raw materials were safeguarded for the economy of the Third Reich. Militarily the relationship between the Soviet and German forces appeared to be a highly beneficial one, but in reality, beneath the smiling façade, it was clear that the alliance was tenuous at least, and with political ideologies that were worlds apart, it was unlikely to be a lasting arrangement.

On the Russian agenda, Stalin was carefully constructing a buffer zone between his country and the west, and he soon began pushing troops into ports around the tiny Baltic States, which crumbled under Soviet pressure.

· · ·

Then early in October 1939 Stalin began to make demands on Finland. He wanted to secure land near Leningrad, islands in the Gulf of Finland, and use of the Hang Naval Base, and in exchange he offered the Fins Soviet territory on their eastern border, but the Fins were far from convinced. Finland and the Soviets had a long and complicated history. Up until the beginning of the nineteenth century Finland had been part of Sweden, until the Russian Tsar, Alexander the First, had driven his troops across the frozen Baltic Sea and into battle with the Fins in 1808. A year later Sweden lost the eastern third of their country, which was established as the Grand Duchy of Finland, a part of the Russian Empire.

Little changed until just over a century later new revolutionary ideas began to seep into the consciousness of millions of working-class Russians, and the borders of the Empire began to crumble.

With millions of Russian soldiers dying on the battlefields of the First Great War and dreadful food shortages on the home front, revolution swiftly engulfed the country in 1917. Soon the Red Army was marching through the streets of St Petersburg championing the Bolshevik cause and it didn't take long for the Tsarist Regime and its mighty empire to collapse into ruin leaving the country embroiled in a bloody civil war.

The chilling reverberations swept throughout the land and affected all nations that were part of the Empire, and while in Russia, the Red Army and Communism would prevail, as civil war engulfed Finland, the White Army supporting the monarchy, were victorious. As Vladimir Lenin seized the reins of power and the Soviet Union rose from the ashes of the old regime, Finland became an independent state and freed itself from the shackles of the Russian Empire.

· · ·

But there was no doubt that the Soviets were still a dangerous adversary, just across Finland's Eastern frontier. The man who had led Finland's White Army to victory, Baron Carl Gustv Emil Mannerheim, had wanted to march as far as St Petersburg to beat back the Bolsheviks, but in the end the Fins settled for building great fortifications close to the Soviet border. Named the Mannerheim Line, in honor of the Baron, it would prove vital in the defense of Finland as the Second World War gathered momentum.

By the end of November 1939 while negotiations continued between Finland and the Soviet Union, Stalin had grown impatient and the Red Army was ordered to invade.

Baron Mannerheim was once again called upon to take command, this time against the Soviet General Meretsov, who had predicted that his men would reach the Finnish Capital, Helsinki, within ten days. But while Soviet commanders scoured maps and worked out strategies, they had little imagined how difficult the fight against the Fins would prove to be.

Without winter uniforms and lacking provisions for a long campaign the Soviet troops marched towards the Mannerheim Line, as the second coldest winter in over a century swept across northern Europe. Though vastly outnumbered and poorly equipped the Fins were well used to winter fighting and soon had the upper hand. Wearing white camouflaged suits and swiftly traversing the familiar wintry terrain on skis, they had a considerable advantage, and the Soviet casualties were escalating.

| The Mannerheim Line

As January 1940 progressed, one of the most famous battles of the Winter War, the Battle of Suomussalmi was coming to a close. Advancing from the north and the south, two Russian Divisions planned to link up at the village of Suomussalmi before heading west to the city of Oulu, thereby cutting the country in half. With the prospect of facing the Russians attacking on two fronts the Fins fought determinedly. Ski troops made wide circling flanking movements and caught the rear end and middle of the northern division by surprise. Meanwhile to the South, frozen lakes became death traps. Once crossing the waters, the Soviets dark uniforms made them easy to spot against the white snow, and Finnish home guard troops, many of them being expert shots, were able to pick them off, one by one, with the Fin, Simo Hayha emerging as the deadliest sniper in history with over five hundred kills.

Meanwhile despite the Fins lack of sophisticated anti-tank weapons, improvised petrol bombs called Molotov cocktails, named after the Russian foreign minister, proved equally deadly, destroying nearly two thousand tanks during the course of the war.

Faced with tough opposition the Red Army were forced to retreat, again becoming easy prey for the Finnish ski troops. Suffering in the freezing cold temperatures, the Russian armies were divided into isolated groups, and as they huddled around fires, they were swiftly encircled and eliminated. The forests, snow covered lakes and roads of Finland were soon littered with the frozen corpses of Russian soldiers as more and more fell victim to the bitter cold and the constant attacks from the Fins.

By January 8th it was clear that the Russians had lost the Battle of Suomussalmi. Finland had not only achieved a decisive victory but could also take their pick of Soviet munitions and tanks left abandoned across the landscape. But this was one battle in a bitter war, and Finland would not be able to hold off for long without the assistance of the Allies. In Britain and France emotions were running high as the brave Finnish soldiers captured the public imagination; even in the United States, still adamantly neutral, there were many who supported the Fins and were keen to help. Some even went as far as going to Finland to fight as volunteers.

But as the winter war continued, Hitler was all too aware that the Allies might well come to the aid of the Fins, and the thought of British and French soldiers venturing closer to the Nazi sphere of conflict was a cause for concern.

· · ·

Finland was uncomfortably close to neutral Sweden and Norway, countries that were of vital importance to the Nazi war machine, supplying it with precious iron ore. If they decided to send troops into Finland, the allies would have to cross these two countries and with a foothold in the area could easily seize ports and stations so vital to the economy of the Third Reich.

It was clear that the Allies would have to be kept at bay and German commander, Gerd von Runstedt urged the Führer to begin preparations to seize strategic bases in Scandinavia, before the British and the French could get there. However, the British Government were still reluctant to take any positive action, preferring to take a defensive stance. The lone voice of Winston Churchill, The First Lord of the Admiralty, continued to warn of Hitler's evil intent, and he lauded the bravery of the Finnish troops and was keen to send assistance as soon as possible. He also criticized Norway and Sweden for remaining neutral, saying, *"Each one hopes that if he feeds the crocodile enough, that the crocodile will eat him last." .*

However Prime Minister Neville Chamberlain who had worked so hard to secure peace for Europe before the outbreak of war, following a policy of appeasement right up to the moment Hitler marched into Poland, was hesitant to come to Finland's aid. In diplomatic terms this would not only mean a hostile act against Nazi Germany, but the Soviet Union as well and the Allies simply did not have the military strength to fight both. Since Poland had been invaded the British had been preparing for war, stepping up military production and conscripting men into the forces, but the Germans had enjoyed years unchallenged building their military strength and were far superior.

The longer the British could spend building up the army, navy and the air force, the more chance they had of surviving a long war.

Military drill and training days were organized to make sure people were at the peak of their physical condition should they be sent into battle or be needed to defend the home front. There were also Allied troops pouring into Britain from the dominion countries all over the globe. From Australia, New Zealand, and Canada soldiers streamed off the boats to take up arms and fight for the Allies.

As well as preparations for battle, precautions were taken against a Nazi bombardment of the British mainland. Gas masks were distributed to quell fears of the kind of gas attacks that had been used on the battlefields of the First World War. Searchlights were installed around the major cities to illuminate enemy aircraft and night-time blackouts became a way of life.

After the damage caused by the German Zeppelin raids of World War I every effort was also made to safeguard Britain's national treasures. Sandbags were used to protect important buildings, stained glass windows were taken away, paintings were removed from the National Gallery and along with priceless manuscripts from the British museum were stored in bombproof shelters.

There was also the civilian population to consider. Many children had been evacuated to the safety of the countryside from Britain's cities the previous autumn, but by January 1940 with little evidence of any immediate threat, the children had returned to their homes, leaving many wondering if a real war would ever be fought against Hitler and Nazi Germany.

Nonetheless despite a lack of fighting on the home front, the citizens of Great Britain were beginning to feel the effect of the European war. The nation imported 55 million tons of food every year from abroad and the German Government believed that if they could cut off food supplies and disrupt trade, the country would be brought to its knees. Nazi U-Boats and battleships had been attacking British merchant ships since autumn 1939 and even with a convoy system introduced to protect shipping, there were still heavy losses.

· · ·

Hundreds of British merchant seamen had to bail out of sinking ships in these first months of the phony war, and those who didn't die at sea were taken prisoner by the Nazi aggressors. It was a conflict that would become the longest military campaign of the Second World War and would be named by Churchill as The Battle of the Atlantic.

Meanwhile back on dry land, food stocks were beginning to run low in Britain. The government decided that rationing would have to be introduced in the first weeks of January 1940. Everyone was issued with ration books and as the queues formed outside the shops, people waited patiently in turn to receive their carefully weighed out portions of butter, bacon and sugar.

As the months went on more and more goods would be added to the ration books as supplies dwindled and as food imports dropped to less than a quarter of the normal amount this was only the beginning of the dramatic changes that people would have to get used to in wartime Britain. But if Hitler hoped to crush the spirit of the British he would quickly learn that it would take a great deal more than personal hardship to dent their morale.

| Ration books introduced

It was inevitable that the situation would deteriorate as the war progressed and, in an attempt to prepare for a further decline in imports the British Government called for every man and woman in the country to grow their own food on allotments, even if that meant turning front lawns, sports pitches and even formal public gardens into vegetable patches. Flowers were replaced with cabbages, and while the politicians made their impassioned pleas for people to do their bit, the acreage of British land used for food production had increased by 80 percent.

Posters were soon seen everywhere from tube stations to offices, encouraging everyone to '*Dig for Victory!*' and many other catchy slogans were used. But while home grown food production increased, it became evident that after decades of migration to urban factory work, Britain was in dire need of agricultural labour. There was a shortfall of around 50,000 workers and with more and more men being recruited into the forces, it was now up to the women of Britain to play their part.

The Women's Land Army was quickly mobilized to keep the farms of Britain working and would actually mark a major turning point for women in the twentieth century, as they cast off their traditional roles in society and stepped into positions usually filled by men.

And it wasn't only work on the land that women were encouraged to take up, because as the war progressed they would also be recruited to work in factories and even join the army, air force and navy, becoming every bit as important as their fathers, husbands and sons fighting for King and country.

However, while Britain focused on how to survive with reduced food supplies and stepped up the preparations for war, the Nazi threat was looming closer than they could possibly imagine. The valuable raw materials of Scandinavia were not Hitler's only priority, because to the west of Germany, and within easy reach of France, lay what the Führer described as the Third Reich's Achilles heel, the Ruhr Valley.

After Germany's defeat in the First World War, France had occupied this territory, which with its valuable coal, iron and steel production had been the richest region in all Germany. The French occupation of the Ruhr had contributed to Germany's economic collapse at the end of the 1920s and despite the fact that a decade later French troops had already left the Rhineland, in 1936 Hitler had made it a priority to send Nazi troops into the territory to safeguard it. The progress of the war depended upon the possession of the Ruhr and one of Hitler's greatest fears was that it would be taken from him once again.

In a speech to his followers he warned that:

> *"If England and France push through Belgium and Holland into the Ruhr, we shall be in the greatest danger".*

As a consequence, he was ready for action, declaring:

> *"I shall attack France and England at the most favorable and quickest moment. Breach of the neutrality of Belgium and Holland is meaningless. No one will question that when we have won."*

What Hitler proposed would in fact be a well-rehearsed battle plan, as German troops had invaded Belgium only two decades earlier during the First World War, and the outcome on that occasion had been far from satisfactory in Hitler's view. He had fought in the trenches for his adopted homeland and had been devastated by the news of Germany's humiliating defeat as the Entente claimed their victory.

With a burning desire for revenge Hitler prepared to send the German army back to Belgium to achieve the hopes that had been dashed by the armistice of 1918. With fears of losing the precious Ruhr Valley growing by the day, Hitler ordered the conquest of the Low Countries, to be executed at the shortest possible notice to prevent France from occupying them first. A Nazi presence in Belgium and Holland would also provide a basis for a successful long-term air and sea campaign against Great Britain, a nation that Hitler feared. Although he was not afraid of Chamberlain, who was still dragging his heels as Prime Minister, it was the First Lord of the Admiralty, Winston Churchill that gave the Führer most cause for concern. Hitler was without doubt banking on the element of surprise, but as Britain continued to watch and wait, the German plans were unexpectedly revealed.

On January the 10th 1940 a German reconnaissance plane took off from Berlin with Hitler's invasion plans onboard and headed for a staff meeting in Cologne. The plane would never arrive at its destination, and its fate according to some, would change the very outcome of the war. Lost in the fog, the pilot mistook the Meuse River running through Belgium for the Rhine and when the plane suddenly ran into difficulties it was miles off course.

Forced to make a crash landing on the outskirts of Mechelen in Belgium, the pilot was a very long way from home. While the two officers onboard climbed from the wreckage, Belgian border guards soon discovered the documents and when they were passed to Allied intelligence the plans for an attack on Belgium and the Netherlands were revealed. Within hours the shocking news was passed on to the relevant military and political leaders who were in the line of Nazi fire.

Once informed of Hitler's plans King Leopold the Third of Belgium immediately telephoned the Dutch Queen, using the code phrase "Be careful, the weather is dangerous", and then told the Grand Duchess of Luxembourg to "Beware of the flu". The strange words indicated that a German attack was imminent. More importantly he was also quick to inform the French Supreme Commander Maurice Gamelin, who swiftly gathered his army commanders together to decide upon a course of action. Although there were doubts as to whether or not the documents might be the work of counterintelligence, Gamelin decided that this was the perfect opportunity to pressurize the neutral Belgians into allowing a French advance into their country.

. . .

Indeed, the French as Hitler had rightly anticipated, intended to eventually execute an offensive against Germany, as soon as they had built up sufficient military strength. With just days before the predicted invasion date Gamelin ordered the First Army Group and the Third Army to march towards the Belgian frontier. News also reached Lord Gort, the commander of the British Expeditionary Force, already stationed in France, who were awaiting the call to arms.

In Germany meanwhile word had filtered back to Berlin that the precious documents may have fallen into enemy hands. Hitler was furious and removed all those he believed to be responsible from their posts, while his Chief of Operations, General Alfred Jodl, concluded that the situation was catastrophic. The Belgians however were doing an excellent job of keeping the extent of their knowledge secret, and as yet the Germans had no idea as to the whereabouts of the documents and whether they had fallen into enemy hands.

Nevertheless, back in the Allied camp there were complications. In return for allowing French and British troops across their borders, the Belgians wanted guarantees that in the event of war their territorial integrity and colonies in Africa, would be protected and that they would receive financial aid. Although the French Premier Daladier was happy to confirm the guarantees, the British government was not prepared to do so.

As the weather deteriorated in Belgium and heavy snow began to carpet the border territory it looked increasingly unlikely that the Germans would attack at all, and as Prince Leopold, a staunch neutralist received Britain's reply he decided upon a new strategy. Ordering Belgian border troops to stop removing border obstacles and to repulse by force any foreign unit which violated Belgian territory, no matter what their nationality, he made a determined stand. Gamelin was furious and pleaded with Daladier to force the Belgians to face up to their responsibilities, but for now Belgium remained neutral.

. . .

In Germany, Jodl was surprised to note that Allied forces had been suddenly put on alert and realized that the Belgians must have had access to the invasion plans captured at Mechelen. The element of surprise had been lost and on January the 16th Hitler was persuaded to call off the invasion. For the time being at least, the phony war would continue.

The Mechelen incident was far from being a total disaster for the Nazis however, for they now knew how the Allies would react to an attack. Hitler insisted that new invasion plans be drawn up and his most experienced commanders began to develop a ground-breaking new offensive, which involved invading not only to the north, but marching the bulk of their troops further south through the Ardennes Forest. What became known as the Sickle Cut Plan would see the obliteration of all Allied resistance and lead to the inevitable fall of France.

Back in the Allied camp, the commanders were content that the danger had passed, and the focus of attention was shifted from the Belgian border back to events in Finland. After the disastrous defeat the Russians had faced in January, Stalin had demoted and shot most of the commanders responsible and placed the entire operation in the hands of Marshal Semyon Timoshenko. Finland had to be defeated at all costs and colossal reinforcements were now ordered to march into Western Karelia. A Soviet army a million strong began to advance, with support from their air force, and as February began, the Fins came under fire from the skies as the Russians started a campaign of blanket bombing that aimed to obliterate civilian and military targets.

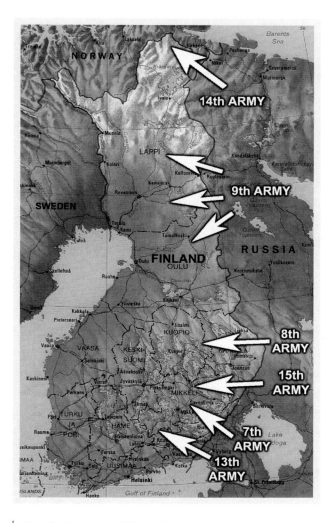

| Russian invasion of Finland

On the global stage emotions were running high as the world watched the plight of the Fins, and British politician, Anthony Eden condemned the Soviet Attacks saying:

> *"Not Russia only but Germany also, bears a terrible responsibility for what is happening in Finland at this hour. Hitler and Ribbentrop, these men and their policies alone made Stalin's aggression possible".*

Finally, in Paris on February the 4th 1940, help seemed to be close at hand as the Supreme Allied War Council made plans to send an Anglo-French force to Finland. However, they still had the problem of neutral Norway and Sweden to contend with. The troops were scheduled to disembark at the Norwegian port of Narvik and support Finland via Sweden while securing supply routes along the way.

While the Allied politicians deliberated and the Finns found themselves very nearly out of ammunition, the Soviets used an enormous concentration of artillery fire to break Finland's defensive position until on February the 14th they were forced to withdraw. As the Nazis continued to perfect their attack plans for the invasion of France, they were also keeping a very watchful eye on events taking place in Scandinavia. Matters came to a head in mid-February when a German tanker called the Altmark passed through Norwegian waters. On board were hundreds of prisoners from the merchant ships that had been sunk over the previous months.

Unfortunately, Norwegian search parties failed to inspect the hold and allowed the ship to pass, but a British plane soon spotted the tanker and raised the alarm.

The British Navy were put on full alert and one of their ships, the Cossack, began to give chase. Then on February the 16th the Royal Navy managed to board the German vessel armed with bayonets, and after hand-to-hand fighting managed to overwhelm the crew. After months in captivity, the

British seamen were finally set free and despite the freezing Norwegian weather awaiting them, were delighted to leave their floating prison.

But they were soon back at sea, and the next day HMS Cossack approached a Scottish port, her decks packed with the British seamen that had been rescued. The Navy had achieved a rare victory for Britain in the quiet months of the phony war, but it was destined to trigger the Nazis to make a further step towards the complete domination of Western Europe.

Hitler had been alerted to the fact that the British had no intention of observing Norwegian neutrality and two days after the rescue, he made the invasion of Norway and Denmark, codenamed *Operation Weserubung* a priority; and for the time being the invasion of France would have to wait.

Britain's flagrant entry into the territorial waters of a neutral country also had further repercussions, infuriating the Norwegians, and when the Allies requested transit rites so they could assist Finland on March 2nd they were refused. The Swedish King was equally concerned that his country would become a battleground between Germany and the Allies, and he too refused the Allies transit rights to come to the aid of the embattled Fins. Despite the promises of assistance from the Allies, it seemed clear to Finland's Commander Mannerheim, that with rapidly depleting troops and ammunition, the longer help was in arriving, the worse the losses for the nation would be.

By the 5th of March, the Soviet army had advanced 10–15 kilometers beyond the Mannerheim Line and had entered the suburbs of Viipuri. For Finland there was little point in fighting on and they admitted defeat on March the 12th, signing a peace treaty and surrendering valuable territory. Military troops were evacuated, and thousands of civilians began the long journey to make new lives for themselves. Barbed wire marked out the new boundaries between Finland and Russia, and an enraged Churchill wrote: *"Now the ice will melt; and the Germans are the masters of the North."*

Churchill had again been proven right in his assessment of Hitler and the dangers that the world faced, but as First Lord of the Admiralty, despite holding well-informed opinions, he was without power. Prime Minister Chamberlain had been as hesitant as ever to make a stand against Hitler, but public confidence in him was waning, as Chamberlain's reputation suffered a terrible blow. The French Prime Minister Deladier was also viewed as having failed to come to the aid of Finland, and he was actually forced to resign over the affair. What had happened in Finland was extremely worrying for the Allies, and while in Europe and Scandinavia events were gathering pace, across the Atlantic in America, the people of the USA were also watching to see what would happen next.

At this stage relations were rather strained between the American President and the British Prime Minister. However, Franklin D. Roosevelt had made every effort to strengthen the ties between the two countries.

Just months before the outbreak of war he had invited King George the sixth and Queen Elizabeth to make a state visit and this had certainly helped to improve public relations. But Roosevelt's concerns over Hitler's activity in Europe went way beyond a traditional feeling of goodwill towards Britain. It was thought that with conflict in Europe, a New World Order might not favor American interests. With such concerns playing on his mind, FDR decided to send an envoy, Sumner Welles to the continent to see if anything could be done to secure peace before the phony war escalated into a global conflict.

Sumner Welles' first destination was Italy at the end of February, as he attempted to prevent Mussolini from entering the war on the side of the Germans. The Italian Foreign Minister, who also happened to be Mussolini's son-in-law, openly disliked the Germans and gave Welles reason to hope that the Italians could be drawn away from their alliance with Berlin. But Mussolini was far from willing to denounce his German friends and driven by his desire to recreate the Roman Empire, it seemed it would be difficult to steer the dictator towards a peaceful solution.

By March the 10th Welles had reached London, where he had a number of meetings with senior statesmen, an audience with King George the Sixth and the Prime Minister. Welles was surprised by the anger Chamberlain demonstrated towards the Germans, but his policy had always been one of avoiding conflict and Welles was heartened by the fact that the Prime Minister was considering appeasing Berlin further with colonial concessions in Africa. A visit was also made to the Admiralty to meet with Winston Churchill, but this was less successful.

As far as Churchill was concerned the only course open to the Allies was to fight to the bitter end, and he doggedly rejected any peace solution that would not have at its heart *"the elimination of Herr Hitler"*.

As it happened Winston Churchill's comments could not have been better timed, because during the American envoy's visit Nazi bombers crossed the North Sea to the Scottish Coast, where the British fleet had been secretly anchored at Scapa Flow. On March the 18th one hundred bombs were dropped in twenty-five minutes, hitting warships, injuring navy personnel and killing a man who would become the first civilian to die on British soil during the Second World War.

As RAF pilots leapt into action and flew towards Germany to retaliate it seemed that while the phony war continued, peace was far from the thoughts of those living in Europe. Flying over enemy territory the RAF targeted the German air base on the island of Sylt. The damage turned out to be minimal, but it was clear that the peace Roosevelt had hoped to promote was no more than an impossible dream. In fact, on the very same day that air strikes were being made on German and British territory, Hitler was in talks with Mussolini in the Austro-Italian Alps at the Brenner Pass. It was their first meeting since Munich in 1938 and contrary to America's hopes that Italy would refuse Germany their assistance, Mussolini informed Hitler that he was now ready to join Germany and its allies in the war against Britain and France *"at the decisive hour."*

All attempts to promote peace had been in vain. While the political arena became increasingly heated France and Britain began to discuss invading Norway and Sweden to seize Germany's supply of iron ore.

On March the 28th the Anglo-French Supreme War council decided to begin mining Norwegian waters, but by then it was too late. Hitler had given the command and the German warships were already on their way. The phony war was about to come to an abrupt end and battle was about to commence.

With spring 1940 came the realization that the conflict ahead would be long, hard and bitterly fought. All hopes of anyone being able to make peace with Adolf Hitler were at an end, and as he gathered his Axis partners around him, a global war became inevitable. What had gone before in Austria, Czecho-slovakia and Poland would change the course of history. The watching and waiting were over in the European Theatre of war, the battle lines had been drawn.

3

FIRST BLOOD

April – June 1940

| Churchill comes to power

The spring and early summer of 1940 proved to be a very eventful few months in the history of the Second World War, which until this point had seen acts of Nazi aggression followed by periods of watching and waiting on the part of Great Britain and the Allies. But by April and into May, Adolf Hitler's troops were storming through Scandinavia and across Europe, employing ever more aggressive new techniques to invade Norway and Denmark to the north, and the Low Countries and France further south.

· · ·

It was at this point in the war, six months after the Nazis had invaded Poland that Allied soldiers were finally sent fully into battle and as the struggle became progressively more brutal there could be no clearer indication that the phony war had come to an end, and Europe was now in the full throws of bloody conflict. Nevertheless, for the Allies the horrors and heartbreaks of this period would also be marked by moments of triumphant glory. When thousands of Allied troops were rescued from the beaches of Dunkirk in northern France, while Nazi troops edged ever closer as the German planes of Goering's Luftwaffe screamed overhead, it was one of the most inspiring moments of the entire war.

While Hitler's armies stormed across the continent this extraordinary event gave the people of the occupied nations a glimmer of hope, and for the British there could have been no better boost to morale. Early in May Winston Churchill took on the mantle of leadership, giving Adolf Hitler and his Third Reich an enemy to be reckoned with that would fight doggedly until the bitter end.

This chapter will explore the dramatic events that lead to the Nazi invasion of France as Europe was thrown into increasing turmoil and you'll understand one of the major turning points of the Second World War, when for the first time since September 1939 Adolf Hitler's plans were thwarted. The importance of this event cannot be underestimated, for it was during this period that the "spirit of Dunkirk" was forged from the fires of despair, and it was this strength that would ultimately save Britain from the icy grasp of the Third Reich and change the course of history.

In April 1940 all eyes were fixed upon Scandinavia, which was of great strategic value for both the Allied forces and Hitler's Axis of Evil. The Kingdom of Norway was especially important to the Nazi war machine, as ninety percent of Swedish iron-ore was being shipped to Germany through the Norwegian port of Narvik. The western ports of the nation were also of great value to the Nazis, offering the potential for creating strategic bases to launch U-boat attacks from the North Sea and the Atlantic.

This point had been picked up by the head of the German Navy, Grand Admiral Raeder. Recognizing the importance of Norway early on, he had argued for the country's occupation just after the outbreak of the war in the autumn of 1939, and by spring, Germany had made this an objective.

Meanwhile back in Britain, Chamberlain and the government were still trying to avert war at any cost, and Churchill was becoming ever more frustrated at there being no attempt made to prevent Norway from falling into Nazi hands. Every suggestion Churchill made to support Britain's Nordic neighbors was outvoted by Chamberlain's cabinet, and although the Prime Minister's motives were understandable, Hitler was becoming ever more dangerous.

The scars left by the First World War still lingered in the memories of those governing the United Kingdom, and the idea of pushing the nation into another bloody land war was an unthinkable concept.

Neville Chamberlain had been elected Prime Minister in 1937 in preference to Churchill and his outspoken concerns about Adolf Hitler's rise to power in Germany, and Chamberlain was committed to peace, following a general policy of appeasement with the Führer despite Germany's increasing belligerence.

It was not because he sympathized with Germany; far from it. In a letter to his sister he wrote: *"On the whole I hate Germans"* but he was very concerned that the nation simply was not ready for war.

Alone Britain lacked the industrial infrastructure and financial strength to win an arms race with Germany, and as America, Britain's traditional ally, presided over by Franklin D. Roosevelt, remained reluctant to become involved in a European war, there were simply insufficient funds to redress the balance. But while the presence of U-Boats in the Atlantic became ever more menacing, a sense of foreboding had begun to grow, and it was clear that the British government would not be able to watch and wait for much longer, the time for action had come.

As pressure mounted Chamberlain and the foreign secretary Viscount Halifax approved a plan to occupy the port of Narvik and control the rail link to Sweden, but Norway and Sweden were unwilling to collaborate in a scheme that might lead to war with both Germany and the Soviet Union.

As an alternative Churchill suggested *Operation Wilfred*, a plan to mine Norwegian waters and force German shipping out into the open sea where the Royal Navy lay in wait.

Allied troops could then be sent in to occupy Norway, but the government repeatedly rejected the idea. Churchill's hands were tied, and he could do no more than stand by and watch in horror as events unfolded. Meanwhile Hitler had spent his time during the phony war very wisely, drawing up plans for dominating Europe and while the Allies hesitated, his Nazi forces stood poised to attack. By April warships, air force and armies were ready to invade not only Norway but also its neighbor Denmark, which would prove a valuable staging post for operations. Chamberlain's caution had given the Nazi leader the breathing space he needed and by the time *Operation Wilfred* was finally approved and the British began mining Norwegian waters on April the 8th it was already too late.

With complete disregard for the non-aggression pact signed with neutral Denmark only one year earlier, at 4.15 in the morning, on April the 9th 1940 German forces marched in. Within 3 hours, after threats to bomb Copenhagen, the Danish government surrendered and the occupation was so sudden that most Danes had no idea that their country had even been invaded. And all the while, Hitler's General Falkenhorst with the twenty-first Army Corps was already on route to invade Norway.

The initial German invasion force, transported by several groups of ships, planned to attack six Norwegian ports simultaneously including Oslo, Narvik and Trondheim. As Norwegian coastal defense ships were torpedoed, German airborne forces parachuted into the country's major cities carrying out the first paratrooper attack in history. Within 24 hours most of the strategically important Norwegian towns and cities were in Nazi hands. Better late than never, Britain's Royal Navy arrived to battle back against German naval forces two days after the start of the invasion, but their efforts were futile. It was too late.

As Hitler became ever more aggressive throughout Europe, with the loss of Norway inevitable, Allied troops were withdrawn to fight elsewhere and the Norwegians were left to fight on as best they could alone.

Back in London, emotions were running high after the failure of the British expedition to Norway, especially as Winston Churchill had seen this disaster coming. It was clear that a passive strategy up to this point had been too cautious and it was time for Chamberlain to go. In a debate in the House of Commons, one of Chamberlain's closest friends turned to history and the words of Oliver Cromwell to express the view of the British people:

"You have sat too long here for any good you have been doing. Depart, I say, and let us have done with you. In the name of God, go."

With honor and dignity Chamberlain accepted his fate and resigned, but now an alternative leader had to be found, one who wouldn't be afraid to lead the nation through another World War. The Conservative politician Anthony Eden was one possible candidate, but at just forty-three years old, he was considered too young. Another option was Viscount Halifax, a senior conservative politician, the foreign secretary, and Chamberlain's choice as a replacement, but the prospect of running a wartime coalition did not appeal to the world-weary Halifax. By a process of elimination, the only possible candidate for Prime Minister was Winston Churchill, the First Lord of the Admiralty, whose fearsome reputation and correct analysis of what Hitler would do next improved British morale dramatically.

Winston Churchill took up office on May the 10th 1940, and while a new coalition government was swiftly formed, Adolf Hitler would have been all too aware that Churchill was going to be a much tougher adversary than Chamberlain had been. The phony war had given Hitler the upper hand without a doubt and Churchill quickly set to work in order to redress the balance. However, nobody, not even Churchill, could have predicted just how quickly the new Prime Minister would have to stand up and be counted.

For the time being Hitler was working towards the invasion of France, a nation that he had come to hate after his experiences as a soldier during the First World War and from this moment onwards he was determined to see the French bow to the power of the Third Reich. The conquest of France would be the crowning glory in the Nazi domination of Europe.

The most brilliant German military minds were now put together to come up with the ultimate attack plan for achieving the occupation of the Low Countries and Northern France. Described as "Fall Gelb", Field Marshall Erich von Manstein devised a highly elaborate operation, which would be later described by Winston Churchill as the "sickle cut" technique.

· · ·

Using three army groups, A, B and C, the Nazis would push into the Low Countries and France, using great military ingenuity to break the Allied line in two, trapping enemy troops on the French beaches at Dunkirk. Army Group B was to be led by Field Marshall Feder von Bock and their orders were to feign an attack through neutral Belgium and the Netherlands to draw as many Allied troops as possible northwards.

Group C had the task of attacking France along the defensive Maginot Line, again keeping Allied troops fully engaged.

Meanwhile Army Group A would instigate the main attack, led by Field Marshall Gerd Von Runstedt, clearing a path to advance through the Ardennes Forest, crossing the River Meuse and then using a blitzkrieg sweep to push across France towards the English Channel, trapping Allied forces in Belgium and across the Flanders fields where so many had died during World War I.

It was an ingenious yet risky plan, but Hitler was so confident of its success that the very evening before the attack he told his staff *"Gentlemen you are about to witness the most famous victory in history!"*

It was destined to be the very same day that Winston Churchill became Prime Minister, May the 10th, that saw the Nazis start their advance towards France.

At just after four in the morning when the first attacks took place, the neutral countries of Holland and Belgium found themselves in desperate need of aid from the Allies with the phony war well and truly at an end. The Dutch hoped that should any invasion take place, the Nazis would leave the main cities, which were protected by flooded low level areas and fortifications intact, and proceed through the southern parts of the country, and on into Belgium.

. . .

However, Herman Goering, the Commander of Germany's air force, the Luftwaffe, was determined to capture the Western Dutch airfields fearing that the British might take control of them, creating a base from where the RAF could attack the Fatherland. Consequently, Goering demanded a complete conquest of the Netherlands.

Though poorly armed with artillery, relying on Howitzers and machine guns that dated back to the First World War, the Dutch fought bravely and efficiently against the modern tanks and weapons of the German Army. But Hitler was adamant that all resistance had to be crushed and as his Panzer tank divisions gathered outside Rotterdam, Holland's second largest city, the nation was given an ultimatum. If they surrendered, their cities would be spared. If not, they would be bombed.

While negotiations commenced, what followed would go down in history as one of the great atrocities of the Second World War as waves of Goering's bombers darkened the skies, above Rotterdam. The onslaught of bombs that ensued tore out the heart of the city, making eighty thousand people homeless and leaving a flat and desolate landscape in their wake. Almost a thousand people were killed and with other major cities threatened with the same fate, the Netherlands had no choice but to surrender. On May the 14th the battle for Holland was over, and as the Nazis took the strategically vital airfields, the Dutch Queen, Wilhelmina, fled to London where she would continue to rally support for the fight against Germany.

While Hitler had vanquished the Netherlands within four days, the battle for Belgium would prove to be an altogether tougher affair. The country was protected by Fort Eben-Emael, a huge fortress that was virtually impregnable, and considered to be one of the most modern in the world at that time. The Germans yet again resorted to more unconventional strategies to invade the country and used gliders to land and unload assault teams.

. . .

Within hours Nazi paratroopers and Panzer tank divisions were occupying Belgium and their French neighbors along with the British were convinced that this was the main attack, just as the Nazi commanders had hoped, and responded by throwing as many Allied troops as possible into the path of the Germans.

French citizens after a long trek

French and British forces began to move forward to make contact with the Belgian army and create an unbroken line of resistance from the English Channel to the borders of Switzerland. But little did they know that further South, the bulk of the Nazi forces in Group A were steadily advancing through the Ardennes Forest unchallenged and about to storm through the allied lines.

Back in London, Winston Churchill and the government watched events unfold with ever increasing concern. The British Expeditionary Force, more commonly known as the BEF had been in France since Germany's invasion of Poland in 1939, and after waiting patiently throughout the phony war, battling the bitter cold winter as they built trenches in preparation, these soldiers were now called upon to provide vital reinforcements for the Belgian and French troops.

As the BEF poured into Belgium in their thousands they were given a tremendous welcome, but as Holland fell and the Nazi troops broke through all lines of defense, Churchill could see the difficult fight that lay ahead for the soldiers of the BEF. The situation however was graver than the British Prime Minister could possibly have imagined.

The Nazi army pushing through the Ardennes comprised of divisions led by some of the greatest Generals in Germany, most notably Erwin Rommel and Heinz Guderian. The latter was one of the first to develop and advocate the ground-breaking principles of blitzkrieg, which translates into English as lightning strike. This technique was a new revolutionary form of warfare using mechanized forces to pierce a small section of the enemy front before proceeding onwards, without regard for their flanks. Guderian believed that the tank was the decisive weapon of war and stated that in his opinion, *"If the tanks succeed, then victory follows"*.

Guderian's strategy during the invasion of France would prove a great success, but despite the impressive Nazi maneuvers the Allies still had many valuable opportunities to thwart the Germans. However, they failed to make the most of the chances that they had, leaving Hitler in the ascendency as his troops seemed ever more invincible as the days went on.

While the Germans were making their way across the wild territory of the Ardennes, poor roads did somewhat hinder the progress of the vast armada of Nazi vehicles and troops struggling to make headway on their way to the River Meuse.

. . .

The Meuse was one of the biggest defensive lines protecting the French from invasion, forming a natural barrier between France, Belgium and Holland, flowing for over five hundred miles. It was vital that this line be defended no matter what the cost.

As the progress of Nazi troops began to slow, the French Commander Maurice Gamelin, now fully aware of army Group A's advance, had the perfect opportunity to attack by air, but he elected not to do so.

Gamelin was reluctant to risk using strategic bombers so close to the German border and instead ordered reinforcement divisions to the Meuse sector by the comparatively slow means of night trains. The French were convinced that the Nazis wouldn't even attempt to breach the Meuse Line to the west of the Ardennes, until they had a large infantry and artillery support available. There was little sense of urgency amongst the French commanders, as they believed they had at least until the 20th of May to get reinforcements in place.

Underestimating the efficiency of Hitler's offensive was a grave mistake. Just three days after invading Belgium on May the 13th, German forces were already at the Meuse line. As Panzer tanks and troops attacked, forging ahead on land, Goering's Luftwaffe roared overhead bombarding Allied troops, flying almost four thousand sorties. The bombardment lasted from eight o'clock in the morning until dusk and was the heaviest the world had ever seen. Morale on the Allied side quickly plunged, troops began to abandon their posts while Panzer tanks attacked relentlessly pushing through the first lines of defense and towards the river.

Before long the Nazis had made considerable progress, pushing some five miles into the French defenses. By seven o'clock that evening, as false rumors abounded from fleeing soldiers that German tanks were already behind them, the remaining troops left defending the line also fled. It was a fatal mistake and one that would shatter all hope of saving France. Left unprotected, the next morning German troops and anti-tank units swept over the River Meuse.

Although Allied forces desperately tried to destroy the bridges with air attacks to prevent the Nazi advance, German fighter planes battled ferociously and along with anti-aircraft guns, shot down around ninety Allied bombers in just one day. The Luftwaffe described the event as "The Day of the Fighters" and with the bridges still intact, the Panzer divisions under Guderian, now ranged freely around the landing areas until all real resistance was neutralized. It was at this point that the blitzkrieg tactics of the highly trained Nazi military machine proved most effective. Despite instructions to consolidate a small bridgehead, Guderian and Rommel disregarded orders and began to strike out in all directions, taking French troops all around the country by surprise.

As Rommel's Panzers pushed deeper and deeper into France it became virtually impossible for even German High Command to determine their whereabouts, and they became known as the "Ghost Division". This was blitzkrieg at its most reckless, infuriating many of the Nazi commanders, but the swift progress was undeniable. By the 17th of May, Rommel had taken ten thousand Allied prisoners and had lost only thirty-six of his own men.

In Paris panic began to set in as the government realized that Allied defenses were all too swiftly crumbling to dust. Archives were burnt and the French Prime Minister Paul Reynaud telephoned Churchill on May the 15th, declaring, *"We have been defeated. We are beaten; we have lost the battle"*. Churchill rushed to Paris the next day, and when he asked Reynaud where the strategic reserve was, that had saved Paris in the First World War, the devastated French Premiere confessed: *"There is none"*. It appeared France was doomed.

While the government of France was thrown into disarray a future French leader was beginning to make a name for himself. General Charles De Gaulle hastily assembled forces for a counterattack, and it was one of the few positive successes for the beleaguered nation, but it was not enough to push back the German advance. Nevertheless, despite De Gaulle's inability to save the country, the brave attempt would see him promoted to the position of Brigadier General and he would become a figurehead for the Free French thereafter. Even when the Third Reich had much of the nation within their grasp General De Gaulle would continue to inspire the French Resistance to fight for freedom from the London base he occupied after fleeing France.

While the Germans pushed ever onward, by May the 17th Rommel and Guderian's forces actually found themselves in a dangerous position. The tanks were low on fuel, the troops were exhausted and after the quick dash into France without waiting for support, their flanks were now unprotected.

The Nazi advance slowed down completely giving the French a golden opportunity to attack, but once again they failed to take action. The Panzer Corps were given the luxury of time to repair tanks, eat, sleep and even shave and take a bath.

The blame for missing so many opportunities firmly rested with the French government and its military commanders. Since the Treaty of Versailles in 1919, following the end of the First World War, the French government hoped that Germany's warmongering days were over. As the depression of 1929 hit hard, France had put off rearmament while Germany flouted the Treaty of Versailles and secretly began to build up their armies and invest in new weaponry.

Now as the Nazis swarmed into France with their highly equipped forces, the French lacked just about everything from modern tanks to light weapons and even clothing. Badly prepared and poorly led many of the fighting men were now convinced that defeat was imminent.

· · ·

Meanwhile, once refreshed, the panzers began to push towards the coast and the advance became more intense than ever. Using integrated ground and air assaults the sheer strength of the Nazi charge was terrifying; they destroyed everything in their path as thousands of refugees began to flee the country rather than live under German occupation. But for the Allies worse was still to come. In the North they were now being encircled with no possible escape route. The situation was disastrous, instead of a Franco-Anglo-Belgian line containing the Nazi attack there was now a German line stretching from Germany to the sea, quite literally cutting the Allied forces in two.

On May the 20th, the French Prime Minister Paul Reynaud sacked Gamelin for his failure to contain the German offensive, and replaced him with Maxime Weygand, a Major General renowned for his role in the First World War. But not even Weygand would be able to muster the forces necessary to stop the advance.

Seeing the situation was becoming increasingly desperate, Lord Gort, the Chief Commanding Officer of the BEF, ordered a retreat towards the channel on the 23rd of May, hoping that the troops could be evacuated. While the Nazis blockaded Calais and Boulogne, Dunkirk, lying just 6 miles from the Belgian border, was now one of the last major ports available to the Allies.

British, Belgian and French forces headed for its beaches but as Guderian's troops advanced, the Allies were being encircled and before long three hundred thousand men were trapped with nothing but sea ahead of them and the enemy to the rear.

A disaster on an epic scale was now brewing, as Churchill and the British navy were faced with the stark reality that there simply weren't enough vessels to rescue the number of soldiers steadily increasing on the beaches of Dunkirk. The most they could hope to save would be around forty-five thousand men, leaving two hundred and fifty-five thousand active Allied service personnel to the mercy of the Germans.

There was however just the smallest glimmer of hope. On May the 14th a message had been broadcast to the British nation requesting that all owners of seaworthy craft, that hadn't already been requisitioned for the war effort, be registered with the admiralty. The call for assistance reached owners of yachts, pleasure cruisers and even fishing boats and the response was phenomenal. Soon a huge civilian fleet was on standby, some manned by trained volunteers, others captained by their owners and all ready to cross the channel to sail into the battle of France and save as many Allied soldiers as possible. They would become known as the Little Ships of Dunkirk and would play a crucial part in one of the most daring rescue missions in history.

It was now up to Vice Admiral Bertram Ramsey, who was in charge of the defense of the Dover area of British operations and the protection of cross Channel military traffic, to finalize the plans, which were codenamed *Operation Dynamo*.

This was an immense challenge and staff worked around the clock, in underground tunnels deep beneath Dover Castle, to finalize every final detail. By May the 26th the operation was ready to be launched and the vast fleet set off across the Channel towards France.

Few knew what to expect with battles raging so close to the French coast, and the Nazi troops swiftly progressing, but when they finally arrived within sight of Dunkirk the crews manning the ships found to their amazement that Guderian's forces were nowhere to be seen.

As far as the coastline stretched thousands upon thousands of Allied troops, as yet untouched by the Nazi onslaught, were sitting patiently waiting for help to come. Considering the incredible success of the German's blitzkrieg sweep across France it seemed incredible that the tanks of the Panzer divisions had not reached this part of the coastline, but two days earlier a pivotal moment in the battle for France had taken place.

Quite extraordinarily it was Adolf Hitler himself who had intervened in the fate of the thousands of Allied soldiers and his actions undoubtedly resulted in so many of them escaping. While the Panzers stood poised to attack the encircled troops, he had given the order for the tanks to hold their position. The reasons behind this seemingly strange decision remain to this day something of a mystery, but we do know that Goering had told the Führer that his Luftwaffe alone could prevent an evacuation, while Runstedt had warned Hitler that further Panzer activity would result in an extended repair period, jeopardizing the second stage in the battle of France, and the plans to seize Paris.

There is also another theory however, namely that Hitler did not want a war with Britain and still hoped to be able to negotiate a settlement with Churchill, which after the conquest of France would allow him to focus his energy on Russia and the Eastern Front.

Soldiers queue in the Dunkirk dunes

In the meantime, while the Nazis waited, the British vessels sailed closer to the French coast and the mass evacuation began. Troops waded deep out into the water to meet the rescue teams and clamber on board to safety. Thousands upon thousands of men now lined the shores and waited patiently for the ships to take them away. Orderly queues formed for the boats and even though many knew that they would perhaps never make it off the beaches they still waited their turn.

The little ships now played their vital part, as one of the main problems Ramsey had to overcome was the fact that the shallow waters around Dunkirk, meant that many of the larger naval vessels could not be used to get men from the beaches to the ships waiting offshore. While the evacuation continued, and more men clambered aboard the boats, the Nazi commanders soon became aware of what was happening. As Hitler realized his terrible mistake in calling off the attack, he ordered a full-scale air and land assault on May the 27th to wipe out the troops and sink the evacuation ships that had come to save them.

. . .

The RAF swiftly flew in to protect the boats and troops on the ground and the air became a mass of swooping planes as they fought long and hard to counter the relentless attack staged by the Luftwaffe. While enemy bombs kept falling from the skies the role of the British fighter pilots would prove crucial to the success of the mission.

Meanwhile on the ground the Allies were all too aware that some of their number would have to form a stronghold to keep Hitler's men away from the beaches to protect the ships for as long as possible. Hundreds would sacrifice their lives so that others could live, willingly obeying the order to "fight till the last bullet".

To make matters worse news reached the Allies that on May the 28th Belgium had surrendered to the Germans, leaving the BEF dangerously exposed. As troops battled on, with Dunkirk under such heavy attack, the evacuation was becoming increasingly difficult, and even with the vast fleet of little ships, there were simply not enough boats. In the first forty-eight hours of the evacuation only 8,000 soldiers had been saved from the French beaches alive. Soon Dunkirk was swathed in clouds of black smoke billowing up from the heavy shelling, but despite the Nazis best efforts to take control, the Allied soldiers, protecting the beaches dug in even deeper, keeping the enemy at bay.

As news of what was happening reached Britain, more boats joined the rescue mission to try and help and from yachts and lifeboats to holiday steamers, more and more seaworthy craft began to sail towards the battle torn coastline. Once the rescued troops had been safely set down on British soil from the first wave of little ships, many of the boats simply turned around and went back to France again, to rescue more men.

While the German guns continued to fire, on May the 29th nineteen thousand soldiers were rescued from the beaches. Morale was now steadily rising amongst the Allied troops in France, and just one day later as the men coming back to Britain were counted in, the overall number of troops rescued had risen to forty-seven thousand.

As the mood amongst the British and French improved, the weather also began to play a part in aiding the evacuation. On the fourth day of *Operation Dynamo* a thick fog fell and shrouded the channel. It was now virtually impossible for the Luftwaffe to continue the attack and their planes lay grounded while the Allies struggled towards the ships waiting for them.

As the evacuation drew to a close on the 4th of June, and the last boat left the shores of France, more than three hundred and thirty thousand men had been saved, and despite the odds stacked so heavily against them, only two thousand Allied servicemen had been lost on the beaches, throughout the entire operation. It was an incredible achievement for the Allies and even the Nazi commanders were impressed. Erwin Rommel praised the staunch resistance of the Allied forces, despite the fact they were under-equipped and had little ammunition for much of the fighting.

For Nazi Germany however, the failure to swiftly capture Dunkirk and destroy the British Expeditionary Force was one of the biggest mistakes they would make in the Western Theatre of war. They may have won the battle for Dunkirk, but the mistakes they had made would in the months and years ahead cost them dear.

Back across the channel, as Allied troops reached the south coast of England, the next phase of the operation was set in motion as soldiers had to be relocated as quickly as possible. Train stations quickly filled up with the soldiers hoping to get home and see their loved ones, before being assigned to new duties.

| A very British welcome home with mugs of tea.

Hundreds of volunteers worked around the clock to ensure that the soldiers were comfortable, and they were welcomed home as returning heroes as the nation showed its gratitude to the men who had survived to fight another day.

While Britain rejoiced at the return of their battle weary soldiers, Churchill hailed the outcome of the Dunkirk evacuation as a *"miracle of deliverance"*, but he also had a warning for the public: *"we must be very careful not to assign to this deliverance the attributes of a victory. Wars are not won by evacuations"*.

Valuable artillery and weapons had been lost on the beaches and roads of France that would result in an even greater dependency on the United States throughout the course of the war. In addition, many of the Allied soldiers that had been left behind were now Prisoners of War and back in France the mood was understandably bleak. After the evacuation at Dunkirk, General Weygand was in a difficult position. France had lost their strongest and most modern forces in the North, as well as their best-armored formations and heavy weaponry. Their manpower was depleted, and with a front to defend from the Channel to the Sedan, without as they perceived it any Allied support, many French leaders openly lost heart. To them, Dunkirk had been an abandonment.

Adolf Hitler could now begin the second phase in the battle for France, *"Fall Rot"* which translates as Case Red in English. Just one day after the last ship had left Dunkirk on June the 5th 1940, the German offensive was renewed, and the Nazi forces began to march towards Paris.

Without the support of the British air force, the French air resistance soon collapsed and while Germany enjoyed total air supremacy across the country, the French government fled, declaring Paris an "open city". On the 14th of June the Wehrmacht marched into the beautiful French capital, and as a deep dread filled the hearts of the Parisians who witnessed the loss of their city, it was a triumphant moment for Nazi Germany.

This was the jewel in the European crown for Adolf Hitler, and one of the defining moments he had been waiting for. When Paul Reynaud, the Prime Minister, resigned his position he was succeeded by Marshall Phillipe Petain, who immediately requested an armistice with Germany. Still raging at the way Germany had been treated after the First World War, Hitler had the original train carriage, where the 1918 armistice had been signed, removed from a French museum and placed in the exact same spot in the Compiegne forest, where Marshal Foch had accepted Germany's surrender.

On June the 22nd Hitler sat in the chair where the French commander Foch had completed Germany's humiliation over two decades earlier, but after only listening to the preamble, disdainfully he left the rest to his Chief-of-staff, General Keitel. France was split into an occupied zone in the north and west, and a nominally independent state in the south at Vichy. The Vichy government, led by Petain, accepted France was a defeated nation, and attempted to gain favor with the Germans through passivity.

Meanwhile as Hitler greedily seized French territory, a new player had joined the theatre of war. Benito Mussolini the leader of Fascist Italy declared war on France and Britain on June the 10th and would soon put pressure on British troops based in Northern Africa.

With countries to their east and south swamped by the Nazi enemy and Stalin's Red Army and Mussolini allied with Hitler, Britain was now in a grave situation. The island nation stood alone.

However, Dunkirk had instilled hope into the people of Britain, and after Winston Churchill's *"miracle of deliverance"*, every man, woman and child believed that anything was possible. In fact, as it became evident that Britain would be Germany's next target, they even began to believe that Adolf Hitler and his Axis of Evil could be defeated if they all pulled together. Winston Churchill had instantly made his mark as a great leader, and whether they knew it or not, the triumphant Nazis now had a real fight on their hands, as Churchill declared: *"The Battle of France is over. The Battle of Britain is about to begin."*

4

BRITAIN UNDER ATTACK

July - September 1940

Hitler and Hermann Goering plan the British attack

As the winds of change blew through Europe, by June 1940 Nazi Germany had invaded almost every country to the north, south, east and west of its borders, terrorizing civilians, obliterating cities and driving back the Allied troops that tried to halt their advance. It seemed that little stood in the way of the Nazis and their total domination of the continent and when Adolf Hitler marched victoriously into Paris on June the 14th the world could do nothing more than look on in total dismay.

But while Nazi forces flooded into France and Hitler's commanders began to enjoy the fruits of their success, there was one nation that refused to capitulate to German domination.

Across the Channel Great Britain was simply not prepared to contemplate peace with Nazi Germany and as the planes of the Third Reich began to swarm towards British air space, Adolf Hitler was about to discover that he faced an entire population determined to defend its beaches, towns and cities, no matter what the cost.

While the British Prime Minister Winston Churchill, rallied the public to fight to the bitter end, the Battle of Britain got underway and Hitler's military supremacy faced its biggest challenge to date. The story of this most historic battle, and the brave souls who fought to defend their island, protecting it from a regime that threatened freedom and democracy in Europe, marked a turning point in a war that had so far seemed impossible for the Allies to win. And as the spirit of Dunkirk remained strong, it was the extraordinary bravery of those who struggled through the dark days when Britain stood alone, that would ultimately save not only the United Kingdom but also their fellow Allies from the overwhelming force of Hitler's Third Reich.

From the terror of the blitz, to the extraordinary battles fought in the air, not forgetting of course the events unfolding further afield in the Far East and the deserts of North Africa, this chapter will chart the first real evidence of the world fighting back against Adolf Hitler and his Axis of Evil.

In 1938 the British public had watched King George the Sixth lay a wreath on the Cenotaph in memory of the thousands of lives that had been lost in The First Great War.

At this stage few people realized how close the nation now was to facing bitter conflict and that the peace the world had cherished for almost two decades was about to be shattered. However, from the rubble and ruins of the First World War, new and dangerous forces were beginning to emerge. The Italian dictator, Mussolini was eager to create a new Roman Empire and Adolf Hitler was rallying the German people to support his demands for more territory, and his dream of a world run by an Aryan master race.

When the Nazis marched into Czechoslovakia in March 1939, past Allies France and Great Britain were left clinging precariously to the comfort of tradition. The French President, Albert Lebrun made a state visit to Britain, reassuring the public that the established empires were more than a match for the new dictators, but it was soon clear that fine words and rash promises would never be enough to withstand the terrible storm that was brewing on the continent. On September the 1st 1939 Adolf Hitler seized his opportunity and invaded Poland and two days later Britain, swiftly followed by France, declared war on Germany. As the full horror of the Nazi occupation cast its shadow across Poland, on British soil, sandbags were put in place and children were evacuated from the major cities.

But even as the Nazi U-Boats prowled the high seas attacking at will, causing food to become scarce, the then British Prime Minister Neville Chamberlain, still hoped to find a peaceful solution. However, by the spring of 1940 it was clear that Adolf Hitler had no intention of backing down and on April the 7th Denmark and Norway were invaded as the Nazis secured precious raw materials for the Third Reich, and the phony war that had defined the autumn and winter of 1939 was well and truly over.

What's more Hitler's stormtroopers didn't stop at Scandinavia, because on May the 2nd the Low Countries came under attack, with France being the Nazi's next target.

While the British Expeditionary Force, the BEF, along with armies from Belgium and France rushed to defend their borders, back in Britain the public believed that Chamberlain's tentative and hesitant policy of appeasement had let them very badly down indeed. As nations were toppled like dominoes across Europe, it was evident that peace was not a word that had any place in Hitler's vocabulary, and the only option was to stop taking a defensive line and go on the attack. Chamberlain had no choice but to step aside as a new leader took to the floor of the House of Commons, at the head of a wartime coalition government, ready to change the course of history. It was none other than Winston Churchill, a statesman who had been no stranger to conflict his whole life long. He was also a descendent of one of the greatest military commanders Britain had ever known, Lord John Churchill, who had crushed the forces of the French King, Louis the fourteenth, at the Battle of Blenheim in 1704.

Winston Churchill as a child had been fascinated by war strategies and battle maneuvers, and proudly upheld the position of school fencing champion. After attending the Royal Military Academy at Sandhurst, Churchill graduated eighth out of 150 cadets, and was commissioned as a Second Lieutenant in the 4th Queen's Own Hussars in 1895. From the Boer War in South Africa to battles in Cuba and India, Churchill travelled far and wide, sometimes fighting and sometimes writing news reports and on occasion doing both simultaneously.

It was clear that the young man seemed to be most at home when he was at the heart of the action, and even when he became a politician as the twentieth century dawned, from skirmishes with the suffragettes in 1910, to gangster battles in the East End, it seemed that wherever there was a battle to be fought Churchill was never far away.

Nevertheless, as the First World War loomed on the horizon Churchill's actions were frequently controversial and not always successful. When he was appointed First Lord of the Admiralty in November 1914 his strategy of securing a sea route to Russia by capturing Constantinople proved problematic from the start. The campaign was an unmitigated disaster and thousands of troops, many of whom were volunteers from New Zealand and Australia, were slaughtered at Gallipoli as the attack commenced. Always unpopular in political circles due to outspokenness, Churchill was made the scapegoat for the disaster, although others had equal responsibility. The First Lord of the Admiralty was removed from his post in disgrace and Churchill would find himself in the political wilderness for the next two decades before fate finally granted him another opportunity to prove himself to the British public.

When the battle of France commenced in May 1940, Winston Churchill, as Britain's new Prime Minister, had the chance to win back the credibility he had lost as a result of the events at Gallipoli, and it was a chance he was determined to exploit to the full. On May the 2nd as Winston accepted the role of Prime Minister he told the nation that he had nothing to offer but his blood, toil, tears and sweat, and that the intention of the new government was, *"to wage war by land, sea and air. War with all our might and with all the strength God has given us"*.

His skillful rhetoric prepared the British people for the battle that lay ahead and when Allied forces were trapped in their hundreds of thousands on the beaches of Dunkirk just weeks later, Prime Minister Churchill was as good as his word.

· · ·

While Hitler's troops encircled the Allies, leaving them no escape, one of the most miraculous events of the war took place, with military and civilian personnel all playing their part. Beneath the very noses of Hitler and his generals, three hundred thousand Allied troops were evacuated from the beaches of Northern France by a flotilla of ships, fishing boats and yachts, along with all manner of other seaworthy craft, and returned safely to Britain, ready to fight another day.

It proved that the Nazis were not infallible, but while Britain celebrated and welcomed their troops home, Churchill was quick to warn the nation that with valuable artillery and weapons lost and their French allies left to face the enemy alone, this was far from being a victory. As France fell in June 1940 Churchill gave a stark warning to the nation worth repeating here: *"What General Weygand called the Battle of France is over. I expect that the Battle of Britain is about to begin"*. They were wise words indeed. Britain was about to come under the fiercest of attacks.

But compared to the situation faced by the countries that had already been vanquished by Hitler's sudden blitzkrieg tactics, at least Great Britain had been preparing for war for nearly a year. Barrage balloons had been put up, factories had increased production, and as more and more men poured into the army, women had been stepping forward to take their places on the production lines as well as on the nation's farms.

Meanwhile volunteers from the Commonwealth and those fleeing countries now occupied by the Third Reich began pouring into Britain, ready to join the Allied cause. While all measures were taken for the defense of the nation, security was of paramount importance, and Churchill, fearing there may be spies amongst the foreigners living on British soil, demanded that all Germans, Austrians and Italians be interned without trial.

He famously demanded, "Collar the lot", and by the summer of 1940 thousands of foreigners had been sent to the Isle of Man to live in bed and break-fast accommodation and hotels that had been cordoned off into camps. It was a move that many criticized, and the vast majority of those interned were completely innocent, but with a bitter battle ahead Churchill could not afford to take any risks. It was the first of many controversial moves that he would make over the course of the war, and by the beginning of July 1940, yet another difficult decision had to be made.

With the majority of France under the control of the German's puppet regime, the Vichy Government, there was a real risk that Hitler would use the French fleet, the fourth largest naval force in the world, against the British. The Commander of the French Navy, Admiral Darlan, had given a personal guarantee to Churchill that this wouldn't happen, but the British Prime Minister was all too aware that Darlan may have no choice in the matter and such a dangerous threat could not be overlooked. Wary of Hitler's next move, just days before the Battle of Britain began, Churchill proved that he was determined to defeat the German Führer whatever the cost. Codenamed *Operation Catapult,* a fleet of British warships from Gibraltar sailed to where the largest concentration of French Naval power was based, at Mers-el-Kebir in French Algeria.

Their task was to take control of the French fleet, and although attempts were made to use diplomacy to secure the ships, the commanding Admiral in Algeria refused to hand over control to the British. On Churchill's instructions, the British fleet opened fire and one thousand two hundred and ninety-seven French sailors were killed, with more than 350 left wounded.

The desperate measures taken by the British Prime Minister triggered a huge debate in the House of Commons and not surprisingly also soured relations between the British and the French for some time. Nevertheless, what some considered to be ruthlessness on the part of Churchill served as a stark warning to Hitler that he had better not underestimate the British. It demonstrated that Great Britain was prepared to continue the fight against Nazi

tyranny alone if necessary, and Churchill later declared that for *"high government circles in the United States ... there was no more talk of Britain giving in."*

Interestingly, while all this was going on, Hitler had been convinced that after
the evacuation of the troops at Dunkirk, the war was practically over and that
the British, defeated on the continent and with no European allies, would
soon agree to a peaceful surrender. Although some members of Churchill's
government, most notably the foreign secretary Lord Halifax, had been
willing to negotiate with Hitler, Churchill's defiance in Algeria was a sign that
Britain would never surrender without a fierce fight.

So, the gloves were off. Hitler was now in no doubt whatsoever that the
British would have to be conquered by force if the Nazi domination of
Western Europe was to be total, and with Churchill obstinately standing his
ground, back at Nazi headquarters all attention was now focused on drawing
up a plan of attack. As Hitler and his Generals plotted, he hoped it would
take no more than a month to bring Great Britain into line, but his commanders were very wary of the problems that lay ahead; invading an island was a
very different proposition to storming across a borderline with tanks.

During the Norwegian campaign of April 1940, the German naval forces had
come close to being destroyed and they stood little chance of being a match
for the powerful Royal Navy, if an invasion was launched. Grand Admiral
Erich Raeder informed his Führer that invading Great Britain could only be
considered as a last resort, and only then, if the Luftwaffe had neutralized the
RAF, to give Germany supremacy in the air.

So, the decision was taken to direct all efforts towards the destruction of the
Royal Air Force in the first phase of *Operation Sea Lion,* the codename for the
invasion of Britain. Then when the RAF had been destroyed a massive sea and
airborne assault along the length of the south coast could take place, and this
would then be followed by a full-scale invasion. One hundred thousand

troops, along with Heinrich Himmler's terror force, the SS, would storm into Britain with orders to destroy all opposition.

The responsibility that now lay with the RAF was immense, and despite it being the oldest independent air force in the world, having been founded in 1918, the policy of appeasement that had prevailed during the 1930s had meant it was far from being as prepared for war as the German Luftwaffe. The focus had been on building bombers rather than fighters to defend the country and it wasn't until 1938 that Fighter Command was given full priority.

Air Chief Marshal Dowding, in charge of British Fighter Command since its formation in 1936, had very little time to prepare for the battle that lay ahead. The RAF's main weakness was a shortage of experienced pilots, especially after the Battle of France and the losses incurred during the evacuation of Dunkirk.

| Battle of Britain air observer

Farm boys, teachers, doctors, bank clerks and shop assistants, alongside hundreds of other young men with everyday jobs, little training and virtually no combat experience, were now called upon to face the rigorously trained Luftwaffe pilots. Nevertheless, they were being led by experienced commanders who certainly knew what was required. First World War ace, Air Vice Marshal Keith Park from New Zealand was responsible for defending the southeast of England and the critical London approaches. Park's Number 11 Group would bear the brunt of the attacks, while Air Vice Marshal Trafford Leigh-Mallory commanded Number 12 Group, covering the Midlands and East Anglia, playing an equally vital role.

The main German attack came from two Luftwaffe Air Fleets, commanded by

Field Marshals Albert Kesselring and Hugo Sperrle. However, although the Luftwaffe had many more aircraft and experienced pilots than their British counterparts, the outcome was anything but a foregone conclusion.

For a start, the German air fleets had not been designed to fight in their own right, but to support the army on land operations. The tactic had been used brilliantly in the conquest of Western Europe with the famous blitzkrieg or lightning strike attacks.

But being given total responsibility for a battle was a huge undertaking for the Luftwaffe. The Battle of Britain was the first campaign to be fought solely in the air, and all previous rules of engagement no longer applied. Equally the Germans also faced the major disadvantage of fighting a battle far away from their home bases, leaving them little time to spend in the skies over Britain, with refueling always a major issue.

During an air battle, if a German plane was hit, the pilot, if not killed was immediately captured, whereas the British pilots could parachute onto home territory and fight to fly another day. For the Nazis what on paper had looked to be straightforward was anything but, as the Luftwaffe quickly realized what they were up against.

There had been German air raids made on Britain since 1939, but nothing on this scale. Luftwaffe bombers had been shot down over the Firth of Forth and Scapa Flow in mid-November 39, and during further attacks in the New Year.

But as Churchill and the nation watched and waited for Hitler's next move, on July the 10th 1940 the Battle of Britain began in earnest. Wave after wave of Nazi fighter-escorted bombers headed for the ships and harbors of the south of England. Despite being vastly outnumbered, five squadrons of Hurricanes and Spitfires rose from the runways and took to the skies to challenge Germany's modern, state of the art planes.

With unsurpassed bravery and courage, the pilots gave their all for King and country in an epic battle of Churchill's David against Hitler's Goliath.

Incredibly the Germans lost twice as many planes as the British, and contrary to Hitler's belief that it would take no more than four days to defeat the RAF, the Luftwaffe soon discovered that they had a major fight on their hands. Not only were they up against the sheer bravery and determination of the enemy pilots but the British also had a revolutionary top-secret technology that would make a major contribution to the outcome of the battle.

What would later become known as RADAR gave British controllers early warning of Luftwaffe raids, as the great towers scanned the skies along the English coast and out to sea. And further inland the British Observer Corps continued to employ more traditional methods, peering heavenward, day and night, ready to phone control command as soon as an enemy aircraft came into view. Both the Observer Corps and RADAR provided an invaluable part of Britain's defense as the controllers who watched the tables twenty-four hours a day would send out warnings to the nearest fighter bases as enemy planes came into sight, so they in turn would be ready to fly into action.

Soon the Luftwaffe began to wonder why the Spitfires and Hurricanes were always waiting for them, but nonetheless they continued to underrate the value of the RADAR towers. Ironically back in 1939, just before war broke out, the Germans had sent the airship Graf Zeppelin on a spy mission to scour the British airwaves for RADAR transmissions. While the vast airship flew up and down the east coast, British RADAR operators saw the largest echo they had ever witnessed appear on their screens, but the German scientists onboard were oblivious to the commotion below and concluded that RADAR in Britain was in fact primitive and inefficient.

Radar trials in Southern England

As the airship floated back to the fatherland RADAR wasn't the only thing German intelligence had failed to pick up on. In the heart of the Buckinghamshire countryside at Bletchley Park, codebreakers were working day and night to decipher messages sent through the German Enigma Machines. The Nazis transmitted their most secret and tactical information, coded through Enigma, and Project Ultra was dedicated to decrypting the messages.

Eventually ultra-intelligence became so successful that the British had to ration its use to avoid undermining Nazi confidence in their Enigma machines. The Germans would only discover the extent to which Polish and British cryptographers had broken the Enigma codes after the war, but while ultra-intelligence was helping the battle on the home front, further afield there were threats that Ultra could not be of any assistance with.

With the remnants of Queen Victoria's Empire, the British still had colonies in all corners of the globe, having once been the largest formal empire the world had ever known, with its power and influence stretching far and wide. As the Axis tightened its grip, outposts of the Empire from the Far East to the deserts of North Africa, as well as territory in the Mediterranean, were all coming under threat. As a result, Britain had a great deal more than the home front to be concerned about.

On the other side of the globe, Japan had long been waiting to seize its opportunity to create an Empire on the scale of the great dominions of the British and the French. Up until now Tokyo's focus had been on China and since 1937 Japanese armies had been plunging deeper into its territory, seizing land and cities, terrorizing the civilian population. While the Chinese continued to counter the attacks, and tales of atrocities grew, there was increasing sympathy for China's plight from abroad and Britain and the US were doing all they could to send aid and supplies for the war effort.

Nevertheless, the battle between China and Japan was prolonged and brutal and by 1940 still showed no sign of coming to a close. By now the Japanese had seized territory on the South Coast of China, cutting the provisional capital Chongqing off from the sea and it was becoming increasingly difficult for aid to get through.

Only a few tenuous supply routes were left, and Tokyo's generals were eager that they be cut off as soon as possible, so that the battle for Southern China could be swiftly won.

· · ·

One of these routes was the Burma Road, which ran from Lashio in the north of British controlled Burma to the Chinese city of Kunming, and Japan demanded that Churchill have it closed with immediate effect. Britain was in a difficult and vulnerable position as some of its most valuable colonies, including Hong Kong and Singapore, were in the Far East and with the Battle of Britain in full swing, could not afford to spare precious ships for their defense.

Japan certainly seemed to have the upper hand, already having taken advantage of the Germans' victory in France by putting pressure on French Indochina to close *their r*outes into China, and it appeared that the British were now equally helpless to protect their interests.

Prime Minister Winston Churchill had a grave decision to make, and for the time being at least he had no other options open, forcing him to reluctantly agree to Japanese demands. On July the 17th the Burma Road was temporarily closed, amid cries of "Shame!" from the politicians in the House of Commons. And while these events were taking place, in Africa yet another belligerent was making his presence felt.

The Italian dictator, and Nazi Germany's ally, Benito Mussolini was keen to expand Italian territory and had already begun the task of creating a new Italian Empire. In 1936 he had seized Abyssinia in East Africa, today known as Ethiopia, and had added the nation to his already established colonies of Italian Somaliland, namely Somalia and Eritrea. In North Africa, the Italians already held Libya and Mussolini was now plotting to capture the valuable ports of Egypt and the Suez Canal, so he could link up his forces in Libya with those in Italian East Africa.

Britain was in a better position in Africa than in the Far East however and was already one step ahead. When Mussolini declared war on Britain after the evacuation of Dunkirk, thirty thousand allied troops had stormed into Libya on June the 14th, signaling the start of the North African campaign. After capturing Fort Capuzzo on June the 16th and winning the first tank battle in the Western Desert at the Battle of Girba, it seemed that for the time being Egypt and the Suez Canal were secure in Allied hands.

Meanwhile in East Africa the Italians were enjoying rather more success and after some minor incursions into British territory in the Sudan and Kenya, in August 1940 the Italians and their German allies attacked British Somaliland. In response the British garrison was evacuated by sea to Aden, a French protectorate, and Mussolini was left to celebrate his first victory over Britain and the Empire.

As the Luftwaffe continued their bombardment of Britain, Adolf Hitler also had an eye on the British colonies. The Island of Gibraltar had been under British rule since the eighteenth century and served a vital role in both the Atlantic and Mediterranean Theatre, controlling virtually all naval traffic into and out of the Mediterranean Sea from the Atlantic Ocean.

While continuing preparations for *Operation Sea Lion,* Hitler began planning to seize the British colony, which would close the Mediterranean to British shipping leaving merchant ships a long and perilous route along a U-boat infested Atlantic highway. The operation was code-named *Operation Felix,* and if it succeeded would put greater pressure on the British mainland as they struggled to fight off the Luftwaffe attacks.

Hitler did however have one obstacle to overcome; the attack would have to be launched from Spain and to do this he would have to win the allegiance of the Spanish dictator, General Franco.

Franco was as yet poised gingerly on the edge of the European conflict and was not as eager as the Italian dictator Mussolini to make an alliance with the

Nazi Führer. In return for his help, Franco told Hitler he wanted Gibraltar, French Morocco, part of Algeria including Oran, as well as oil and full compensation for the cost of a British blockade. Whether by design or not, Franco's demands were beyond what Hitler was prepared to pay, and throughout the war he would continue to thwart the Nazi Leader's plans.

By the time negotiations with Spain were concluded, Hitler would famously tell the Italian dictator Mussolini that he would prefer three or four of his teeth pulled out than to speak to Franco again. Unable to use Gibraltar to create his blockade, and still unable to bring the Battle of Britain to a swift conclusion as more and more Luftwaffe planes were being shot down, Hitler now decided to step up the attack. It was time to collect together all the force he could muster to obliterate the RAF and the nation's air defenses, to crush the British spirit once and for all.

On August the 1st 1940 Hitler ordered the German Minister of Aviation, Herman Goering to summon all the might of the Luftwaffe to overpower the RAF in the shortest time possible, so preparations for *Operation Sea Lion* could be completed. The date for the invasion was set for September the 15th but before that could happen the RAF had to be beaten.

As the battle commenced 1,485 plane sorties were flown against the ports and airfields of southern England, and although British Fighter Command gave their all, the losses in the skies and damage to airfields on the ground brought the RAF to the very brink of defeat.

| Londoners going to work during the blitz

With no choice but to fly by day and night, the British pilots were exhausted and as the bombs continued to fall, a Nazi victory seemed imminent. On August the 16th while the battle raged, Winston Churchill visited Number 11 Group's Operations room and was deeply moved by the valor of the young men fighting in the skies. He was so overcome with emotion he could barely speak but the words he did utter would become the basis of his speech to the House of Commons four days later when he praised the bravery of the RAF.

"The gratitude of every home in our island, in our Empire, and indeed throughout the world, except in the abodes of the guilty, goes out to the British airmen who, undaunted by odds, unwearied in their constant challenge and mortal danger, are turning the tide of the World War by their

prowess and by their devotion. Never in the field of human conflict was so much owed by so many to so few".

And still the battles in the skies continued as the Luftwaffe ventured further inland seeking to destroy RAF bases and industrial targets where planes and other vital supplies were being produced. Many major airfields were seriously damaged and those working in factories were now at great risk. But people were determined to do their bit for the defense of the nation and worked doggedly throughout the attacks so that the war effort never faltered.

Meanwhile more and more Polish pilots were joining the RAF to help with the fight against the Nazis. 303 Squadron would famously bring down more enemy planes than any other squadron during the Battle of Britain, but despite the resilience of the men fighting in the skies and the immense effort of all those working around the clock to support them, the margins were beginning to narrow, and Fighter Command was beginning to struggle. The Luftwaffe came dangerously close to destroying Britain's air defense, but then suddenly there was a change in Hitler's battle plan.

Hitler had made it clear that the civilian population of Britain should not be targeted without his express permission, but when on August the 24th a German bomber crew accidentally dropped their bombs on London, the consequences changed the course of history. Churchill's retaliation was swift and the very next day British bombers were loaded and sent to Germany, to exact revenge on Berlin. Despite there being little damage inflicted upon Berlin in the air raids, the psychological effect on the German people was dramatic.

Herman Goering had given his assurance that the cities of the fatherland would not, and could not be bombed, but it was a promise that he evidently couldn't keep. Hitler was furious, and it seemed that he allowed anger to color his military strategy. The Führer was determined to avenge the attack on Germany and ordered that bombing now be focused with immediate effect on Britain's cities rather than Fighter Command and its airfields. Unbeknown to Hitler he had given the RAF the respite that they desperately needed, but as the blitz got underway it was the people of Britain who would find themselves under attack.

On the 7th of September 1940, in the late afternoon, sirens began to wail across the British capital as enemy planes were spotted flying towards London. As the warning rang out, people began rushing for safety, hurrying to the basements of buildings or guided to the nearest air raid shelters. Then as the streets and buildings fell silent a blanket of bombers, two miles wide were seen flying up the Thames and the onslaught began. 348 German bombers escorted by 617 fighters swarmed above the city and within moments bombs began to scream through the air, shattering the calm.

The RAF fighters who flew to defend the capital were overwhelmed as in the words of one squadron leader, the sky became a *"seething cauldron of aeroplanes"*. London was thrown into complete and utter turmoil, but while explosions continued there were even graver concerns troubling Churchill's War cabinet. Reconnaissance flights over the French channel ports, from Le Havre to Calais, had shown a substantial buildup of barges that very same week and with moonlight favoring a landing that very night, it seemed increasingly likely that the Invasion of Britain was about to take place. As the blitz began the decision was taken to issue the code word "Cromwell" nationwide, which meant that invasion was imminent. The forward coastal divisions were put on alert all over the country, and coastal artillery sites were manned, as those charged with the defense of the realm donned steel helmets and waited for the first sight of the enemy.

Home guard units manned their pillboxes, but panic started to set in, and some began ringing church bells believing that the Nazis had already landed.

. . .

As the sound of bells, silenced since the outbreak of the Battle of Britain, began to echo throughout the land, the Nazi threat suddenly seemed very real and truly terrifying.

Back in London by 6pm the first wave of bombers having dealt their deadly blows departed. But two hours later, while fire fighters battled the blazes raging throughout the city, a second group of 133 raiders, guided by the flames of London burning, continued the onslaught throughout the night. People cowered underground as the earth shuddered and shook, with no idea of what awaited them above. The second attack lasted until 4:30 in the morning and by daybreak when people began to emerge from their shelters many were met by scenes of utter devastation.

As the search for survivors amongst the rubble began, it was soon revealed that over four hundred people had been killed and more than three times that number had been injured. However, despite the human tragedies for the people of London, to the relief of those watching the coast, there was still no sign of the Nazi barges and it was clear that for the time being at least *Operation Sea Lion* had yet to be launched.

Then, in true British style as the dust began to settle, the Sunday roast was cooked whether at home or in a neighbor's oven, tea was brewed, and morale did not waver. Meanwhile a classic radio broadcast from Churchill praised the fighting spirit of Londoners as they survived the first terrible days and nights of the blitz, serving notice that Hitler's bullying tactics would never shatter the British resolve.

For the next 57 days consecutively, London was bombed either during the day or through the night, and the fires raged relentlessly. Germany began to target many other cities, from Coventry and Cardiff to Belfast and Birmingham, with attacks that were devastating. Within a few weeks the daily bombing sorties had become nightly raids as Hitler tried to weaken the spirit of the British by depriving them of their sleep. But while the onslaught continued the British fought back in every way that they could.

The government tried to confuse the German bombers by enforcing a "blackout". Street lamps were switched off, car headlights had to be covered and air raid wardens would ensure that everyone kept their lights off or concealed behind blackout curtains. Shelters were built in gardens, and as the bombing intensified, people began to gather in underground stations to sleep.

As the war continued whole communities began to develop the most extraordinarily strong sense of unity. Shops still opened despite being surrounded by the rubble of neighboring buildings and those fortunate enough to find their houses still standing rallied to help those who had not been quite so lucky. The way the British coped with the onslaught was admirable and despite their disturbed sleep in London, people continued to get up and go to work in the factories, determined to supply the Commander of the RAF, Sir Hugh Dowding, with the planes and ammunition his fighter pilots so desperately needed. People from all walks of life stood shoulder to shoulder in the fight against Hitler.

Despite fears for their safety the King and Queen were determined to remain at Buckingham Palace, showing solidarity with the British people. They even travelled around the country to boost morale and console those who had lost homes and loved ones. Buckingham Palace suffered no less than nine direct hits during the war, but once the Palace had been bombed the Queen said that she could at last look the people of the East End in the eye, and rather than shattering the nation's morale, directly attacking the monarchy had quite the opposite effect. The British were heartened that their Royal Family shared their suffering and the Kingdom was united.

. . .

As the Battle of Britain and the blitz continued, back in Germany controversy had been growing over the planned invasion of the United Kingdom and *Operation Sea Lion,* with the Army and Navy unable to agree on a landing procedure. Hitler's faith in the plan seemed to be wavering and the invasion date was postponed from the 15th of September until later in the month. Even so, on September the 15th Goering launched his final major offensive to destroy RAF Fighter Command. However, with the help of Ultra Intelligence the RAF were forewarned of the attack and in the end the Luftwaffe lost 60 aircraft to the RAF's 28; it was to be the last engagement of the Battle of Britain.

After this defeat, *Operation Sea Lion* was called off and with sea conditions deteriorating as winter approached it would be spring before it could even be considered again. The Battle of Britain was over, but Hitler would continue his efforts to bomb the nation into submission. During the blitz, some two million houses would be destroyed, with 60,000 civilians killed, and many more were injured.

Elsewhere in the world, the threat of Fascism and tyranny was spreading at an alarming rate. By September the 13th Mussolini had revived his invasion plans in North Africa and ordered the Italian Tenth Army to advance on Egypt. Within two weeks, on the other side of the globe, the Japanese had invaded French Indochina, and were ready to agree a formal alliance with Nazi Germany.

On September the 27th 1940, the Axis powers united in Berlin as Japan signed the Tripartite Pact joining Germany and Italy in the fight against the Allied forces. Hitler, who was already planning to renege on his non-aggression pact with the Soviet Union, had not invited Stalin. Russia was destined to become another target in Hitler's conquest for world domination, but for the time being, defeating the British remained his major objective.

· · ·

The war in Europe was reaching global proportions, but Britain's fight to stave off the Nazi attacks had been admired across the world and as the words of Winston Churchill *"We shall never surrender"* reverberated around the globe, they would provide inspiration not only for the people of Britain, but also for every occupied nation, terrorized by the Nazi regime. However, the British would not have to stand alone for much longer, as the consequences of Hitler's Tripartite Pact would directly bring the Americans into the conflict, at last making the Allies a real force to be reckoned with.

5

FIGHTING FURTHER AFIELD

October – December 1940

Rounded up in Warsaw

I n the history of World War II, 1940 was a year of dramatic change. At the outset people watched and waited to see what Adolf Hitler would do next, but for the Allies, as the Führer employed his blitzkrieg tactics across Europe, swallowing up the Low Countries and France into his ever-expanding Nazi Empire, it was too late to stop him. Next, Hitler turned his attention towards Britain, and as summer turned to autumn, the island nation, quite literally, had to fight for its survival. As everyone looked skyward the Battle of Britain raged overhead, until Hitler was finally forced to face defeat, at which point London bore the brunt of his anger.

The blitz saw Londoners relentlessly bombed, night after night, at the mercy of Herman Goering's Luftwaffe. But the spirit of Great Britain, now under the Premiership of Winston Churchill, never faltered. With autumn giving way to winter, as you'll discover in *Fighting Further Afield,* the British not only held their ground on the home front but were soon making headway in North Africa, and while Hitler's Italian ally, Benito Mussolini edged his troops into Egypt it was the Axis who suddenly found they had a fight on their hands.

As countries around the globe began taking sides in the conflict, what began as a European war showed every sign of becoming truly global. While Japan joined forces with the Nazis, the Americans began sending aid to the British and took precautions to defend their country.

In the meantime, the unlikely pact between Nazi Germany and the Soviet Union, forged at the beginning of the war, was under threat and before the year was out Adolf Hitler was preparing for a course of action that was destined to shock the world.

By the beginning of October 1940, the boundaries of nations across Europe had changed dramatically. Before the war had even started, Czechoslovakia had effectively ceased to exist, with much of its territory carved up between Germany, Hungary and Poland, while the western powers, continuing their policy of appeasement did nothing. It would soon become difficult to ignore the threat that Nazi Germany posed however, as when Adolf Hitler ordered the invasion of Poland on September 1st 1939, within two days Great Britain and France were drawn into a war, which would last for six long years.

Meantime mid-September, Adolf Hitler realized that the invasion of the country, codenamed *Operation Sea Lion* would have to be postponed, and that Germany had lost the battle of Britain. Although the Nazis would continue to bombard Britain's towns and cities during the blitz, by the autumn of 1940 with most of Europe occupied by the troops of the Third Reich, Hitler had other matters to preoccupy him. He was keen to begin working on the ideologies he had described in his autobiography *Mein Kampf*. This would draw his attention to the east, where in his opinion the two greatest evils in the world resided; the communists and the Jews. In *Mein Kampf he* had made no secret of his hatred of the Jewish race, and as early as 1922, he confessed *"Once I really am in power, my first and foremost task will be the annihilation of the Jews".*

By the beginning of October, it was clear that Hitler's determination to carry out earlier threats had not wavered, and in Poland a country with the largest Jewish population in Europe, the horror of the Nazi master plan could not have been more evident. Prior to mass deportation to concentration camps, the Jews were collected into ghettoes in the cities and on October the 3rd 1940, Warsaw's Jews were instructed to move into what would become the biggest ghetto of all.

It held 380,000 people, amounting to thirty percent of the entire population of the city, crowded into only two and half percent of the land area. By November the 15th it was cordoned off from the rest of the city and the people crowded within were left to face disease and starvation. Those who were thought they were lucky enough to survive the ghettos, faced an even worse fate, and were deported to death camps.

Although the public perception of the Holocaust is Hitler's attempt to eradicate the Jews, many other groups were also targeted. It was decided at a conference in Berlin, to expel 30,000 gypsies from Germany and send them to Poland. Here they would be put into death camps such as Auschwitz, where they were cordoned off from the other prisoners.

Heinrich Himmler the Chief of the Gestapo took charge of their deportations and executions, and it's estimated that up to half a million gypsies were killed during the war, which was almost the entire gypsy population of Eastern Europe.

In the Nazi concentration camps, prisoners would be given symbols to wear, which showed their status within the prisoner hierarchy, depending on race, or religion among many other factors.

The Gypsies were branded with black triangles and held the lowest status in the camps along with the Jews, who had the identifying symbol of the star. People were also targeted depending on their political allegiances and communists were especially hated by Hitler and identified by a red triangle.

Hitler's experiences of the First World War shaped his attitude to many of the groups who would suffer when he came to power. In Hitler's opinion, the First World War had not been lost by Germany's inability to fight on, but by intentional sabotage of the war effort by Jews, Socialists and Bolsheviks. In 1917 revolution had torn through the Russian Empire while the First World War was still raging, and a communist leader Vladimir Lenin had taken center stage, advocating equality and universal brotherhood.

· · ·

When the Tsar was overthrown however, the country became divided in a bloody civil war which brought death and suffering to millions of people. There was a genuine fear in Germany that the Bolshevik revolution would spread further afield. In fact, by early 1919, it was evident that communist ideologies had crept into Germany when two attempted Communist revolutions took place in Berlin and Munich.

Both were brutally crushed, mainly by the Freikorps, a paramilitary group of returned war veterans who hated the Communists; many of these men would go on to become senior figures in the Nazi Party and indeed one of the main reasons for the existence of the Nazi Party was to fight communism.

In Hitler's *Mein Kampf,* he made no secret of his hatred of the Soviet Union also. He considered the Soviets sub-human and ruled by Jewish Bolsheviks and saw a war on their nation as an unavoidable part of his master plan. Unlike the Nazis the communists believed in a universal brotherhood and equality and to Hitler their destruction would be inescapable on the path to world domination.

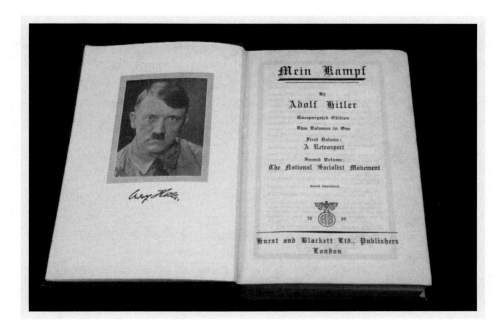

Mein Kampf English language version 1939

It was therefore surprising to say the least, when in late August 1939, the Nazis and Soviets signed a 10-year non-aggression pact, commonly called the Molotov-Ribbentrop Pact, after the Foreign Ministers of the two countries. The agreement renounced warfare between them and pledged neutrality by either party if the other were attacked by another.

Each signatory promised not to join any grouping of powers that was *"directly or indirectly aimed at the other party"*. When the Soviet press broke news of the Pact, it was met with utter shock worldwide, but it was only a ruse by Hitler, and it would not be long before he attacked his old ideological enemy.

By mid-August Hitler had already began discussing the prospect of taking on the Bolshevik menace with his military commanders and he would soon begin putting pressure on countries around Eastern Europe to join the Axis, so he could expand his resources and prepare for a full-scale war to the east. In the meantime, in October 1940 he focused on cementing relationships with countries around Western Europe. While the British continued to fight back and refused to surrender to Nazi Germany, Hitler's aim was to create a "continental block" of powers, leaving the island isolated from the rest of Europe.

The Italian dictator Benito Mussolini had already joined the Axis, signing the Tripartite Pact with Germany and Japan, in September 1940 though he had begun collaborating with Hitler long before. The British owned valuable territory in North and East Africa and while the Battle of Britain was in full swing, Mussolini, encouraged by Hitler, had begun edging his troops into Sudan, Kenya and British Somaliland to the east and the British protectorate of Egypt to the North.

The Suez Canal in Egypt was of great importance to the Axis as this was the pathway to the rich oilfields of the Middle East. To seize these would increase Axis oil supplies considerably and even more importantly cut off fuel supplies from the Allies. Not only this, but the Suez was also vitally important to Axis dominance in the Mediterranean Sea, an area that still had a strong allied presence.

On September 9th, 1940 The Italian 10th Army had launched their offensive on Egypt and succeeded in pushing the British back beyond the village of Sidi Barrani to the east of the Libyan border. Here the Italian commander, Marshal Rodolfo Graziani dug in and established several fortified camps just eighty miles west of the British defenses at Mersa Matruh. But when Mussolini pressurized Graziani to press on, he refused; waited to be re-supplied and here the Italians would stay until December 1940.

While the Suez for the time being remained in British hands, there was another strategic point in the Mediterranean that Hitler was keen to seize from the allies, namely the island of Gibraltar which lay between North Africa and Spain. In order to send troops onto the island Hitler was well aware he would first have to gain the support of the Spanish dictator, General Francisco Franco, so Nazi forces could launch their attack from the Spanish coast. With high hopes the Nazi leader travelled to Hendaye on the French border to discuss the matter with the Fascist leader on October 23rd 1940.

During the Spanish civil war which began in 1936, both Italy and Germany had provided Franco with aid, sending planes to bomb cities fighting for the republican cause. The German Condor League and the Italian Air Force had attacked Barcelona and the town of Guernica in the Basque region, but although Franco had happily accepted assistance from the Nazis in the past, he was uneasy about inviting the Germans to camp on his doorstep.

When he met Hitler, he produced a long list of conditions for participation, including a claim on Gibraltar, territory in Portugal and Vichy French territory in North Africa. While Hitler hoped to consolidate relations with Vichy France, he had no choice but to refuse the Spanish leader. Nevertheless, Spain's supposed neutrality in the Second World War would not stop the country from providing the Axis with aid.

The Spanish helped build observation posts round Gibraltar for German spies and allowed German U-Boats to be resupplied at their ports and Italian bombers to refuel at their airfields. Members of the Spanish embassy in London even collected intelligence information for Berlin. Meanwhile Hitler would be considerably more successful in forging an alliance with the French Prime Minister Marshal Phillipe Petain, who he met on October 24th, just one day after his meeting with Franco.

Petain had been a successful military leader in the First Great War, and after an impressive victory in the Battle of Verdun, he had become a public hero and was made a Marshal of France.

. . .

But though Petain was held in high regard by statesmen both at home and abroad, by 1940 public perception of him would change dramatically. As the Nazis marched into Paris the French Prime Minister Paul Reynaud had refused to surrender to Germany and when he was forced to resign Marshal Petain took his place as head of state.

It was Petain who would sign the armistice with Germany on June 22nd 1940 which gave the Nazis control over the north and west of the country including the entire Atlantic coastline. A new administrative center was set up in the spa town of Vichy and while Petain tried to gain favor with the Nazis by accommodation and collaboration, both occupied and unoccupied France would suffer. Petain blamed France's liberal democracy for the defeat of the country and set up a more authoritarian regime, changing the motto of the French Republic, from Liberty, Equality and Fraternity to Work, Family and Fatherland, introducing many harsh measures to the country, including anti-Semitic laws.

Six days after the secret meeting with Adolf Hitler on October 30th the French would realize the extent to which their new leader had betrayed them, as Petain declared in a radio broadcast speech *"I enter, today, into the way of collaboration"*. It was clear that his alliance with Nazi Germany had been sealed.

Although Hitler was now assured of the allegiance of Vichy France, old allies were threatening to undermine his plans for the Eastern Front. In preparation for the invasion of the Soviet Union, the German dictator had made moves to secure Balkan territory to the south of the Soviet border where he hoped to create a waiting zone for his troops.

On October 12th, Nazi soldiers were moved into Rumania to secure the precious Ploiesti oilfields, which would be a valuable source of fuel for the Nazi war machine. It was a step too far for Hitler's Axis partner Mussolini however, who deemed Rumania as being within his sphere of influence. The fascist leader was infuriated when he heard the news and felt even more side-lined on hearing of Hitler's talks with Vichy France in late October.

Hitler and Mussolini in closer times

Increasingly frustrated with Germany's failure to consult Italy on military moves he announced *"Hitler always gives me a fait accompli. This time I am going to pay him back in his own coin. He will find out from the papers that I have occupied Greece".*

Greece lay to the southern extreme of the Balkan Peninsula, and while British ships anchored in its ports and used the country to refuel, its collaboration with the allies had concerned Mussolini for some time. Keen to prove that he was on his way to creating a new empire on the scale of the Third Reich, Mussolini decided that now was the moment to strike.

Without consulting Hitler, on the eve of October 28th the Italian leader sent his ambassador in Athens, with an ultimatum to the Greek government; allow free passage for Italian troops into Greece or face war. The Greeks had a good relationship with the British, and their King, George the Second was an ardent anglophile, keen to keep close ties with the country. Hardly surprising then, that when faced with Mussolini's ultimatum the Greek response was: *"Then it is war"*.

The next day Italian forces crossed the Albanian border, assured by military leaders that the Greco-Italian War would last no more than two weeks. But the Greeks would not yield easily, and Italy would soon be retreating into Axis territory. Meanwhile as war tore through the peninsula, Hitler's hopes of ensuring that the Balkans remained a quiet waiting area before he attacked the Soviet Union had been dashed.

While events unfolded on the continent, across the Atlantic Ocean the United States of America was keeping a close eye on European affairs. In 1940 it was election year and President Roosevelt was attempting on the one hand to play down the possibility of America joining the war, and on the other quietly trying to aid the allies. In the interwar years the American people were very hesitant to involve themselves in another distant war, having lost many young men in World War One.

Nevertheless, while the Nazis continued to bombard Great Britain, Winston Churchill had sent delegates to America to plead for help and Roosevelt felt compelled to assist those fighting the Axis. On September 3rd 1940 Congress agreed to amend the Neutrality Act to allow munitions sales to the British and French; fifty over-age destroyers were sent to Britain in exchange for bases in the Atlantic and Caribbean, marking the beginning of America's moves towards belligerency.

In another bold move on September 14th, Congress passed the Selective Training and Service Act of 1940, which required young men to register with local draft boards. This was the first peacetime conscription in United States history and by October 16th as the Secretary of War Henry Stimson drew the first draft capsule, while the nation looked on, registration had begun.

Thousands of men would now be called into the military services, but as young draftees fought mock battles with make believe weapons, the United States was not prepared to fight in a full-scale war just yet.

Meanwhile Roosevelt had a difficult tightrope to walk, with a presidential election due at the end of the year. Though there were those who supported intervention many more supported isolation from the war, and if the President wanted to keep the public happy, he would have to find a way to please both parties.

Roosevelt had not been eager to continue to a third presidency. He had had two exhausting terms fighting the Great Depression in the 1930s and was now keen to retire. However, with war on the horizon, his conscience would not let him leave the political arena and it was evident that the Americans were not willing to part with their president just yet.

In the weeks running up to the election Roosevelt would face a tough battle against his competitor the Republican Party Candidate, Wendel Willkie. Willkie was a corporate lawyer and a former democrat who had never run for public office before. However, he was ready to put up a fierce fight for his place in the White House. A big focus of his criticism was Roosevelt's attempt to break the "two-term" tradition as president, established by George

Washington and he declared *"if one man is indispensable, then none of us is free".*

The issue failed to catch the public's attention however and as republican support dwindled, he turned to criticism of Roosevelt's interventionist behavior.

Willkie claimed that Roosevelt was secretly planning to take the USA into the European war against Germany and stated that *"No man had the right to use the great powers of the Presidency to lead the people, indirectly, into war".*

While the accusations flowed and support for the republicans grew, Roosevelt defended himself admirably and stressed that his intention was to do all he could to keep America out of the war. In the north eastern States, he repeated daily the message *"I am fighting to keep our people out of foreign wars. And I will keep on fighting".* He declared *"I have said this before, but I shall say it again and again and again: Your boys are not going to be sent into any foreign wars".*

But Roosevelt need not have feared that the public would let him down, and when he received 27 million votes to Willkie's 22 million on Election Day it was clear he had won over the Americans once more. On November the 5th 1940 Franklin Delano Roosevelt was duly elected President for an unprecedented third term. Whether he would keep his country out of the war as promised however, remained to be seen.

The news that Roosevelt would remain in the White House for a third term, was met with relief by the British Prime Minister Winston Churchill, who feared that without American support, the fight against the Axis would be difficult if not impossible, to win.

. . .

While bombs continued to rain down on the British, the blitz was not the only cause for concern for Churchill, as the Battle of the Atlantic which had begun when Britain declared war on Germany in September 1939, was taking its toll on Allied merchant shipping.

Britain was an island nation with an overseas empire and its survival and ability to fight depended greatly on supplies from across the Atlantic Ocean and as more boats were lost at sea, goods arriving in the country were rapidly depleting.

Items that had always been taken for granted suddenly began to disappear from the shelves and as early as January 1940 food rationing had been introduced, so everyone could claim their fair share of what was available. Bacon, butter and sugar were the first to be limited, but it wasn't long before many other things, such as tea and meat were added to the list and soon it was commonplace to see people queuing up outside the shops, brandishing their ration books.

Food wasn't the only thing to be rationed however and with limited amounts of fuel, petrol had been the first item introduced for rationing back in 1939. Although fuel production continued in Britain throughout the war, much of it was reserved for the army's trucks and tanks, as well as the planes of the RAF; bombers travelled long distances to Axis territory and needed a huge amount of fuel.

With petrol in short supply, people were encouraged to use public transport rather than their own cars and seeing horse-drawn vehicles rattling through the streets became a familiar sight again. Some however preferred using a more inspired method of getting about, and gas bags were occasionally used to supply cars with fuel.

. . .

The Fall of France in June 1940 had exacerbated the problem of getting supplies to the British Isles. With France beneath Nazi occupation the German U-Boats had direct access to the Atlantic from the western French ports of Brest, and La Rochelle. This placed them a great deal closer to the convoy routes than normal and effectively doubled their range and patrol times. Worse still France had the fourth largest navy in the world and with Petain now collaborating with the Axis, the Allies no longer had this valuable naval force at their disposal.

Meanwhile the battles in Western Europe over the spring and summer of 1940 had taken their toll on British shipping. Six destroyers were lost at the Battle of Dunkirk, a further ten were lost in the Channel and the North Sea between May and July and the Norwegian campaign had claimed six. The fighting in Norway had ended just two weeks before the fall of France on June 10th and now freed up the U-Boats that had been occupied with the Scandinavian battle. From this moment on, U-boat patrols swarmed into the Atlantic from the north and while there were few Allied ships available to protect the convoys, the period from June to October 1940 was coined "Happy Time" by the German navy. Using wolf pack tactics and launching operations from French bases, over 270 Allied ships were sunk during this period.

Meanwhile U-boat crews became heroes at home, and the most successful Captains became celebrity aces. These included Gunther Prien, who had famously sunk the Royal Oak at Scapa Flow in 1939 and sank over 30 Allied ships during the war; Commander Otto Kretschmer who was regarded as the most successful Ace of the Deep and Joachim Schepke who was much admired for his unwavering dedication to the Nazi cause.

Meanwhile as convoys battled their way across the Atlantic to keep Britain supplied, the Mediterranean Sea which had been a traditional focus of British maritime power was also under pressure from the Axis. With Mussolini's troops now pressing into Egypt it was vital to get supplies to the troops defending Allied territory.

But while the Italians were conveniently supplied from the Italian mainland, British stocks had to travel the length of the Mediterranean all the way from the island of Gibraltar. This evidently put the Italian Navy in a strong position to cut off supplies to Allied troops, and British commanders were keen to resolve the problem.

Back in 1935 when Mussolini had set his sights on creating a new Roman Empire and had marched his troops into Abyssinia in Africa, British military strategists had begun examining the possibility of an attack on the Italian naval base at Taranto. Later during the Munich crisis of 1938 when Hitler threatened to seize Czechoslovakia, and the world had waited with baited breath to see if war would be declared, preparations for an attack on the Italian navy had gathered pace.

Admiral Sir Dudley Pound, then commander of the Royal Navy's Mediter-ranean Fleet, was particularly concerned about the Italian naval presence in the Mediterranean and planned an attack which would eventually become known as *Operation Judgement.* Although the offensive had been postponed when Neville Chamberlain, then Prime Minister, appeared to have averted war with Germany, by 1940 preparations for the Taranto attack were once more underway, and by the autumn of 1940 when General Graziani brought his troops to a halt at Sidi Barrani and British ships were freed up for action, the Allies seized the opportunity to strike.

On November 11th RAF reconnaissance flights confirmed that the Italian fleet was in harbor and brought back photographs of the ships positions for intelli-gence officers based on the carrier HMS Illustrious. By 9pm that night, the first wave of twelve Swordfish biplanes were launched from the Illustrious and a second wave of nine followed an hour and a half later.

| Swordfish biplane bomber leaving HMS Illustrious

Carrying a mixture of torpedoes and bombs, the aircraft succeeded in knocking out half the Italian battleship fleet in one night. There was also extensive damage to the docks and facilities, and the next day licking their wounds, the Italian Navy decided to transfer those ships that had survived the bombardment to the port of Naples.

In the meantime, the Royal Navy had greatly increased its control of the Mediterranean. It was the first all-aircraft naval attack in history and would mark the beginning of the end for the battleship, and the rise of naval airpower. While the Second World War would eventually be drawn to fierce battles in the Pacific, this would increasingly be proven to be the case.

The attack on Taranto was also groundbreaking for another reason. It had proven that air-launched torpedo attacks did not require deep water, as previously thought and far away to the east, another Axis partner of Nazi Germany, the Empire of Japan had watched the dramatic events at Taranto with great interest. Japan like Britain, depended on supplies from overseas and while the west, in particular America, condemned the country's war with China, the Japanese feared interference with their plans to build their own Empire.

The Japanese Admiral Yamamoto was particularly impressed by the offensive and saw that if there was no option but to eventually fight America, they could cripple the US Naval fleet before it left for eastern waters. The Taranto bombing would thus become the blueprint for Japan's attack on Pearl Harbor in December 1941.

Meanwhile back in Britain, the success of the Taranto attack was a much-needed morale booster as the Luftwaffe's terror bombing maintained pressure on the population. The blitz which had started early in September 1940, continued unabated, and life was far from easy for those who continued to struggle on the home front.

The man determined to use air attacks to crush British morale, was Field Marshal Herman Goering, who was second in command to Adolf Hitler and the highest-ranking officer in Germany.

As a veteran of the First World War, and one of the earliest members of the Nazi party, Goering had formed a close friendship with Hitler and was appointed commander of the Luftwaffe in 1935. With aircraft boasting the latest military developments, there was no doubt that the Luftwaffe was one of the most powerful air forces on the globe by the outbreak of the Second World War and convinced of its superiority, the Field Marshal had proudly announced *"If an enemy bomber reaches the Ruhr my name is not Herman Goering".*

. . .

But by the autumn of 1940, while the RAF battled to defend their country against invasion, it was clear that the Luftwaffe would have to accept their first defeat in the Battle of Britain.

Nevertheless, Goering was eager to maintain some of his prestige, and proving that the Luftwaffe were a force to be reckoned with, began a terrifying aerial bombardment of the country. The first phase of the blitz from September to October 1940 focused on subduing the British capital, with massive bombardments on London both night anD-Day, but by November 1940 the blitz had taken on a new form, and one raid in particular could only be described as a personal attack of revenge.

While the Luftwaffe targeted Britain, the RAF had also begun to do its fair share of damage, attacking towns and cities around Germany, but on November 8th they went one step too far, as far as Adolf Hitler was concerned. The Nazi leader was enjoying an annual celebration of his 1923 attempted coup in Munich, known as the "Beer Hall Putsch", when the gathering was suddenly interrupted by an RAF bombing raid. The Führer was incensed and determined that an attack on the capital of the Nazi movement would not go unpunished, he ordered Goering to launch *Operation Moonlight Sonata*.

On the night of November 14th, almost 500 German bombers, swarmed over the city of Coventry in the industrial heartland of Great Britain. Before its inhabitants were aware of the terrible fate that awaited them, thousands of incendiary bombs were unleashed on the streets below. Wave after wave of aircraft indiscriminately dropped their lethal payloads on the city in relays until Coventry was completely engulfed in flames.

In ten hours from 7.20 in the evening until dawn, almost 150,000 incendiary bombs and 500 tons of high explosives were released, and by the morning the scene was one of utter devastation.

. . .

Transport systems, gas and water mains had been destroyed, and more than 60,000 buildings had been obliterated. Unlike most British towns and cities, there had been almost no development in Coventry and much of the medieval city had been standing at the time of the raid, only to be flattened in one terrible night. There was barely one undamaged building left in the once beautiful city center, and even the fifteenth century St Michael's Cathedral had been destroyed.

As a cloak of smoke and drizzle hung over the city, the next day people wandered about dazed, taking in the tragic scene of destruction which was all that remained of their city. Meanwhile as the rest of the country awoke to hear the terrible news, within hours of the all-clear the British Home Secretary, Herbert Morrison, arrived and was soon joined by King George VI who made an unannounced visit to give moral support to the destitute citizens.

The biggest tragedy of all was the loss of life with initial reports suggesting that up to 1000 people had died, 400 were so badly burnt that they could not be identified. Hundreds of women and children were among them and as more bodies were pulled from the rubble by November 20th the first mass burial took place, to be followed by another one week later.

While the people of Britain mourned their loss, further afield hope lay on the horizon. Following the Italian advance in North Africa, General Archibald Wavell, the Commander of the Middle East Command had ordered preparations for a British counterattack and the period of relative inactivity in the region was about to come to an end.

On December 7th 1940, the Commander of the Western Desert Force, Lieutenant-General Richard O'Connor, was ordered to commence *Operation Compass* and attack the Italians based at Sidi Barrani. One of the weaknesses of the Italian defenses around the village was that their forces were split up among several fortified camps in the vast desert, spaced widely apart in a chain. This meant that on December 8th British troops could pass unnoticed through a gap in the chain, and attacking from the rear, take one camp after the other.

On December 10th, allied forces were in position, blocking the south and southwestern exits to Sidi Barrani and after launching an attack on the Axis troops, by the evening of the 11th, all resistance had ceased, and the Italians had surrendered. From here O'Connor's troops would go on to take Sallum, Halfaya and Fort Capuzzo in Libya and by December 15th, all Italian forces had been pushed out of Egypt or were prisoners.

It was a black moment for Mussolini, not least, because the Battle of Greece was faring little better and not only had the Italians been pushed out of Greek territory but by mid-December a quarter of Italian occupied Albania was under Greek control. Hitler meanwhile had little time to concern himself with Mussolini's disastrous attempts at expanding the Italian Empire and was busy setting in motion his plans for the Eastern Front and strengthening control of the Balkans.

The Regent of Hungary, Miklos Horthy had entered negotiations with Hitler as early as 1938, and while the Communists loomed close to the border of his country, he saw the Nazis as the lesser of two evils. On November 20th 1940 Horthy committed his alliance to the Axis to print and signed the Tripartite Pact.

Just three days later, on November 23rd Rumania followed suit and then Slovakia. With these three nations all firmly beneath his sphere of influence, Hitler had created a northern Balkan tier, along Russia's southern flank. Within weeks, ignoring all attempts by his most high-ranking officers to dissuade him, the Nazi leader confirmed his plans to invade the Soviet Union, codenamed *Operation Barbarossa,* and a date for the invasion was set for May 15th 1941.

As Hitler moved inexorably towards a showdown with his nemesis the Soviet Union and 1940 ended, on December 29th President Roosevelt delivered one of his famous "Fireside Chats" to the American public. The speech marked a definite decline in the isolationist policy of the United States and it seemed that American intervention was approaching ever closer.

While more nations had been drawn to the side of the Axis, Roosevelt warned the Americans of the risks that the Tripartite pact posed, describing it as *"an unholy alliance of power to dominate and to enslave the human race".*

He warned of the Japanese threat growing in the Pacific, the evils of Nazism and Adolf Hitler and reminded his citizens that the British and their allies fighting across the Atlantic, were still desperate for aid. *"We must be the great arsenal of democracy"* Roosevelt stated, *"For us this is an emergency as serious as war itself".*

Meanwhile even as Roosevelt spoke, the bombs were raining down on the British capital once more, in the most devastating air raid on London to date.

It was only four days after Christmas and Germany had commenced their bombardment with renewed enthusiasm, creating a vast firestorm which would be called the Second Great Fire of London. Around fifteen hundred fires were started, covering an area from Islington in the North to St Paul's Churchyard, and the cathedral itself was only saved thanks to the dedication of volunteer fire watchers.

During all the destruction, vital water mains were shattered so fire fighters had to combat the mud and slime of the Thames River, to feed their hoses. The Nazis had chosen a night when the river was at its lowest ebb on record, making the task even harder. Although the all clear siren sounded by midnight, the battle had only just begun for the London Fire Brigade, who would have to struggle for another fifteen hours to subdue the flames tearing through the city.

While the capital of Great Britain was engulfed in turmoil there was no doubt that the battle against the Axis was far from over, but the New Year promised many changes in the theatre of conflict and though the struggle on the home front and overseas, would continue for a long time yet, the events of 1941 would bring hope to those still fighting Adolf Hitler.

6

ON LAND, IN THE AIR AND ALL AT SEA

January – March 1941

| Rommel the "Desert Fox"

A s the old year of 1940 drew to a close, on the eve of 1941 the air raid sirens sounded once more across the British Isles; the skies thundered with the roar of Adolf Hitler's Luftwaffe planes.

Flying in droves towards London, they were to launch their most savage attack of the aerial war to date, as they continued with the Nazi campaign to crush and shatter British morale.

. . .

While bombs rained relentlessly onto streets and buildings, soon the dark alleyways and crooked passageways of London were illuminated by a fire of vast proportions. Firefighters battled through the dense smoke-filled air, making desperate attempts to quell the blaze as the city was engulfed in flames.

Meanwhile far below in shelters and in the underground stations, civilians cowered in fear, hoping and praying to survive yet another night of the blitz. Since the summer of 1940 the people of Britain had suffered months of terrifying air attacks, and while the death toll rose, it was tragically clear that more civilians than soldiers were falling victim to the ravages of war. By New Year's Day 1941, as the dust settled, and friends and families began to pick their way through the rubble, it's hardly surprising that the British felt more alone than ever in the fight against the Axis.

The year before, France had fallen to Nazi Germany and much of Europe was now occupied by Hitler's henchmen, and while Mussolini's troops continued to fight the British and commonwealth soldiers across the arid African deserts, the planes and U-Boats of the Nazis reigned supreme over the Mediterranean and the Atlantic Ocean.

Nevertheless by 1941 the cracks would begin to show in the alliances that Adolf Hitler had forged, and while the bonds between those fighting for the Allies grew ever stronger, distrust would breed mistrust between those fighting alongside Nazi Germany.

The Soviet Union was becoming ever more powerful, building up its armies and their military machine, while the balance of power between Hitler and the Russian leader Josef Stalin began to shift. Consequently, an unexpected turn of events would have a dramatic impact on the outcome of the Second World War.

. . .

As the story of the conflict continues *On Land, in the Air and All at Sea* will follow the action as it unfolds in the prelude to Germany's invasion of the Soviet Union, while across the Atlantic, President Roosevelt finally rallies support for the Allied cause, giving Britain a fighting chance to make an impact on the Nazi onslaught.

By January 1941 most of continental Europe was occupied by the Axis. France had fallen to Germany in June 1940 despite all attempts to fight off the Nazi advance, with Holland, Belgium and Luxembourg also absorbed into Hitler's Third Reich. To the north, Denmark and Norway had been invaded in April 1940, while Finland had surrendered to the Soviet Union just one month earlier. Meanwhile in Eastern Europe, Poland, the country that Britain and France had declared war against Germany in order to defend, had been neatly carved up between Stalin and Hitler, and its inhabitants were now being subjected to the horrors of Nazi occupation.

The only country unoccupied and still battling against the Axis was Great Britain, and fighting alongside the British troops, were forces from all around the Commonwealth. From Australia and India to Canada, soldiers, mine-sweepers, pilots and sailors arrived to do their bit to help with the fight against the Nazis and their allies. People had also flooded into Britain from countries occupied by Hitler's Axis of evil.

Polish pilots had played a vital part in helping with the fight against the Luftwaffe in the Battle of Britain in the summer of 1940 and Polish cryptographers had been providing crucial information to those working to break the Enigma codes at Bletchley Park. Further afield those still living in occupied countries were forming resistance groups, sabotaging Nazi communications and gathering followers to continue fighting in small pockets around Europe.

But even with support being mustered around the globe to fight Hitler and his allies, the British Prime Minister Winston Churchill was wary that vital supplies and resources were running low. The Battle of Britain had taken its toll with many planes lost in the fighting and many air bases and factories had been damaged by the Nazi attacks. There had also been significant losses of men and precious equipment in the spring of 1940 during the campaign to rescue the BEF, and other Allied troops, from the French beaches of Dunkirk.

The war effort in Britain quickly gathered pace as people were working around the clock to reach production targets in the factories to manufacture desperately needed war supplies. This would be key if there was to be any hope of victory against Nazi Germany and Winston Churchill now laid all his hopes on aid from America. The British Prime Minister had for some time been forging a strong relationship with the US President, and while the Luftwaffe and the RAF had been battling it out over Britain, Franklin D. Roosevelt had made a symbolic gesture by providing aid to the Allied cause in September 1940.

In exchange for territory on British colonies where land or naval bases could be established, American destroyers were transferred to the Royal Navy. Despite America's neutral status Churchill was delighted, seeing the move as *"a decidedly un-neutral act"* and in his opinion the destroyers for bases agreement marked the beginning of the Anglo/American alliance in World War II.

In America however, the general public were not wholeheartedly behind their President and people were reluctant to back any plans that might result in their sons, brothers and husbands being sent into battle in Europe. Many were still haunted by memories of the First World War, where hundreds of thousands of American lives had been lost, on the battlefields of France and out at sea.

When the British went to war against Germany in 1914, few Americans had been willing to join the conflict. It took the threat of German naval attacks on

US shipping, and the tragic sinking of the Lusitania in 1915, to help sway the public mood in favor of intervention.

Over two decades later, Adolf Hitler was all too aware of the danger of drawing America into war, and avoiding the mistakes of his predecessors, he was taking great care not to aggravate the neutral nation. But while almost half the population of America were determined to stay out of the European war, peacetime conscription was already drafting many men into the military and fears began to grow that "their boys" would soon be sent overseas. President Roosevelt was swift to assure the Americans that this was not the case declaring that:

"The people of Europe who are defending themselves do not ask us to do their fighting. They ask us for the implements of war".

However, he did warn that if Britain should fall, Hitler's Axis powers, having avowed their determination to dominate the world, would control Europe, Asia, Africa, Australia and the high seas, leaving all of America living at the point of a gun.

President Roosevelt felt very strongly about the war raging far from American shores and on January the 6th 1941 he made a moving speech to congress that has gone down in history as the Four Freedoms Speech.

In his own words he stated that:

"We look forward to a world founded upon four essential freedoms. The

freedom of speech and expression everywhere in the world, the freedom of every person to worship God in his own way, the freedom from want and the freedom from fear. This is a definite basis for a kind of world attainable in our own time and generation. That kind of world is the very antithesis of the so-called new order of tyranny, which the dictators seek to create with the crash of a bomb."

The speech had a profound impact on the American public and was immortalized in posters and later monuments. It also helped justify the increase in defensive production, but while many Americans seemed to be warming towards the possibility of entering the war, for the British as they continued to fight alone against Hitler and Mussolini, words were not enough.

With bombs continuing to rain down on Britain's cities and ports, and troops now being deployed in Africa, the Prime Minister pleaded with the American President *"Give us the tools and we'll finish the job"*.

Churchill was all too aware that the Allies would need far more than inspiring speeches to help defend British territory from falling into the hands of the Axis.

By now the United Kingdom had reached the stage where it was unable to pay for weapons and fearing the British would surrender to Hitler, Roosevelt asked congress for a law that would limit neither the amount, nor the kind of aid he could send. It would be called the Lend-lease bill, and would authorize Roosevelt to sell, transfer title to, exchange, lease and lend any defense article to any country whose protection the President deemed vital to the defense of the United States.

· · ·

Despite Roosevelt's hopes that the bill could be passed as soon as possible to help Great Britain, there was vehement opposition from the isolationists. In Chicago an organization called America First was gaining popularity and its most famous spokesman, the famous aviator Charles Lindbergh, was determined that the country should stay out of the war.

An array of famous faces had joined the group including the world-renowned film producer Walt Disney, the actress Lillian Gish and Alice Roosevelt Longworth the oldest daughter of Theodore Roosevelt. There were also politicians who supported the organization such as Senator Burton Wheeler who did all he could to undermine the President, circulating charges that the President wished to give away the American navy, enhance his powers, and make war.

With much of the American population nervous about the prospect of taking part in another world conflict, the accusations threatened to jeopardize the Lend Lease bill, and this meant yet more delays in sending aid overseas. Roosevelt was furious, and as the Axis tightened its grip on Europe his concerns grew that Hitler would launch his invasion of the British Isles very soon.

Across the Atlantic however, Adolf Hitler had other concerns and the Nazi leader was planning to send his stormtroopers in a direction that Roosevelt had not anticipated. Although back in August 1939, the German foreign minister Ribbentrop, had signed a non-aggression pact with Russia's minister Molotov, Hitler was now greedily surveying Soviet territory and waiting for the opportunity to crush Stalin and the Red Army.

This course of action was not only motivated by the desire to win more land for the Third Reich, but to satisfy the Nazi dictator's own personal vendetta against Communism; and despite the enormity of the task that lay ahead Hitler was confident he could wage war not only on the west, but to the east.

· · ·

The Germans had been watching Russian activity carefully and had noted the inefficiency of the Soviet military compared to the Nazis who had stormed across Western Europe with relative ease. In the Winter War of 1939 to 1940 great Russian armies had been wiped out by the numerically inferior Fins and the disastrous campaign had convinced Hitler that as far as the Soviet Union was concerned *"We have only to kick in the door and the whole rotten structure will come crashing down"*.

On December 18th 1940 the Nazi Leader had issued the First Barbarossa directive stating his intention to invade the Soviet Union by the spring of 1941 and to prepare for this ambitious plan he had been busily securing a Balkan tier along the Russian southern flank. Hungary, Rumania and Slovakia had all been pressured to sign up to the Axis allegiance just two months after Japan and Italy had signed the Tripartite Pact back in September 1940 and Rumania in particular was now a vital player in Hitler's schemes.

| Map of Rumania

Historically Rumania had been allied with Britain and had fought on the side of the Entente against Germany, during the First World War. The treaty Rumania had signed with the Allies in 1916 had been greatly celebrated, but sadly things did not go according to plan for the Balkan state. Although the Rumanian Army at this time was relatively large with around half a million soldiers, the men had been barely trained and were led by inexperienced officers.

By May 1918 with quarter of a million soldiers dead or imprisoned, Rumania was forced to sign the Treaty of Bucharest with the Central Powers, and the millions of tons of grain as well as the oil the country was forced to provide, would keep Germany in the war, and the Entente battling for victory, until the end of 1918.

It was Rumania's oil that was of special interest to Hitler as well as the country's great strategic value, positioned on the southern border of the Soviet Union.

Hitler was also confident of Rumania's allegiance to the Axis; in September 1940 The King of Rumania Carol the Second had been overthrown by the pro-German anti-Bolshevik regime of Prime Minister Marshal Ion Antonescu who readily signed the Tripartite Pact on November 23rd. German troops soon began swarming into the area, and the country would now become a valuable base for Hitler while the Rumanian dictator became one of Hitler's greatest allies.

While the Nazis quietly and carefully strengthened their control of the Balkans the Russian foreign minister, Molotov was troubled by Germany's failure to uphold its end of the treaty made in 1939. When Russia had exported oil, grain and raw materials to Germany as promised, Germany had only sent modern machinery and weapons to Moscow sporadically. Hostility was building, but while Molotov asked many awkward questions, Hitler managed to detract attention away from the ambitious Barbarossa scheme and he convinced the Russians that the Nazi troops were being moved into Rumania to keep them out of British air range.

Distracting the Soviet Union would soon appear to be the least of Hitler's worries, however. The activities of his Italian ally Benito Mussolini threatened to undermine the plans for a spring offensive to the east and would eventually delay the attack for several months. Mussolini had grown jealous of his partner's success as Nazi troops seized territory from Poland to Norway, and when he heard that the Germans had occupied Rumanian oil fields he was furious. To Mussolini this was an encroachment on south-eastern Europe, an area Italy claimed as its exclusive sphere of influence.

He too wanted to enjoy the spoils of war and extend Italian territory just as his German ally had done, and if Hitler were to rule from the Atlantic to the Urals, he would rule the Mediterranean and all the lands that surrounded it. Against the advice of his Chiefs of Staff and without informing Germany, for he knew that Hitler would object, on October 28th 1940 Mussolini invaded Greece and as the southern Balkan peninsula was thrown into turmoil, Hitler's quiet waiting area would soon become a battle zone.

Invading the cradle of western civilization, would not be the easy task that Mussolini had hoped however, and while the Greeks battled back coura-geously, by the third week of November, not one Italian soldier was left on Greek soil. Greek troops soon began pushing into Italian occupied Albania and high hopes of a victory for the Italian empire, ended in utter humiliation for Mussolini.

In January 1941 both sides had reached a stalemate and while there was world admiration for the unyielding fighting spirit of the Greeks, Hitler was growing increasingly concerned that the Allies would come to their aid and move into Balkan territory. Such a move would spell disaster for the careful preparations of the invasion of the Soviet Union, and Hitler was well aware he may soon have to intervene in the disastrous Greek War himself.

There were also other concerns to occupy the Axis as Mussolini's troops were not only struggling in the Balkans but further afield in Africa. When Italy had declared war on June 10th 1940 against Britain and France, the British posi-tion in North Africa seemed hopelessly outmatched.

· · ·

UK Army General Percival Wavell commanded 40,000 dominion soldiers caught between two hundred thousand Italian troops in Libya and two hundred and fifty to the south in Ethiopia and Somaliland.

The Axis hoped that with a successful campaign in North Africa they could strike north to the oil of the Middle East, cutting off the rich oil fields from the Allies and increasing oil supplies for their own war machine. But when Marshal Rodolfo Graziani on the Axis leaders' orders, invaded Egypt in September 1940, the tides of war swiftly turned.

Despite battles on the home front, Churchill had bravely sent troops to defend Egypt, and on December 9th 30,000 troops under Army General Richard O'Connor were sent to reclaim Sidi Barrani, sixty-five miles inside Egypt's border with Libya. By December 15th 1940 the Italian troops had been completely pushed back out of the country and by 1941 the enterprising O'Connor turned the large-scale raid into a full-scale invasion of Libya.

While the Allies hoped that control of North Africa would be a step towards a second front against the Axis powers in Europe, Hitler and his generals had turned their attention to the Mediterranean Sea. The campaign in north Africa, depended on supplies arriving across the Mediterranean and if the Axis succeeded in blocking off these supply routes it would be disastrous for the Allies.

The Axis already controlled most of the ports along the North African coast. After the fall of France, they had seized Morocco, Oran in Algeria, Tunis in Tunisia and yet the Italians still had control of Tripoli and Benghazi in Libya.

All that was left to the Allies was the Suez Canal in Egypt and the precious islands of Gibraltar and Malta, which were of vital importance in ensuring Allied success. The Axis were aware of their strategic importance, but Hitler had had many problems wrenching the islands from the Allied grip. He relied on the Spanish dictator Generalissimo Franco to provide the land from where he could launch his attack and while Franco remained unwilling to take sides in the war, for the time being Gibraltar remained in British hands.

Malta was even more crucial to the North African campaign, as it not only provided a useful stopping post for Allied convoys on their way from Britain, but the island's position between Sicily and North Africa was perfect to make attacks on Axis supply convoys destined for Africa.

According to Churchill, Malta was the unsinkable aircraft carrier and while German U-Boats continued to attack British ships crossing the Atlantic Ocean, in the Mediterranean the roles were reversed as Allied ships and aircraft based on Malta, were able to bombard the Italian convoys supplying the army in North Africa. The Axis were well aware of how capturing Malta could influence the North African campaign and regular bombardments of the island as well as the growing numbers of submarine Wolfpacks prowling the seas, soon made Allied convoys to the islands suicide runs.

Though naval escorts were sent to accompany the ships and even submarines attempted to get critical supplies to the island, it was a significant challenge to keep the island supplied and when Mussolini requested Germany's help in subduing the island, matters were about to get a lot worse for civilians and military stationed on Malta.

In January 1941 Air Marshal Goring had ordered the cream of the Luftwaffe Fliegerkorps to move down from Norway towards Sicily. As well as thousands of Luftwaffe personnel, warplanes arrived by the dozens in daily flights and by January 8th there were 96 bombers on the island, within flying distance of Malta, and hundreds more on the way.

. . .

The Nazi pilots arriving on Sicily would include Jaochim Muncheberg a young fighter ace who at just twenty-one years of age had received the highest award of bravery, the iron cross, for the many victories he had claimed during the Battle of Britain and with so many skilled Luftwaffe pilots gathering to the north, the risk to convoys heading to Malta had increased considerably.

In early January an Allied convoy carrying supplies and weapons from Gibraltar, was on its way to Malta and Greece. Alongside it sailed a strong naval force of destroyers and the aircraft carrier Illustrious, an important target for the Axis. The Illustrious was the Royal Navy's lone aircraft carrier in the Mediterranean and had already caused considerable damage to the Italian Fleet, launching a devastating attack at the port of Taranto in November 1940. Not surprisingly the Italians and the Germans were keen to remove it from the field of conflict.

Just after noon on January 10th German Air Marshal Hermann Goering's *Luftwaffe* made its Mediterranean debut as forty-three Stukas attacked the convoy, diving in synchronized waves from different heights to confuse the ships' anti-aircraft fire. Highly skilled, the pilots of the Luftwaffe pressed home their attacks with no thoughts for their own safety, and as five hundred-kilo armor-piercing bombs screamed through the air the effects on the ships below would be devastating.

Seven direct hits were scored on the Illustrious, and the aircraft carrier whose flight deck of Fulmars and Swordfish, might have made the difference to which side dominated the Mediterranean, was all but destroyed. Malta was now virtually alone and would suffer the worst bombardment of any country in the entire war; in fact, more bombs would fall on the tiny island than on London during the entire blitz.

Nevertheless, while the Axis could celebrate the destruction of the Illustrious, in Africa there was considerably less to rejoice. O'Conner was still plunging further into enemy territory now heading for the port of Tobruk, and the Italians were swiftly losing ground in the North. Meanwhile in East Africa there was a British counter offensive attacking Italian held Eritrea from the Sudan. Mussolini's dreams of a new empire were disappearing rapidly and on January 18th 1941 he departed for Germany "dark faced and nervous" to meet Hitler at his Berghof Residence.

In the beautiful surroundings of the Bavarian Alps, the two dictators had much to discuss, but while Mussolini was visibly concerned over the deteriorating situation in Africa, Adolf Hitler was adamant that the Italians keep fighting and hold their ground.

Above all the Nazi Führer feared that if the Allies defeated the Italian forces in Africa, the British troops would be free to make mischief elsewhere, and Greece, dangerously close to his precious Rumanian oil fields, would be their next port of call. Tripoli could not fall, he told Mussolini, and as soon as possible he would send reinforcements from Germany to help defend Libya against O'Conner's advancing troops.

But even as the Axis leaders discussed military strategies, British troops were building up forces around Tobruk on the morning of January 21st and under cover of darkness, a fierce assault was launched and soon O'Connor's battalions had breached the line of defense. Hurling grenades and using tank and artillery fire the British troops battered the Italian platoons fighting to defend the city. Within twenty-four hours however the city had been captured and despite the insistence of Mussolini that surrender was not to be considered, the Italian troops had no choice but to lay down their arms.

As the Western Desert Campaign continued, it seemed there was no stopping O'Conner's advance. By January 30th the Allies had seized Derna, one hundred miles to the west of Tobruk; then by February 7th the retreating

Italian tenth Army was cut off and destroyed during the Battle of Beda Fomm. As Libya's second largest city Benghazi fell into Allied hands, the British captured 130,000 Italians and the Italian tenth army ceased to exist. The way to Tripoli and total elimination of Italian dominion in North Africa lay open.

On February 9th as the remaining Italian forces retreated to El Agheila General Graziani sent a message to Rome, pleading nervous exhaustion and begged Mussolini to relieve him of his duty.

Two days later he departed for Italy, while the Allies were left to celebrate their achievements. Praising the incredible accomplishments of the Western Desert Force, the British foreign secretary Anthony Eden paraphrased the words Churchill had used after the Battle of Britain and announced, *"Never has so much been surrendered by so many to so few"*.

In two months, O'Connor, who would be knighted for his achievements, had led his troops over 800 miles, destroying an entire Italian army of ten divisions and had lost only 500 men. Though the Western Desert Campaign had been a great success, back in Britain, the political situation was delicate, and Churchill had much to consider while Mussolini's war against Greece continued. Britain had signed a guarantee with Greece in April 1939 and while the Greeks were still fighting Italian troops, it was seen as politically unacceptable not to support an ally under threat. Failure to act might discredit the British, and with much depending on foreign support, Churchill felt that a token effort should be endeavored.

He agreed with Wavell, commander of the British troops in the Middle East, to move a significant proportion of O'Connor's Thirteenth Corps, from Libya, to Greece in the southern Balkan Peninsula. Wavell had been reluctant to prejudice the campaign in North Africa but with the majority of Graziani's forces captured, he felt it was now safe to transfer some of the men. The decision would have devastating effects on those who were left behind to fight, however.

Adolf Hitler had been paying close attention to the Allies every move and as O'Connor's forces were left considerably depleted, he saw the opportunity to strike.

On February 12th the newly formed German Afrika Korps, fresh and ready for battle were raced to the African desert to prevent the total collapse of the Italian forces. They had better equipment than Mussolini's army and even more importantly they had one of the greatest commanders in Germany to lead them, General Erwin Rommel.

German tank prepared for war in North Africa

Rommel was a highly decorated officer in the First Great War and had already met Allied forces back in 1940 when he made a considerable impact on the success of the Nazi invasion of France. During battle his panzers had pushed deeper and deeper into France moving so swiftly that not even German High Command knew their whereabouts, which is why they became known as the Ghost Division.

By May 1940 Rommel we remember had succeeded in taking ten thousand prisoners as he thundered across Allied terrain, losing only thirty-six of his own men. What's more if he'd been given the opportunity, he would have captured many more of the British and French troops, had they not been saved from the beaches of Dunkirk.

It's no wonder then that Rommel's arrival in North Africa was cause for concern and as German troops began to make their way towards the advanced position of the British at El Agheila, from their base at Tripoli, O'Connor's fortunes were about to take a turn for the worse.

Rommel would prove to be so skilled at desert warfare that he would become known as the Desert Fox, and when on February 20th German and British troops confronted each other for the first time in Africa, the Allies would soon find themselves retracing their footsteps, forced to retreat back towards Egypt.

Meanwhile in the Balkans Hitler was preparing to protect his precious Rumanian oilfields, and with the first British troops deployed for Greece this was becoming a matter of urgency. His goal was now to ensure the Axis had complete control of South Eastern Europe, and he began to pressurize those countries that had not already joined him, to sign the Tripartite Pact.

Any country that failed to comply would face the armies of the Third Reich. The Greek Government as well as the King of Greece, who had rejected a

German offer of immunity, were now treading on dangerous ground and would soon face a war they would find difficult to win. When Bulgaria agreed to sign up to the Axis Powers on March 1st, within a day German Units were crossing the River Danube so that air and ground forces could be deployed in the Bulgarian countryside, ready for an attack on its Greek neighbor. But Greece was not the only Balkan country to hold their ground against the Nazis.

The Kingdom of Yugoslavia, which stretched from the Western Balkans to Central Europe, remained as yet undecided about its allegiance. The Regent, Prince Paul of Yugoslavia, had hesitated about following the Rumanian and Bulgarian example by joining the Tripartite Pact, and was being urged by Great Britain and the United States to resist German pressure and attack the Italians in Albania.

Following the First World War, and the Treaty of Versailles, Yugoslavia had been a friend to the French and was an important presence when it came to maintaining peace in the Balkans.

After the fall of France in 1940 however, Yugoslavia was alone, surrounded by countries that were part of the Axis powers. On March 4th 1941 Prince Paul of Yugoslavia met Hitler and said that he would sign up to the Tripartite Pact, on the proviso that his country was not asked to fight for the Axis, and that German troops would not expect transit through Yugoslavia. Negotiations were destined to continue for weeks, but in the meantime Yugoslavia's future looked uncertain.

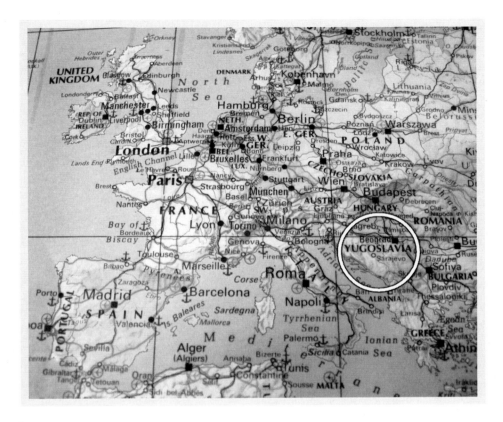

| Map of Yugoslavia

As the Axis cast their shadow across Europe and beyond, Adolf Hitler, as well as keeping the pressure on the Balkan states, was also staying in close contact with his Japanese allies. On March 5th Hitler issued directive number 24, "*Co-operation with Japan*" hoping to persuade the Asian empire to act in the Far East as soon as possible, to further distract the British forces.

Japan at this time was amid a long and brutal war with China and had already used the weakened position of the Western Empires to their advantage. In 1940 Tokyo officials pressured French Indochina to close some of the few routes left which were being used to transport valuable aid into the vulnerable country. That same year, they had also demanded that the British government close the Burma Road, which ran from the British held territory of Burma to the Chinese city of Kunming.

At the time there had been uproar in the House of Commons when Prime Minister Winston Churchill had complied with the demands of the Japanese, but Britain had been in a vulnerable position and there was little else Churchill could have done. Some of Britain's most valuable colonies were in the Far East, including the island of Hong Kong, along with Singapore, which was considered by many to be "the Gibraltar of the East".

There was also Malaya to the north of Singapore, which was an important source of rubber, and of course Burma itself, with the valuable port of Rangoon. By now the Japanese were ready to venture a great deal further afield than China, and if they could snatch the outposts of the once mighty British Empire, not only would they have access to the vital resources themselves, it would also mean that supplies to British troops, already stretched to full capacity, would quickly run dry.

For Winston Churchill, the threat to the Empire was extremely worrying, but there were more immediate concerns far closer to home. As the Luftwaffe continued to bomb the British Isles, Churchill realized that the fight against Hitler and the Axis powers would be a long and bitter one.

Britain had now been subject to regular attacks since September 1940 and there seemed little hope that the Luftwaffe would ever ease their bombardment. During January and February there had been intense bombing raids all around the country, as Hitler had done all that he could to dampen the morale of the British people.

·   ·   ·

But it would take more than the blitz to defeat the British and despite the bombs raining down from the German aircraft, the resolve of the nation remained firm. The Royal Family set an example to the rest of the country when despite the dangers they refused to leave London. Even when Buckingham Palace was hit again in early March, damaging the North side of the building, they remained in the city, and continued to rally support for the battle against the Nazis, giving hope and comfort to their loyal subjects.

As the Axis closed in on land, air and sea and more and more troops left the country to be deployed around the globe, the British government worked hard to keep the Nazis at bay and extreme measures were taken on the home front. The Minister for Labor and National Service, Ernest Bevin made the radical decision to call up the nation's women to help with the war effort and as the adult female population joined the workforce from March 1941 onwards, Britain was transformed with the implementation of a total war economy.

By December Bevin went a step further and ordered the conscription of women into the services. Though at first only single women aged between twenty to thirty were called up, by mid-1943, almost 90 percent of single women and eighty percent of married women were working in the factories, on the land or in the armed forces.

In the 1930s a woman's place was in the home while a man's place was to go out to work, but with the onset of war, traditional social roles in Britain would change dramatically. Though many women without families had jobs before the war, by 1941 mothers and single women alike were being called on to occupy what were considered "men's jobs"; indeed, their immense contribution to the war effort would play a significant role in Britain's success against the Axis.

As the spring of 1941 edged closer there was a change in tactic in the Luftwaffe's bombing raids and rather than targeting cities further inland they followed orders from Hitler to focus on the ports along the coast of Britain. The change came as the successes of the German navy in the Battle of the Atlantic began to wane, and U-boat losses mounted, in part due to the extra destroyers Roosevelt had sent from America back in 1940.

Karl Donitz, Commander of the German Navy, turned to the air force for help and asked Hitler to change strategy so that the swarming planes of the Luftwaffe now headed for ports such as Plymouth, Bristol, Swansea, and Belfast with tragic consequences for their inhabitants.

But while more and more people were killed in the blitz, on March 11th 1941 Churchill was given the news he'd been anxiously waiting for. After months of debate and negotiations, President Roosevelt had finally won over congress and signed the Lend-Lease Act. This meant that vast quantities of war supplies from the United States would soon begin arriving in Europe and those who were fighting Nazi Germany were given real hope that the war could be won.

Adolf Hitler realized that America's days for neutrality were coming to an end, although the United States had not yet made a declaration of war. Nevertheless, Hitler now had powerful allies and his treaty with the Japanese would prove to be of great use. Spies from the country were already surveying the American naval base at Pearl Harbor and by the end of 1941, as relations deteriorated between Washington and Tokyo, the Japanese would launch a devastating attack not only on Pearl but American bases around the Pacific, crippling their fleet for a time.

In March 1941 however, Hitler had little time to contemplate the threat of American intervention with decidedly more pressing matters to attend to in the Balkans. While mechanized German fighter forces were flooding into Bulgaria in preparation for the invasion of Greece Hitler still awaited confirmation that Yugoslavia would side with the Nazis.

. . .

The country's allegiance to Germany was crucial to Nazi success in the Balkans as attacking Greece across the twenty-five-mile-wide Bulgarian frontier would be a daunting task. On the other hand, if the Nazis were able to attack through Yugoslavia's Vardar River Valley as well, they would have more chance of success against Greek resistance.

On March 25th the Regent Prince Paul finally signed up to the Tripartite Pact, but there were thousands of Yugoslavs including government and military officials who were fervently anti-Nazi, and the nation was anything but behind him. On March 27th a coup overthrew the pro-Axis government and Prince Paul was replaced by seventeen-year-old King Peter the Second, who was godson to the British King and Queen. It was a bold act but would bring a terrible fate to the Kingdom of Yugoslavia: and Hitler barely able to believe the news, furiously announced *"Yugoslavia will be annihilated for she has just renounced publicly the policy of understanding with the Axis"*.

As the Nazi Führer now made the decision to go to war with not only Greece, but also Yugoslavia, refugees from Belgium, Holland, Poland and Czechoslovakia, who had escaped into the country while the Axis swept across Europe, now began to flee back across the Yugoslav borders.

On the dawn of April 6th the Kingdom of Yugoslavia's worst fears were realized as the planes of the Luftwaffe were loaded with bombs and set off to begin their intense bombardment of the capital, Belgrade. Thousands of people would be killed in what Hitler referred to as *Operation Punishment*, and meanwhile to the south as the Germany army thundered across the Greek border, Greece would be defeated within weeks.

As the Balkans were engulfed in turmoil, far away to the north, the Soviet leader Josef Stalin was keeping a close eye on affairs. He had already been informed by foreign diplomats, that Adolf Hitler was planning to invade Russia, but could not believe the Nazis would attempt to wage a war on the vast Red Army, while still occupied with battles elsewhere.

Nevertheless, by early summer of 1941, Hitler's troops would be ready for the war against communism and the Second World War would be taken in an entirely new direction as allegiances changed and the Soviet Union joined forces with the Allies. For Hitler, the delay caused by the conflict in Greece and Yugoslavia, would have dire consequences for *Operation Barbarossa,* and when the icy winds of the Russian winter took hold, the tides of victory would begin to turn in the Allies' favor at last.

7

THE BLITZ, THE BISMARCK & BARBAROSSA

April – June 1941

| The guns are prepared for *Operation Barbarossa*

There is no doubt that 1941 was a crucial year, full of developments in World War II for Adolf Hitler and all those who opposed him. With France now controlled by the Germans, Britain had been left to fight on alone, taking the full brunt of the Nazi attack. Despite all expectations however, they had been able to weather the storm and by April, Germany had changed tactics, resorting to the bombing of British seaports rather than targeting the nation's towns and cities, in an effort to dominate at sea after losing the Battle of Britain back in 1940.

In the Mediterranean, Germany was dealt a bitter blow by the Allies at the Battle of Mattapan, but with Hitler's great favorite, General Erwin Rommel beginning his march into Allied held territory in North Africa, the global conflict was spreading. Italian forces under Mussolini had also been drawn into the North African campaign hindering the British in Somaliland and Ethiopia.

For Britain's Prime Minister, Winston Churchill, who had already proved himself to be a worthy opponent for Adolf Hitler, securing support from America was vital and although President Roosevelt had done all that he could, the people of the USA were still staunchly against entering the war to fight for the Allies. Even so Adolf Hitler knew that he had a huge battle on his hands with Churchill on the other side of the English Channel, but as if that wasn't enough the German Führer was ready to look east towards Russia, the nation he had signed a non-aggression pact with before storming into Poland in 1939.

Would Hitler dare go back on his word and attack the Soviet Union before completing his plans to invade Great Britain? The events of April, May and June 1941 were about to answer this question and many more besides.

. . .

As April 1st dawned there was a difficult time ahead for the Allies in North Africa. Rommel, who would become better known as the Desert Fox because of his cunning desert strategies, was already beginning his ruthless assault on the Allied held lines. The German Afrika Korps swiftly gained the upper hand and the British troops given the task of defending the territory went into retreat. Rommel was pleasantly surprised at the ease with which this happened and moved his troops towards Benghazi and on April 3rd took Libya's second city.

Encouraged, Rommel soon set his sights on Tobruk as a prelude to making a German advance into Egypt. North Africa and the Middle East were hot beds of activity during this phase of WWII, as all sides in the conflict fought to maintain access to oil supplies, with Axis supporters in countries like Iraq giving the Allies a real challenge. And while the Nazi cause was being furthered, their fellow Germans were making major advances in Europe. By April 6th forces were employing their incredibly successful blitzkrieg tactics wherever they went, and the Allied troops stationed in Greece were quickly defeated. Again, the Allies were forced into retreat and Hitler's domination was increasing daily.

The first weeks of April 1941 were, from the point of view of military strategy fascinating. As Hitler accelerated his plans to invade Russia, it was Winston Churchill who directed Sir Stafford Cripps, the British Ambassador in Moscow to deliver a message to Joseph Stalin warning of a possible German attack. Just a few weeks later Churchill warned Stalin in person of Hitler's plans, based on "Ultra" intelligence reports, but by this stage the Russian leader was already preparing, drafting in extra troops to defend the nation's borders, while bringing in reinforcements to protect Moscow.

And while Churchill and Stalin were fully occupied, Hitler quickly made a pact with the Japanese, promising that if they found themselves in conflict with the USA, something that was looking increasingly likely, then Germany would join them in declaring war on America. The Soviets signed a similar treaty with Yugoslavia in case of a German attack, while to complicate matters even further Japan and the Soviet Union signed a five-year non-aggression pact.

With so much tactical maneuvering going on and switching of allegiances, it was difficult for anyone to predict what was going to happen next, but for those being targeted by Adolf Hitler, the most imminent threat was all they had time to worry about.

In Northern Ireland, Belfast suffered a brutal German attack, with the Luftwaffe raining down terror from the skies. Ironically Belfast was hit by one of the most devastating air raids of the war on Easter Sunday April 15th on what should have been a day of peace and celebration. More than two hundred German aircraft strafed the city, and through a combination of standard explosive and incendiary bombs, claimed the lives of nine hundred people and injured more than fifteen hundred others. For the Germans, casualties were light with no anti-aircraft guns fired because RAF fighters were believed to be in the area, although they had never actually been scrambled.

And all the while in Africa, Rommel was still making rapid progress, but despite his gains, he drew his troops to a halt at the Fort of Tobruk, which was destined to become a battleground for many a military engagement in the months ahead. Between April 13th and 15th it appeared that the Nazis were on course for another easy victory as his tanks quickly advanced into the city. But his tanks became trapped as the Allies made the most of the situation, marking the beginning of a siege, the outcome of which was never going to be a foregone conclusion.

The Germans were also very active just across the Mediterranean, as Hitler made plans to attack the Island of Crete, which would be codenamed *Operation Mercury.*

. . .

This would consolidate his position having already attacked the Greek mainland and deny the British a convenient base on the island, as by April 24th Greece had fully surrendered to the Nazis, and Hitler's decision to target Crete was a logical next step.

And still the political maneuvering continued. Roosevelt proposed transferring part of the US Fleet to the Atlantic Ocean, and Winston Churchill was happy to support the move. Although the Americans were yet to join the Allies fully in the war effort, their contribution supporting from the sidelines was invaluable. It was now almost impossible for the Allies to predict Hitler's next move, and naturally for Winston Churchill there were still grave concerns that a full-scale Nazi invasion of Great Britain was on the way.

In fact, there were those who suggested that British troops should abandon the fight in the Middle East and return to protect their homeland. But Churchill was opposed to the idea, and he must have been heartened by news that in East Africa the Italians had surrendered, which allowed Haile Selassie to return to Ethiopia's capital Addis Ababa and reclaim his throne.

The tide was slowly but surely turning in many different directions, and as May 1941 progressed there were some astonishing surprises in store.

One of the most incredible of them all came on May 10th when Hitler's second in command, Rudolf Hess, was discovered with a broken ankle in a Scottish field. Interestingly, despite his long and loyal devotion to Hitler, Hess had often been overlooked as praise was lavished upon his more vociferous rivals for the Führer's attention, Hermann Goering and Joseph Goebbels.

Although there is all manner of conspiracy theories, it's generally believed that dissatisfaction with Hitler's leadership caused Hess to undertake a solo mission, flying to Britain to broker a peaceful conclusion to the hostilities with Winston Churchill. By this time there was a growing German Resistance, already working towards assassinating Adolf Hitler, so Hess would have by no means been alone in feeling that the Führer's days were numbered.

When news reached Hitler that Hess's plane had taken off, fighter pilots were dispatched to prevent him reaching his destination. Hess managed to reach Scotland before he had to bail out, which is how he came to break his ankle.

For Hess the war was over after being kept prisoner by the British until the Nuremberg trials and he was eventually sent to Berlin's Spandau Prison where he remained until his death in 1987. But for the Luftwaffe, May 10th proved to be very busy indeed because after Hess made his emergency landing in Scotland a total of five hundred and fifteen bombers attacked London, scoring direct hits on several of the city's great landmarks, including the British Museum, the Houses of Parliament and St. James' Palace. The number of casualties grew to staggering proportions, making this the highest death toll for a single raid throughout the war, claiming one thousand three hundred and sixty-four lives, while over sixteen hundred were left injured.

One of the reasons for the large number of casualties was the lack of bomb shelters for much of the city's population. Public air raid shelters were available, although the government was reluctant to provide too many, in case people become too dependent upon government aid. Consequently, families were encouraged, with the provision of subsidized materials, to build their own shelters, leaving those who were unable, to make their own arrangements to use the London Underground stations as a haven during the raids.

Although the losses suffered by the people of London that fateful night were without doubt devastating there was some consolation. Britain's aerial defenses had improved greatly, and the Germans were certainly not going to be able to continue inflicting such damage without paying a price. At this point in the conflict the average Nazi fighter plane casualties per raid had increased from just twenty-eight in January of 1941 to one hundred and twenty-eight by mid-May.

Despite this there was large improvements in technology, both on the ground and in the air for the British. Radar allowed ground crews to be ready well before the raids began, and with airborne radar fitted to some British aircraft, RAF pilots were able to successfully engage the enemy, especially at night when visibility was severely reduced. Unlike Belfast, London also had a large contingent of anti-aircraft batteries, which allowed for a steady rate of fire against the Luftwaffe, and this certainly made a huge contribution to reducing the German air force's effectiveness.

Hitler's aerial attacks against his enemies, using a blanket of firebombs to cripple industry and destroy housing as he broke the spirit of the people, had brought him great success.

But Londoners were made of sterner stuff. Sadly, in Belfast the bombing of a major water works had meant that the pressure wasn't high enough to fight the fires, but London suffered no such difficulty and crews worked tirelessly to prevent the fires from spreading.

As many of those from the emergency services were now fighting for their country, volunteers took their places and members of the home guard really played a crucial part in stopping London from burning. And there was a great deal of work to be done, so as well as fire fighters and first aiders, these brave volunteers also took on tasks like running for the blitz Scouts, who were responsible for guiding fire engines and ambulances through the worst of the flames and the rubble, to get to the injured.

After this raid on London, a further wave of Luftwaffe bombers hit Birmingham just 6 days later, and thankfully did much less damage. Throughout the blitz, British cities and their people had suffered some of the most destructive attacks of any conflict to date.

However, they were not the only nation to be attacked in this manner during WWII, and as the war shifted more in the Allies favor, British and American bombers would target German cities with equally appalling consequences. Aerial bombardment was one of the more devastating acts of war used throughout the conflict between the Allies and the Axis powers.

While the tactical bombing of troops had been the main aim of air forces before the Second World War, these more strategic terror raids were fast becoming the order of the day.

Focusing on destroying industry and crippling the economy of a country was a major consideration, while terrifying civilians and breaking their spirit was another major aim.

For the British keeping morale high, whatever the German bombers threw their way was of vital importance and Winston Churchill was without doubt a master at lifting the mood of the nation. Wherever he went visiting bombed out cities, the people came out to cheer him and Churchill was able to make even those who had lost everything feel that their sacrifices had not been in vain.

Plymouth Guildhall and St. Andrews

Taking a closer look at what happened in Plymouth demonstrates just how deadly and effective Hitler's air raid tactics were. During the relentless raids on the city, even air raid shelters were no guarantee of safety and when a communal shelter took a direct hit, 72 people were killed as entire families were wiped out. Not surprisingly by the beginning of May, plans were put in place to evacuate the city's children, and they were sent off to the relative safety of North Cornwall on May 3rd the day after Churchill's visit. The good folk of Plymouth had born the fearsome brunt of a sustained Luftwaffe attack, but like the rest of the Great British public, they refused to be intimidated.

When a local headmistress nailed a wooden sign over the door of a badly damaged church, simply saying "Resurgum" she summed up the mood of Plymouth, with the Latin word translating literally as "I shall rise again".

And as Churchill made his way through the rubble of Plymouth, his resolve to stand firm against Hitler must have been strengthened as he encouraged the survivors, assuring them that Plymouth, like the entire nation, would indeed, rise again. But with British cities like London, Belfast and Plymouth to mention but a few, suffering such heavy bombardments, a counterattack against the Germans was inevitable.

Throughout April and early May, Hamburg and Berlin were both hit repeatedly by RAF bombers, although they could not inflict the kind of damage the Luftwaffe had on British cities. Nevertheless, just as Hitler had tried to break the British spirit through the blitz, the RAF certainly dented German morale even though the bombing raids did relatively little damage. From the British perspective, when the Chief of Air Staff, Sir Charles Portal declared that if you could get four million people out of their beds and into shelters it was worth it, he summed up the aim of the mission, considering the limited resources available to the RAF at that time.

Being able to bomb cities as far away as Berlin was in point of fact a new concept for the RAF, because up until this point in history their planes simply didn't have that kind of range without needing to refuel. However, thanks to the development of longer-range bombers, it had become a possibility since the beginning of 1940, although without a doubt these raids took the RAF to the limit of their technology.

Consequently, these attacks on German cities had to be conducted during the summer months, when the hours of light were longer, but this did make the Allied aircraft far more likely to be spotted by enemy defenses.

· · ·

It would be 1942 before the RAF would have the resources to effectively bomb German cities, and longer again before they implemented them fully.

Meanwhile back in North Africa the Siege of Tobruk was continuing, but the Chief of British Middle East Command, General Archibald Wavell saw an unexpected window of opportunity. With so many Axis troops engaged in the Siege, there was a weak defensive front between Egypt and Libya, and quick to take the initiative Wavell instigated *Operation Brevity* on May 15th. The main objective would be to acquire this territory, pushing Rommel and the Germans back from the Egyptian Libyan border and then launch an offensive on Tobruk.

The first part of the offensive involved taking the Italian controlled Halfaya Pass, which was an important strategic location for both Allied and Axis forces. On the morning of the 15th, despite stiff Italian opposition the Allies took the strategically vital pass, and throwing Axis commanders into a state of confusion, gained the upper hand.

However, as the Allies made progress the Germans were swift in pouring reinforcements into the battle zone, without losing their stranglehold on Tobruk. The engagements were hard fought in difficult conditions, and the Allied casualty numbers started to rise dramatically. With Rommel having been so successful in the preceding months, Allied reinforcements would be very hard to come by and rather than sustain further losses *Operation Brevity* was closed down.

Retreating to the Halfaya Pass the Allies did all they could to hold this strategic position, but for Rommel, *Operation Brevity* had actually alerted him to how important this pass was. It gave whoever held it a safe supply route through the region and the Allies were not able to hold it for long as the Germans launched *Operation Scorpion* to take it back on May 27th, in effect reversing all the territorial gains that had been made as a result of *Operation*

Brevity. While conquering Africa had always been a very large part of the Nazi masterplan, Hitler had always known that neutralizing the threat posed by the British Navy was of equal importance.

The main purpose of the Battle of Britain back in 1940 had been to destroy the RAF fighter planes to prevent them coming to the aid of British battle-ships when Germany was ready for a full-scale invasion. In fact Hitler had started building warships to match those of the British Navy back in the early 1930s, and when the pride of the German Navy, the Bismarck, was dispatched on May 19th 1941 it was the ship's first operational sortie. The Bismarck's mission had been to intercept and destroy Allied convoys in transit between North America and Great Britain. With the German U-Boat presence as well, Allied shipping ran terrible risks, particularly as British Intelligence were unable to track the positions of the enemy.

However, on May 9th there was a glimmer of hope, because when Allied forces boarded a captured German U-Boat they were able to recover an Enigma Cipher machine and the German codebooks. Once in the hands of British Intelligence with the code breakers at Bletchley Park in the heart of the English countryside, the Allies' prospects out in the Atlantic improved dramatically as coded German radio transmissions were deciphered, giving British and American ships some warning of where the enemy lay in wait for them.

As the Bismarck along with the Prinz Eugen, a German heavy cruiser, attempted to break out into the Atlantic they were spotted by the British Royal Navy, and the Battle of Denmark Strait began. The major casualty of the engagement was the flagship of the British Home Fleet, HMS Hood, and when news reached Winston Churchill in London, he angrily demanded that the German ship responsible, the Bismarck, be hunted down and sunk.

Two days later as the Bismarck headed for safety, aircraft from HMS Ark

Royal attacked the enemy ship and the damaged craft became an easy target. On May 27th she was finally sunk, and at last the people of Britain, still reeling from the effects of the blitz, had something to celebrate.

The capture of the German Enigma machine and the subsequent breaking of the latest enemy codes certainly proved to be of great benefit to Allied shipping, but the implications were far more widespread. When Adolf Hitler's plans for *Operation Mercury,* the invasion of Crete, were put into action, because of Ultra, the deciphered Enigma coding, the Allies were already aware that an attack was imminent. With the help of the island's civilian population the Allies fought fiercely to resist the German airborne invasion, and they inflicted heavy losses on the Nazi paratroopers.

In fact, by the end of the first day, May 20th it appeared as if the Allies had the upper hand. But the battle was far from over and due to miscommunication, the Germans managed to take Maleme airfield to the west of the island, which meant reinforcements could be flown in, overwhelming the Allies.

After ten days the Germans were victorious and General Wavell had no choice but to authorize the Allied evacuation of Crete, leaving the island under Nazi control.

However, although Hitler decided that there would be no more large scale airborne operations, due to the heavy German losses at the outset of the Battle of Crete, the Allies were very impressed and started to look at using paratroopers in the future, building their own airborne divisions.

While all eyes were focused on the war in Europe, the tension was also building in the Far East. When war was declared in 1939 the Japanese had already been at war with China since 1937 in the Second Sino Japanese War and there were far reaching consequences. Wherever the Imperial Japanese

Army instigated conflict, military personnel and civilians alike faced the most brutal regime.

Just months before World War II began, America had imposed sanctions on Japan after their terror bombing of the Chinese city of Chongqing in May 1939, when more than 5,000 civilians were killed in just two days. An embargo was put upon the export of airplane engine parts to Japan from America and as time went on and the Japanese showed no sign of halting their relentless quest to dominate the Far East, further sanctions were destined to follow.

News of an earlier attack by the Japanese on the city of Nanjing where the most appalling atrocities were committed against a civilian population had also reached the west and as well as imposing sanctions against the Japanese, President Roosevelt had also been providing aid to China.

During WWII Chongqing came under numerous Japanese attacks, and as Germany and Russia prepared for a bitter battle, the Japanese bombed the city yet again.

On June 5th a largely undefended civilian population were targeted as the air force of Imperial Japan flew more than twenty sorties over the city, bombing continuously for more than three hours. The actual numbers of casualties were not recorded, but some four thousand local residents were asphyxiated after a tunnel they were hiding in collapsed, trapping them below ground.

For the people of China, as for those of any nation the Japanese conquered, these were truly terrible times, with Japan's policy of the "Three Alls", Kill all, burn all, loot all, no quarter was ever given, and for the Americans still poised upon the sidelines of the conflict, the alarm bells over Japan's barbaric behavior were now ringing loud and clear.

. . .

But for the time being the mighty USA had to be content with ever increasing sanctions and an embargo on trade with Japan. Oil would soon become a major issue as the Americans were preparing to stop supplying the Japanese, who of course had no natural resources of their own. They desperately needed American oil to keep the cogs of their military machine turning, something President Roosevelt was well aware of; however, backing the Japanese into a corner would have consequences that he could never have imagined.

While Japan remained an ominous presence to the East, Roosevelt was also concerned about developments in the European War to the west.

The American people had been fiercely opposed to joining the war against Nazi Germany, but while the British continued to struggle through bomb raids and the blitz, public opinion regarding the war in Europe had started to thaw a little.

Daily radio broadcasts gave the Americans the opportunity to follow their progress in extraordinary detail. Reports were often conducted at street level as Londoners rushed for their bomb shelters, and while British resolve remained as firm as ever, the American people began to foster a deep respect for the beleaguered nation.

The Battle of Britain that had taken place during the summer of 1940 had also proved an inspiration to many Americans, as the bravery of the RAF captured the public imagination. Hundreds of US citizens had started volunteering for service in the RAF hoping to play their part in the attempt to stop Hitler in his tracks and ensure Nazism did not become a dominant force in the world.

. . .

Even famous actors signed up to do their part, with James Stewart registering for service with the US Air Force in early 1941 and Clark Gable a year later. Soon support for the British increased to the point where an *"all aid short of war"* system was implemented, providing much needed back up for the Allies. Earlier in 1941 Churchill had called on Roosevelt for help, imploring that the US President, *"give us the tools and we'll finish the job"*, and by March congress had passed the Lend-lease Act.

| War torn London appeals to the USA

American warships were also sent to escort Allied merchant-shipping crossing the Atlantic Ocean so that much needed supplies could reach the British mainland, while the Nazi U-Boats continued to prowl the seas. Support for the European war was extended even further when steps were taken to freeze German and Italian finances.

• • •

As the Nazis had marched through the nations and cities of Europe, they had seized gold from many banks and more hauntingly had even confiscated money and possessions from concentration camp victims and other civilians. Much of what they had stolen was now being stored in the US and was a major part of their wartime funding.

When all assets held by Germans and Italians within the United States were frozen on June 14th it dealt a major blow to the Nazis, as tensions on a global scale continued to rise. Nevertheless, while the American President did all he could to help Britain and the Allies, there were many of his countrymen who were strongly against Roosevelt's moves to aid the European war.

Public figures like Charles Lindbergh, the famous American Aviator, believed that the war with Hitler was a European affair, and that the real enemy of the United States was Communist Russia. He believed that sending any sizable force to the aid of the British would leave America open to attacks from the Soviet Union, which he was convinced would result in the destruction of western civilization.

But Lindbergh couldn't have been any further wide of the mark, because while Britain braced itself for the invasion Hitler had promised on the heels of the Luftwaffe's aerial bombardment, the Soviet Union was about to become the next victim of Adolf Hitler's master plan for world domination.

Despite the non-aggression pact signed between the Soviet Union and Germany in August 1939, and their joint invasion of Poland, Hitler always had an Eastern Campaign on the agenda. His perception of the Soviet Union was as a nation populated by ethnic Slavs, ruled by Jewish Bolshevik masters.

Way back in the mid-1920s Hitler's book, Mein Kampf, presented his view of world order, and even in those early days of his rise to prominence he had stated that Germany's destiny was to turn *"to the east"* as it had done *"six hundred years earlier"*. Consequently, under Hitler's direction the Nazis made it a priority to kill, deport or enslave Russian and other Slavic populations, in order to repopulate their homelands with pure blooded Germanic peoples.

However, strong as Hitler's hatred of Jews and Bolsheviks was, there were other driving forces that motivated his persistent desire to conquer nations to the east of Germany as well as to the west. Hitler undoubtedly recognized the enormous wealth of the Soviet Union, a land rich in precious resources, which he was convinced could serve as the equivalent of India to the British, for the Third Reich. So as Stalin continued to build up his Red Army using the very same materials that Germany were coveting for their war effort, the urgency for an attack on the Eastern Front began to grow.

The fact that Stalin had control of materials vital to the Nazi war machine was far from ideal as far as Hitler was concerned, and when the Soviet foreign minister Molotov visited Berlin in November 1940, the Führer's disquiet about the Russians power escalated. With the Soviet Union in such a strong economic position Hitler realized that he may be forced to bend to any demands Stalin chose to make, and he was determined not to lose a moment in his preparation for an eastern campaign.

On December 18th 1940 Hitler had ordered Führer Directive Number 21, and from the opening statement it was obvious that he meant business.

"The armed forces of Germany must be prepared, even before the conclusion of the war with England, to defeat Soviet Russia in one rapid campaign". The campaign was to be code named *Operation Barbarossa* in honor of the medieval German King and Holy Roman Emperor, and even Hitler had to acknowledge that it would be a monumental struggle between two opposing world views.

. . .

For the campaign to be successful Hitler was aware that timing was everything. This would need to be blitzkrieg tactics at their swiftest, because not only would the Red Army be extremely dangerous once they started retaliating, but also if Russia hadn't been conquered by the onset of winter, the bitter cold weather would become a major factor.

On their home territory, in extreme conditions, the Red Army would have the advantage. German Reconnaissance planes were rapidly deployed to survey the vast Soviet territory in order to gather intelligence, and as the Nazi Generals were busy formulating battle plans, Hitler's troops were beginning to build up in Poland.

As mentioned earlier, the British Prime Minister, Winston Churchill had attempted by various means to warn Stalin of the impending attack, but just as Churchill didn't trust Stalin, the Russian leader felt exactly the same way about his British counterpart. Also of course Stalin was well aware of Germany's dependence on Russian resources, and as a consequence did not believe it possible that Hitler would take such a rash course of action.

And all the while he and his generals had agreed upon a strategy for the daring advance. Three separate army groups would attack along what were old historical invasion routes, as the Germans were not the first to have had ambitions to conquer Russia.

The Emperor Napoleon had attempted just such an invasion back in 1812, and although he'd reached Moscow, in the end the strength of the Russians combined with the bitter winter weather had resulted in a humiliating defeat. Yet Hitler believed he could triumph where Napoleon had failed. The German's "Army Group North" was assigned to march through the Baltic States of Estonia, Latvia and Lithuania, and progress into Northern Russia with the aim of either taking, or destroying, the city of Leningrad.

· · ·

Hitler's "Army Group Center" would be given the task of advancing to Smolensk and then Moscow, marching through the region that today is known as Belarus. In the meantime, "Army Group South" was to strike the heavily populated and agricultural heartland of the Ukraine, taking Kiev before continuing to the east, all the way to the River Volga and the oil rich region of the Caucasus.

And all the while as May 1941 progressed to its conclusion, it was evident that bombing Great Britain into submission with the blitz was not working. A German occupation of the island nation was for the time being at least unlikely, and Adolf Hitler looked for alternative ways of bringing Winston Churchill and the people of Great Britain into line.

As bizarre as it may now sound Hitler's plans to attack Russia were finalized with him believing that if Germany demonstrated its might by defeating Stalin's Red Army, the British would be intimidated into capitulating peacefully to any demands the Führer might make. However, in effect attacking Russia was destined to actually allow Britain some respite as resources were re-directed eastwards. Despite Stalin's determined belief that Hitler was not going to attack the Soviet Union, the evidence was fast suggesting that the Russian leader was being naïve.

As his commanders, including the extremely competent Marshal Zhukov urged him to act, Stalin eventually bowed to their requests for reinforcements, and began moving divisions of the Red Army in preparation. Also, towards the end of May Stalin called up 800,000 reserve forces, but he persisted in his belief that Hitler would not attack.

This was all to the German's advantage through the early weeks of June 1941, and even when the German ambassador to Moscow informed the Head of Soviet International Affairs that Hitler intended to go to war with Russia on

June 22nd Stalin dismissed the report as disinformation. Just days later Hitler issued further directives, preparing for an attack on the Soviets.

The German armaments industry was to focus on the Navy and Air Force in the Mediterranean and Western Asia, where Nazi troops were to continue fighting in Egypt and Turkey, while plans were put in place to capture Gibraltar. Hitler also received good news from North Africa, because as the British launched *Operation Battleaxe* attempting to lift the Siege of Tobruk, it only lasted three days, between the 15th and 17th of June, and failed miserably.

German officers inspect abandoned Russian plane.

With Hitler's confidence in the ascendancy, a treaty of non-aggression was signed with Turkey, as his final preparations for *Operation Barbarossa* were maneuvered into place. However, it wasn't only in the European theatre of war that the pressure was mounting.

Roosevelt and the American Government had by this time suspended petroleum exports to Japan from east coast and gulf ports, an action that would leave the Japanese military machine in a precarious position, with no viable fuel supply to fall back upon. But the consequences of America's sanctions were still months away, and Stalin and the Russians were about to get the shock of their lives.

In the early hours of Sunday June 22nd, just as the Russians had been previously told, *Operation Barbarossa* began with the bombing of major Soviet cities by the Luftwaffe. On the ground some three million German troops went into action, with the element of surprise very definitely on their side. When news of the invasion reached Stalin, he evidently found it very hard to believe what was happening, despite the 90 separate warnings he had been given of Hitler's intentions since July 1940.

In fact, when Marshall Zhukov telephoned to speak to Stalin directly, the Russian leader was by all accounts completely silent. Zhukov asked, "Did you understand what I said Comrade Stalin?" and when it was evident that he did not, Zhukov had to repeat the information all over again.

Consolidating their position, the Luftwaffe also worked extensive reconnaissance, monitoring the Soviet response, and having destroyed almost 4,000 Russian aircraft in the first three days, were able to support German troops moving at devastating speed on the ground. The Soviet Defense Minister, Marshal Timoshenko was swift to call for men, horses and vehicles to be supplied for the war effort, as well as directing what was left of the Soviet air force to target German aircraft.

. . .

It's interesting to note that Winston Churchill responded with an evening radio broadcast on the day of the invasion, offering help to the Russians fighting for their homeland. However, in the days that followed, the American response was perhaps less sympathetic, if the thoughts of the future US President, Harry S Truman were anything to go by when he remarked that is was a very good thing for Germany and Russia to be at war, and that he sincerely hoped they would finish each other off.

As the military implications of Germany's attack on Russia were played out across the wide expanses of the Soviet Union, the political minefield suddenly became just as treacherous. There was no doubt that Hitler had awoken a sleeping giant, although it would be some months before the Germans would fully realize the enormity of the task that they had been charged with.

However, even at the time of the invasion the German Foreign Minister, Von Ribbentrop looked to his Japanese allies for assistance, urging them to attack Russia from the north. But Japan was busy formulating a major offensive against the USA and made it clear that they would wait until the Germans had at least captured Moscow and reached the Volga river, before joining the battle against the Soviets.

Even so, as the weeks of June passed, the Russian Red army had quite enough to contend with as the German thrust gathered momentum. At this point the Russians were still in a state of chaos and disarray, and when the city of Minsk fell on June 27th, Hitler's tanks were already a third of the way to Moscow.

As 1941 reached its halfway point, nobody could have predicted what was going to happen next. Suddenly for the British, the Russians were no longer fighting alongside the Germans, and the beleaguered Winston Churchill was keen to hold out an olive branch to Joseph Stalin.

. . .

In peacetime they would have been on opposing sides of any argument, but throughout history, war has always made for strange alliances, and this was no exception. With Roosevelt's help from the sidelines Churchill had come a very long way, but without America fighting fully for the Allies, the British Prime Minister would welcome the Russians into the fray, if not with open arms, then with a grudging acceptance of Britain's situation.

Churchill was convinced that destroying Hitler and his Nazi regime as quickly as possible was vital, and if an alliance with Russia made this more likely, that was how he would proceed.

Hitler's objective to intimidate the British into capitulation had ironically served only to strengthen their resolve and their position, with the mighty Russians as allies, and as the Nazi dictator planned his next move, events in the Pacific theatre of war were poised to dominate the remainder of 1941.

Before the year was out Hitler would be at war with the three major world powers, Great Britain, Russia and the USA, as the Japanese prepared to alter the course of history.

8

RUSSIAN ROULETTE

July – September 1941

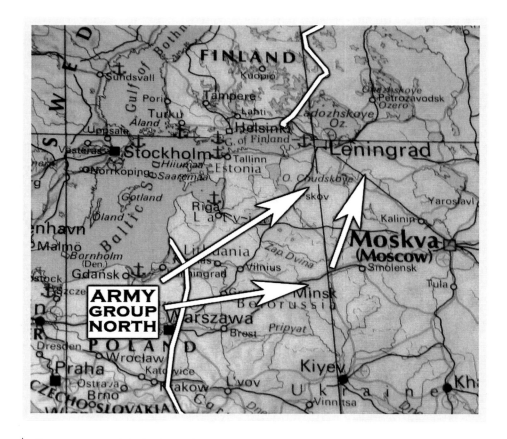

| German approach to Leningrad

As September 3rd and the second anniversary of the outbreak of World War Two rapidly approached, the events of 1941 were rapidly gathering momentum. In Europe the course of the conflict had veered dramatically as Adolf Hitler, after failing to invade the British Isles, turned his attention eastwards.

On June 22nd 1941 the Germans had invaded Russia as Hitler gave the order for *Operation Barbarossa* to commence. Anticipating a rapid victory, by employing the blitzkrieg tactics that had seen Poland, Denmark, Norway, the Low Countries and France all fall to the Nazis, Hitler truly believed his troops would conquer the mighty Soviets before the onset of winter.

It would prove to be a huge error of judgement, as the German Führer vastly underestimated the strength of his enemy.

What's more any hopes he had of his Japanese allies attacking Russia from the east as the Nazis advanced from the west were soon dashed, as the Empire of the Rising Sun became rather more pre-occupied with their ongoing war with China, and awakening a sleeping giant of their own, namely the United States of America.

The months of July, August and September 1941 were set to become very interesting indeed, and as the world watched and waited to see what would happen next, it wasn't just the Soviet Union preparing to play Russian Roulette.

For many people looking back at the history of World War II, the position of the Russians in the events, as they unfolded, is often tricky to understand. Even Winston Churchill the British Prime Minister described Russia as being *"a riddle wrapped in a mystery inside an enigma"*, and as we look in depth at what was going on in July 1941, stepping back further in time will certainly help us to understand matters more in context.

Traditionally, as the 20th Century dawned, the Russians had close ties with Great Britain, not least because the Tsar, Nicholas II, was married to Queen Victoria's granddaughter, Alexandra. And as another of Queen Victoria's grandchildren, the German Kaiser Wilhelm threatened the peace of Europe, the Russians joined forces with the British when World War I began in 1914.

· · ·

But as the battlefields of Ypres and the Somme became soaked in the blood of the young men fighting in the trenches, the mighty Russian Empire was crumbling fast, and on the streets of Moscow Russian blood was being spilled in equal measure.

As World War I raged on, the Russian Revolution of 1917 saw the working classes revolt against their capitalist overlords, triggering a brutal Civil War.

With heavy losses to the Germans on the Eastern Front and deteriorating conditions on the home front, tensions ran high.

The glittering decadence of the Royal family was in stark contrast to the meagre existence of the peasant classes, and as Lenin came to fore as the Bolshevik leader, the Romanov Dynasty was toppled as the Tsar and his family were captured and then executed.

It was a desperate time for the people of Russia, which saw the rise of Communism and the Red Army, named in honor of those whose blood had been shed in the war against capitalism. Then when Lenin died in 1924, his place was taken by Josef Stalin.

Ironically Lenin had warned against the threat that Stalin posed, but his wise words went unheeded. As far back as the 1920's Winston Churchill could sum up a situation with the most telling of words, and a staunch opponent of communism, he declared that when it came to Lenin, for the people of Russia, *"their worst misfortune had been his birth"*, while *"the next worst was his death"*.

It proved very much to be the case, as the Russians were left floundering without Lenin, and when Stalin came to power, on human rights issues, there was little to choose between the new Soviet Leader and Adolf Hitler.

Stalin's "Great Purge" of the 1930s left the world, and his own people, in little doubt about what he was capable of.

More accurately described as "The Great Terror", Stalin launched a purge of the Communist Party to ensure he faced no opposition, just as Hitler was doing with his government in Nazi Germany. Those who had ever shown dissent were either sent to forced Labor Camps or executed, while millions of ethnic minorities were deported.

Of the five first Marshals of the Soviet Union, only two would survive the Purge, Budyonny and Voroshilov, both of whom would have their part to play when the world went to war for a second time. With on average an estimated 1,000 executions of Russians a day, the Red Army became a fierce military machine hardened by dogma and governed by terror, capable of committing the most dreadful atrocities without questioning orders.

Although vehemently opposed to Stalin, Hitler had much in common with him, and when the German Führer realized he needed to secure Russian co-operation before invading Poland in 1939, despite hating Communism with a vengeance, he made a pact with them that he had no intention of keeping.

It was always going to be one of history's most uneasy pacts, and as we return to July 1941 Hitler's cavalier abandonment of it may have come as little surprise to the Allies, but was a complete shock to the Soviets, despite the fact that they had been repeatedly warned about the imminent Nazi invasion by Allied Intelligence. Further east again though, events were taking place that were destined to have dramatic repercussions before the end of the year.

· · ·

On June 2nd, 1941 an Imperial Conference was held in Japan, as Hitler's most powerful ally evaluated their position. With *Operation Barbarossa* putting Russia and Germany at war, the Japanese were reluctant to be drawn into the conflict as they had issues of their own that demanded more immediate attention. Japan had been at war with China since 1937, which was a major undertaking, but diplomatic tensions with the USA were also escalating.

It's worthwhile at this point in the proceedings to re-cap on events to date from the Japanese perspective, so that it's possible to put what happened throughout the latter part of 1941 into context.

The Japanese had a history of disputes with America and Russia and having spent many centuries of its existence with its ports closed to the outside world, it was a nation of great mystery. When the American Naval Commodore, Admiral Matthew Perry finally forced the Japanese to open trading links with the west, as the 19th Century drew to a close the Empire of the Rising Sun without doubt felt they were being taken advantage of. What's more with America buying the vast expanses of Alaska from the Russians and winning the Philippine Islands and Guam from the Spanish, Japan was all too aware of the growing dominance of the USA. Hawaii was also annexed with the Americans creating a Naval Base there, from which they could easily reach their newly acquired territory in the Pacific.

It will come as little surprise therefore that the Japanese took steps to improve their military power, modelling their army on the French and the Prussians, and their Naval Fleet on the British. This proved invaluable when Imperial Russia edged ever closer to Korea, a country Japan viewed as a safety buffer. When the Japanese Navy attacked the Russian Fleet at Port Arthur in 1904, they won a resounding victory.

However, the new century was fast becoming diplomatically precarious, and just ten years later a melting pot of conflicts on a global scale had exploded into the First World War.

After bitter and bloody fighting in the trenches and great battles at sea, when peace eventually prevailed in 1918, treaties were fast put in place to prevent such a war ever breaking out again. But just as the Treaty of Versailles and its draconian measures against the defeated German nation fired Adolf Hitler and other likeminded patriots into action, another treaty caused discontent for the Japanese.

The strength of the largest naval powers in the world came under scrutiny in the aftermath of World War I and the Washington Naval Treaty was signed between America, Britain, France, Italy and Japan agreeing limits for each signatory's Navy. However, the Japanese felt they had been unfairly constrained by the Americans and it was the start of a period of conflict between the two culturally diverse nations.

Prince Fumimaro Konoe, who would eventually become Prime Minister of Japan, was skeptical of western intentions at this time and he was particularly concerned about the lack of natural resources available to his tiny island nation. Konoe believed that the nations in the west were protecting their own self-interests and remarked that unless every country had equal access to international markets the *"resource poor"* nation of Japan *"would have no resort but to destroy the status quo for the sake of self-preservation"*.

Within a decade the fragile foundations of peace that the Treaty of Versailles had attempted to construct were under threat and Konoe's predictions were to become reality. The Wall Street Crash of 1929 sent the world spiraling into an economic depression and Japan was forced to look further afield for supplies of raw materials to feed the country's dying economy.

· · ·

There were already Japanese colonies in Manchuria in north eastern China, and tempted by a land rich in natural resources, the Imperial Army marched its troops into the region, in September 1931. Within six months a Japanese victory had been secured and on March 1st the last Emperor of China, Puyi, who had been removed by Chinese warlords in 1924, was placed at the head of the new puppet state of Manchuria. The region itself was re-named Manchukuo and soon the army began to draw up plans for settling five million colonists in China within twenty years.

In the meantime, the new settlers set to work building mines for gold, coal and iron ore which would help fuel Japanese expansion. The timber industry thrived, and farmers were encouraged to grow opium poppies, the sale of which would help fund the Imperial Army. Before long there was a dramatic increase in opium smoking and soon a quarter of Manchuria's population were addicts.

But while Japan reaped the benefits of their venture into China, their actions were condemned by the west. The League of Nations set up after the First Great War to prevent further acts of aggression around the world refused to recognize Manchukuo as an independent state and instructed Japan to pull out of the area.

However, in February 1933, a Japanese delegate, Yosuke Matsuoka responded to the representatives of nations from around the world, telling them that Manchuria was a matter of life or death for Japan.

As Matsuoka marched from the hall, it marked Japan's withdrawal from the League of Nations and the beginning of increasingly fraught relations with the west.

By 1936 Japan had renounced the Washington Treaty and by 1937 after six years of sporadic battles, the conflict between China and Japan had escalated in size and intensity.

On July 7th as tensions heightened between the troops of the Chinese leader Chiang Kai-Check and the Imperial army of Japan, an incident at Marco Polo Bridge to the south of Beijing, led to full scale war between the two countries.

Beneath the watchful eye of the west, Japanese troops began to pour into China led by the military leader Hideki Tojo and were soon mercilessly ravaging the vast nation. There were many in Tokyo who were appalled that the army seemed to be pushing forward on their own initiative and Prince Konoe, who had by now become Prime Minister of Japan realized that his government had little or no control over the army.

By December 1937 the Japanese army had reached the capital of China, Nanjing and launched a terrifying attack on its inhabitants that would see hundreds of thousands of innocent civilians massacred.

There were westerners in the city at the time, who like the Chinese, began to flee for their lives and while the city was engulfed in chaos one particular event would mark the beginning of even greater hostilities between Japan and America. Many military personnel and civilians had boarded the USS Gunboat Panay to escape Nanjing and on December 12th 1937 to the horror of those on board, Japanese naval planes began to dive towards the ship bombarding it with explosives.

While bomb blasts tore through the deck, many were injured, and three Americans were killed. It was a grave moment for diplomatic relations between America and Japan, and to make matters worse a news reel of the event was soon on its way to President Roosevelt in Washington.

· · ·

With such an open demonstration of hostility the American President had every reason to declare war, but while the memories of the First Great War still hung over the nation, the United States had been keen to take an isolationist stance and steer clear of conflict for the time being. Meanwhile many of the Japanese had expressed their remorse for the incident.

Vice-Admiral Isoroku Yamamoto made a formal apology to the United States for the Panay Incident. He was a Harvard man who had spent time as a naval attaché in America and was aware of the considerable naval power that America wielded. He was also more aware than anyone else of the dangers of going to war with a nation as powerful as the United States.

| Vice Admiral Isoroku Yamamoto

To the relief of the Japanese government, on Christmas Eve 1937, the President accepted the apology from Tokyo, but while the war continued in China, Roosevelt was increasingly disturbed by the tales of atrocities, filtering back to the west.

. . .

The Japanese military had little respect for human life and their use of biological weapons and terror bombing was killing millions of civilians throughout China.

After the Japanese firebombed Chongqing in May 1939, killing five thousand people in two days, America made decisive moves towards preventing further Japanese brutality.

In July that year an embargo on the sale of aircraft to Japan was put in place, and served as a warning to the country, that America would do all it could to hinder its expansionist policies. By the time war had broken out in Europe, Roosevelt took further measures and by signing the Lend Lease Act in March 1941, promised aid not only for the British in their fight against Nazi Germany, but also for the Chinese as they battled against the Imperial Army.

The leader of the Chinese National Front, Chiang Kai-Shek had also requested air support and by the summer of 1941 the First American Volunteer Group, popularly known as the Flying Tigers were in training on Chinese airfields. Though the pilots would not be in combat until early 1942, the fact that Roosevelt had approved their deployment was once again proof of where America's sympathies lay.

Japan in turn made it clear that while war was waged in Europe their sympathies lay with the Axis. In September 1940 they had signed the Tripartite Pact with Nazi Germany and Italy, and by the spring of 1941, Frank Matsuoka, the delegate who had marched out of the League of Nations in 1933, was waving triumphantly from Mussolini's balcony in Rome.

Matsuoka who was by this time the Japanese foreign minister, had been educated in America, and had lived there for nine years.

But despite his western upbringing Matsuoka was obsessed with the idea of an Anglo-American conspiracy aimed at Japan, and it was these fears which had drawn him closer to the belligerent nations of Nazi Germany and Fascist Italy.

To the surprise of the Japanese government, the Japanese Foreign Minister did not stop at Italy and Germany however and on April 13th 1941, after a successful meeting with Josef Stalin he had signed a Neutrality Pact with the Soviet Union.

It was certainly not what the Japanese government had expected, and officials were left bewildered by their Foreign Minister's radical new policy. Russia was Japan's hereditary enemy and had penetrated into the folklore of the people even before Commodore Perry's expedition in 1853 signaled the beginning of hostilities between east and west.

Japan regarded Russia as the great power against which it was destined to fight for its survival and it's worth looking back at one particular battle between Russia and Japan to better understand the rivalry that existed between the two nations.

Barely two years before Matsuoka signed the neutrality pact with Stalin, there had been fierce battles between the Soviet Union and Japan. Mongolia which bordered Japanese owned Manchuria, had been a soviet puppet state since the 1920s and it seemed there was little hope of a peaceful co-existence between the two regions.

The border between the two territories was hotly disputed and while Japan claimed that the border ran along the Khalkhin-Gol river, the Soviets argued that it ran near Nomonhan village, some 10 miles east of the river. The argument continued throughout the 1930s and there were frequent military clashes between Japanese troops, and Mongolian and Soviet troops; but the most decisive engagement of the Soviet-Japanese border War, would be The Battle of Khalkhyn Gol.

In fact, this particular battle would also have a major significance in the history of the Second World War.

By the spring of 1939 both the Soviet and Japanese nations had been building up forces on either side of the Khalkhyn Gol and by July, Japanese troops had ventured across the river and were advancing along the west bank. They faced fierce opposition however, led by a relatively unknown Soviet Commander at the time.

Georgy Zhukov was the son of a village cobbler and had led the life of a peasant until conscripted into the army. During the first World War however he proved his military expertise and was soon promoted to the rank of officer for his bravery in battle. Later Zhukov joined the Bolshevik party, where his background of poverty became a great asset, and he was one of the few officers who survived Stalin's great purge of the Red Army.

Renowned for his detailed planning, discipline and "never give up" attitude in battle, Zhukov would eventually become one of the greatest generals in the Soviet Union, and certainly dissuaded the Japanese from ever picking a fight with the Soviets again.

In August 1939 Zhukov launched his counterattack at Khalkhyn gol, with

50,000 Soviet and Mongolian troops and tank and motorized artillery divisions which would prove more than a match for the Japanese. By the end of the month, the northern task force had been completely destroyed, and while the surviving Japanese soldiers were taken prisoner, Zhukov was praised for his outstanding victory.

By the time a ceasefire agreement was signed on September 15th however, the Soviets had other matters to attend to. Stalin had new commitments in Eastern Europe, having agreed to take part in the Nazi invasion of Poland and the Red Army was now drawn to an entirely different field of conflict. Just over two weeks after Hitler's initial invasion of the country, on September 17th 1939 the Soviets thundered into Eastern Poland to the horror of those already battling against the German forces.

Meanwhile, back in Japan, the events in Mongolia would have a profound effect on the politics of war. The Imperial army had long favored a North Strike Group and had advocated marching deep into Siberia to further extend the empire of Japan for years. In fact, propaganda had begun circulating as long ago as 1919, encouraging the Japanese to support the occupation of the Russian Far East. The battle at Khalkhyn Gol however, had changed matters somewhat. The disastrous defeat now convinced the Imperial General Staff in Tokyo, that rather than following the North Strike Group to extend the boundaries of the empire, they should instead focus on a South Strike Group.

This strategy, favored by the navy, would lead Japan to the rich territories of the South Pacific, where many outposts of the British Empire and the United States lay and would ultimately change the course of the Second World War. In the meantime, by the summer of 1941, although the Soviets were assured that there was no longer a Japanese threat to their eastern borders, Hitler had renounced his non-aggression pact with the country and there was a vast Axis army now crossing their southern borders.

. . .

Hitler had waited many months for the opportunity to strike out at the evils of communism and finally by June 22nd, 1941, the invasion of the Soviet Union, *Operation Barbarossa* was well underway.

The German armed forces were divided into three army groups, north, south and center and had the overall objective of reaching the Ural Mountains in the north and the Volga river in the south. Army Group North would march through the Baltics and either take or destroy the city of Leningrad, now known as St Petersburg.

This group would be commanded by Wilhelm von Leeb, a General disliked by Hitler for his anti-Nazi attitudes, but who had earned his place at the helm of Barbarossa after his great success during the Battle of France.

Meanwhile Army Group south would strike through the agricultural heartland of the Ukraine, taking Kiev before continuing eastwards in the direction of Stalingrad on the Volga River and the oil-rich Caucasus. Group South would be led by Gerd von Rundstedt, who had seen action in Poland and France and had also helped plan the invasion of Britain, *Operation Sea Lion.*

Feder van Bock who had led an army into the north of Poland in 1939 would command Army Group Center, and it was Bock's Army which, would advance to Smolensk and then towards the glittering prize of Moscow. From a military perspective there were a number of factors which made Moscow an important objective in the campaign against the Soviet Union. The city was the state capital and its capture would not only disrupt the government but would be hugely symbolic in the battle to conquer the country.

Moscow was also a large industrial center and an important hub in the Soviet railway network, which meant that if it was lost to the Nazis, links with the rest of the country would be cut off.

. . .

Leningrad would be left vulnerable to the north west and Soviet contact would be severely weakened to the South, threatening the defense of the Ukraine.

But while the Nazi Generals were convinced that Moscow should be attacked first, Adolf Hitler believed that Leningrad should take priority over the Soviet Capital. During the planning stages of *Operation Barbarossa,* Hitler believing himself to be a military genius had frequently ordered, *"Leningrad first, the Donetsk Basin second, Moscow third",* while his generals quietly harbored doubts about the capabilities of their Führer when it came to military strategy. But though the differences in opinion would eventually prove damaging to the campaign in Russia, the initial invasion was hugely successful.

An Axis Army of three million men swiftly broke Soviet defense lines and while forces advanced more than twenty miles a day, by July Army Group North had charged through the Baltic States closing in on Leningrad, Army Group Center had encircled Minsk and Army Group South was marching on Kiev.

Stalin in the meantime sat in Moscow, paralyzed by the rapid advance of the enemy, still barely able to believe that Hitler had taken on the might of the Soviet Union. It took almost two weeks for the Soviet dictator to resume control but finally on July 3rd the disorganized forces of the Red Army were given direction, as Stalin addressed the entire country and called for "a Great Patriotic War" against the invader. In his speech he appealed not only to communist ideals, but to Russian nationalism, and as the Soviet people heard the voice of their leader for the first time, soldiers and civilians alike, rallied to defend their country.

On July 10th the Soviet defense forces were reorganized into a three-group command structure. Kliment Voroshilov, who had led the Red Army to disaster in the winter war against Poland, was designated the Northwest force. Semyon Timoshenko who had fought with considerably greater success in Finland was assigned the West Force and Semyon Budyonny was assigned the Southwest Forces.

Budyonny was one of the two First Marshals of the Soviet Union to survive the Great Purge of the 1930s along with Voroshilov. Zhukov in the meantime, had been promoted to Chief of Staff and would coordinate the defense of the Soviet Union.

Since Russian officers lacked the expertise or authority to direct large-scale operations, the Soviet Groups would be nothing like the German Army Groups; however, they soon began to put up fierce resistance to the invading forces. In the meantime, just four weeks into the campaign, problems were beginning to arise in the Nazi advance. Bock's Army Group Center had managed to seize Smolensk by July 15th, but the panzer units were further ahead of the infantry than had been expected.

Hitler had hoped that Soviet troops could be trapped using a huge pincer movement to the north and south of Smolensk, but while German motorized forces had raced ahead of the pursuing infantry, there was a noticeable strain on German supply lines. The gap between the two armored pincers was unable to close until it was too late, and thousands of Soviet soldiers had escaped.

There were now fears that the Russians might push reinforcements between the panzers of Army Group Center and their supporting units, and while Army Group South was encountering problems on its way to Kiev, with heavier opposition than expected, Hitler made a radical decision.

| Ambushed German convoy on Russian soil

To the dismay of the commanders in the Central Army Group, Hitler decided to halt the advance on Moscow and focus all military strength on the attack on Kiev to the south and Leningrad to the north. On July 19th Hitler issued Directive 33 instructing panzers from the central army force to join Rundstedt's troops to the south.

The plan was not popular with the German Army High Command and in the following weeks there were many meetings to debate the issue.

From mid-July to mid-August the discussions would continue, and as time slowly slipped away, the Germans were wasting the most favorable weather for the war on Russia.

While the debate continued, Stalin, wary of the great threat to the Soviet cities now turned to Winston Churchill for assistance and suggested the British open a war front in the west, by attacking France. But although the Nazi bombardment of the British Isles had eased by now, Churchill was in no position to help the Soviets fight their battles, and he reminded Stalin that Britain had been alone in the fight against the Axis for one year.

British resources were stretched to full capacity with battles continuing in Africa and the Atlantic. German troops led by Erwin Rommel, continued to batter Allied defenses as they pressed on towards Egypt and the precious Suez Canal and while the Royal Navy focused their energies on protecting supply ships crossing the Atlantic Ocean, there were growing concerns for the unprotected outposts of the British Empire in the Pacific.

Malaya, Burma, Singapore and Hong Kong were all precious British colonies, and these lay vulnerable to attack while Japan remained allied with Germany. The Japanese had already put pressure on Britain to close the Burma Road, one of the few routes left open to deliver aid to China, and it was clear that as the war continued against Germany, the might of the British Empire was diminishing considerably in the region.

The Japanese in the meantime remained skeptical about their alliance with Adolf Hitler.

As a member of the Tripartite Pact, Japanese politicians had been shocked that

Germany had not informed them of the attack on the Soviet Union, which put them in an awkward position after their agreement with Stalin.

Foreign Minister Matsuoka however was quick to side with Hitler, and dismissing his earlier treaty with the Soviet Leader, now urged Japan to go to war with Russia from the east as Germany advanced across its borders from the west. The government were by now exasperated with their Foreign Minister and keen to be rid of him so Prime Minister Konoe along with the entire cabinet resigned in July 1941, to be reformed into a new government without him.

But although Matsuoka's absence was a relief to many in Tokyo, Konoe was wary that Japan was moving rapidly towards the brink of a war which would soon be unavoidable. The Eastern Empire had already been spreading propaganda in support of a Greater East Asia Co-prosperity sphere to rally support for its venture to the south Pacific. The government claimed that this enterprise would place the people of South East Asia and China under the protection of Japan.

Western Empires had long taken advantage of the wealth of the Pacific and Japan would now free Asia from European and American Imperialism, but while those in the Pacific Islands began to truly believe that the Empire of the Rising Sun would be their salvation, the Co-Prosperity Sphere was no more than an excuse for aggressive military expansionism.

In early July, American intelligence picked up a message from an Imperial Conference held in Japan, which stated that preparation for a southward advance should be reinforced and by July 18th it was clear that Japan was preparing to venture further afield.

Their first target would be part of the French colonial Empire, French

Indochina, which included a large part of Vietnam, as well as Cambodia and Laos and had been administered by the pro-Axis Vichy regime after the Fall of France in 1940.

The Japanese had been making demands on Indochina for months, but finally Vichy officials gave in to pressure and reluctantly signed a treaty with the belligerents on July 24th allowing them to occupy airbases in the south of the country. This now placed the Japanese within easy reach of British colonies and American military bases.

Meanwhile as the threat of a Japanese attack in the east began to grow, Roosevelt made another bold move in the economic war he was waging on Japan, placing an embargo on Japanese trade in oil and steel. Giving Japan an ultimatum to withdraw entirely from China and from Indochina and to renounce its treaty with Germany and Italy, the embargo took effect from August 1st.

The British Empire and the Dutch in Indonesia swiftly followed suit, and the Japanese who had traditionally been dependent upon the west for vital strategic raw materials now faced a global embargo which would have devastating consequences on their economy.

Japan had only stored enough oil for two years and with no hope of replenishing these stores from America, the Chief of the Imperial Japanese Naval General Staff, Osami Nagano announced that there was *no choice left but to fight, in order to break the iron fetters strangling Japan*. He was adamant that if Japan were to go to war it should do so quickly.

As the Japanese high command formally endorsed the "Go South" strategy, to strike the weakly defended islands of the Pacific, on August 4th Winston Churchill boarded the battleship Prince of Wales and set off to meet President

Roosevelt in Placentia Bay, Newfoundland to discuss the situation in Europe and the Pacific.

On August 9th the two leaders met for the very first time, and during this encounter they would create a draft of documents, which set goals for the post-war world. The Atlantic Charter advocated freedom from want and fear, the disarmament of aggressor nations and global economic cooperation.

Atlantic Charter – Churchill and Roosevelt first meeting

It was indeed, the first step towards the creation of the United Nations, but while the British and Americans celebrated their quiet alliance against the Axis, to the Japanese the Atlantic charter may as well have been a declaration of war and was considered a blueprint for Anglo-American world domination.

An Imperial Conference on September 6th concluded that unless negotiations resolved the issue of oil supplies, hostilities would commence against the United States, the Netherlands and Great Britain by mid-October.

The Japanese navy had already begun preparations for war and Admiral Yamamoto, who had been eager to avert conflict with America back in 1937, had concluded that if war was truly unavoidable, the only way to succeed against the immense naval forces of the country was to attack the American fleet before it reached the Far East.

Spies in Hawaii had been sending information back from the American naval base at Pearl Harbor, so the attack plan could be perfected and while the United States focused on increasing forces and defending their bases in the Pacific, it seemed they had little idea of the risks closer to home. In the mean-time, there were some in the Japanese government who were still reluctant to go to war with America.

The Prime Minister Konoye, urged a meeting with President Roosevelt so matters could be negotiated, even offering to travel as far as Hawaii at a moment's notice. But until Japan accepted the ultimatum set, Roosevelt's secretary of state Cordell Hull concluded that there was little reason for the two leaders to meet.

As events gathered pace in the Pacific, and Japan stood poised for war, in Russia the pause for debate that had caused delay in the German offensive had finally ended. Hitler had refused to back down in the face of military opposi-tion to his plans and as the panzers of the Center Army Group now moved south to meet Runstedt's army advancing on Kiev, by August 23rd the attack had resumed.

By September 19th Kiev had fallen to the Nazis and four Russian armies were surrounded in what is now considered the largest encirclement of troops in history.

According to German claims, 600,000 Soviet troops were captured in an unprecedented defeat for the Red Army; left to the mercy of the Nazis, the fate of many of these men would be worse than death as they were sent to Buchenwald Concentration Camp in Germany.

This was one of the largest camps the Nazis had built, and its prisoners would suffer unimaginable horrors as they now faced starvation, summary executions or human experimentation. Of all the prisoners at Buchenwald, the Russians would be treated particularly badly, as in Hitler's opinion they were a sub-human race which should be wiped off the face of the earth.

The loss of so many Soviet troops as Kiev fell would be disastrous for the Red Army, and as the Nazis made headway in the North East, there was now the added danger that Leningrad would be lost. The Nazi General, Leeb, leading Army Group North had received tank support from Army Group Center as well, and by the end of August the Fourth Panzer Army had broken through Soviet defenses and was within 30 miles of Leningrad. Meanwhile the Finnish Army closed in from the north around Lake Ladoga.

The soldiers of Finland played an important part in the success of the campaign on Leningrad and on September 6th Baron Mannerheim, Commander in Chief of the Finnish Defense Forces received the Order of the Iron Cross from Hitler for his command in the campaign.

However, when urged to continue the attack on Leningrad, Mannerheim and the Finnish government were reluctant to commit themselves fully to an Axis war and declined. Their aim had been to gain more territories in the east, and reclaim land lost to the Soviets during the Winter War of 1939 to 1940 - not to capture Leningrad.

But even without the aid of the Fins, Leningrad's fate already appeared to be sealed. The Soviet city which stood on the Neva River, at the head of the Gulf of Finland, was one of the most precious cities in Russia and Hitler was eager to destroy it and annihilate everyone within it. German forces surrounded the city, cutting off all supply routes to Leningrad and facing defenses organized by Marshal Zhukov, began to lay siege to the city.

In the chaos of the first months of war no evacuation plan had been prepared for the inhabitants of Leningrad and as food supplies diminished soon hundreds of thousands of people were dying of starvation. People were reduced to eating anything they could find, and in some cases, some even reverted to cannibalism.

On September 22nd Hitler announced, *"we have no interest in saving lives of the civilian population"* and ordered that the city be erased from the face of the earth. The siege would continue for 872 days and by the end of this time over a million people would have died in Leningrad.

With both Kiev and Leningrad facing destruction by the Nazis, by the end of September, Hitler ordered the advance on Moscow to commence, declaring:

"After three months of preparations, we finally have the possibility to crush our enemy before the winter comes".

But while the Soviets continued to stand their ground and the first snow had begun to fall on the eastern Front a German victory over the Soviet Union was still a long way off. The bitter Russian winter, would promise disaster for Hitler's War on Communism and the battle that the Nazis had hoped would be over within months, was only just beginning.

In the meantime, as Japan's deadline, to end negotiations with America approached, it seemed that the winter of 1941 would see the most dramatic turn of events in the Second World War to date.

9

AMERICA AT WAR

October – December 1941

| Pearl Harbor looking southwest Oct 1941

By the winter of 1941 war had been raging across Europe, Asia and Africa for over two years. Millions were living in fear throughout occupied Europe, while many were suffering unimaginable atrocities in concentration and prison camps. In Africa fighting continued between the Allies and Hitler's Axis powers, while in China terror bombings by the Japanese continued to ravage the vast nation.

Meanwhile Britain had survived the onslaught of German bombs rained down upon them during the blitz, and taking advantage of some much-needed respite, Winston Churchill and the British people looked on as Hitler turned his attention to the eastern Front and the Soviets.

. . .

While it seemed that the entire world was falling under the dark shadow of conflict, the United States of America had also been watching events unfold from afar. Even though preparations had been underway to join the Allies in battle for some time, it wasn't until December 1941 that events drew President Roosevelt and the American people into the war.

When Japanese bombers swarmed above Pearl Harbor, unleashing a devastatingly violent attack, thousands of servicemen were killed as the US Naval fleet based there was decimated.

The reaction from Washington was swift and the Empire of the Rising Sun had woken a sleeping giant, opening a new chapter in the history of the Second World War. From the drama of the Japanese attack on Pearl Harbor, to the battles in the jungles and islands of the Pacific, this chapter reveals the reasons behind America's late entry into the fight against the Axis powers and how their economic and military strength shone a ray of hope on those fighting desperately for freedom all around the world.

The United States had long been known as the land of plenty and from rivers glistening with gold deposits, to vast territories rich in natural resources where great towering cities exuded new wealth, the country had boasted its affluence from coast to coast. For many flooding into America as immigrants from overseas, the USA was seen as a place where dreams really could come true, but despite an abundance of jobs, land and resources, after the First World War, even the mighty "Home of the Free" had its problems.

When the Wall Street Crash struck in 1929 it dealt a devastating blow to the once booming economy and as queues of poverty stricken folk seeking work began to form on the streets, other nations were soon to follow the USA into a dark period of turmoil, as the world faced the desperate days of the Great Depression.

The economic problems were far reaching, and across the Atlantic in Europe, Germany, still reeling from having to pay reparations after being defeated in the First World War, was hit particularly hard. Inflation rocketed, and as the economy froze, millions were made bankrupt.

The German nation was plunged into poverty, and a discontented population was attracted to the promises of the Nazi Party, led by the fervently patriotic Adolf Hitler, who vowed to create a new age of wealth and affluence. His rousing speeches soon began to captivate the German people and Hitler quickly rose to a position of unassailable power.

In 1936 the Nazi dictator proved he was a man of his word, and when he ordered Nazi troops to march into the Rhineland, territory seized from Germany after WWI, he was able to secure precious raw materials to feed his empire building ambitions. Within three years Hitler's thirst for power and dominance had seen Nazi troops dispatched further afield, but when on September the 1st 1939 the Germans stormed into Poland, it meant the start of a Second World War.

While nations fell to Hitler, toppling like dominoes across Europe as the Nazis pushed further west, far across the world in the Eastern Pacific the Japanese were watching the Western Empires crumble.

Their tiny island kingdom had also been affected by the depression engulfing the world, and following the crash of 1929, Japanese incomes had dropped by two thirds, and banks had foreclosed on many businesses.

. . .

As the value of the Yen continued to fall, with few natural resources of its own, Japan had faced a crisis on the scale of Germany, and just like the Germans, the Japanese had started to fight for their survival. Right wing propagandists began pressing for the invasion of Manchuria in Eastern China, to ensure a supply of raw materials to feed the economy and in 1931 The Imperial Army of Japan took their first steps towards creating a great Eastern Empire.

While the Leader of the Chinese National Front, Chiang Kai-shek faced the invading Japanese, by 1937 the battles had escalated into a brutal campaign to conquer the rest of China.

As 1938 drew to a close Japan had within its grasp nine tenths of the nation's railway system and controlled the entire coastline of China. Chinese cities had also been devastated by Japanese terror bombings, leaving a trail of horror in their wake. Soon stories of massacres and atrocities perpetrated by the Japanese in China began to reach the west and after more than 5000 civilians were killed at Chongqing in May 1939 America imposed its first economic sanctions on Japan.

On a global scale these were indeed dark days, as Nazi and Japanese expansionism began to shatter the status quo, and although America had passed a policy of non-intervention, it was becoming increasingly difficult to sit by and watch the emerging powers of Germany and Japan claim one victory after another.

Matters came to a head when Japan sealed its alliance with Adolf Hitler and the Italian dictator Benito Mussolini, in the Tripartite Pact of September 1940.

It was clear to the American President, Franklin D. Roosevelt, that America's policy of neutrality and non-intervention may not be sustainable, and he had a stark warning for the people of the US:

"We are determined to keep out of war, yet we cannot insure ourselves against the disastrous effects of war and the dangers of involvement".

American Military and financial aid to China was increased and by October 1940 the selective training and service act was passed by Congress, to bolster the armed forces.

It was the first peacetime conscription that had ever taken place in the country, as all males aged between 21 and 36 could be called up for military service for 12 months, but if war was declared, they would have to serve their country for the duration of the conflict. Also with American territory such as The Philippines and Guam to safeguard in the Pacific, a program was also embarked upon to increase military presence in the area. With the influx of men into the American forces, during the next year further moves were made by the US to halt Japanese expansionism.

In the summer of 1941, the White House decided to freeze Japanese assets, so they could no longer purchase oil in America. With eighty percent of their oil imports being met by the United States this was disastrous news for the Japanese.

Emperor Hirohito was informed that the nation's oil stockpiles would be completely depleted within two years, which in turn of course meant that the Japanese military machine would no longer be able to function.

· · ·

Matters deteriorated for the Japanese yet again, when they saw British Prime Minister Winston Churchill meet America's President Roosevelt on a warship anchored off Newfoundland to discuss the situation in Europe and the Pacific in August 1941.

This gave rise to the treaty known as the Atlantic Charter, and advocated freedom from want and fear, the disarmament of aggressor nations and stated that all people had a right to self-determination. To the west this was a blueprint for the brave new world that the Allies prayed would emerge after the war had ended, but to the Japanese it was a blueprint for Anglo-American world domination, and even a formal declaration of war couldn't have been more provocative.

With the future looking increasingly dire for Japan, at an Imperial Conference in Tokyo on September 6th 1941 it was decided that unless America agreed to withdraw all political and economic support for the Chinese Nationalist Government, and to lift their economic and oil embargoes on Japan, negotiations with the country would come to a close. The deadline given was for mid-October and in the meantime the Imperial army began to prepare their battle plan.

They were already well placed to launch attacks on the colonies of the British, Dutch and the Americans, having already invaded French Indochina. From here the military could occupy territories rich in raw materials such as tin and rubber, along with many other commodities. But most important of all, from here they were within easy reach of a rich and sustainable oil supply.

With war looming on the horizon, the people of Japan were encouraged to support a battle with the west, which was glorified as a fight for *"The Greater East Asia Co-Prosperity Sphere"*. It was an enterprise that intended to free the people of South East Asia and China from western domination.

· · ·

They would be under the protection of Japan, which would reign with justice and morality throughout a new kingdom, but although the principles of the Co-Prosperity Sphere appeared to be noble and just, once the Pacific War began, the reality would be very different.

Civilians throughout the east would discover that Japanese brutality was considerably worse than western Imperialism, which had for so long dominated their countries, and the horrors of war would soon destroy any illusions that Japan's intentions were honorable.

With future battles edging ever closer, interestingly not everyone in Tokyo was keen to rush into a war. The Prime Minister of Japan, Fumimaro Konoe had at one time supported the notion of the Co-Prosperity Sphere, but as the conflict continued in China he feared that a war on two fronts would be impossible to win and was therefore keen to continue negotiations with the United States. He pressed for a summit meeting with President Roosevelt to discuss the issues and to keep the pro-war factions in Japan at bay, until a peaceful solution could be found, but Roosevelt refused to meet until Japan had left China.

Meanwhile for the Japanese military, the concept of retreat could not even be considered, and would forever be perceived as a humiliating stain on the glory of their Empire.

And as oil supplies gradually dwindled and the October deadline approached, it looked unlikely that a compromise would be reached.

Anxious to begin their conquests of territories across the Pacific, the Japanese military machine once again pressed for war, and at a cabinet meeting on October 14th, the Army Minister, Hideki Tojo, announced that negotiations had failed and the deadline for an agreement had passed.

. . .

Nothing more could be done to avert going to war with the west, and Konoe, frustrated with his failure to negotiate a settlement saw no other option but to resign. On October 18th, as the war mongering General Tojo replaced Konoe, and the militarists assumed total control of Japan, the time for negotiating was over, and the battle was about to begin.

Throughout history the Japanese were renowned for their fierce fighting and had once been led by Samurai warriors who instilled the idea of Bushido or *"freedom from fear"* in their soldiers. A true Japanese warrior should have no fear of death, pain or defeat and no regard for himself, with his only purpose being to serve his master. But even with this extraordinary fearlessness instilled in the population, the fight ahead was going to be challenging.

The United States had built up immense naval fleets and armies and would be a formidable opponent. The Admiral of the Japanese Navy, Isoroku Yamamoto was aware of what the country was up against and knew that to begin a war with America, the Imperial Army would have to do a great deal more than simply seize their outposts.

Yamamoto had studied at Harvard University as well as spending time serving as a naval attaché in America, and he was one of the few Japanese commanders who really understood the immense naval power of the USA, and he told his government in no uncertain terms what was required:

"It is not enough that we take Guam and the Philippines, or even Hawaii and San Francisco. To make victory certain, we would have to march into Washington and dictate the terms of peace in the White House".

But despite his well-founded concerns about picking a fight with such a powerful nation as America, Yamamoto was loyal to his Empire, and dutifully began searching for the best way to overcome the US navy. In October 1940 he had observed the British bombard the Italian fleet based at Taranto with torpedoes, especially developed to work in the shallow water of the Italian bay.

| Midget submarines at Kure dock

It was the first attack of its kind and had proved an inspiration to the Japanese Admiral. He realized that rather than waiting for the American destroyers to come to the Pacific, the planes of Imperial Japan could be mobilized for a surprise strike on the American fleet, crippling it before it could set sail for the Pacific theatre of war.

In the spring of 1941, Japanese carrier pilots began training in the special tactics that would be essential in the attack plan, which would target Pearl Harbor in Hawaii, and by the autumn, as Tojo took on the role of Prime Minister, Yamamoto saw that there was now no turning back. At the beginning of November, he assigned Vice Admiral Chuichi Nagumo as Commander of the mission and set a date for the planned attack, December 7th 1941.

Earlier, back in Washington, President Roosevelt was concerned about deteriorating relations with Japan and the risk this posed to American territory in the Pacific and had elected to move the American fleet from its base in California to Hawaii where it would be closer to the Pacific arena.

Here on the largest island of the archipelago, at Pearl Harbor, the sailors soaked up the sun and enjoyed the beaches with little idea that they were far closer to the troubles brewing overseas than they could possibly have imagined. But while the sailors enjoyed their Hawaiian paradise western intelligence had made some disturbing discoveries.

On November 18th 1941 the US Navy cracked a secret code enabling them to decipher information sent to the Japanese ambassadors in Washington. It revealed that in the event of an emergency, coded warnings would be added to the middle of the daily Japanese news broadcast. "North wind, cloudy" would mean war with the Soviet Union. "West wind, clear", meant war with Britain and its colonies, and "East wind, rain" represented war with the United States. If Japanese delegates on foreign soil heard this weather report, they were ordered to destroy all coded papers.

· · ·

While intelligence was on full alert listening out for the messages which would give them early warning of an attack, the ships that would make up the Pearl Harbor attack fleet had begun to disappear from Japan's home waters. They were heading for their rendezvous point in the freezing Kurile Islands to the north of Japan, but although shipping movements were being monitored, western intelligence still only suspected the attack on the Pacific, and had little idea of the terrible danger the US Naval Fleet at Pearl Harbor was in.

Meanwhile the charade of diplomacy continued between Japan and America, and on November 20th, the Japanese ambassador to the United States, Nomura, presented Japan's final ultimatum to the Secretary of State, Cordell Hull, demanding a resumption of oil supplies to Japan and the cessation of aid to China. Hull refused to comply and once more demanded that all Japanese troops be withdrawn from China.

With negotiations ending, on November 26th the Japanese task force, comprising of six aircraft carriers accompanied by 24 supporting vessels, departed from Tankan Bay in the Kurile Islands in the strictest secrecy. Keeping radio silence to avoid detection, they crossed the North Pacific avoiding the normal shipping lanes as they headed towards their destination, two hundred miles northwest of Hawaii. It was from here that the attack on Pearl Harbor would be launched.

Having received Cordell Hull's reply on December 1st, the Japanese Emperor, Hirohito, held an Imperial meeting to announce that the decision to go to war with America had been taken, and that the time for negotiation was over. With Japan now fully committed to war, the next day, Admiral Yamamoto, sent a coded message from his base in Hiroshima, to vice-admiral Nagumo, the commander of the task force, ordering him to launch the attack on December 7th.

With intelligence services desperately deciphering communications around the globe, suddenly Japanese diplomats in Washington, London, Manila, Hong Kong and Singapore were ordered to burn their codes. This not only meant that diplomatic relations had been severed, but war was about to begin. And for the Allies, the all-important question was where?

While the British and Americans watched for the first signs of belligerence from the Far East, in Nazi Germany, officials were jubilant about the prospect of a Japanese attack on Allied territory. The German foreign minister, Von Ribbentrop, had assured the Japanese ambassador in Berlin that Hitler would support its tripartite pact ally and declare war as soon as Japan went to war with the United States. Tokyo had in turn informed Germany that *"the time of this war may come quicker than anyone dreams"*.

While Roosevelt understood a peaceful conclusion to negotiations between Japan and America looked more tenuous by the day, he could hardly have imagined that a full-scale airborne attack was just a week away. Unaware of the task force lining up close to Hawaii, on December 6th the American President made a final appeal for peace to Emperor Hirohito. Ominously, there was no reply, but later that day, U.S. intelligence intercepted a fourteen-part Japanese message and deciphered the first thirteen parts. They revealed that Secretary of State Hull's offer had been rejected, but the message was incomplete, and it wasn't until the next day that the crucial fourteenth part arrived.

Meanwhile, in Hawaii life went on as normal. American sailors were ashore, enjoying their tropical paradise as they played football or golf and on the night of December 6th, as sailors relaxed in the bars and clubs many were dancing to the sounds of the navy's musicians in a battle of the fleet dance bands. Staying up until the early hours, few would be prepared for the onslaught that lay ahead, but as night gave way to day, the first warning signs were breaking over the horizon.

At 4.50 a.m. on Sunday December 7th Japanese midget submarines stealthily entered through the harbor gates but though they were spotted, no general alarm was given. Back in Washington the tension was building as General George C Marshall, Roosevelt's military advisor, had received the decoded fourteenth part of the message from Tokyo.

It confirmed that negotiations with Japan had ended and realizing the potential implications, the U.S. War Department immediately sent an alert to Pearl Harbor. But problems with radio communications would delay the message and tragically the vital warning would arrive too late.

While Washington was aware that hostilities were about to commence on the other side of the Pacific, events were gathering pace as Japanese ships loaded with five thousand troops from the war-torn battlefields of China, approached British controlled Malaya. Soon soldiers were storming onto the beaches and onto Allied territory, and the war on the west had begun.

While the fury of the Japanese military was unleashed in the Pacific, radio transmissions between the Japanese carrier fleet near Hawaii and Tokyo ceased, and at 6.15 a.m. vice-Admiral Nagumo gave the order to release the planes. As the aircraft carriers pitched and rolled on the stormy seas, the first wave of 183 fighters, bombers and torpedo planes, commanded by Captain Mitsuo Fuchida, took to the sky.

The vast formation included bombers, which would target the battleships and aircraft carriers, followed by dive-bombers to attack the land-based aircraft and hangers at Ford Island and Wheeler Field.

Then came the Japanese fighter aircraft, assigned the task of destroying the planes on the airfields before they could take off and defend the harbor.

. . .

Using music from a Honolulu radio station as a guiding beam to navigate, the enemy planes began to close in on their target. Meanwhile at the Hawaiian naval base the alarm still had not been raised, and people were either asleep or enjoying the tranquility of a lazy Sunday morning. Then to the amazement of those at the harbor, just before 8am the first Japanese assault wave darkened the skies and the calm was shattered.

Commander Logan C. Ramsey at the Command Center on Ford Island sounded the alert, *"Air raid on Pearl Harbor – This is not a drill"* while the Japanese fighter planes began to swoop over Hickam and Wheeler airfields, rallying to the battle cries of commander Fuchida. The Americans, believing there was no imminent threat, had made little effort to prepare themselves for attack and the aircraft were neatly parked out in the open, wingtip to wingtip.

Ammunition lockers were locked, and even the guns that could have provided some protection against the aerial onslaught were unmanned.

As showers of bombs were released onto the airfields below, the Japanese could barely believe their luck, the element of surprise so crucial to Yamamoto's plan could not have been greater. There weren't even any torpedo nets to protect the American battleships, and as waves of bombers began to close in on the fleet, the torpedoes, developed to slice through the shallow depths of Pearl Harbor, devastated one target after the other.

Of the more than ninety ships at anchor in Pearl Harbor, the main objective of the Japanese had been to strike the vessels moored on Battleship Row along the south-east shore of Ford Island. As tornadoes screamed through the air hitting their targets with precision, the men aboard awoke to a tumult of smoke, fire and deafening explosions.

The battleships had little chance to defend themselves and within the first minutes of the attack, all of the seven vessels anchored along the shore had been bombed or torpedoed. Two sank, while the USS Arizona exploded in a giant ball of flames after an armor-piercing shell ignited the ship's forward ammunition magazine.

Although a lucky few were able to jump overboard and swim to safety, as the ship was engulfed in flames over one thousand crewmen were killed, including one of the bands that had competed the night before. It was the greatest loss of life on any ship that day and the casualties of the USS Arizona amounted to half the total number of Americans killed at Pearl Harbor.

As the naval base was thrown into pandemonium, thirty minutes after the first attack there was a short lull in the furious onslaught, before a second wave of Japanese planes, appeared over the harbor. By now all-around Pearl Harbor, civilians who had at first thought the explosions were part of military maneuvers, quickly became aware that they were under attack. The element of surprise had passed however, and the US troops were now aware of what they were facing.

Anti-aircraft fire began to fight off the attacks and some sailors even turned to machine guns and pistols as they battled desperately against the hail of missiles from the sky. Many heroes would emerge on this historical day and one of those who fought bravely to defend the naval base was Doris Miller, a mess attendant aboard the USS West Virginia.

Despite having no training, he seized one of the anti-aircraft guns and began firing at Japanese planes until there was no ammunition left. But despite the bravery of Miller and all those fighting off the onslaught, the casualties suffered by Nagumo's pilots would be few compared to the devastating losses of the Americans.

. . .

By 10 am, as the skies over the Hawaiian Harbor fell silent two hours after the initial attack had begun, a trail of destruction lay around Pearl Harbor. As nurses and doctors rushed to tend the wounded it was clear that the US Fleet had been dealt a devastating blow. Over two thousand four hundred Americans had been killed, including a number of civilians. Over twenty-one ships had been sunk or disabled, and almost two hundred aircraft were destroyed, while over 150 were damaged, as they stood on the ground. Virtually none had been able to take off to defend the base.

However, the US could well have suffered much greater losses had Nagumo's junior officers had their way. When the second wave of planes returned from Hawaii, they had pressed for a third wave of attacks to destroy the American fleet's repair capabilities and the vast oil reserves that remained untouched. But with fuel running low and the risk of American bombers retaliating, Admiral Yamamoto was reluctant to incur further losses and had ordered the ships to turn around and head for home.

It was a decision that would cost Japan dearly as although the scene at Pearl Harbor was one of utter devastation most of the ships on battleship row would be miraculously salvaged, and eventually re-join the battle against Japan in the Pacific theatre of war.

| The USS Pennsylvania, Cassin and Downes

As well as the failure to order a third strike, there was also another blow to Yamamoto's plan, as three U.S. Pacific Fleet aircraft carriers, Lexington, Enterprise and Saratoga, were not in the port during the raid. The USS Enterprise under the command of Admiral Bill Halsey had been delivering planes to Wake Island and was 250 miles west of Hawaii. Halsey himself was furious when news of the attack reached him, and after vowing to avenge the Americans who died that day, he spent the next three years pursuing the Japanese around the Pacific.

· · ·

Far away in Washington news of the attack at Pearl Harbor had reached Roosevelt, and the Secretary of State Cordell Hull. Yamamoto had wanted to abide by the military laws of engagement, giving notice of an attack, and had ordered the Japanese ambassadors to take a message saying negotiations had failed to the White House by 1pm. This would mean 7am in Hawaii, giving a full hour's notice.

The message arrived one hour late however and as envoy Nomura presented the formal document, the planes were already swarming above the Hawaiian naval base. Secretary of State Hull was furious and announced:

"In all my fifty years of public service, I have never seen such a document that was more crowded with infamous falsehood and distortion".

Soon the American public joined the Secretary of State in his fury as they heard of the "sneak attack" on radio bulletins, with many popular Sunday afternoon entertainment programs being interrupted to announce news of the tragic events at Pearl Harbor. The news stunned and angered America, but finally the nation was united behind the President, and the United States was ready to go to war.

On December 8th 1941, as crowds gathered outside the White House the moment the Allies had been waiting for had come. President Roosevelt made an address, which was broadcast around the world, and the global conflict was now truly underway.

The American Senate was unanimous in its decision to go to war with Japan and a determination to avenge the attack on Pearl Harbor swept far and wide, across the whole of the USA. The anti-war and isolationist movement collapsed. Even President Roosevelt's fiercest critic, Charles Lindbergh, declared:

"Our country has been attacked by force of arms, and by force of arms we must retaliate".

Recruiting stations were jammed with a surge of volunteers, inspired by the words of the President and as the country rushed to mobilize troops, soon news of Japanese aggression and Roosevelt's declaration of war made a dramatic impact on the battles raging in Europe. On the eastern front, the Nazi troops advancing on Moscow were battling against Stalin's Red Army which fought fiercely to defend the capital.

With temperatures plunging below freezing, thousands of Germans were falling victim to the bitter Russian winter and for Adolf Hitler it was far from being an ideal moment to be drawn into conflict with another nation, especially one as powerful as the United States.

Nonetheless on December 11th Adolf Hitler honored his Tripartite Agreement with Japan and declared war on America. Speaking out at the Reichstag in Berlin, he furiously insulted President Roosevelt and blamed him for the outbreak of war in 1939 and of even plotting to invade Germany. Confident of the backing of Imperial Japan he boldly announced that Germany could never lose a war with an ally that hadn't been conquered in 3,000 years, which the Japanese so proudly boasted. The hopes of the Nazi leader were at the very least naïve, and his rash decision to take up arms against the United States would ultimately see his hopes of a thousand-year Reich crushed and destroyed.

. . .

While Germany remained apprehensive about Hitler's decision, the third member of the Axis, the Italian Dictator Benito Mussolini, also declared war on America, standing proudly on the balcony over the Piazza Venezia in Rome. As the crowds cheered he pledged that the *"powers of the pact of steel"* were determined to win, and as the so-called axis powers of Japan, Germany and Italy united against America, Britain, France, and their Allies, the world had entered a truly global and very dangerous conflict.

For the British who had been struggling against the might and terror of the Nazi onslaught for over two years, there was immense relief at the news that America had joined the war. Finally, there was a real possibility that the Allies could defeat the Axis, and the borders of Europe could be rebuilt once more.

There can be no doubt that the news was met with joy by those in occupied Europe, but as the people of Britain breathed a huge sigh of relief, there was now another enemy to face, and while Japanese troops began their Pacific advance, the outposts of the British Empire were under serious threat.

After the Japanese invasion of Malaya, the Royal Navy had dispatched the valuable battle cruisers, HMS Repulse and HMS Prince of Wales from Singapore to offer support. However, the Japanese intercepted the advance and on December 10th an air attack destroyed and sank both ships. The British Prime Minister Winston Churchill received the unhappy news and his concern was evident when he said:

"Over this vast expanse of water Japan, is supreme, and we everywhere are weak and naked".

There was little doubt that the situation was grave for the future of the British Empire and as the Japanese marched unchallenged across Malaya soon more outposts were under attack. On December 11th the Japanese invaded the British territory of Burma from their stronghold in Thailand and two days later they made their way to Borneo. The news from the Far East was getting more worrying by the day, and as the relentless Japanese advanced closer to the precious outposts of Hong Kong and Singapore, Winston Churchill's concerns that the Empire was swiftly slipping from Britain's grasp were now a stark and unavoidable reality.

Back in the United States President Roosevelt was equally concerned about the fate of American territory in the Far East. Nine hours after the first strike on Pearl Harbor, the Japanese had begun bombing the American base in the Philippines, which would suffer even greater devastation than the fleet at Pearl. As the Japanese won the battle for control of the skies above the islands, thousands of troops began pouring onto the northern beaches and the gulfs of the western coast.

| Aground – The USS Nevada

The task facing the inexperienced and poorly equipped Philippine and American troops was challenging to say the least, as they tried to defend whatever ground they could against the battle hardy Japanese. The Philippines was of vital importance to the Japanese and by seizing the island nation they could prevent the Americans using it as a base of operations.

But more than this, with the string of islands under their command Imperial Japan could control all lines of communication between the Philippines and other Japanese occupied territories in the region. This really did consolidate their position of strength, while providing the perfect stepping stone to reach the Dutch East Indies. It was on Dutch territory that precious oil reserves could be found, and within weeks the Japanese would be making their advance to snatch the supplies they so desperately needed to ensure a successful campaign.

For the time being though Japanese troops marched further inland, as the American commander charged with the defense of the Philippines, General Douglas MacArthur, prepared to resist with all the forces he could muster. However, as the enemy advanced on the capital, Manila, the situation was looking increasingly dire.

While Allied forces retreated to the Peninsula of Bataan, other American outposts had already fallen to the Japanese. After an aerial bombardment on December the 8th a large invasion force had swarmed into Guam, swiftly overcoming resistance from American personnel stationed on the island. By the New Year, Wake Island would also be taken, and the United States was fast losing its Pacific foothold.

As the relentless advance across South East Asia continued, it seemed nothing could stop the Japanese military machine, and as troops spread around the Pacific and more countries were absorbed into the new Eastern Empire, there were concerns that even India and Australia would soon come under attack from the Japanese. And all the while, as the conflict grew, Admiral Yamamoto's decision to recall the ships from Pearl Harbor before landing a third and potentially decisive blow to the US naval fleet, was rapidly proving to be a grave mistake.

As the smoke settled over Pearl, salvage operations had begun to repair and re-float the ships that had been damaged in the surprise attack. Incredibly, only the USS Arizona, Utah and Oklahoma were beyond repair, while the rest of the fleet would soon be ready to re-join the battle in the Pacific, reclaiming territory that was being lost to the Japanese, while exacting revenge for those Americans who had died on that fateful day.

. . .

But as the ships were hauled from the shallow waters of Pearl, questions were still being asked back in America. Why had the commanders at the naval base not been better prepared?

Scapegoats were soon found and the Commander of the US Military in Hawaii, Walter Short, along with the Commander in Chief of the US Pacific Fleet, Husband E Kimmel, were demoted and blamed for the lack of an adequate defense plan to counter the Japanese attack with.

On December 17th Admiral Chester W. Nimitz took over as Commander of the Fleet and his role in the Pacific War would prove crucial for the Allies, and awards were presented to those who had displayed great personal bravery during the attack on the harbor. The decorated included Doris Miller, who became the first African American to be awarded the Navy Cross, as the Allied leaders began planning their next move in the fight against the Axis powers.

On December 22nd 1941 Winston Churchill flew to Washington to attend the Arcadia Conference and discuss strategies with President Roosevelt. The situation in the Pacific was deteriorating by the day and just as the Prime Minister had feared, the Japanese were now marching on Hong Kong.

Despite the domestic pressure to avenge the Japanese attack on Pearl Harbor, and all the outposts falling into Japanese hands in the Pacific, the US Government believed other issues needed to be dealt with first. The main priority was to defeat Adolf Hitler and Nazi Germany, and after Hitler's declaration of war on the United States in the days following the Pearl travesty, such a course of action became more politically acceptable.

Churchill would remain at the White House until January, but while strategies were perfected, and the weeks passed, the people living and fighting in the Pacific were all too aware of the terror that the Greater East Asian Co-Prosperity Sphere was beginning to symbolize. After seventeen days of resistance the battle was lost in Hong Kong and on Christmas Day, 1941, the Governor of the British outpost surrendered to the Japanese. Meanwhile the situation in the Philippines was also deteriorating at a rapid pace, and just one day after Hong Kong surrendered, Manila was declared an open city.

As 1941 drew to a close, the major military powers of the world were lining up against each other in a territorial battle to the death, and over the next four years armies comprising of millions would fight it out in the air, at sea, in cities and in the jungle. For Roosevelt and Churchill, the fight was for democracy against tyranny, but as more Pacific colonies fell, and more prisoners were taken, the first few months of 1942, would demonstrate that tyranny had the upper hand.

However, once the vast American military machine was let loose into the theaters of operation, while GIs flooded into the Pacific and Europe, it was clear that the Second World War had truly gone global and for the first time since the outbreak of hostilities the Allies were in with a real chance of stopping Hitler and his Axis of evil once and for all. As the Pacific struggle gathered pace, Pearl Harbor was only the beginning of a conflict in which some of the most brutal battles of the war would be fought.

But while the diminutive Japanese Empire had achieved small miracles in their fight against the western giants in the winter of 1941, Admiral Yamamoto, the man who had masterminded the attack on Pearl, was all too aware that the dreams of Imperial Japan would soon be shattered, and in point of fact, their war was already lost.

THE FALL OF SINGAPORE

January – March 1942

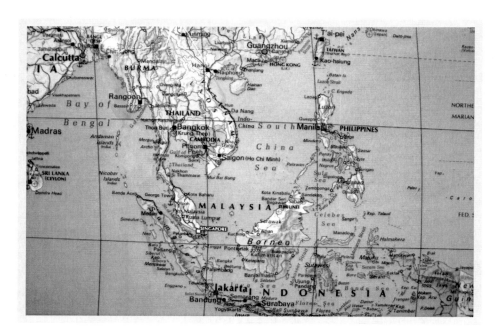

| Map of the Philippines and Singapore

In the early weeks of 1942, as battle raged in western Europe and North Africa, the Japanese threat to invade Malaya and Singapore became a reality. It was unthinkable to the British that the island they'd nicknamed 'the Gibraltar of the East' could fall - and yet fall it did, with dire and terrible consequences. Some eighty thousand prisoners of war were taken in Singapore, fifty thousand more in Malaya. No wonder British Prime Minister Winston Churchill described it as the:

"worst disaster and largest capitulation in British history".

But before the events of 1942 unfolded, the Japanese had had to neutralize the possibility of American intervention. They were thirsty for resources. They had no source of oil to speak of and had lost a shattering 93 percent of their supply after US President Franklin D. Roosevelt ordered an embargo in July 1941. Although the Japanese enjoyed an oil treaty with the Dutch, that too was broken as the Netherlands joined the embargo. Starved of oil, metal and other resources Japan could either draw back and lose face or seek to find the resources it needed elsewhere. Those resources lay in the South Pacific.

The U.S. Pacific Fleet was the only force capable of challenging Japan's Navy. The Americans had bases in the Philippines which could threaten lines of communication between the Japanese home islands and the East Indies. Every oil tanker heading for Japan would have to pass by American-held Luzon. On December 7th, 1941 the Imperial Japanese Army Air Force laid waste to much of the American fleet and Air Force stationed at Pearl Harbor. It was a strike of such audacity it almost defied belief. President Franklin D. Roosevelt described it as *"a date which will live in infamy"*.

. . .

No longer could America take an isolationist view. The War could no longer be seen as a purely European conflict. On December 8th, the US Congress had voted that a state of war existed between the United States and Japan. On December 11th, the Axis countries of Germany and Italy declared war on the United States. Congress immediately recognized the existence of a state of war with Germany and Italy. The US was now at war on all fronts.

The conflict in the Pacific and the war in Europe had different causes. Part of the reason they became entangled, was Adolph Hitler's decision to declare war on America in the hours after the Japanese attack on Pearl Harbor. And yet the Japanese had requested no help from him, and even if they had, he had none to offer. There were those in America who did not relish the prospect of fighting in the Pacific **and** in Europe and yet Hitler's decision to declare war meant that the world's two greatest military and industrial powers, America and Russia, were now aligned against him.

The main cause of war in the Pacific, as we shall see, was Japan's decision to spread its Empire further. What Britain had done a hundred years before, Japan now sought to copy.

Both are island countries; both need raw materials from abroad. Britain fought and conquered foreign lands and brought their rich resources under their Empire banner. Japan now sought to do the same.

For the Japanese there was no such thing as the Second World War. For them it was the Greater East Asia War; a conflict that had begun not in 1939 but in 1931 with the invasion of Manchuria. China was the great enemy. With 65 million mouths to feed Japan's military decided the only way to support the population was expansion. The Japanese had been cruel invaders of China, seeking the glory of Empire, but also the wealth that lay beyond her borders in larger markets for her industry. However, the wealth Japan sought to take by invasion belonged at that time to European colonial powers.

. . .

The French were in Indochina, the Dutch in the East Indies and Britain in Malaya, Singapore and Burma. With the colonial powers fighting a war in Europe their military capabilities were stretched. Japan chose this moment to pounce. But if Japan was to be successful in moving against these old colonial powers it had to keep the American Pacific Fleet from coming to their aid. The assault on Pearl Harbor gave them the edge they sought.

Japan struck hard and fast, attacking American possessions in the Pacific; the Philippines, Wake Island and Guam. Midway Island was shelled by Japanese warships. It was a pattern to be repeated over and over again. They then moved on mainland Asia. Hong Kong - what the Japanese called the *"citadel of British Imperialism in China"* - was hit by air and sea. Airfields in Malaysia felt the full force of the Imperial Japanese Army Air Force. Singapore was bombed. Japanese troops landed in the north of Malaya and Southern Thailand.

America's main air base in the Philippines, Clark Field, came under attack. In the Philippines the main island of Luzon was hit, as was British Borneo where the only Allied ground unit, an outnumbered Indian battalion of the 15th Punjab Regiment, managed to resist for 10 weeks before it was overwhelmed. After a week of fighting, on Christmas Day 1941, the British garrison at Hong Kong fell. It had held on longer than anyone had expected. Isolated at the south-eastern tip of China, Hong Kong had been considered expendable, yet six thousand defenders had held off forty thousand Japanese. The end came when the colony's reservoirs were taken; there was nothing to do but surrender.

The Japanese campaign in Burma took much longer. Burma was a prize highly sought. It provided the British with a gateway to India, the jewel in the colonial crown. What's more since 1938 the Burma Road, that ran from Mandalay to Kunming, had been the only overland supply route for the

Nationalist forces fighting the Japanese in China. With the Americans wrongly believing that China would contribute a mighty force to help the defeat of Japan, it was essential that the road remain open and China was kept supplied.

With China joining the Allies and declaring war on Germany, Italy and Japan, the American general Joseph Stilwell – Vinegar Joe as he was known — joined the Chinese nationalist leader Chiang Kai-Shek as his chief of staff. Though they were successful in repulsing a Japanese attack in China on January 15th their success was short-lived. The Japanese were already in Burma and they did not let the dense jungle hinder their ambitions.

Where roads were blocked, they simply took to the undergrowth. British trained Burmese forces were unable to halt their advance. Japan's first objective was Rangoon, Burma's only port. They reached it and took it in early March. When Japanese forces gained control of the Burmese end of the road, they had succeeded not only in gaining the rich resources of oil and rubber Burma had to offer, but also in closing China's land links to the Allies. Burma would remain in Japanese hands until May 1945.

In the Commonwealth of The Philippines, the Allied forces were commanded by General Douglas MacArthur. The Philippines had been officially made a territory of the United States as far back as 1902. In the months leading up to the war days were languid, given over to ceremonies, inspections and training. Officers and their wives occupied their evenings and weekends with social events and rounds of golf while the soldiers enjoyed the delights on offer in the bars of Manila.

Defending the thousands of islands that comprised the Philippines was a nightmare. They lay 8,000 miles from the American west coast, but only 200 miles from Japanese-held Formosa. To defend them, General MacArthur had the equivalent of two divisions of regular troops — 16,000 U.S. regulars and

12,000 Philippine Scouts. He could call on additional thousands of Philippine militia, but they were untrained and ill equipped; hardly a force strong enough to stand up to the might of the Imperial Japanese Army.

American strategists had developed two plans to counter possible Japanese aggression, one for the Navy - another for the Army. The Navy planned to fight across the central Pacific for a climactic and decisive battle with the Japanese fleet.

The Army saw no way to save the Philippines and favored a strategic defense along an Alaska-Hawaii-Panama line. But writing off the Philippines was politically impossible. As war drew ever closer, frantic efforts were made to strengthen the commonwealth's defenses.

Both General MacArthur and Army Chief of Staff General George C. Marshall, who commanded US forces in Hawaii, overestimated the abilities of their own forces and greatly underestimated the strength and ability of the Japanese. In particular, they grossly exaggerated the power of the new B-17 "Flying Fortress" bomber, a few of which were rushed to the Philippines in the last days of peace. Their efforts proved too little, too late.

With the US Pacific Fleet paralyzed at Pearl Harbor the Japanese Imperial Army Air Force now turned their attention to the Philippines and caught the US Air force on the ground. Japan had total air supremacy. A stockpile of torpedoes was destroyed; US submarines were rendered useless. Only MacArthur's beleaguered American-Filipino army held out on the main Philippine island of Luzon.

The Japanese army landed in the North on December 22, 1941 and began to push southward toward Manila. At first, MacArthur was inclined to meet the Japanese on the beaches, but with no air force, and only able to call on the

Navy's tiny Asiatic fleet he was in no position to challenge Japan at sea. Though the U.S. Regulars and Philippine Scouts were excellent troops, the reality was they were truly outnumbered.

After two weeks hard fighting the American and Filipino troops withdrew to the Bataan Peninsula on the west side of Manila Bay. There MacArthur could pursue a strategy of defense and delay, shortening his lines and using the mountainous, jungle-covered terrain to his advantage. Furthermore, he could deny the Japanese the use of Manila as a port. Perhaps he could even hold out long enough for a relief force to be mounted in the United States.

But it wasn't just bullets and shells the Allies were faced with. The Japanese launched a propaganda war in the skies over the Philippines, dropping thousands of leaflets on Allied troops insisting they had no hope, pressing for their surrender. But there was no capitulation.

On 26th December 1941, MacArthur declared Manila an open city; it would not be fought over. On January 2nd, Manila and the U.S. Naval base at Cavite were captured. MacArthur directed operations from his base on the island fortress of Corregidor. Though the Bataan peninsula was well fortified it was horribly overcrowded; one hundred and six thousand troops and civilians. There was too little food and too little ammunition. Sickness and malnutrition set in. The American-Filipino force, wracked by dysentery and malaria, continued to fight but disease and lack of proper sustenance claimed more lives than the enemy.

By March it was clear that help from the United States was not coming. Nevertheless, The Allies valiantly held out for four months. Though the attempt to hold the Philippines was gallant it was inevitably doomed. In February General MacArthur received the order from president Roosevelt to leave. On the 12th he boarded a motor torpedo boat, under new orders to take command of the communications lines between Australia and America that were now coming under threat.

As he left the Philippines he famously declared *"I shall return"*. The phrase became a rallying cry for the Allies.

General MacArthur (center right)

From his boat MacArthur boarded a plane for Darwin. His B-17 Flying Fortress staggered into the air from Del Monte airfield Mindanao with one engine spluttering. The five-hour flight took him and his staff over the captured enemy islands of the Celebes, Timor, and the northern part of New Guinea. Somehow, they managed to avoid enemy Zero fighters.

· · ·

As they finally reached Darwin, they found that it was under Japanese attack, so they diverted to Bachelor Airfield, about 50 miles away. When they eventually disembarked from the aircraft a weary MacArthur remarked:

"It was close, but that's the way it is in war. You win or lose, live or die — and the difference is just an eyelash".

Some US Navy officers had given MacArthur only a one-in-five chance of escaping the Philippines. Via the radio airwaves 'Tokyo Rose' had boasted that the Japanese would capture him. But MacArthur and his family made it out. It was from this new Australian base that he would conduct the next phase of operations. It would be over two years before he could make good on his vow. In October of 1944 he returned to the Philippines at the head of the American invasion force.

As we've already discovered one of the main driving forces behind the Japanese policy of expansion was its need to replace the oil lost when America enforced its embargo. And so, with barely eighteen months supply of oil in reserve, the Imperial Japanese War machine invaded the oil rich Dutch East Indies on January 11th.

A joint American - British - Dutch – Australian force, under General Wavell, had been formed to protect the curving chain of islands that begins in the north west with Sumatra and continues south and east through Java, Bali, Flores and Timor, the latter just 400 miles off the coast of Darwin, Australia.

When General Wavell took command, the outlook was not good. Dutch forces were scattered across the islands in small garrisons. The air support was meagre. There was no aircraft carrier to provide naval weight. The Japanese attacked southern Sumatra with 700 parachute troops on February 13th. The threat to Java was imminent. On orders from Churchill, General Wavell left for India.

This left Dutch forces under the command of Admiral Helfrich, three Australian battalions, a squadron of British tanks and five squadrons of the R.A.F. Together they engaged the Japanese in what became known as The Battle of the Java Sea. It was a gallant action, but the Japanese would not be halted. By the time the Japanese invasion forces arrived on land the Allied navy in Java ceased to exist. With no air cover or naval support, resistance on land was short. Admiral Helfrich surrendered on March 8th.

Meanwhile the Imperial Japanese forces were moving down through the jungles of Malaya towards the prize that was Singapore. The British had been in residence since 1819 when Sir Thomas Stamford Bingley Raffles founded a trading post there. It soon became an important British outpost and Singapore's rapid growth and importance to the British East India Company ensured that the British were there to stay.

In 1824 the status of Singapore as a British possession was cemented in an Anglo Dutch Treaty that divided the Malay Archipelago between the two colonial powers; the British controlling the area north of the Straits of Malacca, including Penang, Malacca, and Singapore, whilst the area south of the Straits was assigned to the Dutch.

Britain also had interests in Malaya, to the north of Singapore Island. It had become an important source of rubber and tin. By 1910 the pattern of British rule in the Malay lands was established. The Straits Settlements were a Crown Colony, ruled by a governor under the supervision of the Colonial Office in London. Their population may have been fifty per cent Chinese, but all residents, regardless of race or creed were British subjects. Subjects that now faced a Japanese invasion force.

In 1940, as First Lord of the Admiralty, Winston Churchill had been responsible for Singapore's defenses. He was convinced that should the island be attacked it would be by sea. He informed his Cabinet colleagues that *"Singapore is a fortress armed with five, fifteen-inch guns and garrisoned by 20,000 men. It could only be taken after a siege by an army of at least 50,000...".* Furthermore, he noted that Singapore was as far from Japan as New York was from Southampton. He thought it impossible to maintain men and munitions over such a distance.

He also didn't consider it plausible, at that time, that the Japanese, who he described as a "prudent people" would extend themselves beyond the Yellow Sea and China where they were already occupied. Surely, they would not embark on so mad an enterprise so far from home? Churchill was wrong. He dispatched two battleships, HMS Prince of Wales and HMS Repulse.

HMS Prince of Wales was a King George V – class battleship. The Prince of Wales had a brief but active career, helping to stop the Bismarck and carrying Churchill to the Newfoundland Conference.

HMS Repulse was a Renowned class battle cruiser, the second to last one built. She too had taken part in the chase of the Bismarck. The Admiralty had planned for an aircraft carrier to accompany the two ships, but the action never materialized. HMS Repulse left Singapore in company with HMS Prince of Wales and four destroyers, to try and intercept the Japanese invasion convoys heading towards Malaya.

But their hunt for invasion forces proved fruitless and they turned south. It was at this point that Japanese aircraft were spotted. The fleet was attacked by

86 planes. Without the protection of an aircraft carrier the ships were very vulnerable. The force the British thought to be an "unsinkable deterrent" was sunk, leaving the coast of Malaya exposed.

General Yamashita could now make a move. His assault on Singapore would be down through Malaya and as the British had been slow to send troops north from Singapore, Malaya was badly defended. The Japanese first encountered resistance from the 3rd Corps of the Indian Army defending the coast. These were quickly isolated and forced to surrender. Although the Japanese Twenty-Fifth Army was outnumbered by the Allies, General Yamashita concentrated his forces. He had just thirty thousand men, the Allies one hundred thousand more.

But despite their numerical inferiority the Japanese pressed forward hard. On January 14th, a company of Australians ambushed Japanese bicycle-mounted troops who were passing through a cutting that led to the bridge on the Sungei Gemencheh River. Despite inflicting heavy casualties in their first major confrontation with the Japanese, the Australians were eventually forced to withdraw. The Allies were unprepared when the Japanese left the roads and moved swiftly through the jungle. The jungle had been expected to slow the Japanese advance, but the Japanese didn't ride in trucks, they walked and rode bicycles.

With superior close air support, armor, coordination - tactics and experience played to their advantage. The British had underestimated the military capabilities of their foe. The assortment of untrained pilots and inferior Allied equipment in Malaya, Borneo and Singapore at that time were no match for the Imperial Japanese Army Air Force. Their fighter aircraft, especially the Mitsubishi A6M Zero was instrumental in achieving air superiority.

Whilst fighting continued in Malaya the Japanese continued the strategic bombing of Singapore. The British did their best to keep the bombers at bay with anti-aircraft fire for as long as ammunition was available. The governing powers began the evacuation of women and children. Some would never see their fathers and husbands again. As defeat loomed, all available ships were hastily loaded with fleeing civilians. *The Empire Star*, designed to carry a small number of passengers, was crammed with 2,000 refugees. But co-ordination broke down and the evacuation became chaotic. Enemy planes attacked the fleeing ships and thousands of civilians drowned. Others survived drowning only to be murdered by Japanese troops as they struggled ashore on Bangka Island.

With the Japanese advancing on Singapore let's take a moment to look at events as they were played out in Europe. From the time that Hitler rose to power in 1933 he began to pass 'The Nuremberg Laws', stripping Jews of rights and citizenship. He had made no secret of his antipathy towards Jews and spoke often of their removal by any means. By 1941 the first extermination camps were being built: Belzec, Sobibor, Treblinka, Chelmno, Majdanek and finally Auschwitz-Birkenau.

On January 20th 1942 The Wannsee Conference was convened at Wannsee Villa, Berlin; a meeting to discuss the practicalities of mass murder. Though no order directly linking Adolph Hitler to the extermination of the Jews has ever been found, Rudolf Hess, commandant of the camp at Auschwitz, and Adolf Eichmann, who has been described as 'the architect of the Holocaust', both said such an order existed in the early summer of 1941.

Writing in his dairy Joseph Goebbels, Hitler's Reich Minister of Propaganda, noted:

"Regarding the Jewish question, the Führer is determined to clear the table... Now the World War has come. The destruction of the Jews must be

its necessary consequence. We cannot be sentimental about it. It is not for us to feel sympathy with the Jews".

At Wannsee the plans for the final solution were laid. The mass extermination of Jews began soon after. But the Nazi war machine would soon have an expanded Allied force to reckon with. The Americans were already fighting the Japanese in the Pacific and now they were about to enter the fray in Europe, with some four thousand troops landing in Northern Ireland.

These were the first US troops to set foot on European soil since the American Expeditionary Troops left at the end of The Great War. They were greeted by Sir Archibald Sinclair, Secretary of State for Air with the words:

"Your safe arrival here marks the new stage in the World War. It is a gloomy portent for Mr. Hitler; nor will its significance be lost on General Tojo".

In truth the deployment of American troops in Britain had been in the planning since April 1941, eight months prior to the Pearl Harbor attack. U.S. contractors had already been hard at work building bases for the 87,000 Americans the US war Department planned to send. For the GI's life in Britain took some getting used to. For a start they drove on the wrong side of the road - and the BBC's wireless programs were not exactly what they'd been used to.

The United States War Department distributed a handbook *"Instructions for American Servicemen in Britain"*, to advise them on the peculiarities of "The

British, their country, and their ways." The guide was intended to alleviate the culture shock for soldiers taking their first trip to Great Britain, or, for that matter, abroad. One passage read…

"The British don't know how to make a good cup of coffee. You don't know how to make a good cup of tea. It's an even swap".

There were explanations of everything the G.I. might encounter, from weights and measures to money, rationing and sports. Baseball may have been the national pastime back home, but in Britain cricket was the summer sport. For some Americans the nuances of the game were just a little too exciting.

The arrival in Britain of rich relations from across the Atlantic meant the arrival of American supplies. Suddenly Brits, especially young women, were being offered items that had been rationed since 1940; butter and bacon, sugar, jam and eggs. Cheese and canned fruit appeared on the kitchen table. And suddenly there was a plentiful supply of nylon stockings and chewing gum. On February 9th the old saying 'cleanliness is next to Godliness' became a little harder to achieve. Soap went on the ration. But the Americans travelled with a plentiful supply.

Everyone was keen to be seen to be doing their bit. The British Royal family were no exception. On February 25th Princess Elizabeth, the future Queen Elizabeth, signed up for war service.

6,000 miles away the Allied forces were falling back from Malaya. Their 54-day campaign was over. To the consternation of the British the Japanese were closing in on Singapore. As well as being an important strategic port, Singapore was the home of many who were supporting China. Financial support had come from the ethnic Han Chinese, support that contributed to the stalling of the Japanese advance in China. Yet one more reason for the Japanese to invade the island.

The Allies hung on, facing a determined Japanese assault. For General Yamashita it was a nervous time, as he would later recall:

"My attack on Singapore was a bluff - a bluff that worked. I had 30,000 men and was outnumbered more than three to one. I knew that if I had to fight for long for Singapore, I would be beaten. That is why the surrender had to be at once. I was very frightened all the time that the British would discover our numerical weakness and lack of supplies and force me into disastrous street fighting".

Singapore lay under the command of Lt-General Arthur Percival. At his disposal he had roughly 100,000 military personnel from Australia, Great Britain and India, as well as soldiers raised in Malaya and Singapore. They prepared their defense. The Japanese strategy was a wily one - at midnight on February 7th, Japanese troops landed unopposed on Singapore's north-east coast and they gave the impression of an impending attack from that direction. However, the next day they began a strategic air and artillery attack on the north-west coast instead.

By 9.30 that night, the first Japanese amphibious assault on Singapore was launched. Undeterred by heavy casualties suffered from Australian machine-gunners, wave upon wave of Japanese troops landed successfully. By midnight the Australian defense was broken. The following day the Tengah Airfield fell to the Japanese. Singapore turned her famous large-caliber coastal guns inland.

At least those that could turn. But the guns were supplied with mainly armor piercing shells, necessary to penetrate the hulls of armored war ships – the very reason the guns were there. Had the guns been well supplied with high explosive shells the Japanese attackers would have suffered heavy casualties. The guns would have helped repel the Japanese advance. They didn't.

| IJN Kuma – A critical vessel of the Japanese navy

With his troops well established on the northern shores, Yamashita's next objective was Bukit Timah, commanding the north-western approach to Singapore town. Yamashita called upon Percival to surrender. But Percival had strict orders to "fight till the end."

. . .

A bitter battle was fought where the Japanese 18th Division faced the 1st and 2nd Battalions of the Malay Regiment supported by men from the Australian forces. The Allies fought stubbornly and kept the Japanese onslaught at bay until midnight of February 12th. But as the odds grew too great the Malay Regiment retreated.

Up on Bukit Chandu, Allied soldiers ran out of ammunition but refused to give up. They engaged the Japanese in hand-to-hand combat, but it was no use. By the afternoon of February 14th Bukit Chandu was taken. Enraged by the stubborn stand put up by the Malay Regiment soldiers, the Japanese exacted revenge. They stormed the nearby Alexandra Hospital, bayoneting and killing patients and staff on sight. More than 200 died in the senseless massacre.

By this time, the Japanese advance had forced British troops to fall back to a perimeter around the municipality. This was their last defense. Around this the Japanese converged. The end was imminent. The water supply fell to a critical level and supplies including food, fuel and ammunition were also running low. These reasons along with mounting civilian casualties, led Percival to make the momentous decision to surrender.

On February 15th 1942 at 6:15 p.m., in a makeshift conference room in the Ford Motor Company factory in Singapore, General Arthur Percival for the Allies surrendered the island to Lieutenant General Yamashita Tomoyuki. It was a magnificent victory for Japan, for the capture of Singapore signaled the end of British power in the Far East. On the part of the British, Percival's telegram to the Supreme Commander of the American-British-Dutch-Australian Command read:

"ALL RANKS HAVE DONE THEIR BEST".

Of the 50,000 white troops captured in Singapore, 18,000 would die of disease or mistreatment in the next three years and eight months. The Japanese made the island the headquarters of the Southern Army renaming Singapore "*Shonan*" meaning "Light of the South." The Japanese now had the riches of Malaysia at their disposal and had gained control of the Straits of Malacca, the main sea-lane between the Pacific and Indian Oceans.

Following the British defeat at Singapore nationalist movements began to realize that the old colonial powers were not the superior unbeatable force they had believed; a point that marks the beginning of the decline of the Empire. From here we can trace the downward spiral of British colonial powers. With Singapore fallen, elsewhere the British Empire was under attack. Just before ten o'clock on February 19th, 188 Japanese planes descended upon Darwin in what was to be a precision strike.

It marked the beginning of raids against Australia that would last into 1943. The Australians saw it as their Pearl Harbor and although Darwin held nothing like the same significance as the American target in Hawaii a greater number of bombs were dropped.

Darwin was unprepared. Eight ships in the harbor were sunk, including an American destroyer, the USS Peary. A further thirty-five ships were damaged. None of the small number of available Allied planes managed to take off. All were destroyed or damaged. In just forty minutes, the Japanese planes had achieved their goal and they turned for home. But another wave was to come.

This time there were 54 Japanese bombers. Their target: the town and Darwin Airfield. Two hundred and fifty dockside and port workers lost their lives that day, somewhere between three and four hundred were wounded. The true casualty figures were suppressed by the Australian government for fear of mass panic but nonetheless chaos ensued.

Although February 19th was a day for Japanese rejoicing before the summer was out, the four Imperial aircraft carriers involved in the attack would in fact be sunk during the Battle of Midway.

Whilst the Japanese forces were winning the day in the Pacific, their countrymen were experiencing something very different in America, where thousands of their citizens had made their home. After Pearl Harbor a Japanese face in America was not a welcome face. In reality relations between the Japanese community and the wider American public had been crumbling for years.

| Japanese-American children pledge of allegiance

Farmers who resented competing against immigrant labor could now argue loyalty to the United States as a reason to mistrust anyone with a Japanese background. Even before Pearl Harbor, President Roosevelt had ordered the names and addresses of each American-born and foreign-born Japanese to be collected. All enemy aliens in California, Oregon, Washington, Montana, Idaho, Utah, and Nevada were ordered to surrender what was described as contraband.

This included short wave radios, cameras, binoculars, and various weapons such as hunting knives and the dynamite used by farmers to clear land. Los Angeles congressman Leland Ford wrote:

"I do not believe that we could be any too strict in our consideration of the Japanese in the face of the treacherous way in which they do things".

California voted to bar all "descendants of natives with whom the United States is at war" from all civil service positions. Prohibited zones were established; places forbidden to all enemy aliens. German, Italian, and Japanese were ordered to leave the San Francisco waterfront areas.

Soon anyone designated an undesirable alien was moved from coastal locations of the U.S. California's Attorney General, Earl Warren, called Japanese Californians the *"Achilles heel of the entire civilian defense effort."* And warned, *"Unless something is done it may bring about a repetition of Pearl".*

Farms were transferred from the hands of Japanese Americans to Caucasian tenants and corporations. Of primary concern was the continuation of production at full capacity. Japanese American farmers were told to continue their farm activities in the time before eviction and that destruction of crops would be punished as sabotage. On February 19th 1942, President Roosevelt signed an Executive Order that began the round-up and 'evacuation' of 120,000 Japanese Americans to one of 10 internment camps - officially called "relocation centers".

While Japanese Americans comprised the overwhelming majority of those in the camps, thousands of Americans of German, Italian, and other European descent were also forced to relocate there. Though conditions were not good, they were nothing like the concentration camps set up by the Nazis.

. . .

In Europe the Nazis were not having it all their own way. Although German troops continued to lay siege to the Russian city of Leningrad, the city refused to fall. Leningrad was one of the primary targets of Hitler's *Operation Barbarossa,* and he had expected it to "fall like a leaf". The first shells fell on Leningrad on September 8th 1941. The Red Army had been outflanked when the Germans encircled the city. But the city did not fall as Hitler imagined it would. It fought back and continued to fight back for 900 days. The city's almost 3 million civilians (including about 400,000 children) refused to surrender; instead they endured rapidly increasing hardships.

January and February saw Leningrad plunged into the depths of an extremely cold winter. Lack of fuel meant that the use of electricity in homes was banned - industry and the military took priority. Kerosene for oil lamps was unobtainable. Wood became the major source of heat in homes with furniture and floorboards being burned in most of them. The food needed to fight the cold was simply not available. If bread was obtainable, people had to line up in the bitter cold in the hope that some might be left by the time they got to the front of the queue.

Over January and February 200,000 people died of cold and starvation. Despite these tragic losses and the inhuman conditions, the city's war industries continued to work.

With no heating, no water supply, almost no electricity and very little left to eat, the city still refused to succumb to the Nazis. The Germans were discovering that their enemies still had a lot of fight left in them and while the Russians were holding out against Hitler, Winston Churchill was plotting the next phase of the war against him.

In the corridors of power, the British Prime Minister's words rang loud in the ears of his military strategists *"The Navy can lose us the war,"* he said. *"But only the RAF can win it. … our supreme effort must be to gain overwhelming mastery of the air. The fighters are our salvation, but the bombers alone provide the means of victory".*

On Valentine's Day 1942 Bomber Command issued Directive No.22, which ended the recent period of aircraft conservation by the RAF, although attacks were still not to be pressed in the face of bad weather or 'extreme hazard'. With the new Lancaster bomber entering service and equipped with a new navigation device called GEE, Bomber command hoped that locating targets would be made much easier. Nine days later one of the most influential figures of the Second World War took up his new command.

Air Marshall Arthur "Bomber" Harris was appointed Commander in Chief of Bomber Command. Harris had a reputation of being a determined and forceful character. Harris was totally convinced that the bombing of Germany could bring the Nazis to their knees and strike a decisive blow towards winning the war.

In early March his bombers hit the Nazi held Renault plant in the Paris suburb of Billancourt. Serious damage was done to the production facilities, although many French workers were killed. However, this successful raid was a much-needed morale boost for the bomber crews. On this same night, the Lancaster bomber made its operational debut, laying mines off the French port of Brest. Of the 235 RAF planes that took off, only 1 failed to return.

Five days later the RAF made a raid on Essen, home of a Krupp's factory. Krupp's produced submarines, tanks, artillery, naval guns, munitions and other armaments for the German military. Though the results were disappointing the bombers returned again and again. Not only was the factory a target but under the new directive so was the city. It was a prelude of what was to come.

. . .

Under the new tactical doctrine of area saturation bombing, the RAF launched 234 planes and a massive incendiary attack against Lübeck on the Baltic. It devastated the old city. Hitler was so incensed he ordered the Luftwaffe to bomb historic British towns and cities in retaliation. But Harris did not waver from the belief in his plan. By the end of May, 900 bombers would be dispatched to lay waste to Cologne.

With the bombers now taking the fight to Germany, the war in Europe began to turn in the direction of the Allies. Hitler would discover that the Allies were not prepared to lie down. He now faced a resurgent R.A.F., the might of America and an obstinate foe in Russia.

Although the Allies had suffered badly at the hands of the Japanese in the Pacific the foundations of a fight back there were already being laid.

With the arrival of American troops in Noumea, New Caledonia, plans were already taking shape that would see the American conquest of Guadalcanal, the first of a catalogue of amphibious assaults on Pacific islands.

With both the Battle of the Coral Sea and the Battle of Midway on the horizon the Japanese would soon realize that the relatively easy-ride they had in taking their new possessions, would come to an end.

The Allies were fighting back.

11

THE BATTLE OF MIDWAY AND BEYOND

April – June 1942

Jimmy Doolittle second from left

With the focus in the early years of World War II on Europe and North Africa, Adolf Hitler's actions had been the main driving force, while the Allies fought to resist the Nazi advance across the continents. However, as 1942 progressed the Second World War was taking on global proportions, with the ramifications of the surprise Japanese attack on the American Navy at Pearl Harbor, in December 1941, becoming increasingly evident.

Events in the Pacific Theatre of War were escalating, as the Empire of the Rising Sun, extended its reach further south, expanding its defensive perimeter towards Australia, and to the north east, began venturing danger-ously close to the western coast of America.

. . .

The seemingly unstoppable force of Japanese expansionism was nevertheless about to face a serious challenge and as we look a little more closely at the months of April to June 1942, you'll discover that the Japanese didn't have things their own way for long.

A sleeping giant had truly been awakened at Pearl, and as the Americans fully entered the arena of war, they quickly began to make their presence felt. From the daring American "Doolittle Raids" on Tokyo, through to the battle of the Coral Sea, and the dramatic events at Midway, any advantages gained by Japan at Pearl Harbor, were about to be countered in some style by US forces, as the tide of the war in the Pacific slowly but surely began to turn.

The creation of an East Asian Co-Prosperity sphere, free from the shackles of the Western Empires had long been the desire of those ruling Japan, and by April 1942 it seemed that the Empire of the Rising Sun was vaster than it had ever been before.

The war in Southeast Asia and the Pacific had been highly successful and the Japanese were now in control of the most strategically important parts of the Chinese coast, and had occupied Malaya, Thailand, the Dutch East Indies and most of Burma. In the Pacific they held Wake Island, New Britain, the Gilbert Islands and Guam, and while the drive to seize new territory continued, the outlook was grim for the Allies.

In the first few months of the war with Japan, valuable British and American outposts had swiftly fallen to the invading forces, and thousands of people were now prisoners of war, helplessly caught behind enemy lines. Even Singapore, once regarded an impregnable British fortress had been crushed by the Japanese, dealing a devastating blow to allied commanders.

America in the meantime had lost valuable military bases and would soon lose its foothold in the precious Philippine islands.

After invading the capital, Manila, the Japanese were now advancing further south, hot on the heels of the retreating Allied troops, and there seemed to be little in the way of halting Japan's drive to completely dominate the Pacific.

With a string of victories to boast of, many of the Japanese troops were in fact so satisfied with what they had accomplished so far, that in some regions of the new empire, they took time out to relax. For the time being, the western threat to their Pacific domain seemed to have been eliminated, and the Japanese were confident that they could hold their newly won territories with ease.

Britain and America were however preparing to strike back and would not take such belligerence without some form of retaliation. Days after the attack on Pearl the British Prime Minister, Winston Churchill, had rushed to Washington to begin discussions with President Roosevelt, and on December 26th, 1941 in a speech before the US Congress, he stated his unwavering determination to crush the new eastern enemy.

Britain had been alone in its fight against the Axis since the Fall of France in the summer of 1940, and the entry of America into the global conflict, had been met with great relief by Churchill. Now Roosevelt, Churchill and the Soviet Leader, Josef Stalin, who had been fighting the Nazi forces since June 1941, were united against the Axis, and there was at last real hope that the allies could win the war.

. . .

As commanders were allocated to the Pacific Theatre of war however, there was no doubt that the challenges that lay ahead were great.

Fleet Admiral Chester W. Nimitz had assumed command of the Pacific Fleet two weeks after the Japanese attack on the American naval base in Hawaii, and with many battleships and destroyers sunk during the raid, he was well aware it would take time to salvage the ruins and reinstate the US fleet to its former glory.

Faced with coordinating an attack across the Pacific, an ocean that covered over 65 million square miles, there was no doubt that in the early months of the war Nimitz was operating at a considerable disadvantage. However, there was one thing that the Americans had in their favor. The aircraft carriers that were destined to play such a vital role in the battles of the Pacific hadn't been at Pearl Harbor when the Japanese planes had swarmed in, creating an advantage that the US Navy would exploit to the full.

Meanwhile, as fears grew that Japan would soon move further south towards Australia and New Zealand, the first response from the Allies called for the establishment of bases in the far reaches of the Pacific so a counterattack could be launched. The remote islands of New Caledonia, Fiji and Espiritu Santo, which lay to the north east of Australia, had long been within the western sphere of influence and work was soon underway to establish military bases there. With fierce battles being undertaken in the European theatre of war, finding sufficient air and naval reserves to send to the Pacific proved extremely challenging for the Allies, and valuable supplies came at a less than ideal pace.

And all the while the Japanese raced to expand the boundaries of their Empire, as Allied engineer units raced against the clock to complete *their* work, often attempting to accomplish the impossible as they negotiated the difficult terrain.

. . .

There would inevitably be the occasional setback, but the Allies never wavered in their determination to halt the Japanese in their tracks, and by April 1942 the situation could not have been at a more critical point.

Since the invasion of the Philippines on December 8th 1941, American and Philippine forces led by General Douglas MacArthur, had been fighting a desperate battle against the Japanese invaders. As the situation had deteriorated, President Roosevelt had ordered MacArthur to leave, to take command of operations in the southwest Pacific from the relative safety of Australia, and although he had been reluctant to leave his men, MacArthur finally obeyed his President's orders on March the 11th, but not before he had vowed to return.

It was of little consolation to the troops left in the Philippines who had been backed into a corner on the Bataan Peninsula off the main island of Luzon by the beginning of April. Allied naval forces in the area had been destroyed in a series of battles around Java, and with almost all neighboring territories under Japanese control, the troops were now cut off from most of their supplies and surrounded by the enemy.

When the Japanese launched their new air and artillery assault, breaking through Allied defenses, the men, who were worn out from malnutrition, sickness and combat fatigue, were too weak to counter-attack and surrendered. Some of the Allied servicemen managed to escape to Corregidor Island to the south of Bataan, but battalions of Japanese infantry swiftly moved in and pushed the defenders back to Malinta Hill.

To the despair of all those left fighting, the American flag was soon lowered and General Jonathan Wainwright, who had taken over from General MacArthur, had no choice but to accept General Masaharu Homma's terms of surrender. As a result, by May 8th, 1942 the Philippines had been officially lost.

· · ·

But there was an even greater tragedy for the Allies to face as the Philippines fell. The Japanese had captured 80,000 allied prisoners, all of whom needed to be transported to prison camps, and faced with such a huge task, it was decided they should walk sixty miles, to a railhead at San Fernando.

| Bataan death March – Burial duty

What was soon dubbed the Bataan Death March began on April 10th, and it proved to be a terrible ordeal for the men who were already malnourished and sick. Thousands lost their lives as a result of exhaustion, hunger, dehydration and sickness, while many others were brutally murdered by their captors. It was a stark warning that going to war with Japan would be costly in terms of casualties, as the POWs were treated with bitter contempt by the Japanese soldiers, who regarded surrender as dishonorable.

• • •

Meanwhile, as the news of the brutal treatment of the men at Bataan reached America, posters were circulated to advertise the atrocity, and emotions were soon running high amongst the American population. The resolve of the allies to crush the Japanese was now more determined than ever and President Roosevelt had already set in motion plans to strike at the very heart of Japan by bombing its capital city: Tokyo.

After the attack on Pearl, Roosevelt had been keen to restore public morale and considering the later events in the Philippines he was now eager to demonstrate to the Americans, and to the people of Japan that the Empire of the Rising Sun was not invulnerable to attack.

With such an ambitious project in mind, Lieutenant Colonel Jimmy Doolittle, one of the most famous aviators and aeronautical engineers in America, had been chosen to plan and execute the attack. Over the years Doolittle had won an array of awards for his achievements, and had made many important contributions to aviation technology, but the task that lay ahead would be one of his greatest challenges yet. The main problem he faced was that America had no bases within bomber operating range of Tokyo, and although an attack could be launched from aircraft carriers, planes which were typically used with these ships, would not be able to cause a great deal of damage.

After long deliberation an idea was eventually conceived to adapt giant B-25 bombers, so they were light enough to take off from carrier decks, and by the beginning of April these highly modified planes, were aboard the USS Hornet, and on their way to the Pacific. Vice Admiral Marc Mitscher captained the carrier from which Doolittle would launch his attack, while the task force would be led into enemy waters and protected by Vice Admiral William Halsey, aboard the USS Enterprise.

Halsey in fact had a particular bone to pick with the Japanese. When Pearl Harbor had been attacked, Halsey had been delivering planes to Wake Island

and was 250 miles West of Hawaii. On hearing of the strike, he had vowed to avenge the thousands of Americans killed at the naval base and his determined drive to defeat the Japanese soon earned him a reputation.

While the USS Hornet and the USS Enterprise ventured close to the gates of the Japanese Empire, Halsey would however face a drawback in his quest for revenge. On April 18th a Japanese picket boat spotted the task force and while warning signals were sent back to Japan there was now the danger that Japanese land-based planes could be launched, putting the precious American carriers at risk. Halsey decided that the attack on Japan should commence immediately and soon the crew aboard the USS Hornet were rushing to prepare their planes.

The aircraft had less than 470 feet of runway, and none of the pilots, including Doolittle, had ever taken off from a carrier before; in fact no one had ever attempted to launch a bomber the size of a B25 from the deck of a carrier before, making the task a challenge to say the least.

But the rigorous training the volunteer Army crews had received had clearly paid off, and all sixteen B-25s carrying their deadly payloads of incendiary bombs and high explosives, were launched successfully. Although the Japanese alert meant the planes were now setting off 180 miles from their original launch site, favorable weather would help them along the way, and the bombers would soon be closing in on their targets with Doolittle's plane at the helm.

| B-25s on the deck of USS Hornet

Six hours after takeoff, the planes reached Tokyo and at noon they began dropping bombs on the capital and the surrounding areas. They met with little resistance and the impact made, was exactly what Roosevelt had hoped for. The Japanese were so shocked by the attack that high level military commanders began blaming each other and the mortified commander of Tokyo's air defense was shamed into committing suicide.

In the meantime, Japanese fighter squadrons were returned home, and a carrier group was withdrawn from the Indian Ocean to protect home waters.

While America hailed the pilots of the Doolittle raid as national heroes, not all the men who had braved the attack would make it back alive. Two crews would be imprisoned by the Japanese after landing in enemy territory, and three of these men would eventually be executed. Meanwhile Doolittle along with many of the other crews, were helped by Chinese military and civilians in the east of China, who sheltered them and ensured they reached safety.

This would however have tragic consequences for the Chinese as Japan launched a campaign in retaliation, which would kill a quarter of a million villagers in the region. Such vicious retribution revealed just how much the attack on Tokyo had injured Japanese pride and although the damage to Japan itself was not as severe as Doolittle had hoped, the fact that US bombers had reached the homeland at all would have a profound effect on Japan's decision making, in the next step of their pacific war.

As the boundaries of the empire had grown ever greater in the early months of 1942, there had been much disagreement among senior Japanese commanders, over the next course of action to take. Fleet Admiral Osami Nagano, head of the Naval General Staff had keenly supported spearheading further territorial gains, a strategy which had the full support of the Imperial Japanese Army.

They wanted the next attack to be centered on isolating Australia, which could be used as a potential American base, and it was proposed that as part of its empire building, Japan should occupy Port Moresby, in New Guinea, and Tulagi in the Solomon Islands. This would strengthen Japanese defensive positions in the South Pacific, and provide a base from which to attack Australia, which would then be within the range of land-based aircraft.

The Japanese had already begun edging close to the Australian mainland and after seizing New Britain, the largest island in New Guinea, back in January 1942, they had established a major base at the city of Rabaul. The Australians were well aware of the dangers that this posed to their country and in February 1942, their fears were more than justified as Japanese planes, gathered from the same task force that had attacked Pearl Harbor, flew towards the northern coast of Australia.

These were soon joined by powerful land-based bombers and as they closed in for the attack, the port of Darwin faced a bombardment which would be even more devastating than the attack on Pearl.

By seizing new bases in the Solomon's and New Guinea, Nagano hoped that Australia would be further isolated and the occupation of Port Moresby and Tulagi would not only ensure the defense of Rabaul but would serve as jumping-off points for the conquests of New Caledonia, Fiji and Samoa.

This in turn would cut supply and communications lines between the United States, Australia and New Zealand.

Not everyone in Japan was in accordance with Nagano however, and Admiral Isoroku Yamamoto, who had masterminded the attack on Pearl Harbor, believed that rather than continue to drive for more territory, Japan should concentrate on creating a defense buffer for their new empire.

There was now an endless supply of resources at the disposal of the Japanese, which could be gathered from the territory they held around the Pacific, and beyond. The supply routes between the Japanese mainland and the occupied countries needed to be protected however, and to do this Yamamoto was eager to eliminate the threat of American intervention.

The Japanese admiral was aware that the failure to destroy valuable carriers at

Pearl had been a fatal mistake and to ensure the survival of the empire and indeed of Japan itself, it was essential to finish what he had started in December 1941 and complete the destruction of the American fleet. Yamamoto began to conceive a plan to lure US carriers within range of a Japanese task force, for a monumental battle which would ensure Japanese control of the Central Pacific.

He selected as his target, Midway Atoll, two tiny coral islands which lay on the extreme northwest of the Hawaiian Island chain. The American base here, was far enough from Hawaii to lessen the risk of heavy land-based air power threatening Japanese ships; and not only would valuable US carriers be sent out to protect the atoll, if captured, Midway would further extend the Japanese defensive perimeter and even provide a useful base to launch attacks on the west coast of America.

Yamamoto had however struggled to convince Admiral Nagano that an attack on Midway should take priority, and until April 18th 1942 preparations had been focused on advancing further south towards Australia, rather than on destroying the American fleet. It was only when Jimmy Doolittle launched his daring raid on Tokyo that opinion swung in favor of an attack on Midway.

With fears growing that the homeland was vulnerable to air attacks, the Prime Minister of Japan, General Tojo, agreed that resources should be focused on the defense of the Empire and the elimination of the American threat. Nevertheless, by mid-April, it was too late to withdraw the forces preparing to advance on Port Moresby and Tulagi, and for the time being the Battle of Midway would have to wait.

The drive towards Australia, codenamed *Operation MO,* was scheduled for the beginning of May and the entire campaign was placed under the command of Yamamoto's protégée, Admiral Inoue. He in turn would coordinate several groups which included a Carrier Strike Force, commanded by Vice Admiral Takagi; a Tulagi Invasion Force commanded by Rear Admiral Kiyohide Shima and there would also be a Port Moresby Invasion Force.

What the Japanese didn't realize however was that the Americans had cracked their codes and as signal traffic was intercepted by US and British intelligence, Admiral Nimitz was informed of the imminent attack on Port Moresby. The news was treated very seriously by the American commander who was aware that Australia would be left vulnerable if the Japanese established bases so close to the country.

After consulting Admiral Ernest King, head of the US Navy, it was decided that the invasions should be opposed with all the aircraft carriers the allied forces could muster. A fleet centered on two carrier groups was rapidly assembled and included Task force 17 based around the carrier USS Yorktown and Task Force 11 based around the carrier USS Lexington.

Rear Admiral Frank Fletcher, who had already seen action in the Pacific, after the Marshall and Gilbert Islands Raid back in February, was placed in command of Yorktown, and would also be in overall command of the mission. Meanwhile Rear Admiral Aubrey Fitch would command Lexington and there would also be a joint Australian-American cruiser force to provide additional support: Task Force 44, would be commanded by Rear Admiral John Crace of the Royal Navy.

As the ships headed towards New Guinea and the Solomon Islands, they would encounter many dangers along the way, with high seas and heavy winds to combat, but there was no doubt that every man on board was willing to brave the worst of storms, if it meant he was given the opportunity to strike back at the Japanese. While the carriers moved further west, soon preparations were made for the attack; bombs were loaded onto planes and pilots prepared for the mission ahead; then finally, on May 3rd news arrived that Shima's invasion force had arrived in the Solomon Islands.

As Japanese troops began to pour onto Tulagi, Fletcher altered course to head due north towards the enemy, and on May 4th sixty aircraft were launched in three waves from Yorktown, taking Shima's forces completely by surprise.

The attack was a success and as well as hitting three minesweepers, and four seaplanes, the Americans managed to sink an important Japanese destroyer. Nevertheless, the Japanese would continue to hold Tulagi as they set to work establishing a seaplane base on the island.

After inflicting a considerable amount of damage on the Japanese fleet, Fletcher took his task force due south to meet up with Crace and Fitch's ships, but now the Japanese were aware of the presence of American carriers in the area. Eager to accomplish what Yamamoto hoped to do at Midway, it was now Admiral Takagi's turn to take part in the action. He led his carrier strike force from its position 350 miles north of the Solomon Islands and entered the Coral Sea to hunt for the allies. It was a journey into the unknown, as the scene was set for the first ever aircraft carrier battle in history.

One US commander would later comment that the battle of Coral Sea, was without a doubt "the most confused battle area in world history", and indeed as search planes were sent from both sides to look out for enemy ships, the Americans and Japanese were playing a game of cat and mouse.

In the confusion of the hunt, some planes would fire on their own forces, others would try to land on enemy ships, but finally, on May 8th the decisive battle was fought. At about 8.20 that morning, each side spotted the other almost simultaneously and rushed to launch their aircraft; the Japanese in a combined strike, and each American carrier in separate strike forces.

. . .

By 9:25 all aircraft had been launched and as the carriers headed for each other, Yorktown's strike force attacked at 11am, to be met by sixteen Japanese Zero fighters, protecting the carrier Shokaku and her sister ship.

While planes lunged and swooped through the air, avoiding anti-aircraft fire, Shokaku was hit by two one thousand-pound bombs, which caused heavy damage to her flight deck, and before long, with further attacks from Lexington, she was out of the battle.

But the Japanese soon struck back, and fourteen planes swept in to attack USS Lexington in a pincer movement. She was hit twice by torpedoes, before dive bombers moved in hitting the ship again. Meanwhile a bomb exploded on Yorktown's deck, but while Fletcher's carrier would survive another day, the Lexington would not be so lucky. The bombs had ruptured a fuel tank, and as sparks ignited the fumes that had built up in the carrier, a series of dramatic explosions followed, leading to uncontrollable fires.

As ships were called up to help with the evacuation, over two and a half thousand men rushed to escape from Lexington. By this stage each side had suffered considerable damage, and as survivors were pulled to safety both the Americans and the Japanese decided to withdraw their forces. The results of the battle had been costly for the Americans, and with the loss of USS Lexington, as well as other ships and many planes, it appeared that the Japanese had won a tactical victory.

However, the Battle of Coral Sea would in fact give the Americans the greater advantage. With a strong allied force in the area, and with two of their carriers damaged, the Japanese now feared that many of their landing crafts might be destroyed if they went ahead with the invasion of Port Moresby. The attack was called off and with it the advance towards the northern approaches of Australia, Nimitz's mission had been a success and for the time being Australia was safe.

Although Japanese progress had been checked in the south Pacific, in the South East Asian theatre of war the advance continued. The British Eastern Fleet had already been driven out of the Indian Ocean by the Japanese, allowing the Empire to further extend its western defensive perimeter, and while Japanese submarines now prowled freely throughout the area the allies could do little to stop the enemy from pushing further west through the British colony of Burma and towards India; the crown jewel of Britain's Asiatic Empire.

By now Britain had lost a great deal of territory to the forces of the Axis and Winston Churchill was clearly concerned about this additional threat to British colonialism. The Indian subcontinent had been ruled by the British since 1858 and Churchill was reluctant to lose such a precious part of the empire; his American ally, President Roosevelt, meanwhile, had other concerns.

Burma provided the supply route for aid and arms into China, and it was important to keep this open so the Chinese leader, Generalissimo Chiang Kai-Shek, could continue his war with Japan unhindered, keeping enemy troops occupied and preventing their re-deployment to the South Pacific.

Chiang Kai-Shek, his wife and General Joseph Stillwell

Roosevelt had assigned General Joseph Stillwell the role of Chief of Staff to the China Burma India Theatre. But while the conflict in Burma continued, it was soon evident that the allies were fighting a losing battle. By the end of April, Lashio in North East Burma had been taken, cutting off the Burma Road, and Stillwell had no choice but to order an emergency evacuation.

On May 6th the American general began to retreat towards India on foot, while British troops tried to slow down the progress of the advancing Japanese soldiers, before crossing over to India themselves. Before long, all hope of holding Burma had been lost, and as the country fell, the buffer protecting India, was no more.

. . .

Despite Churchill's fears of losing more British terrain, the Japanese actually had no intention of invading India, and as May drew to a close it was clear that there were other more ambitious plans to occupy their commanders. Yamamoto was by now finalising preparations for the Battle of Midway and it would soon be time for the next stage of Japan's attack on the American fleet.

Although Yamamoto's superior Fleet Admiral Nagano had finally agreed to the attack on Midway, there were still disagreements between the Japanese naval commanders. Nagano had decided that Yamamoto should launch a separate mission at the same time as the Midway battle, to capture some sparsely inhabited, volcanic islands, which extended over one thousand miles west of the Alaskan Peninsula.

The Aleutian Islands lay far to the north of Midway and Yamamoto realized that the extra mission would extend his vast battle zone to unmanageable proportions, but Nagano would not be dissuaded. The Aleutian Islands appeared to have little economic, military or strategic value because of their barren, mountainous terrain and harsh weather, but seizing them would further extend the defense of Japan and make it harder for ships to slip through the Northern Pacific.

There was also the hope that launching this second attack, far from Midway, might serve as a distraction, leading some American ships north and therefore weakening the US fleet. Yamamoto must have eventually seen that there were some advantages to Nagano's plan and though reluctant, he finally agreed to extend the area of battle to incorporate the islands near Alaska.

The Japanese Admiral now faced coordinating the most challenging naval conflict ever undertaken by the Japanese and set to work gathering the largest fleet to have ever sailed the Pacific Ocean for the mighty battle that lay ahead. The element of surprise was a vital part of Yamamoto's plan, so he split the immense fleet into four separate groups, so the Americans would have no idea how vast the Japanese forces actually were, when the battle commenced.

The First Carrier Striking force would be led by Admiral Chuichi Nagumo, who had led the attack on Pearl harbor in 1941 and had also forced the British to abandon the Indian Ocean, after successful attacks on their fleet in early 1942. Nagumo's force would operate in close support of The Midway Invasion Force commanded by Vice-Admiral Kondo; meanwhile, The Main Force, which followed behind these other two, would be led by Yamamoto himself and would attack the American carriers once they had been lured out into the open.

Finally, the fourth section of the naval fleet, Northern Force was to detach from the main body and head north for the Aleutians, before the Midway battle commenced. Unfortunately for Yamamoto, the disposition of his forces would be the greatest flaw in his plan as the groups would be too far apart to support each other.

Yamamoto's ships would in fact sail three hundred miles behind Nagumo's Striking Force and be of little help when the Americans launched their defense.

Meanwhile far across the Pacific Ocean, the US Navy's Combat Intelligence Unit at Pearl Harbor had once again intercepted Japanese codes and all Yamamoto's efforts at deception would be in vain. By May 1942 Admiral Nimitz had been provided with confirmation that Midway was the next target for the Japanese.

He even had the complete Japanese order of battle, as well as the dates of the attack, which were expected on either June the 4th or the 5th. While the Imperial fleet set sail for Midway with little idea that their mission had already been revealed to the enemy, US forces rushed to prepare for the battle that lay ahead. Midway was second only to Pearl Harbor in the defense of the west Coast of America, and after the devastating raid on the Hawaiian base the Americans would ensure that this time they were more than ready for the impending attack.

Unlike the Japanese, they had the advantage that Midway itself could be used as a launching platform, and as well as their own planes additional air power had been sent from Hawaii, further strengthening defenses. The aircraft carriers were also called up to protect Midway and Fletcher's Task Force 17 was immediately recalled from the Coral Sea.

Although severely damaged Yorktown had survived the battles against the Japanese, and after arriving in Pearl Harbor on May 27th, work crews from the shipyard had worked around the clock to ensure she was repaired and ready to defend Midway within days.

Halsey's Task Force 16, with the carriers USS Hornet and Enterprise were already at Pearl, although Halsey himself would not be well enough to take part in the battle. He would be replaced by Rear Admiral Raymond Spruance who would operate under the overall command of Admiral Fletcher. As well as calling on as many army and naval personnel as he could muster, Nimitz requested photographers so the events at Midway could be recorded. The famous film director John Ford knew Nimitz well, and would capture some of the most memorable footage of the conflict.

By the end of May all possible preparations had been made for the battle that lay ahead, and with defenses in place, American forces could do little more than watch and wait for the Japanese offensive to begin. Air corps units searched the skies for the first signs of a Japanese attack, while far out to sea, Yamamoto's armada edged ever closer to the naval base.

· · ·

Compared to the Americans, the Japanese had little idea of what they were up against. They believed that only two aircraft carriers, the USS Enterprise and USS Hornet would be available for the defense of Midway and were convinced that USS Yorktown had been sunk at the Battle of Coral Sea.

Underestimating the strength of their opponent would be an expensive mistake, as in reality the Japanese faced not two but three American carrier groups, and the challenge that lay ahead would be much harder than Yamamoto had imagined.

By May 30th US search planes were launched from Midway, to hunt for the giant enemy fleet, and after scanning the seas for several days, the ships of the Imperial navy were finally spotted.

As the alarm rang out across Midway in the early hours of June 4th, Nagumo ordered dive-bombers, torpedo bombers and Zero fighters to launch their attack on the American base and within less than two hours, the onslaught had begun.

American planes, flown by marine pilots, scrambled to intercept the attack, and would destroy many of the enemy planes despite heavy losses. Meanwhile as dive bombers from Nagumo's attack force swooped across the island, those defending the ground fought back fiercely, and the anti-aircraft fire would prove much deadlier than the Japanese expected. The base was thrown into chaos as bombs rained down on the island, destroying fuel storage tanks and aircraft hangars, but the defenders continued to battle back against the enemy forces.

As the first attack on the island ended, it was the American's turn to strike back and two torpedo squadrons headed for the Japanese carriers. Without fighter escorts they were no match for the Japanese Zeros, and were almost all shot down, but as the waves of American attacks continued, the Japanese were kept distracted. They were too busy focusing on the defense of their ships to launch a strike against the American fleet, and soon US planes had broken through the Japanese resistance.

The Enterprise air group hit two carriers, including Nagumo's, while York-town's bombers attacked a third. Before long there was only one Japanese carrier, still operational, and she counter-attacked, sending a wave of dive bombers towards Yorktown.

Compared to the Japanese carriers, Yorktown was better prepared for the attack, and swiftly launched her fighters to intercept the enemy planes. Many of the Japanese aircraft were shot down, and although Yorktown was repeat-edly struck by bombs, fires were controlled, and she continued to launch more fighter planes.

While a second wave of Japanese bombers headed for the American carrier, Rear Admiral Spruance launched a final strike on the Japanese fleet, with forty dive bombers. Within an hour they found the last Japanese carrier and despite desperate attempts to defend her, American planes delivered a deadly blow, which left her ablaze and sinking.

By the end of the day it was clear that Yamamoto's mission had failed miser-ably and with casualties mounting, and more and more planes being lost to the enemy he would have no choice but to call off the invasion of Midway.

Four Japanese carriers had been destroyed and their loss would have grave consequences for the Imperial navy, throwing the balance of power firmly in America's favor. There had nonetheless been heavy losses on both sides and

Yorktown, the flagship of Fletcher's Task Force 17, which had been so important at the Coral Sea, and at Midway, would not survive to see another battle. After being hit by torpedoes, the crew was forced to abandon ship amidst fears she would capsize, and after a final deadly blow from a Japanese submarine, Yorktown sank on June 7th.

The Americans had suffered just over three hundred casualties at the Battle of Midway, but the Japanese had lost many more, with over two thousand men killed, and there was little doubt that the Americans had won an overwhelming victory.

As the injured US marines and sailors were tended to and survivors were brought to safety, President Roosevelt congratulated those who had bravely fought off the enemy, clearly relieved that the Battle of Midway had checked the advance of the Japanese.

But far to the north, the threat from the Eastern Empire was not yet over. The Japanese forces that had headed to the Aleutian Islands would have greater success than Nagumo's Midway fleet and on the 3rd and 4th of June their carriers launched air attacks on two military bases on the island of Unalaska.

Hindered by bad weather the planes hadn't caused as much damage as hoped, but on June the 6th and 7th the Japanese had landed at Kiska Island and Attu Island, and had soon established bases there. This now placed the Japanese dangerously close to US territory, and with fears that attacks could now be launched on the west Coast of America, every precaution was taken for the defense of the mainland.

Although a resounding victory had been won at Midway, it was clear that the war against Japan was far from over, and the months that followed would reveal just how hard the battle against the Empire of the Rising Sun, was going to be. From the freezing terrain of the Aleutian Islands, to the sweltering jungles of New Guinea and the Solomon's, the toughest battles in the history of the Second World War were still to be fought, and the Pacific conflict was only just beginning.

12

EL ALAMEIN TO STALINGRAD

July – September 1942

| Bernard Law Montgomery

B y the summer of 1942 the Second World War had been raging for almost three years and showed little sign of abating. The conflict that started back in 1939 when Nazi Germany invaded Poland had now spread far beyond the confines of Europe, and as the Axis powers sought to expand their vast empires, the battlefields of war stretched from Africa to Asia.

With Germany, Italy and Japan now united against the Allies, fighting had broken out in every corner of the globe, and the struggle continued across the war-torn continents, while at sea naval battles were being fought for control of supply routes.

As the Axis tightened their stranglehold on the previously tranquil waters of the Mediterranean, there was an ever-growing risk that the Allies fighting in North Africa would be cut off, and the future of their Western Desert Offensive was far from assured. Italian and German troops were now posing a very real threat to British interests in Africa, as they struck deep into the desert landscape of Egypt, reaching El Alemein just outside Cairo.

Within the shortest of timeframes there was little left standing between the Axis powers and the Suez Canal, which was the pathway to the oilfields of the Middle East. If the Allies were to stand any real chance of victory in World War II, the battles that lay ahead to secure North Africa would be absolutely critical.

Ironically though, the leader of Nazi Germany's attentions would not be entirely focused on North Africa, as Adolf Hitler's determination to destroy communism proved to be rather stronger than his desire to penetrate Egypt.

. . .

On the eastern Front, as the German tanks rolled further into Russia, by July 1942 The Battle of Stalingrad was well underway. Facing a bitter conflict, Joseph Stalin, the Russian leader, called for a great patriotic war against the enemy, and with the full might of the Soviet Red Army to contend with, the troops of Hitler's Third Reich were destined to be occupied for some time to come.

And all the while in the Far East, despite the immense territorial gains of Hitler's Japanese Allies, the tide that had so far been running in the Axis' favor was slowly beginning to turn against them. Out at sea, The Battle of Midway, fought in June 1942, had proved to be a crucial victory for the Allies in the Pacific Theatre of War. The Americans had caused irreparable damage to the fleet of Japan, spurring US soldiers on, who were now ready for their first offensive in the Solomon Islands.

The African continent had been a field of conflict between Western Empires long before the outbreak of the Second World War, and while European colonies were established across the continent, by the early twentieth century there was little left that the native inhabitants could call their own. The last remaining independent states were the tiny republic of Liberia to the west and the ancient kingdom of Ethiopia to the east, but in the 1930s when the climate in Europe became increasingly unsettled and new leaders hungry for power emerged, the autonomy of these countries would also be under threat.

The Italian dictator Benito Mussolini, dreamt of turning Italy into a nation that was *"great, respected and feared"* throughout the world, and wanted to create a *new* Roman Empire, an idea very much celebrated by his supporters. Following the Roman example, Mussolini would strive to repeat what had been done two thousand years earlier, by placing the Mediterranean and North Africa, beneath the Italian sphere of influence once more. He began by consolidating power in Libya, ruthlessly forcing the migration of thousands of Libyans and showing no mercy to those who opposed his new regime. He then turned his attentions to East Africa where Italian Somaliland and Eritrea were already beneath his rule, and seeing the advantage of connecting these two countries, back in 1935 he invaded the Kingdom of Ethiopia.

The country, which was then known as Abyssinia, was swiftly vanquished and despite uproar from abroad, by the spring of 1936 Italian East Africa had been established unopposed, in the first step to Mussolini's empire building.

By the outbreak of the Second World War, as the Nazis swept across western Europe, crushing Denmark, Norway and the Low countries, before moving into France, Mussolini became impatient for further territorial gains. With a French defeat imminent in June 1940, he seized the opportunity to take advantage of the conflict and declared war on both Britain and France. By this time the Italian leader had set his sights on Egypt and was particularly keen on obtaining access to the Suez Canal, which lay beneath British influence.

The Suez was of great strategic importance as it connected the Mediterranean Sea to the Red Sea, providing a pathway to the rich oilfields of the Middle East. It also provided the shortest ocean link between the Mediterranean and the Indian Ocean and had originally been important in helping the European powers govern their colonies.

During the war, its value in the balance of power would make possession of the canal indispensable, and Mussolini was swift to begin preparations for the push into Egypt, rushing to deploy troops to Libya while the allies were occupied in France. But while the Italians prepared for battle, the British had not been idle. A Middle East Command had been set up in Cairo in June 1939 as tensions heightened in Europe and was to be presided over by General Archibald Wavell.

. . .

The British had been wary of the threat the Italians could pose to their supply routes for some time and on the assumption that conflict was imminent Wavell had ordered his commanders to start planning operations at once.

By the time the Italians ventured into Egypt in September 1940, the British would be ready for them, and though their Western Desert Force, would be numerically weaker than the opposition, not only would they prevent Mussolini's troops from reaching the Suez, but by December the allies had succeeded in pushing the Italians back into Libya.

Seizing valuable territory as they went, by January 1941, the Western Desert Force had reached Tobruk, and one month later, they had seized Libya's second largest city, Benghazi.

With vital ports lost to the allies and thousands of Italian soldiers now prisoners of war, it seemed that all Mussolini's hopes of a new Roman Empire were fading into oblivion.

Adolf Hitler in the meantime, urged the Italian leader to hold his ground in Libya, as an allied victory in Africa could have grave consequences for the plans he had for *his* new kingdom; The Third Reich. By early 1941 Axis forces were gathering in the Balkans ready for the attack on the Soviet Union, and Hitler was concerned that if the conflict in North Africa came to a close, British troops might be deployed to Greece in the southern Balkan Peninsula.

This would place them uncomfortably close to the precious oilfields of Rumania, so vital for Hitler's military machine, and fearing that his lifelong mission of destroying communism might be interfered with, he made moves to ensure that the war in North Africa would continue.

.   .   .

In February 1941, the highly trained German Afrika Korps were sent to Libya, accompanied by one of the best commanders in Nazi Germany, General Erwin Rommel. Rommel had risen to fame after leading an armored division across France and trapping the allied soldiers on the beaches of Dunkirk, but his success as a desert general would earn him even greater acclaim.

Renowned for his quick judgement and improvisation in battle, Rommel would become known as the desert fox, presenting a worthy adversary for the allied troops.

Spring of 1941, it appeared that the gains made by the allies earlier that year were about to be lost, and not only would they face Rommel and his troops, but they had the added problem of the axis threat to their supply routes. The Mediterranean Sea was crucial to the flow of supplies to North Africa, and with Vichy France beneath the influence of the Nazis, the Axis already had the advantage of ports in French North Africa.

In April 1941 the situation deteriorated further when the Nazis helped the Italians vanquish Greece and valuable ports were lost to the allies, and in May, there would be an additional blow to the allied naval forces, when the Luftwaffe launched an attack on Crete. Senior Luftwaffe commanders had been enthusiastic about the idea of seizing the island, hoping to regain some of the prestige they had lost during the Battle of Britain.

Although the German army high command felt there was enough on the agenda with the planned invasion of Russia, Hitler was won over by the idea and at dawn on May 20th, 1941 the daring airborne attack was launched. Though the Germans had used parachute and glider-borne assaults on a much smaller scale before, this was to be the first large-scale airborne invasion, and despite fierce resistance from the civilian population, by the end of the month Crete had fallen.

. . .

British troops were taken prisoner and the Swastika flag was raised as yet another Nazi victory was secured. Now all that was left to the allies in the Mediterranean, besides Egypt, and the captured ports of Libya, were the islands of Gibraltar and Malta. Malta was particularly important to the North African campaign, as it provided the only allied base between Gibraltar and Egypt and was the last threat to Rommel's supply lines from Europe.

The British Prime Minister, Winston Churchill regarded the island an unsinkable aircraft carrier, but as Rommel's troops made progress in Libya, beating back the Western Desert Force and heading eastwards towards Egypt, the Axis hold on the Mediterranean would tighten, and by 1942, almost no ships would be able to get through to Malta.

Hitler and Mussolini lacked the resources to take both Cairo and Malta at the same time, so they decided to batter and starve the island into submission. It would become one of the most intensely bombed areas in the war, with around 250 raids per month in the first six months of 1942.

The destruction to the island was unimaginable, and thousands of people were killed or injured in the attacks. Their devotion to the allied cause however did not go unnoticed, and they were awarded the George cross for their heroism, while the American President, Franklin D. Roosevelt, described the island as *"one tiny bright flame in the darkness"*. But while supplies dwindled and allied naval forces struggled to reach Malta, allied commanders realized, it would only be a matter of time before the island surrendered.

Rommel in the meantime was approaching Egypt and after weeks of grueling battle by June 20th, 1942, he had captured Tobruk. Ten days later his panzers reached El Alemein, a railway station on the coast of Egypt, just 60 miles from Alexandria. While the allied position deteriorated dramatically,

Churchill refused to be beaten by Adolf Hitler and was adamant that the battle to crush the axis should continue.

Though Churchill was determined to defeat Hitler, the British situation was by now critical. As well as Axis gains in Europe and Africa, there were grave concerns for the future of the British Empire in the Far East. Singapore had fallen as had Burma and the risk that the Japanese might venture across the border into India, and attack from the east could not be ignored.

Meanwhile as the Germans progressed in Russia, closing in on the Caucasus, there was the possibility that new German armies might descend from the north through Iran. Adding to the threat posed by the Japanese and Rommel, this meant that British forces in the Middle East might have to face the enemy three ways.

By the end of June 1942, in Egypt the panic was already setting in, and in Cairo the British began burning confidential papers anticipating the arrival of Rommel's troops any day; meanwhile all measures were taken to stall the enemy by flooding areas around the river Nile and building defensive positions to the west of Alexandria.

Wavell who had originally headed the Middle East Command had by this time been replaced by Claude Auchinleck, who had previously commanded the Indian Army. Auchinleck had not seen much success since his appointment one year earlier however and was criticized for having little experience or understanding of British or Dominion troops.

The Western Desert Force, which had by now changed its name to the Eighth Army, was made up of divisions from around the British Empire, including South Africa, Australia, and India.

. . .

The confidence that both dominion and British commanders had in Auchinleck was waning by the summer of 1942 however, and relations were considerably strained. Nevertheless, the fate of Egypt now lay in their hands, and Auchinleck's future rested on their success.

| The British infantry charges

The allied desert air force would also play a prominent role in the defense of Egypt, and when Rommel began the attack on El Alamein, on July 1st, 1942 they would cause considerable damage to the advancing units. The RAF planes heavily bombarded the already fragile supply routes and while British mobile columns attacked from the west and from the south, soon Rommel's men were exhausted and running out of supplies. By July 4th the commander took the decision to go on the defensive and the German advance was halted.

For Churchill it was not enough. He urged Auchinleck to attack again and to eliminate the axis threat, but Rommel's defenses held strong, and while battles continued throughout July, by the end of the month, the British commander had no choice but to end the offensive operations.

The failure confronted Churchill at a particularly difficult time for he was about to inform the Soviet leader, Joseph Stalin, that an Anglo-American invasion of Europe, would not be possible until the African campaign had been concluded. Stalin had been fighting Nazi Germany since June 1941, and while the Russians struggled desperately to halt the advance of Hitler's troops, the Soviet Leader had been putting pressure on Churchill to open a second front for some time.

While Stalin hoped for an invasion of occupied Europe, British commanders had however concluded that an allied invasion of north-west Africa, where Vichy France held territory in Morocco, Algeria and Tunisia should be the priority. This would improve naval control of the Mediterranean Sea and help pave the way for an invasion of southern Europe by 1943.

Though the Americans were not as keen as their British counterparts, Roosevelt supported Churchill when he suggested the invasion of North Africa. Nevertheless, with Egypt still under threat the allied position in the region, was tenuous to say the least. Wary that Stalin would be unhappy with the alternative arrangements, Churchill decided to stop off in Cairo on his way to Moscow, in early August 1942, determined to make some changes to the Middle East command.

. . .

By now there was a considerable breakdown of morale amongst those in the Eighth Army and with complaints circulating about Auchinleck, Churchill decided he should be replaced with General Harold Alexander. Alexander had a commendable track record, with awards for heroism spanning both the First and Second World Wars, but more importantly he understood the importance of keeping spirits up amongst the troops and was much respected by the men he commanded.

Together with Admiral Harwood who remained in command of naval operations, and Arthur Tedder who commanded allied air operations, Alexander would now take the allies into a new phase in the Western Desert Campaign. Meanwhile, there was also the leadership of the Eighth Army itself to be considered, which had been commanded more recently by Auchinleck himself.

Churchill was keen that one of the Eighth Army corps commanders, Lieutenant General William Gott, take on this role but when the plane Gott was travelling in on his way to Cairo was shot down by a German fighter ace, Churchill was forced to rethink.

Sir Alan Brook, the Chief of Imperial General Staff had initially recommended that Lieutenant General Montgomery, who had led troops in the battle of France, should command the eighth army, and although Churchill had dismissed the suggestion earlier on, with the loss of Gott, it seems he was left with no choice.

On August 7th, Montgomery took on his new role as leader of the Eighth Army, and his dedication to his troops and popularity amongst his men, would help transform not only the army, but the fortunes of the allies in Africa. Although the changes in the Middle Eastern Command would certainly improve the allies' chances, Churchill still had to confront Stalin with the news that Africa would take priority over Europe.

. . .

He arrived in Moscow on August 12th to discuss the situation with the Soviet leader, but although Stalin initially argued for an attack on France, the British Prime Minister managed to reason with him. He explained that by taking North Africa, they could threaten the belly of Hitler's Europe by striking at Germany through Italy, and he assured the Soviet leader that in the meantime American and Commonwealth forces would be assembled in Britain ready for the eventual invasion of France across the channel.

After days of discussions Stalin eventually gave the invasion of Africa his blessing and assured Churchill that the Soviet troops could hold out until the winter.

But as Churchill returned to London the Nazis were already advancing on Stalingrad and the Soviets were about to face their most difficult battle to date.

When Adolf Hitler had ordered the invasion of the Soviet Union back in 1941, he had a number of strategic objectives, which included seizing Leningrad to the north west of the country, Moscow, the capital of the Soviet Union to the center and Stalingrad to the south, but as yet the conquest of Russia was proving more difficult than the Nazi leader had expected.

Although Hitler's troops had reached Leningrad by September 1941, those defending the city had refused to surrender, and the siege of Leningrad would continue for another two and a half years. The battle of Moscow in the meantime had come to a close in January 1942 and had been a decisive Soviet victory, although over a million Soviet soldiers and civilians had been taken prisoner or killed in the process.

. . .

Having failed to capture Moscow or Leningrad, Hitler had now placed all his hopes on vanquishing the city, which bore the name of the Soviet leader; Stalingrad. Stalingrad provided vital transport routes between the Caspian Sea and Northern Russia and seizing the city, would effectively sever the transportation of supplies to the north. It was also hoped that the capture of Stalingrad would secure the right flank of the German armies as they advanced into the Caucasus, a region which was rich in oil and minerals and vital to Hitler's war against the allies.

But perhaps one of the greatest reasons Hitler had for attacking Stalingrad was its significance to the Soviet Leader. Stalin had played a part in defending the city against the White Army in 1919, when the Red Army was battling for the survival of Bolshevism; and when he had come to power as leader of the communist nation in the 1920s he had decided to change the city's name which was originally Tsaritsyn to Stalingrad to celebrate his role in the Russian revolution.

Such symbolism was not lost on Adolf Hitler, but while the Nazi dictator was driven by his desire to destroy communism, his General Staff wanted to attack in the direction of Moscow again, in the hope they could crush the remainder of the soviet military forces.

There was little hope of dissuading Hitler once his mind was made up however, and the attack on Stalingrad and the Caucasus, codenamed *Operation Blue* took priority over all other military plans and was scheduled to commence by the end of May 1942.

In the meantime, the Soviets had been given a strong indication of the latest Nazi scheme. A briefcase containing the plans for *Operation Blue* had been discovered after a German plane was shot down over Russia. But while the soviet generals poured over the papers, Stalin was convinced that the appearance of the plans were no more than a deliberate ploy to fool the commanders of the Red Army and to draw Soviet troops away from the real target, which *he* believed was Moscow.

For the time being the protection of the capital, remained Stalin's priority, but while Nazi troops prepared for the advance Hitler's true motives would soon be clear.

One month later than planned, on June 28th 1942, *Operation Blue* had finally commenced, and the troops of Army Group South were thundering across the desolate Russian plains towards their objective.

The Axis forces had been split into two groups: Army Group South A, which was commanded by Wilhelm List and included the seventeenth army and the First Panzer Army which advanced towards the Caucasus in the far south. Meanwhile Army Group South B which included General Hans von Salmuth's Second Army, the Fourth Panzer Army and General Friedrich Paulus' Sixth Army marched east towards Stalingrad and the Volga River.

There had been concerns amongst the Nazi commanders that the decision taken to run two operations simultaneously would put a strain on supply lines and put the entire offensive at risk, but in the early stages of the advance, Army Group B's progress towards Stalingrad went so well that Hitler decided to make some changes to the order of battle.

Believing that Army Group B didn't need the fourth panzer army any more, he ordered the tanks south to join the troops advancing on the Caucasus. The change in strategy resulted in a huge traffic jam as the panzers crossed the path of the motorised sixth army, and Paulus's advance was delayed. While the Sixth Army waited, the days passed by and the element of surprise evaporated.

· · ·

With the accumulation of traffic to the south, the Soviets now realized that the target of the next Axis attack was Stalingrad, not Moscow, and all available troops began to rush towards the city, to prepare for its defense.

Red Army General Andrei Yeremenko was placed in command and consolidated what forces he had on the eastern bank of the Volga, to prepare for their approach.

But once Army Group B was ready to advance once more, their progress was swifter than ever and soon Paulus's sixth army, had reached the River Don, which lay only forty miles west of Stalingrad and the Volga. Fierce fighting ensued as the Soviet soldiers in the area did all they could to check the Axis advance, but all their efforts would prove futile.

By July 21st more than one hundred assault boats began crossing the Don, and within hours a beachhead had been established on its east bank. The Soviets put as many men as they could muster into the 40-mile margin which separated the Don from the Volga, but soon Russian defenses were crumbling, and it appeared that little stood in the way of the Axis advance into Stalingrad itself.

In a desperate attempt to stop the Soviet collapse, Stalin ordered that every granule of Russian soil be defended to the last drop of blood, threatening those who retreated with death. Meanwhile anyone strong enough to hold a rifle was sent to defend the city, and civilians were ordered to dig trench works and fortifications around its outskirts. No one was exempt from the effort to save Stalingrad, and women and children worked as hard as the soldiers to prevent the Nazis seizing their city.

However, by the end of August the battle was about to become harder than ever as the German air force, the Luftwaffe began their attack from the skies.

. . .

As the city was reduced to rubble and ruins, the Axis troops moved steadily closer, and soon the spearhead of the Sixth Army had reached a section of the Volga to the north of the city.

By the beginning of September Stalingrad was surrounded on three sides, and the real battle was about to commence. Two months after the offensive had begun, the city limits were finally penetrated by Paulus's troops and axis forces broke into the city in a dozen places. Not long after, the Nazis cut the rail line that travelled across Russia from Stalingrad to Moscow, destroying one of the country's most important supply routes. Troops and supplies could now only reach Stalingrad from across the Volga, behind the city.

As the situation deteriorated, Stalin ordered one of his greatest commanders, General Zhukov to leave Moscow and head south to coordinate the defense of Stalingrad. Meanwhile General Vasily Chuikov, who had fought off the Nazi attack as they advanced across the Don, was placed in command of the Russian 62nd army, which was now responsible for holding Stalingrad.

Before long, Chuikov's situation would become desperate however as the 62nd Army were penned into the city in the grip of the Germans. By mid-September the Axis troops had taken the highest point in the town, an ancient tartar burial ground, known as the Mamai Tumulus, giving them a huge advantage over the Soviets. From here they could attack strategic targets around the city and there was little doubt that whoever controlled the high ground, commanded the battle.

The Soviet thirteenth Guard Rifle division arrived across the Volga, to reinforce the 62nd Army and were ordered to charge the strongpoint by Chuikov. Few would survive the ordeal and thousands of Soviet soldiers would die in the battle for the summit. But soon it was once more beneath Russian control, and the fighting now descended into the streets of Stalingrad.

The first tank into Stalingrad

The battle would become one of the bloodiest of the Second World War, as the axis fought the soviets for every ruin, cellar and staircase in the city. There were no battle lines; only brutal skirmishes between one street and the next, while buildings ridden with snipers turned the area into a vast killing zone. For those fighting within, life would become an endless hell of gunfire, hunger and fear and the casualties on both sides would be immense.

While Stalin's war against the axis continued, it was clear that a second front to take the pressure off Soviet troops could not come a moment too soon, but the invasion of North Africa which Churchill had promised the Soviet leader, was as yet in the early planning stages and disagreements between American and British commanders were beginning to threaten the progress of any invasion at all.

Concerns at this stage revolved around *where* the landings in French African territory should be. Churchill wanted to land troops as close as possible to the base of Rommel's Afrika Korps, and advocated landing on the eastern border of Algeria close to Tunisia, but the American Army Chief of Staff, George C. Marshall wanted to limit landings to Western Algeria and appeared to be planning an attack on a much smaller scale than Churchill had envisaged.

Disconcerted, the British Prime Minister reminded President Roosevelt that the allies had promised Stalin a *serious* diversion to draw German efforts away from the Soviet Union, and ever the diplomat, Roosevelt ensured that a compromise was found which would please both American and British commanders.

It was decided that there would be three simultaneous landings; American forces would land in Casablanca in Morocco, as well as Oran in Algeria, while a combined British and American force, would land in Algiers, which lay further to the east of Algeria, and closer to Rommel's troops.

The invasion itself would however take time to prepare, and while US soldiers and marines were mobilized for the attack and began arriving in Britain ready for their first European offensive, it seemed unlikely that American forces would be ready for the invasion until the late autumn.

In the meantime, American commanders had more than just the European theatre of war to contend with. Although the priority of the United States had been to defeat Nazi Germany when they had entered the war in December 1941, in the Far East Hitler's Japanese allies were posing a considerable threat to allied interests.

During the first six months of the Pacific War, the Japanese had conquered hundreds of thousands of miles of territory, spanning from Burma in East Asia to the islands of the south Pacific. But by May 1942, American forces had started to make some progress in checking the Japanese advance.

During the Battle of Coral Sea, they had successfully prevented the Japanese from taking further territory in New Guinea, and the following month a major naval battle had been fought around the island of Midway in the north Pacific, which had inflicted heavy losses on the Japanese fleet.

Nevertheless, the Empire of the Rising Sun showed little sign of easing their campaign to seize new territory and by mid-1942 they were constructing a large airfield on Guadalcanal in the Solomon Islands. From here they could launch attacks on American bases in Fiji, New Caledonia and Samoa and threaten allied supply and communication lines to Australia, which lay to the south of the Solomon Islands.

New Zealand troops in the Solomon Islands

While allied concerns grew, Admiral Ernest King, Commander in Chief of the United States Fleet proposed an invasion of the island of Guadalcanal and other strategic points around the Solomon's and the Combined Chiefs of Staff had soon agreed to launching their first American offensive in the Pacific.

After spending six months on the defensive, the allied counterblow was soon underway and by late July 1942, the first marine divisions had left their training areas in New Zealand ready for the battle. They moved north in deep secrecy and as a cold front swept across the Pacific, they were able to use the weather as a cover. By the time they reached the Solomon Islands on August 7th the seas were calm, and the Japanese had no idea that an attack was about to be launched.

. . .

The landing force then split into two groups, with one group assaulting Guadalcanal, and the other attacking Tulagi and Florida Island. At first there was little resistance from Japanese troops, who began to flee after aerial bombing from allied planes had paved the way for the invasion, but by the seconD-Day the battle had begun.

While troops fought back on the ground there were heavy air attacks from Japanese planes based on Bougainville and other nearby islands, but despite the bombardment, American forces had reached the Japanese airfield on the seconD-Day of the offensive. They renamed the airbase Henderson Field, after a marine who'd been killed during the Battle of Midway and from here the Americans could launch their own attacks on the enemy.

Throughout August, US aircraft and their crews would continue to arrive at Guadalcanal to beat back the enemy, and air battles between the Allied aircraft at Henderson airfield and Japanese bombers and fighters from Rabaul in New Guinea, continued daily. While the Japanese Commander defending the island ordered his troops to *"rout and annihilate the enemy"* the battles through the dense and disease-ridden jungles of Guadalcanal, would be some of the worst the American GIs would encounter during the Second World War.

In the meantime, eight hundred miles to the west there was an equally difficult conflict underway, coordinated by Supreme Allied Commander of the South West Pacific area, General Douglas MacArthur. It had been decided that the invasion of Guadalcanal would be carried out at the same time as an allied offensive in New Guinea where the Japanese were threatening to seize territory once more.

Lessons had been learnt at the Battle of Coral Sea and rather than launching an amphibious invasion, this time the Japanese decided to mount an overland assault across the towering Owen Stanley Mountains in late July. Their target was a strategic town on New Guinea's southern coast, by the name of Port Moresby and from here they could launch further attacks on the North-East of Australia.

The Japanese had already inflicted severe bombardments on Australia, and MacArthur, who was renowned for his determination, decided to launch a bold counter-offensive which would ensure the country was protected from further attacks. If the Japanese dared to venture across the Owen Stanley mountains, so would the allies and MacArthur ordered the battle-hardened troops of the Australian 7th division who had returned from fighting Rommel's troops in Africa earlier in the year, to venture deep into the jungle to beat back the Japanese invaders.

The track they followed was the Kokoda Trail or Track, and it would take them through some of the most hazardous terrain in the south pacific. Through disease-ridden swamps, plunging gorges and dark humid jungles the Australians embarked on a deadly mission to fight back the Japanese. There was little opportunity for rest, while they remained on constant alert for the enemy both day and night.

In the meantime, US planes flew overhead to drop supplies to the troops battling on the ground, though the smoke signals the Australians sent out would not always be easy to find.

Fortunately, the native people of New Guinea would play a vital part in the Kokoda Track Campaign, looking after supplies for the troops when they were dropped in the local villages, and taking care of the soldiers when they were injured.

. . .

While the campaigns in the Solomon's and New Guinea continued into the autumn of 1942, it was clear that the battles to vanquish the Japanese were yet in the early stages, and as Australian and American troops attempted to wrench territory from the enemy's grasp, inch by inch, it was evident that the war in the Pacific would be a long and bitter conflict.

In Africa and the Mediterranean, there was however already a glimmer of hope on the horizon as the battle continued against German and Italian forces. In August an operation had been launched to get supplies through to those desperately struggling on Malta and fourteen merchant ships had set off from Gibraltar, protected by two large forces of warships.

Throughout the voyage the allied forces suffered heavy bombardments from axis planes, and many of the allied ships including destroyers, aircraft carriers and the merchant ships themselves were sunk or badly damaged during the voyage to Malta.

Nevertheless, by August 15th, five merchant ships had managed to reach the island, and although the siege of Malta had by no means come to an end, the supplies that they brought meant that for the time being the island could continue to fight back, and the Axis conquest of the Mediterranean was not yet complete.

Meanwhile in Africa the morale of allied troops protecting Egypt had been lifted considerably by the presence of General Montgomery. After he had taken command of the Eighth Army on August 13th, he became a whirlwind of activity, regularly appearing before the troops and announcing to his officers *"If we are attacked, then there will be no retreat. If we cannot stay here alive, then we will stay here dead"*.

At the end of August Rommel made a last and desperate bid to reach the Nile, but proving he was a man of his word Montgomery checked the Nazi advance in two days fighting in the battle of Alam el Halfa. From this moment onwards, Montgomery's focus would be on the preparation for a counter-attack which he was determined would lead to a decisive victory against Rommel's forces.

The British commander decided to move his field headquarters, closer to the Air Force command post in order to better coordinate combined operations, so the Army, Navy and Air Forces could fight their battles in a unified, focused manner. His aim was to deny Rommel the strength to withstand the eighth army when they launched their counter attack, and he ordered the allied air force to destroy every enemy strip they could find in the Eastern Mediterranean as well as bombing the sea routes to Rommels' Front.

The British commander also focused air strikes on enemy ports in North Africa, so if supplies did make it through, they would find it virtually impossible to unload the ships when they arrived. Meanwhile from Benghazi to El Alemein, there were regular bombardments of Rommel's troops. The combined effort had the desired result, and within a month less than half of Rommel's supplies would be getting through.

Soon the tables would be turned in North Africa, and while preparations continued for the invasion of North West Africa before long, the Axis would be facing an attack on two fronts.

Rommel knew full well that the British Commonwealth forces would soon be strong enough to launch an offensive against his army and his only hope now was that the German forces fighting in the Battle of Stalingrad could swiftly defeat the Soviet troops. The Germans advancing through the Caucasus could then threaten Iran and the Middle East and draw British troops away from his front line.

. . .

But Rommel's hopes would all be in vain, for in Stalingrad the Russians were planning a momentous counterattack and as the winter of 1942 drew near, the tides of war were about to turn.

13

THE TIDE BEGINS TO TURN

October – December 1942

| Martin A-30A light bomber aircraft

A s the Second World War entered its third year, Adolf Hitler and his axis allies continued their advance into new and unconquered terrain. In 1942 the vast armies of the Third Reich were plunging ever deeper into Russia, battling the Red Army in the war-torn streets of Stalingrad, while further south they had reached the icy mountains of the Caucasus.

In North Africa German and Italian troops had crossed the border into Egypt and were edging closer to the oil fields of the Middle East.

In the Far East, Hitler's Japanese allies, had extended their influence far beyond the confines of their tiny island empire, and commanded great tracts of land and ocean that stretched from South East Asia to the remote islands of the Pacific.

Millions of people were to suffer unimaginable horrors as the axis powers encircled the globe, casting a reign of fear and terror across every nation they occupied. But for those who continued to struggle beneath the shadow of the New Order, by the autumn of 1942 hope lay on the horizon.

The strength of the Allies was growing and with the Soviet Union, America and Great Britain now united, the balance of power was beginning to shift. By November the allies would finally be ready to launch their invasion of North Africa, and while the Eighth Army beat the enemy back out of Egypt, German and Italian forces in the Western Desert would soon face an attack on two fronts.

In the meantime, the Soviet soldiers fighting the Great Patriotic War in Russia were ready to launch their counter offensive at Stalingrad and as the city fell beneath the icy grip of winter, the German Sixth Army, would soon be trapped with no hope of escape.

. . .

From the frozen plains of the Soviet Union, to the darkest jungles of the Pacific, the fight against the Axis was gaining momentum and at last the tides of war were slowly but surely beginning to turn in the allies' favor.

No one could have foreseen however the speed at which Japan would create its new empire and by 1942 the eastern enemy had claimed territory, which stretched out from the western border of Burma at the gates of India to the freezing Aleutian Islands near Alaska and had conquered islands as far south as New Guinea and the Solomon Islands in the South Pacific.

While the conquests mounted, by 1942 some felt that more should be done in the Pacific theatre of war and American naval commanders were particularly keen that the attack on Pearl should be avenged. Determined to strike back at the Japanese, Admiral Ernest King insisted that an offensive should be launched on the island of Guadalcanal, which was part of the Solomon Islands, to the North East of Australia.

The Japanese had begun building an airfield here and their presence in the area was posing a considerable threat to Australian ports.

King was concerned that the sea routes between Australia and America would soon be severed and with troops already arriving in the Pacific this could have grave consequences for the possibility of an allied counterattack.

Despite the directive that gave the European war zone priority, the Joint Chiefs of Staff in Washington eventually agreed to King's campaign and by August 7th 1942, the first US amphibious landing of the Pacific war had taken place, marking the beginning of America's change from defensive operations to offensive action. The battles in the dark and humid jungles of the Solomon

Islands would nevertheless be long and bitter, with more men losing their lives to deadly diseases than to the enemy.

Out at sea in the meantime fierce naval battles would continue to rage, causing heavy losses to both sides. On October 26th the carrier USS Hornet, which had launched the first attack on the Japanese mainland during the Doolittle raids in April, was hit during the battle of Santa Cruz Islands. It would be a major loss for the American fleet, but little could be done to save the carrier, which suffered heavy bomb and torpedo damage.

Nevertheless, the Americans had an important advantage, having seized the airfield on Guadalcanal from the Japanese during the first days of battle. Henderson airfield was now being turned into a sizable air base and would pose a considerable threat to any attempts by the enemy to ship fresh troops to the island.

As the Americans continued their grueling battle for supremacy, the Japanese prisoners mounted, and by December it was evident that King's campaign in the Solomon Islands had been a success.

While the enemy retreated further back towards the west coast of Guadal-canal, it was decided that the weary US marines could finally step down and let the army divisions take over. By the end of the winter, in February 1943, Guadalcanal would be secure, and the Americans would be ready for their next step in the Pacific War.

Meanwhile, over four thousand miles to the north of the Solomon Islands, US soldiers were faced with a very different challenge. The Aleutian Islands, which lay off the coast of Alaska in the North Pacific had been invaded by the Japanese in June 1942 placing the enemy uncomfortably close to Canada and the west coast of America.

. . .

With the risk of aerial attacks on the American mainland becoming a real possibility, it was decided to send a small number of troops to occupy the island of Adak just a few weeks after the invasion of Guadalcanal. From here it was hoped that strikes could be launched on Japanese forces based on the islands of Kiska and Attu.

The bitterly cold weather and freezing terrain would pose as much of a problem to the US soldiers in the Aleutians, as the heat and disease-ridden jungles of the Solomon's had posed to US marines. From thick fog and high winds, to plunging temperatures and icy conditions, the Americans based on Adak would have much to contend with, nevertheless their determination to defeat the Japanese kept them battling through the worst of the weather and they would soon be ready to launch their first attacks on the enemy.

The key to victory in the Aleutians would be airpower so building a suitable airfield to ensure that the bombardment of Japanese bases could begin as soon as possible had been top on the list of priorities.

Although conditions were not always ideal for flying, once the airbase was ready for use American pilots would begin to brave the bitter weather and inflict as much damage as they could on Japanese forces in the area.

The battle to oust the enemy would nevertheless take some time and it would be 1943 before American troops could venture onto Kiska and Attu to ensure the Aleutians were cleared of the invaders.

While events in the Pacific focused primarily on the invasion of Guadalcanal, the war in the Aleutians would become known as the forgotten war.

. . .

The men who fought here would still play an important part in the global conflict however, and many lives would be lost as they battled to protect the American mainland and the Pacific sea routes from the threat of attack.

Both the campaigns in the Aleutians and Guadalcanal nonetheless remained secondary to the more pressing issue of defeating Nazi Germany. By 1942 hundreds of thousands of Soviet soldiers were being killed on the battlefields of Russia, and the urgency of opening up a second front in Europe was growing by the day.

There had been much debate amongst allied commanders about where to launch their attack and back in 1941 Winston Churchill and Franklin D. Roosevelt had discussed the possibility of an ambitious cross-channel invasion from Britain into occupied France.

The venture was widely supported by American commanders, but the British were more reticent, wary of the strength of the Nazis in France.

The armistice signed between France and Germany in 1940 had placed northern and western France, including the entire Atlantic coastline beneath the control of Hitler's troops, and sending British and newly trained American forces to face the battle hardy Nazis was considered a suicide mission.

In August 1942 such fears had been justified when a small-scale raid launched on Dieppe in northern France had disastrous results. The port was fiercely defended by the Germans and of the 6000 Canadians and British troops who had taken part in the landings over 4000 were killed, wounded or missing by the end of the campaign.

The tragedy made it evident that the Nazis would not give up an inch of the territory they had conquered without a tough fight. Although the experiences of Dieppe would contribute to better preparations for the eventual invasion of France, it was clear that more time was needed before a large-scale attack could be launched, and soon an alternative mission began to gain greater popularity.

| The aftermath of Dieppe

As well as France itself, the Nazis had control of French colonies in Africa, and these were playing a key role in the axis battles being fought out in the western desert. Ports in Algeria and Tunisia ensured that crucial supplies for Italian and German troops were arriving unhindered across the Mediterranean Sea to North Africa and this was posing a considerable problem for British and Commonwealth troops protecting Egypt.

. . .

Despite all attempts to stall the enemy advance by June 30th axis troops led by General Erwin Rommel had crossed the Libyan border and had reached El Alamein just 60 miles from Alexandria.

There was now a real danger that the Nazis would seize the Suez Canal, which was vitally important to the balance of power in the Second World War. The Suez connected the Mediterranean to the Red Sea and the rich oilfields of the Middle East, and if seized by Hitler it could have devastating consequences for the allied war effort.

While the situation deteriorated in Africa, it was proposed that rather than a cross channel invasion into France, an invasion of North Africa should be undertaken. The plan was to seize key ports and airfields in Morocco and Algeria in a simultaneous attack on Casablanca, Oran and Algiers.

Allied troops would then advance into Tunisia and seize the port of Tunis which would prove an important move in restricting Axis supply lines. British naval commanders felt that seizing these ports would be a vital step in gaining control of the Mediterranean which would in turn be crucial if there was going to be any hope of pushing the enemy back out of occupied Europe. It was hoped that after the invasion of North Africa the allies would then be able to advance on the soft under belly of Europe and invade Italy.

American commanders were initially reluctant to agree to the invasion of North Africa, fearing that the British wanted to postpone a large-scale invasion of northern France indefinitely, but President Roosevelt had formed a close friendship with Winston Churchill and supported the move.

General Dwight D. Eisenhower was selected to coordinate the invasion which was codenamed *Operation Torch,* and in the summer of 1942, he arrived in London to commence preparations for the attack.

. . .

Meanwhile in North Africa the fight to stall the Nazi advance continued. General Bernard Law Montgomery, otherwise known as "Monty", had taken over the command of the Eighth Army in Egypt in August 1942, and was determined that Rommel and his troops would advance no further than El Alamein.

The Eighth Army had fiercely defended their position in the Battle of Alam el Halfa at the end of August, and now formed a defensive line which stretched from the coast to the impassable Qattara Depression, and this would ensure that the Germans and Italians were held at bay for the time being.

There was little doubt that Rommel's troops would soon attack again however and Montgomery's focus in the early autumn of 1942 was on preparations for a dramatic counterattack which would expel the axis from Egypt and drive them back into Libya.

Vast quantities of weapons and ammunition were stockpiled to give Montgomery's troops superior firepower; additional tanks arrived from America and while more forces arrived to join the Eighth Army, Montgomery soon had almost two hundred thousand men at his disposal.

In the meantime, allied planes were doing all they could to destroy the axis supply lines. Forces from Malta intercepted ships in the Mediterranean while the Desert Air Force kept up a relentless campaign against Axis supply vessels bombarding Libyan ports close to the border with Egypt.

This meant that most of Rommel's supplies had to be shipped to Benghazi and Tripoli which were much further west and an enormous distance from El Alamein.

Rommel meets up with Rüdiger von Wechmar

Soon the flow of supplies crossing the Mediterranean to the axis armies had fallen to a dismal level and Rommel began to realize that the war in Africa would not be won without more air support. The planes of the German Luftwaffe were however occupied in the battles of the Soviet Union leaving allied air power unchallenged in the Western Desert.

By October 1942 less than half of Rommel's supplies were getting through and to make matters worse the commander's health had begun to fail. He decided to take sick leave and departed for Germany to recover from his illness, leaving his troops to the command of General Georg Stumme.

· · ·

But the departure of Rommel couldn't have come at a worse time because Montgomery was about to launch his counterattack. Months of meticulous planning were finally over and on October 23ʳᵈ the allied troops were bracing themselves for their greatest battle yet. In the silence of the desert all took heed of Monty's simple message, that each and every officer and man should enter the battle with the determination to see it through, to fight and kill, and finally to win.

At 9.40 in the evening the onslaught began, with the largest artillery bombardment since the First World War. Nine hundred artillery guns fired at the axis lines for fifteen minutes, so that the ground was soon shaking with the sheer power of the attack. As the shells pounded Rommel's defenses the infantry advanced and were soon clearing the way for the armored divisions.

The battle would continue for fourteen days and nights, and although Rommel made his way back to North Africa to help stall the allied advance, by November 2ⁿᵈ he knew he was beaten.

Despite orders from Hitler to fight to the last, the Nazi commander started his retreat two days later. Thousands of his men had been killed, wounded or taken prisoner, and although a portion of Rommel's army had escaped to Sallum near the Egyptian border, allied troops would soon be arriving from the west, and the depleted axis forces would have to face the enemy on two fronts.

Back in Britain the news of Montgomery's victory at El Alamein was to be rejoiced across the nation and for the first time since the beginning of the war church bells rang out across the country to celebrate. No one was more relieved by the news than the Prime Minister, whose popularity had begun to suffer as the allies were defeated in battles from Dunkirk in France to Singapore in the Far East.

. . .

The news of Montgomery's victory came not a moment too soon, and while Rommel was beaten out of Egypt faith was restored in Churchill who was finally able to boast of an allied success. Speaking to the House of Commons in early November he announced *"this is not the end. It is not even the beginning of the end, but it is, perhaps, the end of the beginning."*

Churchill had no doubt that the Battle of El Alamein marked an important turning point in the Second World War and many years later he would write: *"Before Alamein we never had a victory, after Alamein we never had a defeat".*

The British finally had good reason to celebrate but many difficult battles still lay ahead and *Operation Torch,* the invasion of North Africa would prove to be a diplomatic minefield long before British and American troops had the opportunity to land in Algeria and Morocco.

For the campaign to succeed it was important to persuade the Vichy French forces in North Africa, to collaborate with the allies, and Roosevelt was concerned that British involvement in the invasion could jeopardize the entire campaign.

Although France and Great Britain had fought together in the First World War and were allied at the beginning of the Second World War, when Paris fell to the Nazis in 1940 the friendship between the two countries became strained to say the least.

The French government led by Paul Reynaud, had tried to escape the advancing Nazis after the French capital was invaded, relocating a number of times until reaching Bordeaux in South Western France; but some politicians urged for an end to hostilities, and despite Reynaud's objections, by June 22nd an armistice was signed between the French and Adolf Hitler. Reynaud resigned and was replaced by 84-year-old Marshal Petain who set up a new government in Vichy.

The Vichy regime was granted full diplomatic recognition by America, who hoped to use gentle persuasion to draw the Vichy French back to the allied side, but Great Britain took a different stance. The collaboration of the French with Nazi Germany presented many risks to the country and there were fears that the French fleet which was one of the most powerful in the world would soon be controlled by the Nazis.

The repercussions of this would be catastrophic for Great Britain, which was already struggling to survive as the Nazi U-Boats tightened their stranglehold on the Atlantic.

To recap Churchill who had been Prime Minister for less than two months ordered that the French Navy should either join forces with the British Royal Navy or be neutralized in some way to prevent the ships from falling into German or Italian hands.

There were already French vessels in British ports and these were swiftly boarded, but the most powerful concentration of French warships was at the port of Mers-el-Kebir in French Algeria and it was this squadron which was Churchill's greatest concern.

Despite assurances from Admiral Darlan, the Minister of the French Navy, that there was no danger of the Germans seizing the ships in North Africa, the British prime minister was determined to eliminate any possible risk to Britain's security. Churchill made one of the most controversial decisions of his career when he ordered that the French fleet be attacked unless it sailed from its base in Algeria to allied waters. After negotiations failed the British opened fire on July 3rd, 1940.

· · ·

There were many who condemned Churchill's decision and the Admiral who had been ordered to make the attack said that it was *"the biggest political blunder of modern times"*. But while politicians chastised the Prime Minister, the attack had proved to the world that the British would put up a fierce fight to the threat of the Nazis, no matter what the cost.

In 1942 however the events of the summer of 1940 posed a problem to the planned attack on Vichy French territory in North Africa. Roosevelt felt that the French would react better to American troops and suggested that all landing forces should be US troops or marines.

The British who were keen on encircling the remainder of Rommel's troops were not to be left out however and it was finally decided that while the attack on Casablanca in Morocco, and Oran in Algeria would be launched by purely American forces, a combination of British and American forces would invade Algiers.

The British troops in the meantime were instructed to sew the American flag to their uniforms in the hope that this would appease the French. President Roosevelt also made many other moves to ensure that the Vichy French forces, which far outnumbered the allied units, would collaborate with the invasion plans.

He wrote a personal letter to Marshal Petain, urging him to support the Allies; he even tried to win over the Arab population in North Africa by commissioning a proclamation stating that the American Holy warriors had arrived. *"Pray for our success in battle, and help us, and God will help us both."* was part of this unusual message, but it's unclear whether it had much impact on the local population.

· · ·

In the meantime, Roosevelt had sent a diplomat by the name of Robert Murphy to Algiers as his personal representative in North Africa.

Murphy had the task of contacting all potentially friendly political elements in Tunisia, Algeria and Morocco and was assigned the task of finding a French figurehead for the attack.

Murphy soon became convinced that General Henri Giraud, who had recently gained fame after escaping from a Nazi prison was the man for the job. Giraud had been held captive by the Nazis for two years and although he was a supporter of Vichy France, he refused to collaborate with the Germans; a fact that boded well for the allies.

The alternative for the French command in North Africa was General Charles de Gaulle who had been based in London since the Nazis had occupied France. De Gaulle was considered the leader of the Free French, but Roosevelt felt that if there was to be any hope of winning over Vichy French Commanders, Giraud would be the better alternative.

For the time being De Gaulle was to be kept in the dark concerning all operations, although he would later become an important presence in the allied effort against Germany. While the delicate political situation was negotiated hundreds of allied ships began heading towards North Africa. The central and eastern task forces left the British Isles to head for Algeria, while the western naval task force of 102 ships and over 24,000 American troops left the United States to cross the U-boat infested waters of the Atlantic.

Their destination was French Morocco and virtually all the men aboard were going into action for the first time. Just a few months earlier they had been working as clerks, lawyers, salesmen and garage mechanics but soon they would face the overwhelming demands of battle.

. . .

When the ships were several days out at sea they were briefed on where they would land and taught basic phrases of the language spoken there.

Instruction in French was supplemented with lessons in elementary Arabic and while some learned languages, infantrymen worked endlessly on preparing the weapons on which their lives might depend.

All 3 task forces involved in the invasion were proceeding with the utmost secrecy and although there were many concerns that U-Boats would attack, German command didn't appreciate the significance of the convoys, and the threat they posed to North Africa; in fact, some commanders believed that the ships were supply convoys heading for Malta.

But although the U-Boats failed to detect the allied threat, there were other dangers the invasion forces had to contend with. Stormy weather made for rough seas around the Atlantic coast near Casablanca, and it was decided that the Western task force should be diverted to Gibraltar, where the other ships were congregating.

The allied island base, which lay between Spain and North Africa was where General Eisenhower had his headquarters buried deep beneath the base of the Rock. But the ships preparing for the invasion weren't the only newcomers in Gibraltar; on the eve of the invasion General Giraud was smuggled to the base by submarine.

Giraud believed he would be commanding the invasion and there were moments of confusion while Eisenhower explained the mission through his interpreter.

. . .

Eventually Giraud agreed to be a spectator and would be ready to step in later as administrator of French North Africa.

By the early hours of November 8th, the ships had sailed to their positions in preparation for the three-pronged attack on North Africa and the landing forces were launched from their mother ships. The Eastern task force was split into three groups, two heading for beaches to the west of Algiers and one to the east. There was practically no French opposition here and some French generals even greeted the American forces.

In the meantime, five hundred American paratroopers had been flown in from the British Isles to aid the attack on Oran. Not all reached their targets south of the city however and the central attack force was left to deal with the opposition alone. After a naval engagement in Oran harbor the troops started ashore in the early morning of November 8th with one combat group landing to the east of the city and another to the west.

Their aim was to then converge and capture the city by a double envelopment. Some units faced resistance, but before long all fighting had ceased and the French surrendered to the allied troops.

The second part of the three-pronged attack had been successfully accomplished, but the third landing to the north and south of Casablanca would be a different story. A coup to overthrow the pro-Vichy commander in Casablanca had failed and French defenses were now in wait for the eastern task force. The Americans were fired on by elements of the French fleet and a fierce naval battle ensued off the coast of French Morocco.

| US M3 Lee tank crew standing by

Although four of the French ships were eventually sunk, in the meantime the troops landing ashore were encountering heavy opposition. But while the battling continued, there was a turn of events that would have a profound effect on the future of the north African campaign.

When the eastern Task force had entered Algiers, it had been discovered that the Vichy French commander, Admiral Darlan, was in the city on a private visit. With the opportunity to deal with a senior Vichy representative who had greater authority than Giraud, Eisenhower began negotiating with the Vichy

Commander and offered him the chance to stay in control of French forces if he joined the Allies.

Keeping the Vichy Commander would mean the Vichy regime, with its Nazi laws and concentration camps would be maintained and for many this was simply unacceptable.

De Gaulle who had now learned of events in North Africa was furious and General Giraud was not enthusiastic about working alongside Darlan.

As news of Eisenhower's collaboration with the Vichy commander spread overseas there was much confusion in America about where the loyalties of the allied commanders lay, and many were dismayed by the negotiations being made with Vichy France. But the fact remained that without the collaboration of Darlan and a permanent peace agreement between the allies and France, many more lives would be lost during the battle for North Africa.

Hundreds of French planes and pilots stood poised for an attack on the allied troops now moving towards Tunisia, and it was vital that Darlan's cooperation was obtained so that the rest of the campaign could succeed.

Finally, on November 10th after coming to an agreement with Eisenhower, Darlan ordered a ceasefire and the French troops laid down their arms.

The fighting ended in Casablanca, and allied forces could now continue their march towards Tunis; but the consequences for Darlan would be grave.

Marshal Petain immediately ordered his dismissal from the French navy and

Hitler, furious with the news that Darlan had collaborated with the allies, ordered troops to march into unoccupied France on November 11th.

However, the Nazi leaders' invasion of Vichy France only hardened the resolve of the French to support the allies, and their troops soon joined the British and American units heading for Tunisia. While the allied tanks rolled further east, 1,200 miles away the Eighth Army were making swift progress from the opposite direction having driven the axis out of Egypt.

Montgomery's troops continued to seize strategic ports along the Libyan coastline, and it was hoped that Rommel and his troops would soon be encircled by the two allied armies. As the battle for North Africa continued Adolf Hitler feared that southern Europe would soon be under threat and he ordered thousands of troops and tanks to be sent to Tunisia, to fight back the allied attack.

Meanwhile General Kenneth Anderson from Great Britain was leading the allied race for Tunis with the First Army. His troops were made up of American and British soldiers from the eastern attack force as well as French soldiers and their aim was to reach the Tunisian capital before axis reinforcements arrived.

By November 22nd Anderson's troops were ready to launch a major assault on Tunis, but the weather began to hinder their advance.

Within a week torrential December rains had transformed the arid landscape into a quagmire and the allies faced a slow and difficult struggle across the unstable terrain.

While mud now became as much of an enemy to the First Army as the troops of the axis, the allies arrived too late to seize Tunis. Nazi reinforcements had already consolidated their positions and began launching their counterattack, and it was clear that the fight for North Africa was not going to be as swift as initially hoped.

The inexperienced American soldiers would face a difficult fight before they could seize Tunisia but while the eighth army made steady progress from the east, General Eisenhower was convinced that the Axis, would soon lose their foothold in the area.

Back in Great Britain Winston Churchill was jubilant and celebrated the events of the past month in a speech to the British population. The invasion of North Africa had achieved what the allied leaders had hoped for, and while combat continued, some of the pressure was now taken off the Soviet soldiers, battling around Stalingrad.

In early November, Hitler had boasted that *"Stalingrad is in our hands"*, but while attention was focused on events in North Africa he seemed unaware that the Russian General Georgy Zhukov had begun amassing an enormous force to the north of the city in preparation for a crushing counter attack. By November 16th the first snows of winter had swept across the Russian battle-fields and fate was on the side of the Soviet soldiers.

The Volga River became a frozen bridge and the troops of the Red Army could now cross over into the battle zone. Within days they were ready for their dramatic counterattack and Russian artillery opened a gigantic enveloping maneuver with one army to the north of the Germans and another to the south.

Half a million Russian soldiers and 15,000 tanks advanced in vast columns while across the steppes a band of 50,000 Cossacks stormed across the winter landscape.

Under the onslaught the German line began to bend, and then the Russians made a breach, smashing through the 6th Rumanian corps on November 20th. Zhukov's aim was for the two Russian forces to meet far southwest of Stalingrad in order to encircle the entire German 6th army and to cut its supply lines.

Within four days he had achieved his goal as the two spearheads of the Russian pincer movement met 100km west of Stalingrad: 250,000 German troops were now trapped inside the city. To prevent the sixth army from breaking the encirclement the Russians began creating a corridor to a width of over 100 miles, which would separate the army from the rest of the German military; hundreds of tanks were soon moved into the area along with 60 divisions of soviet troops.

But instead of urging the Sixth Army to escape while they still could, Adolf Hitler ordered their commander, General Friedrich Paulus, to remain in position and to hold the city at all costs. On November 23rd Hitler declared that Stalingrad was a fortress to be defended to the last.

Herman Goering, Hitler's deputy and head of the Luftwaffe, had assured the Nazi leader that his planes could drop supplies to the sixth army, but, providing for such a vast number of troops was beyond the capabilities of the German air force.

Appalling weather conditions, technical failures and soviet anti-aircraft fire all limited the abilities of the Luftwaffe and while all attempts were made to get supplies to the soldiers in Stalingrad, before long those trapped inside the city began to run out of fuel, ammunition and most importantly, food. As soviet forces consolidated their positions around Stalingrad, battling to shrink the pocket of axis soldiers, the situation for the thousands of Germans within became desperate.

It was increasingly evident that the Luftwaffe could not carry out their mission to supply the sixth army and plans were made for a rescue attempt. The operation, code-named *Operation Winter Storm* aimed to break through the encirclement and relieve the trapped German forces. On December 12th the German fourth panzer army under the command of General von Manstein began their relief effort and initially took the Red Army by surprise.

They made large gains on the first day and the spearhead forces successfully defeated the soviet counter attacks, but by December 13th the advance had slowed considerably and three days later the Russians launched their second offensive.

As resistance and casualties increased, Manstein appealed to Hitler and to General Paulus to begin the Sixth Army's breakout operation but both refused.

The decision would prove fatal for the hundreds of thousands of men still inside Stalingrad.

Although the Fourth Panzer Army continued to attempt to open a corridor to the Sixth Army between December the 18th and 19th, two days before Christmas Manstein was forced to call off the assault. By Christmas Eve the Fourth Panzer Army began to withdraw to its starting position and the Sixth army were left to their bitter fate.

The final stages of Nazi Germany's attempt to conquer the Soviet Union had failed, and by January the soldiers still left alive in Stalingrad would have no option but to surrender to the enemy.

Around the world the armies of the axis were fighting desperate battles and it would only be a matter of time before the allies achieved their final victory. But while many had real cause to celebrate during the Christmas of 1942, the allied commanders, had little time to pause in their continued drive to defeat the enemy.

The fight for Tunisia would continue far into the New Year and it would be spring before the allies could claim their prize and march into Tunis; and after Tunis there would still be another two years of fighting before the Nazis surrendered.

Meanwhile in the Pacific the struggle to vanquish the Japanese would be long and bitter, as the Americans fought some of the bloodiest battles of the war to wrench one island after another from their control.

Although the tides of war had turned there were still countless battles to be fought across the globe, and the fight for victory was far from over.

14

FACING THE MUSIC

January – March 1943

Guadalcanal patrol river crossing

As the Second World War entered its fourth year, it had become a confrontation that was truly global. By 1943, more and more nations had been drawn into the conflict as they aligned themselves either with the Allies or with the Axis powers or were held powerless under military occupation. By invading the Soviet Union, Adolf Hitler had taken on a formidable enemy. In the bitter cold of a Russian winter, amid the ruins of a city that had suffered through too many long months, German forces would make a humiliating surrender and many thousands would trudge away as Soviet prisoners of war.

The loss of Stalingrad proved a turning point, as the Red Army was emboldened to begin a new push against the German occupiers, reclaiming their vast nation piece by piece. Ordinary Germans were increasingly aware of the weighty advantage that the Americans were bringing into play for the Allied war effort.

American Air Force bombers joined the RAF in bold raids on ports, industrial centers and larger cities, sending a message of defiance and determination to Hitler and his generals, and also seeking to further undermine waning public confidence in the Führer's leadership.

In 1943, there was also room for optimism in the Pacific War against Japan. For young US marines, the South Sea Island of Guadalcanal was synonymous with anything but a tropical paradise. It had come to mean nights broken by screaming bombs and artillery fire, savage fighting in the sodden jungle, marines diving for cover into foxholes as Japanese planes strafed the landscape, while the Americans below battled malaria and dysentery as well as dodging sniper fire. But Japan's once tenacious hold on Guadalcanal was slowly but surely being loosened, and victory came sooner than the American and Australian commanders had dared to hope.

Across Southeast Asia, Japanese militarism was still holding diverse nations and populations under its harsh rule, belying Japan's promises that it would lead Asian nations into a bright new future. The Second World War posed a real dilemma to anti-colonial nationalists in the region; should they believe in Japan's promises, or throw their lot in with the Allies?

However, the often-barbaric treatment of local populations by their new Japanese overlords helped settle the matter, and colonialism definitely seemed the lesser of two evils. What's more America's President Roosevelt was carefully building a relationship of cooperation with China, a nation at war with Japan since 1937. The Chinese were firmly on the side of an Allied victory, despite reservations about cooperating with the west.

. . .

Also, in North Africa the Allies received a favorable reception from the indigenous population. They watched as largely mute observers as the tides of war ebbed and flowed across their lands. A clash between European Titans was being acted out, that thankfully was largely fought in the barren deserts beyond their cities.

For the Allies, success in the sands and rocky hills of North Africa gave hope that an end to Hitler's brand of National Socialism and its evil ideology of racial purity was now in sight.

As 1943 began, the US and British troops that had made surprise landings along the coasts of Morocco and Algeria at the onset of winter were still attempting to push eastwards, hoping to link up eventually with the forces under British Field Marshal Bernard Montgomery. Montgomery's Eighth Army was advancing along the Mediterranean coast from the other direction, hot on the heels of the retreating Germans led by Field Marshal Erwin Rommel, Hitler's Desert Fox. Montgomery's hard-won victory over Rommel's forces on the desert battlefield at El Alamein, in Libya, had been a huge boost to British morale.

Nonetheless, the Allied breakthrough at El Alamein had prompted Hitler to give greater strategic importance to North Africa. Along with his Italian ally, Benito Mussolini, Hitler had sent more men and equipment into the region by sea and air from Sicily. Also, Allied successes in North Africa had prompted Hitler to order the direct occupation of the south-eastern part of France, which until this point had been administered by the pro-Nazi French government based in the town of Vichy.

All France was now directly under the iron hand of the Nazis, and most of the rest of Europe was either under direct Nazi rule, or was ruled by governments that had fallen into line with Hitler. And the Führer's plans for a new order based on ideas of racial supremacy were escalating.

The focus of Hitler's hatred was Europe's Jews, and in the previous nine months, five death camps in Nazi-occupied Poland had started their murderous operations.

In America, meanwhile, public opinion remained united behind President Roosevelt in support of the war against Germany and the Axis powers, including, of course, Japan. The devastating Japanese attack on Pearl was not something that would be easily forgotten, or ever forgiven.

The Japanese were seeking to eliminate US naval power in the central Pacific in order to secure access to the oil fields of the Dutch East Indies, as modern-day Indonesia was then known, as well as other resource-rich territories to the south. A resurgent Japan had aligned itself with the Nazi drive for supremacy in Europe, while in Asia, the Japanese government considered that they were the only nation with the industrial and military might to end centuries of western dominance.

By January 1943, Japan had already wrested control of the Philippines from the American and Filipino defending forces. The Japanese had also taken Hong Kong, Malaya and Singapore from the British, and Indonesia from the Dutch. In Burma, bordering India, where agitation for independence from Britain was growing, Japanese forces had marched in, facing little opposition. But for months American and Australian troops had been battling with the Japanese by land and sea in the Solomon Islands, north of Papua New Guinea.

Eventually the Japanese military commanders decided to cut their losses and evacuate what was left of their forces from the key Solomon Island of Guadalcanal. As the Japanese head of state, the Emperor Hirohito, gave his formal approval for the retreat, the Allies were given hope that perhaps the string of Japanese victories in Southeast Asia might be coming to an end.

And on the other side of the world, amid the snows of a Russian winter, the Germans were also meeting tough opposition as Soviet and Nazi troops were locked in a war of attrition. The momentous confrontation between Hitler's Germany and the Soviet Union, which had started when the Nazis had marched across the border from occupied Poland a year and a half earlier, was by January 1943 entering its final, tragic act.

Hitler had expected the Communist regime of Joseph Stalin to crumble from within, but this eastern Front had proved an ever more perilous drain on the human and military resources of the Third Reich. The Germans had discovered to their cost just how determined the Red Army was to resist them. Now a second harsh Russian winter was sapping the morale of the cold and exhausted German soldiers, and nowhere more so than at the city of Stalingrad, on the mighty Volga river.

Stalingrad, today known as Volgograd, lies a full 600 miles south of Moscow, but its position allowed it to control the shipping of supplies by river to the north of the Soviet Union. The factories of its industrial zone had continued to produce tractors and armaments despite war and invasion. And beyond the city to the south lay the oil-rich Caucasus region, which the Soviets considered a vital part of their empire.

For all these reasons, the city of Stalingrad had attracted Hitler's attention, and the previous summer it had endured a massive bombardment from the Luftwaffe while the German Sixth Army attempted to encircle it by land. As the city was reduced to rubble, the death toll mounted into the tens and then hundreds of thousands.

· · ·

Russians, both civilians and military personnel alike, bore by far the heaviest burden of casualties. But then in November 1942 a counter-offensive by the Red Army had trapped the German forces, along with some contingents from Rumania and Italy, in a pocket of land on the west bank of the river and had prevented German reinforcements from breaking through.

Supplies were dwindling fast and typhus was spreading among the German troops and the other national contingents fighting alongside them. Just nine days into the New Year of 1943, as the winter drifts still lay thick outside the city, a Russian captain appeared before German lines with a white flag. He was offering General Friedrich Paulus, commander of the German Sixth Army, the opportunity to make an *"honorable surrender"*.

Paulus was an experienced strategist, having begun his military career before the First World War, who was doing his best to carry out the Führer's orders to hold Stalingrad at all costs. However, there was little he could do, and Paulus and his men realized that they would be expected to fight to the death. After the Germans had held out for as long as they could, on the evening of the last day of January, the Red Army battered its way into the city, forcing Paulus to retreat into a former department store.

But the Russians soon captured him in the basement of the building, lying fully dressed on his camp bed. He and his men had no more fight left in them. To all intents and purposes the nightmare that had been the battle for Stalingrad was over.

Elsewhere the signs were equally ominous for the German invaders. On January 18th their blockade around Russia's second most important city, Leningrad, modern-day St Petersburg, had been broken. The Russians freed up a narrow corridor of land through which more supplies could at least be brought in for the city's famished and disease-ridden population, and more civilians could be evacuated to safety.

. . .

Stalin had for some time been pressing the United States and Britain to open a front in Western Europe to take some of the pressure off the Soviet Union. Although a second front in Europe was not yet possible, Allied progress in North Africa had already diverted some of the Axis military resources away from Russia. As Allied forces in North Africa took a time-out, bogged down by the winter rains, on the highest political level moves were afoot to agree upon what should be done next.

As the fighting in Stalingrad was entering its last desperate phase, two men were booked into the Anfa Hotel in Casablanca, Morocco's main seaport, under the false names of "Admiral Q" and "Mr. P". Hotel staff were astounded to see that the two were in fact America's President Roosevelt, who had flown in via West Africa, and Prime Minister Winston Churchill, who arrived from London in a converted bomber.

Stalin had been invited to join them but had sent a message saying he could not leave his country at such a crucial moment, however he made sure he reminded the two leaders that they had promised to open a second front in Europe that spring.

Morocco was a French protectorate previously controlled by commanders loyal to France's Vichy government. It now represented a secure meeting place for the two leaders, as after the Allies had arrived, senior French commander Admiral Darlan had renounced his loyalty to Vichy and formally ceded to the United States the right to oversee all ports, transport and troop movements.

When Darlan was assassinated by a dissident Frenchman just weeks later, his place as administrator of North Africa had been taken by another former Vichy supporter General Henri Giraud. He had been groomed for this role by the Americans, much to the displeasure of another French General, Charles de

Gaulle. He'd opposed Nazism and the Vichy government from the start, and as commander of the Free French forces based in London had become a symbol of French resistance.

| The Casablanca Conference - FDR & Churchill seated

The two French generals were also persuaded to attend the nine days of talks at the Anfa Hotel, that would go down in history as the Casablanca Conference, where they were obliged to keep their hostility within diplomatic bounds. Between Roosevelt and Churchill, relations were far easier as it was the fourth time that the two leaders had met since the war began. As the Casablanca Conference ended, Roosevelt told the press that he and Churchill had agreed that the war would continue until the Allies secured an *"uncondi-tional surrender"*.

There would be no deals with the enemy and those responsible for atrocities would-be put-on trial. In fact, the Allies had decided on this policy before Casablanca.

There was criticism in the US and Britain over the policy of working in North Africa with former Vichy commanders, who had previously collaborated with the Nazis. Roosevelt and Churchill therefore needed to re-emphasize that their goal was the total defeat of Nazism and all its grotesque ideology.

And as a signal to Stalin, Roosevelt also told the listening reporters that he wanted to pay tribute to the "enormous weight of the war" that Russia was bearing. However, some of the most important decisions taken at Casablanca had inevitably to be kept out of the public arena. The first was the decision that the second front to be opened against Nazi Germany in Europe would initially be via Sicily or Sardinia and onto mainland Italy, rather than through northwestern France.

It had also been decided that an invasion across the English Channel would not be possible in 1943. There were as yet not enough American troops in England, nor sufficient boats ready for there to be a major landing in France. Nevertheless, serious planning for this invasion to take place in 1944 began. Another unpubli-cized outcome of the meeting at Casablanca was an agreement that bombing raids over Germany by American and British bombers would aim to draw German fighting power away from the Russian and Mediterranean theatres of war.

The bombing would also be targeted to destroy Germany's military and indus-trial infrastructure, and in the words of the agreement *"undermine the morale of the German people to a point where their capacity for armed resistance is fatally weakened".*

As for the two French generals, they reached their own resolution at the conference, agreeing to share authority in French North Africa, which they hoped, from now on, would remain under Allied control. Even so North Africa was proving far from accommodating for the newly landed Allies, and the road through Tunisia to link up with Montgomery's men was challenging to say the least.

They had crossed the border into Tunisia weeks earlier but had been held in check by German units and winter rains, which had made the roads impassable.

In the capital, Tunis, which lay so temptingly close to the Italian island of Sicily, the Germans and Italians had been building up a new military presence, redeploying transport planes from the eastern Front. The French commander in Tunis remained loyal to Vichy and was allowing the Germans to use Tunisian airfields for this airlift.

While the Italian navy struggled with a shortage of oil, the Allies suffered from a lack of enough ships to transport their troops down across the Mediterranean, even with civilian craft such as cruise liners pressed into service.

After the Battle of El Alamein, Rommel would never again be able to hold a firm front against Montgomery and his men, who included South Africans, Indians, New Zealanders and others alongside British soldiers. At first light on January 23rd, a British tank with seven Gordon Highlanders clinging to it rumbled into the deserted Libyan capital of Tripoli, after coming along an empty but heavily mined coast road, where every bridge had been demolished by the retreating Axis forces.

The Allied tanks that followed found that Hitler's Desert Fox and his men had already retreated, and Montgomery was able to accept the surrender of the city from its Italian mayor, who donned his full regalia for the occasion. The capture of Tripoli meant Rommel, now falling back towards Tunisia, had lost his main supply base, and the Italians had lost the last part of their African empire.

However, although the Nazis were losing their stranglehold on North Africa, they were still dominant throughout Europe, and there was no stopping their reign of terror in the nations they occupied.

By early 1943, five death camps were in operation in occupied Poland. Unlike the concentration camps, where the Nazis imprisoned a range of political and religious opponents and people, they judged socially deviant, the death camps were expressly built for the purpose of carrying out killing on an industrial scale. Victims of the death camps included Poles, Hungarians and Soviet prisoners of war, but it was the Jews, often transported there from all over Europe, who were the main target.

Presiding over this genocide was Heinrich Himmler, one of the most powerful of Hitler's henchmen. Himmler's SS operated police and military units alongside the regular German army, and its members were recruited for their ideological commitment to Nazism, and their supposed racial purity. The SS was a prototype of the master race that Hitler dreamt of.

In Poland, the capital Warsaw had been home to the majority of the country's Jews. More than two years previously the Germans had forced all Warsaw Jews to move into a designated walled area, known as the ghetto. All movement in and out was controlled by armed guards, effectively cutting the Jews off from the outside world, where in overcrowded conditions typhus and tuberculosis spread like wildfire and malnutrition was rife.

Some 330,000 Jews had by 1943 already been deported from the Warsaw Ghetto, but about 60,000 remained. So, it came as a shock for the German guards when in mid-January a small rebellion broke out, a precursor to the more famous uprising. For the first time the Jews held in the Warsaw Ghetto, which had become in effect a waiting room for the death camps, had attempted to strike back and it gave the Nazis a taste of what lay ahead.

Back in Germany, ordinary people going about their everyday lives were also beginning to feel disillusioned with Hitler and the Nazi regime, particularly as by the end of the month both the American air force and the RAF had been bombing major targets, including Berlin. On January 16th the RAF had returned to Berlin after 14 months away. The city was hit by 8,000 sizable bombs and thousands of smaller incendiaries and the intensive bombing continued for a second night.

Ten days later, American bombers made their first raids on the German home-land, in a daylight raid on the Wilhelmshaven naval base, on the North Sea west of Hamburg. Next Hamburg itself came under fire and on Saturday January 30th the RAF marked Nazi Germany's 10th anniversary with two daytime bombing raids over the country.

The second, in the afternoon, was timed to spoil a radio broadcast of a celebratory speech by Hitler's propaganda minister Josef Goebbels. Whatever doubts the people of Germany might be having, and any questions asked by Hitler's closest associates about his state of mind, Goebbels was the most constantly loyal of them all.

. . .

And never had the eloquent skills of Josef Goebbels been more in demand, particularly as news of Germany losing the Battle of Stalingrad started to filter through. Stalingrad was the Nazis' first large-scale military defeat, and there would be no hiding the scale of the losses from the already disheartened German public. On February 2nd the last Axis units in the Russian city's industrialized zone finally followed General Paulus' example and laid down their arms. The tally of casualties at Stalingrad speaks for itself.

On the Axis side, at least 120,000 men had died while 91,000 soldiers, including 24 Nazi generals, had been taken as prisoners-of-war. Only about 5,000 of these prisoners would ever make it home; more than a quarter perished in the immediate days after their capture, weakened by disease, malnutrition and lack of medical care. On the Russian side, the civilian population of Stalingrad had been decimated, while the Red Army's casualties were even higher than the Germans.

Some estimate that up to a quarter of a million Russian troops had been killed, captured or wounded in the city.

In his field headquarters at Rastenburg in East Prussia, Hitler berated his generals. The crushing defeat at Stalingrad had heightened his distrust of his senior officer corps, many of whom had been career soldiers long before they were Nazis.

And Hitler's unease was well-founded, not least because after Stalingrad, General Paulus became one of the leaders of a Soviet-sponsored League of German Officers, making radio broadcasts in which he urged his fellow officers to overthrow Hitler.

. . .

In Berlin, Goebbels addressed a mass rally in a rousing speech broadcast across Germany by radio. The audience that packed the stadium had been carefully selected, and roared approval as Goebbels urged the German nation to redouble its efforts against what he described as the Bolshevist threat from the east.

Only now, after Stalingrad, was the full scale of this threat understood, he said, but the German people would follow Hitler *"through thick and thin"*, as he put it. *"Do you want total war?"* he bellowed. *"If necessary, do you want a war more total and radical than anything we can yet imagine?"* The audience rose to its feet chanting their support.

But approval for Hitler was fading. Shoppers in Munich city center were stunned to see anti-Nazi graffiti on the walls, and at the city's university, students even dared to protest, chanting *"Down with Hitler"*.

An underground student group, the White Rose, had been circulating anti-Nazi letters in several cities for some months.

The White Rose students were non-violent. Some had seen service on the eastern front, and one of them had witnessed the treatment of Polish Jews in the Warsaw ghetto by the German oppressors and could not get the images out of his mind. *"Isn't it true that every German is ashamed of his government these days?"* the first letter read.

"Who can imagine the degree of shame… when the awful crimes that infinitely exceed any human measure are exposed to the light of day."

Not surprisingly the Nazis quickly crushed the movement before it could grow into something more dangerous. The Gestapo secret police were tipped off, and the two ringleaders, Hans Scholl, a 25-year-old medical student, and his sister Sophie, a biology student aged just 21, were executed in late February along with a third student. Three more White Rose activists would share their fate before the year was out, paying the highest price for voicing what many in Germany were by now thinking.

While defeat at Stalingrad had dealt a mighty blow to the prestige of the German military in Europe, in the Pacific the image of the Japanese army as an unbeatable, efficient military machine was also beginning to crumble. The Allies had chosen the little-known string of Solomon Islands in the South Pacific, as a starting point for their fight back against Japan.

When the Japanese occupied some of the larger islands, American and Australian troops made their own landings on one of them; Guadalcanal.

The island had an airfield under construction, and if the Japanese could seize control and get it operational, they would most certainly be able to threaten supply routes between the US, Australia and New Zealand. Throughout the autumn and winter of 1942, the Japanese put up a fierce fight, by land, sea and air, while islanders sympathetic to the Allies kept a lookout for the movements of the Japanese military.

Early in 1943, American troops were advancing along the north of Guadalcanal. The airfield was already in US hands, but they feared a renewed Japanese offensive.

Little did they suspect that the Japanese commanders had already received their Emperor's blessing for a withdrawal, and the naval maneuvers were actually in preparation for an evacuation of thousands of Japanese troops. By the end of the first week of February, more than 10,000 Japanese soldiers had been taken off the island, before the Allies even realized that the battle for Guadalcanal was over.

From this point on, Guadalcanal would be a major Allied base, with new runways and a port. It had cost American lives of 1,700 soldiers and 5,000 were wounded, but the eventual goal, the re-taking of the Philippines, no longer looked quite such an impossible task. What's more American shipyards were working at full steam, producing warships that the Japanese could not hope to match.

Guadalcanal Japanese casualties

For Japan the loss of 860 aircraft and 15 warships with their highly trained crews was going to be a major issue.

. . .

The defeat led the Japanese military to carry out a major reappraisal of their strategy, as they resolved to hold onto central New Guinea, and take a defensive stance along the southern perimeter of their area of control.

Despite the setback at Guadalcanal, Japan's determination to present itself as the leader of a newly awakened Asia had the potential to seriously undermine the Allied war effort. Nowhere was this more so than in India, once considered the jewel in the crown of the British Empire, where the British army had traditionally been supplied with large numbers of Indian recruits. But the battle for an independent India was already gathering pace.

By 1943 the Indian nationalist leader Mahatma Gandhi had been detained because he had declared that India should be granted immediate independence if it was to carry on supporting the Allied war effort. Consequently, there had been mass arrests of Gandhi's supporters, while police released a barrage of lethal gunfire against unarmed demonstrators.

In eastern India, the local population was no longer in awe of their British overlords, having seen their humiliating retreat from Burma the previous year, and had resorted to sabotaging railways and telegraph lines. The loss of Burma had at a stroke deprived India of 15 per cent of its supply of rice, the staple upon which India's poor so depended. Therefore, the British quickly realized that it was vital to regain control of Burma to quell the rebellions in India, as well as to defeat the Japanese.

With Japan controlling much of China's eastern seaboard, the famous Burma Road had been the main route for getting supplies to Chinese nationalist forces deep in the country's interior.

. . .

But with this road now closed by the Japanese, the Allies needed to open another route to make sure that supplies to China could be maintained.

America's President Roosevelt believed firmly that China's assistance was vital in the battle against the Japanese, and had persuaded the Chinese leader, Chiang Kai-shek, to accept American Lieutenant General Joe Stilwell as his military advisor, with the title of commander in chief. At a meeting in New Delhi on February 7th, Chiang Kai-shek agreed to provide manpower to help re-conquer Burma in exchange for US aid.

Stilwell was already supervising the building of a new road from Ledo in India to link up with the final stretch of the Burma Road.

Work on this ambitious feat of engineering was making slow progress through early 1943, drawing on the labor of some 15,000 US soldiers, most of them African Americans, and 35,000 Indians.

Tropical diseases took their toll, hundreds of US soldiers died during the construction of the Ledo Road, as well as many of the local people who were also involved. US air force commanders thought the road would never be as effective as the hazardous airdrops of supplies they were organizing across the mountains to the Chinese, and over time, unfortunately, they would be proved right.

| A group of the Chindits pose for a picture

A British land offensive against the Japanese on Burma's western Arakan coast, on the Bay of Bengal, was making similarly slow progress. The British and Indian soldiers were finding that their Japanese enemies were well trained and battle-hardened. This first Arakan campaign did at least benefit from ground-breaking research that had been done to find a drug effective in protecting troops against malaria.

As February progressed, the British desperately needed a morale boost, and success in Burma would certainly deliver it. With perfect timing a Special Forces Unit that had been training across the border in India found themselves in the media spotlight.

· · ·

Plans were in place for them to get behind Japanese lines in Burma, and generally disrupt enemy supplies by destroying transport systems wherever possible, and their British commander told newspaper reporters that this special force would be called the "Chindits", after a mythical Burmese lion.

Numbering some 3,000 men, the Chindits crossed the border from India deep into Burma but found the terrain much more difficult than expected. The forces did succeed in blowing up a number of bridges, and clashed with Japanese infantry divisions, but by the end of March received orders to return to India. Nevertheless, despite only actually managing to take out Japanese railway communications for less than a week, the story of the Chindits was given plenty of media coverage, and it certainly improved British morale in India and back at home. Evidently it would be possible, with better planning, to actually undermine the Japanese in jungle warfare.

As 1943 progressed the Allies certainly found themselves needing to adapt their military strategy to fit a variety of inhospitable terrains. The Burmese jungle without doubt called for guerrilla tactics, but the wide horizons of North Africa provided the stage for more classic military strategies.

The American General Dwight D. Eisenhower was now given overall authority for the Allied military effort in the whole Mediterranean region, with Britain's General Bernard Montgomery reporting directly to him.

Eisenhower was an unusual military commander in that he had never seen action himself, but with his consummate skill and experience of mediation and diplomacy, he had secured the respect of all the frontline commanders, which was in point of fact quite a remarkable achievement. Nevertheless, Eisenhower had a difficult time ahead of him, and he would need total cooperation from all those he commanded.

· · ·

On February 12th in driving rain, the Allies' 7th armored division crossed the border from Libya into Tunisia. All Libya was now in Allied hands, and Montgomery was able to oversee the unloading of fresh equipment and supplies at the newly cleared harbor in Tripoli. Worryingly, some 17,000 Italian and German forces were now in place in Tunis, and it was imperative to stop Rommel linking up with them.

In mid-February, Rommel drove westwards to head off the Allied forces who had their main supply base in the Algerian town of Tebessa, just over the border from Tunisia. But the road to Tebessa wound along a narrow mountain track known as the Kasserine Pass. This was the setting for the first large-scale meeting of American and German forces in World War II, and the untested US troops suffered heavy casualties.

The Americans' light guns and tanks stood little chance against the heavier German equipment, but within days the Allies had regained control of the pass, thanks to the use of strategically accurate airpower. At last it seemed that time was running out for Hitler's Desert Fox, and back in Britain anything that improved morale was very much appreciated.

In March 1943, the British public was still bearing up under the austerity and the uncertainties of wartime life. So far, civilian casualties in Britain outnumbered those lost in the ranks of the nation's armed forces, but the relentless nightly German bombing of the London blitz was long past. Many of those who had left the capital for safety had returned, and everyone was "making do" the best that they could, amidst all the rationing and shortages.

Government information campaigns had managed to convince the public that rationing was something to be tolerated with good humor, and more and more people were realizing that the best way to have a ready supply of fresh food was to keep chickens and cultivate a patch of ground on the local allotment or in their garden if they had one.

. . .

Ironically the deprivations of war did have one positive side effect in Britain, doing away with the mass unemployment of the interwar years as soaring government spending covered the costs of keeping Great Britain on an even keel.

Lessons were being learned daily as Britain pulled together in order to survive, and proposals were made that after the war a new system should be introduced, that we now know as National Insurance, to provide a minimum standard of living for everyone. Also a National Health Service would be necessary that would offer health care for all, rather than doctors only being available to those who could pay.

The Beveridge Report, which detailed the proposals proved an unlikely best seller and a shortened version was printed for distribution amongst the armed services.

From the cradle to the grave, a new age beckoned, and as people looked forward to the day when World War II would come to an end, one thing was for certain, life would never be the same again.

Keeping morale high both on the home and battle fronts was of vital importance, and although Wartime propaganda is more generally associated with Hitler and his Nazi ideologies, Winston Churchill also kept a watchful eye on what the British press put into print.

A prime example was an event of March 2nd as panic swept through a London underground station being used as an air raid shelter at Bethnal Green, resulting in the deaths of 173 people. Asphyxiated when the only single station exit open became jammed by people thinking the station was being bombed; it was the largest loss of civilian life in a single incident during the war. Many were women and children, and ironically that night the German bombs they had rushed to escape from killed no one. East Enders could not understand why the disaster got so little coverage in the newspapers, but there was in fact a very good reason for the media's silence.

Winston Churchill had decided that to give the story prominence might well damage morale, and worse still, give valuable ammunition to the German propaganda machine, something he was determined should not happen so he issued orders for the news be suppressed.

However, by the spring of 1943, awareness of what was happening to European Jews in areas falling under Nazi control was growing, making the Allies more determined than ever that Hitler had to be defeated, and fast.

On March 23rd Himmler was informed that in the region of one and a half million European Jews had been killed since the outbreak of the war. On that very same day, by pure coincidence, the Archbishop of Canterbury stood up in the House of Lords in London and pleaded with the British government to help the Jews of Europe. *"We at this moment have upon us a tremendous responsibility,"* he said. *"We stand at the bar of history, of humanity and of God."*

The British authorities had known what was going on in the Concentration Camps for some time, thanks to the code-breaking activities at Bletchley Park in Buckinghamshire, which monitored all Nazi communications. Reports also reached them from the Polish underground movement, and the World Jewish Congress in Geneva was doing its best to alert the British government to what was really going on.

Ironically some civil servants and British politicians dismissed the stories as propaganda, while others were concerned about the possibility of what they called a flood of *"alien immigrants"*.

Winston Churchill firmly believed that the best way to help those being treated so appallingly in Concentration Camps was to press ahead with single-minded determination and defeat Nazi Germany. News from North Africa was extremely positive, and by March Montgomery had built up a considerable position of strength.

He had 400 tanks while Rommel only had 160, and the Allies were also superior in the skies, having built new airfields in North Africa, which meant they were no longer reliant on their base in Malta.

The time had come for the Allies to consider an invasion of Italy, and a bombing raid on Sicily left Hitler in no doubt as to what was being planned. The Führer summoned Rommel from North Africa to discuss what was to be done, and at a meeting in the Ukraine, the Desert Fox begged Hitler to allow the evacuation of Axis troops to Italy, where they could be re-equipped.

But neither Hitler nor Mussolini were willing to countenance such an obvious retreat, while Rommel began to tire of the false optimism and failure of the two leaders to be realistic.

Meanwhile back in North Africa Montgomery was making further advances towards an Allied victory in Tunisia. Before the outbreak of WWII, the French, in their occupation of the North, had built a line of fortifications in southern Tunisia. After losing extensive ground in North Africa to the Allies in *Operation Torch* back in the autumn of 1942, the Axis powers had managed to hold onto what was known as the Mareth Line, and using minefields, anti-tank ditches, barbed wire and carefully concealed artillery positions, the Germans and Italians had created a defensive stronghold. But Montgomery's star was most definitely in the ascendancy and by the end of March he had managed to break through the Mareth Line and it literally was only a matter of weeks before the Allies would gain control of Tunisia.

One step closer to a total victory in North Africa, the Allies were already preparing for the invasion of Sicily, and ironically Rommel was destined never to return to Africa again.

For the rest of the war he would be prominent in Hitler's European operations, but even his great military skill and experience would be no match for the Allies, who were daily gaining ground.

The tide really was turning, and even the most downtrodden of Hitler's victims were beginning to feel a sense of hope. In Poland, unbeknown to the Nazis, a major uprising was being planned in Warsaw's Jewish Ghetto, as the resilience of the human spirit shone through the dark and desperate gloom.

As the opening of a new front looked increasingly possible in southern Europe as the German and Italian forces were slowly but surely losing their foothold in Tunisia, Churchill's determination to push towards a speedy victory was gathering momentum. And better news still was coming from the Pacific theatre of war as the Allies were at last beginning to gain the upper hand, as the Japanese were forced to face the prospect that their Imperial Army might not be quite as invincible as they had at first believed.

RESISTANCE IS NEVER FUTILE

April – June 1943

Old town Warsaw

W hen considering the history of World War II, 1943 is of vital importance. Many strategies being implemented by the Allies were starting to come to fruition as gradually Adolf Hitler and the Axis powers' stranglehold in both the European and Pacific Theaters of war were slowly but surely being loosened. The Germans and the Italians faced humiliating defeat on the northern shores of Africa, as the Allied armies, under America's General Eisenhower, forced them to abandon the continent altogether.

The battle for North Africa had already helped draw some of Hitler's military resources away from the eastern Front, where his forces had taken on Russia's Red Army, as all the while the Allies would keep the pressure up on Germany itself, with heavy bombing of the nation's major industrial cities.

At sea, the British in the Atlantic and the Americans in the Pacific would begin to gain the upper hand over enemy submarines, as Allied planes and submarines coming off the production line were equipped with the latest technology, and increasing use was made of patrol planes and light aircraft carriers. The liberation of Europe would never be able to go ahead until the Battle of the Atlantic had been won; for some, an Allied victory could not come soon enough.

The horrific Nazi genocide of Europe's Jews was proceeding with murderous efficiency. As details of the atrocities filtered out to London and Washington, British Prime Minister Winston Churchill and America's President Roosevelt, judged that the only response could be a continued grim determination to defeat Nazi Germany and its brutal ideology. Already focused on the next step, their resolve was further strengthened, as an Allied advance into Italy, using the island of Sicily as a starting point, had more poignant purpose than ever.

· · ·

To set the scene, back in late 1942 British and American forces had made successful landings in North Africa. The Allies had also won over to their side many French commanders there, who had previously been loyal to the French Vichy government that was collaborating with the Nazis.

But in the spring of 1943 Germany and Italy had continued to send reinforcements from Europe across the Mediterranean, and the relatively inexperienced Allied troops, moving from Algeria into Tunisia, had met stiff resistance.

They were having to learn fast, in the most difficult of conditions, but progress was being made.

To the south, the Eighth Army led by British General Bernard Montgomery, had driven the Germans back from Libya and into Tunisia, as Erwin Rommel, who was suffering from the strain of months of combat, had been recalled by the Führer, and replaced.

In the South Pacific, the Americans and Australians had begun what they hoped would be a series of victories against the Japanese in the Solomon chain of islands, north of Australia. With some difficulty and at a cost of many lives, they had taken the first island, Guadalcanal. And with this achieved, understandably, they wanted to give the Japanese no respite.

Japan, Hitler's strongest ally, was in control of a wide circumference, including parts of China, much of south-east Asia, New Guinea, Papua, and in the North Pacific the tiny Aleutian Islands. It was essential to keep the Japanese on the defensive to prevent them from fortifying the Pacific islands they held, building up their air bases and making the Axis position a great deal more secure.

. . .

As we know, back in Africa, there were equally important matters being discussed. Meeting in the Moroccan city of Casablanca in January 1943, Churchill and Roosevelt, with the advice of their commanders, agreed on invading Sicily as soon as practicable, leaving a cross-channel invasion of France for the following year.

This was despite the misgivings of some American generals, who did not want the war in the Mediterranean to use up too much time or military resources. The hope was that Italy could be taken out of the war, and the Allies would be able to buy more time to build up their military strength before any invasion of northern France.

The British knew they were fighting a powerful military-industrial machine that was yet undamaged in its heartland. Hitler and the Axis powers would have to be worn down by a second front in Italy first, before a direct invasion of France could realistically be considered. So, by the time April 1st 1943 dawned, events in North Africa and plans for the invasion of Sicily became of paramount importance for both sides in the conflict.

Germany's military commander in the Mediterranean and North Africa, General Albert Kesselring, could congratulate his forces on having slowed the Allied advance across Tunisia from the west. But time was not really on the side of the Germans and Italians. The Axis forces were slowly but steadily being pushed back in southern Tunisia, towards the capital, Tunis. Their use of Panzer tanks had been impressive, with the model having been upgraded after coming up against heavy Soviet tanks on the eastern front.

Nevertheless, the British and Americans quickly strengthened their position, with increased numbers of tanks and aircraft in North Africa, and with the airfields they now controlled, were able to give their ground forces much better air support.

. . .

In the first week of April, the Allies bombed not only the Italian mainland but also hit Axis transport planes in the air, and ships bringing supplies by sea. Moving cautiously up the coast, Army sappers worked on detecting mines and filling in craters in the road. The troops were glad to be passing through fertile agricultural land and olive groves, after months crossing the rocky tracks of the Libyan Desert, but more importantly, the Tunisian roads provided them with a much smoother driving surface.

Pitting his wits against Kesselring, America's General Dwight D. Eisenhower was in overall command of the Allied forces in the Mediterranean, with Britain's Field Marshal Harold Alexander, as his second in command. Alexander strategically reorganized the Allied front, placing the American forces that were moving in from the west opposite the town of Bizerte, on the northern coast road into Tunis.

Also, the British First Army that had arrived in North Africa with the Americans some months earlier, were ordered to head for the Tunisian capital. One of the last major confrontations for Montgomery's weary men was the battle of Wadi Akarit, about 17 miles north of Gabes. The fighting was bitterly hard fought, but the British infantry supported by plenty of artillery were able to instigate an all-out attack across the plain.

On the evening of April 7th, the Americans along with the British First Army forces at last linked up with the Eighth Army soldiers, many of whom had never even met an American before. The more recent Allied arrivals found the battle-hardened soldiers of the Eighth Army scruffy and poorly disciplined, but with an impressively united fighting spirit. However, all the battle units now brought together in the final push to complete Allied operations in North Africa had by now lost thousands of men, either killed or wounded in the desert sands.

Progress continued to be made as the Allies took the Tunisian town of Sfax, which was quickly followed by Sousse, along the coast. New Zealand and Maori units in Montgomery's army took on Axis troops at the rock of Takrouna, an ancient fortress village in a strategically important location high above the main access route.

Then, with the worst of the fight for North Africa behind them, the Eighth Army, having come so far after battling so hard, found themselves playing a secondary role, pinning down as many troops as possible away from Tunis and Bizerte.

The writing was now on the wall for the Germans and the Italians in North Africa, and for the Italians the cracks in this unequal alliance were beginning to show, as the threat of an Allied invasion of their homeland gathered momentum.

As more and more Italian soldiers were taken prisoner, it became clear that support for the Axis alliance was faltering among ordinary Italians.

There had been little real enthusiasm for war in 1940, and now Libya had been lost, the country that Mussolini had hoped would be the crown of a new Italian empire in Africa, there seemed little to be gained. What's more the people of Italy were unhappy with the treatment of Italian workers drafted into the German factories, and even their leader Benito Mussolini was questioning Hitler's intentions, as the supplies of coal and oil that Germany had promised did not always materialize.

When Hitler and Mussolini met near Salzburg in Austria, both appeared to be visibly strained. Those around Hitler were shocked to see how sick and despondent Mussolini looked, as he urged peace talks with the Allies, but the German Führer would have none of it.

. . .

Eventually Hitler managed to browbeat and cajole the hapless Mussolini into continuing to fight to hold Tunis, convincing his now reluctant ally that this was essential if Fascism was to survive in Italy.

But Hitler's own situation was far from secure and he too faced criticism from his own people, who were by now experiencing great hardship and feeling that the Third Reich was not as invincible as they had been promised.

Propaganda became more important than ever, and for Hitler events in Russia soon gave him an opportunity to justify his position. At a place named Katyn in the Soviet countryside near Smolensk, a Russian peasant made an astounding declaration to the occupying Germans, claiming that the bodies of thousands of lost Polish officers were buried close by in the forest.

For Joseph Goebbels, Hitler's loyal minister for propaganda, it was the best news he'd had to work with for some time. After some exploration of the Russian peasant's story, the Nazis discovered mass graves of more than 4,200 Polish officers slaughtered by the Soviets back in 1939, when Stalin had been in league with Adolf Hitler rather than the Allies.

The Russian position was delicate because since their defection to the Allied cause after the Nazi invasion of the Soviet Union, Hitler's *Operation Barbarossa,* the British and Americans still viewed Stalin with great suspicion. Goebbels was quick to condemn the Russian's brutality against the Polish officers, but conveniently omitted to mention the barbaric treatment of the Poles, particularly the Jews, by the Germans.

Matters were more difficult still because the toppled Polish Government had fled into exile in London in 1939 and wanted the atrocity at Katyn exposed; cooperation with the Russians, ceased.

· · ·

It took a great deal of diplomatic maneuvering to keep what had been an uneasy alliance at the best of times intact, but British and US officials managed to prevent what would have been a disastrous split in the Allied position.

Nevertheless, the spotlight was destined to remain on Poland, as April gave way to May 1943, with events in the capital Warsaw, under German occupation, hitting the headlines. Eastern Europe in 1943 held too many secrets and too much horror. As April began, a new gas chamber had been installed at the extermination camp at Auschwitz, one of six extermination camps operating on Polish territory.

Consignments of prisoners, mainly Jews from various European countries and also non-Jewish Poles and gypsies, were brought in cattle trucks.

On arrival, most of the men, women and children were sent for immediate gassing, with only a minority allowed to live a while longer as slave labour.

In the Polish capital, Warsaw, all Jews had been confined to the traditional Jewish quarter, under guard and shut off from the rest of the city by high walls. Around 400,000 Jews, and some gypsies existed there on minimal rations as the Germans used slow starvation on a community that was also vulnerable to typhus and tuberculosis.

Buchenwald concentration camp captives

Then the pace of deportations to the extermination camp at Treblinka was stepped up. By April 1943 only 60,000 people remained in the Warsaw ghetto, mainly young adults. These people knew by now that they had nothing to lose and some had formed secret resistance groups using arms smuggled in from the Polish underground outside the ghetto.

After a small-scale uprising by the Jewish resistance in January, Heinrich Himmler, head of the Nazi's SS paramilitary, decided the time had come to raze the ghetto to the ground.

. . .

He sent an SS force in on April 19th, with tanks, flame-throwers and dyna-mite squads and though the armed groups resisted desperately with what weapons they had, the Germans soon started burning them out and forcing them into sewers and underground bunkers. 13,000 Polish Jews were killed in the revolt, but the Warsaw ghetto uprising had been a brave and desperate act of defiance, and it gave Hitler and his Generals a taste of what was to come.

Resistance against the Axis was growing stronger by the day and as battles intensified across the globe it was a time of intense planning and strategizing for the Allies. Keeping the seaways open to move troops into position all over the world was of vital importance and while the British navy was taking a lead role in the North Atlantic, in the South Pacific theatre of war US pilots and marines were spearheading the Allied counter-attack against Japan's drive for dominance.

In New Guinea and the Solomon Islands, north of Australia, Japan was now fighting a defensive war under the direction of Admiral Isoroku Yamamoto.

Yamamoto had, unusually, studied in the United States. He had even initially opposed the militarism that led Japan into war. But now he was a marked man for the Americans; it was he who had planned the Pearl harbor attack of December 1941 and while the Japanese public still viewed him as a national hero, the Americans were keen to eliminate the man responsible for thousands of American deaths.

In April 1943, the Americans decoded an intercepted radio message that revealed Admiral Yamamoto would make a flight in the Solomon's on an inspection trip to his troops. The bomber carrying the VIP was to land on an island near Bougainville, in the North. Seizing the opportunity on April 18th four American fighter aircraft took off from Guadalcanal following orders from President Roosevelt and homed in on Yamamoto's flight path. The bomber carrying the admiral was attacked and sent plummeting down into the jungle of Bougainville.

Yamamoto's body was later recovered by a Japanese search party, but Tokyo did not announce his death until weeks later for fear it would affect morale.

The Americans in turn could not boast their triumph immediately as to do so would reveal that they had broken the secret communications code used by the Japanese navy. But while the news of Yamamoto's death remained unannounced, a nationwide address heightened American animosity towards the Japanese.

On April 21st Roosevelt revealed that three members of an American aircrew had been executed in Japan. The three men, two pilots and a gunner, had been among 80 crewmen who had survived a raid led by Lieutenant Colonel Jimmy Doolittle, one year earlier; Doolittle was an aviator who had already been something of a celebrity before the war.

The Americans had hoped to shake the morale of the Japanese with the bombardment of military and industrial targets in cities around Japan. It had been the first Allied raid on Japanese home territory, a bold move that Tokyo had been eager to avenge.

The news of the "barbarous" executions was met with horror by the Americans, and Roosevelt announced that those responsible would not go unpunished; a message that was also intended as a warning to the Japanese over their treatment of some 17,000 other Americans held as prisoners of war.

By May 1943 the focus of the confrontation between the US and the Japanese shifted for a while to the northernmost edge of the Pacific Ocean. There a chain of tiny volcanic islands, the Aleutian Islands, extended out from the US state of Alaska towards Siberia and Japan.

In 1942 Japanese forces had moved onto the two Aleutian Islands nearest to Japan, Attu and Kiska. Thanks to their codebreakers the Americans had ignored this invasion as they knew it was merely a diversionary tactic and that in fact the Japanese intended to attack the strategically important island of Midway in the central Atlantic.

Nevertheless, while Tokyo made much of the invasion of the Aleutians in their propaganda, the Americans were soon looking for a way to oust them, and to this end began to build an airfield on Adak Island, near Alaska. Towards the end of April, US invasion forces had set sail from San Francisco bound for Attu Island, a barren landscape, often so windy that barely a tree could grow.

After two days, the US warships were in position and started to bombard Japanese defenses and by the beginning of May as a dense fog took hold of the island, the infantry were sent in on landing craft hoping to take the Japanese garrison by surprise.

In bitter fighting that would last through May, the US soldiers managed first to reach the valley leading to Chichagof harbor, but the Japanese would not surrender. The last of them broke out of their final positions charging towards the American lines in a suicidal wave, but their last stand would be futile, and by the time the conflict had drawn to a close there were over two thousand Japanese dead.

The Americans themselves lost more than 500 of their own men, and over two thousand had been evacuated suffering badly from frostbite or disease. Attu, back in American hands, now lay between the Japanese mainland and the island of Kiska where Japanese troops still roamed.

The invading armies did not remain on the island for long however, and by the time Allied soldiers set foot on Attu in August 1943, the 5,000-man garrison had already evacuated leaving the inhospitable climate of the Aleutians to the Americans.

In North Africa meanwhile, the German and Italian forces in and around Tunis looked in danger of having no route for a retreat. Despite Rommel's earlier plea to Hitler and Mussolini, to pull their men out of North Africa and prepare for an Allied invasion of Europe, the Germans continued to bring troops and supplies into Tunis, almost until the last minute. In May as Bizerte fell to American units, further south General Alexander unleashed a new offensive with an intensive artillery barrage of Tunis.

Soon the first British armored cars were able to sweep into the capital and before long thousands of people were lining the streets to celebrate, throwing spring flowers at the troops. Beyond the capital, the enemy, though surrounded, continued to fight, rejecting invitations to surrender and to save useless bloodshed.

Kesselring had already abandoned the African continent when finally, at the end of the second week in May, the Germans accepted their fate and made a formal surrender. The Italians soon followed suit and while axis soldiers flooded into prisoner-of-war enclosures those captured amounted to around 125,000 Germans and 115,000 Italians. It was the largest haul of prisoners-of-war in the conflict to date and certainly presented a logistical challenge as far as feeding and managing them was concerned.

Nevertheless, Eisenhower remained unperturbed by this minor complication and was jubilant as he announced to the world that the Axis were now in retreat. Three hours after the surrender, Winston Churchill in meetings with Roosevelt in Washington, received a message from General Alexander informing him: *"The Tunisian Campaign is over. All enemy resistance has ceased. We are masters of the North African shores."* After three years of fighting up and down the desert plains and over mountains the allies had finally achieved their reward and could celebrate the end of the Axis Empire in Africa.

Back in Washington President Roosevelt and Winston Churchill were ready for discussions with senior British and American military decision makers during the conference code-named "Trident". On May 19th Churchill addressed a joint session of both houses of Congress, just as he had done in December 1941, in the aftermath of the Japanese bombing of Pearl Harbor. He was greeted by prolonged cheering even before he began his speech, but with the Axis still at large, Churchill was eager to get down to business. All war plans, he said, must be *"dominated by the supreme object of getting to grips with the enemy."* The defeat of Germany must come first, and this would inevitably bring with it the defeat of Japan.

But there were disagreements between allied commanders over the best course of action to take next. Churchill argued for an invasion of mainland Italy which he believed would serve to draw German troops away from the Russian front, where Stalin's forces were still battling for survival. The Americans on the other hand wanted a full-scale invasion of France launched as soon as possible and believed that no operations should be undertaken which might delay this effort.

After long deliberation an agreement was eventually made between the Allies to invade France in early 1944, with a date tentatively set for May. Churchill would also get his way and a lower priority Italian campaign was planned with immediate effect to take Italy out of the war.

. . .

Meanwhile the focus was on the Atlantic, as vicious convoy battles were being fought out. Before an invasion of France could take place, the Allies knew the Battle of the Atlantic had to be won and with heavy losses through early spring seriously affecting supplies arriving in the British Isles, there were fears that the Nazis were winning the war at sea. Fortunately, by May it seemed the tables had turned and slowly but surely the Allies were gaining the upper hand.

| The sinking of U-Boat 185

By the end of the month a quarter of the total operational strength in the German Navy's submarine wing had been sunk. The son of Admiral Donitz, Commander in Chief of the navy had drowned with the rest of his crew on

May 19th anD-Days later the Nazi commander realized the time had come to withdraw to the south Atlantic.

With only a few U-Boats left roaming the North as a token threat, it seemed the two-year Axis battle to break Britain's supply lines had been lost. Meanwhile the factories continued to step up munitions production and the war effort was beginning to tell not only at sea but in the skies over Germany. Throughout the spring of 1943 waves of British bombers launched attacks on major German cities under the command of Air Chief Marshal Sir Arthur Harris.

Haunted by the memory of years of trench warfare in the First World War, the British, saw aerial bombardment as a way to by-pass fronts on the ground and shorten the war. The heavy bombing was not only targeted at destroying key industries however; it was seen as a valuable weapon in undermining civilian morale in the Fatherland.

During the war hundreds of thousands of Germans were left homeless by the attacks and while conditions deteriorated in the cities, support for Adolf Hitler inevitably began to wane. In May 1943, the RAF were finalizing the details of a particularly daring raid on the country which would focus on the Ruhr valley in Germany.

The aim was to rupture three dams in the area, which was home to much of Germany's heavy industry including steel works, chemical plants and coal mines. Working in the strictest secrecy, a British aircraft designer named Barnes Wallis had developed a drum-shaped bomb that it was hoped would bounce along the surface of the water towards a dam, avoiding the torpedo nets that protected it. The bomb would then roll down the dam below the surface of the water before exploding.

· · ·

On May 16th the raid, *Operation Chastice,* successfully destroyed the first and second dam, though the third would remain intact. Many thousands of gallons of water gushed out from the breaches in the two dams, flooding mines and cutting rail, road and canal links as well as disrupting water supplies. At least 1,650 people drowned, and productive arable land was flooded.

Sadly only nine out of 19 RAF planes returned from the mission and 53 of the aircrew involved were killed in action. But despite the loss, the event was an important boost to British morale, as British cities continued to suffer from raids by the Luftwaffe. Meanwhile for the populations of occupied Europe, the sight of Allied bombers heading for Germany gave them some hope that the Nazis' so-called New Order could not last forever.

As planning continued for the cross-channel invasion of France, the hopes of those living under Nazi occupation were not unfounded. It was beginning to look increasingly likely that a cross-channel invasion of France would be possible in 1944, and with the ambitious task that now lay ahead, Roosevelt was keen to improve contacts with the grassroots French resistance.

| Members of the French resistance

French people had been deeply divided by the coming of the Second World War. Not only were there the divisions between those who supported General Charles de Gaulle, based in London, and those who supported the collaborationist government of Marshall Petain based in the French town of Vichy; there were also many active in the resistance, including the French Communists, who supported neither Petain or De Gaulle.

At the Casablanca Conference in January there had been a rather tense and awkward meeting between De Gaulle and his rival General Henri Giraud who continued to maintain the Vichy regime in North Africa. Nevertheless, in joint leadership of the Free French Forces they called on all loyal men and women to rally to their cause.

. . .

Eventually the National Council of Resistance was set up as an umbrella for the diverse resistance groups who had been carrying out acts of sabotage against the Nazis, and people in occupied France began to do all they could to aid the Allies.

In the meantime, the American secret services began to build their own direct links with the French resistance, through contacts made in Switzerland, hoping that by channelling money into resistance action, they would get access to valuable military and strategic information about the Germans in France. But fighting for freedom did not come without its risks and soon after the first meeting of the new National Council of Resistance numerous leaders were arrested.

During the course of the war many men and women who fought back against the occupying forces in France would be incarcerated, tortured or killed by the dreaded Gestapo but unhindered by the dangers the fight for freedom went on.

In Europe, the systematic genocide continued apace. By the summer of 1943, more than half the Jewish population of Europe had already been killed. Quietly proud of their extermination program, The Nazis did not trumpet the details in their propaganda and referred to killing by euphemisms such as *"special action"* and *"special measures"*.

At Auschwitz in Poland, on average 33,000 people a month were being gassed at the concentration camp and after the elimination of the Warsaw ghetto in May, on June 11th SS chief Heinrich Himmler gave the order that the remaining ghettos in other Polish towns should also be completely emptied and dismantled.

. . .

Poland had had the largest Jewish population of any European state, numbering about three million people and most of this community would be dead by the time the Allies declared victory, along with about three million non-Jewish Poles.

Further east, in those parts of the Baltic States and the Soviet Union occupied by the Nazis, Himmler's mobile killing units, known as Einsatzgruppen had been given a free rein behind the advancing German troops. Whole communities were pitilessly massacred in mass shootings and the Jewish population had been decimated.

But while the Nazis continued with their war of terror, the Allies were slowly closing in and following discussions at the Trident Conference in Washington, preparations for the invasion of Italy had begun. With the Axis cleared from North Africa, Eisenhower now placed all his attention on taking Mussolini and his troops out of the war.

US bombers intensified their attacks on the country, hitting ports, airfields and industrial areas; in Sicily the towns of Palermo, Catania and Syracuse were targeted.

The island of Sardinia, where there was already a sizable garrison of German troops, was also hit and the ports of Messina and Naples on the mainland, suffered intense bombardments. Allied aircraft based on Malta had begun bombing the port of Naples as early as 1940 and the city was no stranger to air-raids, but as the attacks escalated, by the summer of 1943 life was becoming unbearable for its inhabitants. Explosions regularly tore through the city and there were food and water shortages to contend with.

In spite of reinforcements, German air power in Italy was dwindling under the hammering of Allied airpower and as the people of Naples endured a heavier bombardment than they had known before, the Nazis were unable to send the additional planes and anti-aircraft protection that Mussolini was urgently requesting.

With fears growing that the Allies were poised for invasion, thousands of ordinary Italians began leaving their homes in the south of the country and convinced that it was only a matter of time before Allied Commanders launched the attack, the Germans began moving additional troops into Italy from France.

Meanwhile the Allies had spent time deliberating the best course of action when planning their campaign and had finally decided that Sicily would give them the best foothold for an invasion of Italy. The tiny Italian island of Pantelleria on the other hand, which, lay astride the route to Sicily not far from the Tunisian coast, would be a steppingstone to the larger island.

With its sheer cliffs, Pantelleria had been used by the Axis powers as a base for aircraft and submarines, and from here many attacks had been launched on British sea traffic in the Mediterranean. In the words of Winston Churchill, Pantelleria was *"a thorn in our side"*, and the island now posed a real threat to the planned invasion of Sicily.

But keen to ensure that nothing jeopardized the lives of his men or the success of the Italian mission, Eisenhower had an unpleasant future in store for the little island. He and his commanders wanted to see whether by softening up a target from the air, it could then be invaded using a minimal amount of men on the ground.

Using Pantelleria as a testing ground to see the effect of saturation bombing on a defended coastline, Allied aircraft began bombarding the island over five weeks from early May. More than five thousand bombing sorties were flown, and 6,300 tons of bombs were dropped on Italian and German forces there. Barracks, supply dumps and aircraft were hit at the air field, while British naval vessels hit the harbor area and damaged gun emplacements along the coastline.

On June 10th the offensive reached a crescendo, as wave after wave of bombers swept out from Tunisia, bombing the islanD-Day and night, pausing only for the Allies to invite the island to surrender.

Meanwhile in Washington, Roosevelt urged the Italian people to overthrow Mussolini, but though many were keen to be rid of the Fascist dictator, he would remain in power for a little longer yet. Back on Pantelleria, with no surrender offered, a British Infantry Division set off from the Tunisian coast on landing craft.

At about 11 o'clock in the morning of June 11th, Allied airplanes spotted a white cross on the airfield, just before the infantry arrived on the beach. It marked the first time in history that an enemy land force had been bombed into submission before troops could come ashore.

The operation had in no uncertain terms brought home to an already nervous Italian population that the Allied armed forces meant business. As Eisenhower now focused on preparations for the invasion of Sicily, on the other side of the globe battles in the Pacific theatre of war were gathering pace and the Allies were beginning to dominate the seas.

As an island nation, Japan depended on maritime links with the rest of the world, a fact that had been evident in the years leading up to the war. When the United States had imposed sanctions on Japan, to prevent the country from importing raw materials, the tiny Empire had had no choice but to fight for survival.

. . .

By 1943 with new territory to administer and defend around the Pacific, the Japanese now had new concerns and it was vital that shipping lanes were kept open to transport troops and munitions to far-flung garrisons in the south.

After the attack on Pearl in December 1941, with many US carriers and destroyers taken out of action, Japan had made their spectacular entrance into the war from a position of strength, and there was little opposition to their conquest of the islands around the Pacific. While their enemy was still in a state of shock the Japanese did all that they could to maximize the advantage Pearl Harbor had given them.

The crews of the Japanese submarines were expertly trained, and they were equipped with what were called Long Lance torpedoes. These torpedoes had proved vastly more effective than those on the American submarines, which often turned out to be duds, either failing to explode on impact, detonating before reaching their target, or veering wildly off course.

Military planners in the United States had been increasingly focused on the technology and tactics that would allow them to gain the upper hand against the Japanese in the Pacific theatre of war, but the events at Pearl meant they needed to work even harder.

At the beginning of the Pacific war, US submarine commanders had felt ill-prepared for the battles that lay ahead. Eventually though the US military decision makers finally listened to their submarine commanders, and in 1943 redesigned their torpedo, issuing a model with a stronger firing pin at its head. It was time for the rules of submarine warfare to change as the Americans took advantage of the element of surprise.

. . .

Using shock tactics, the Americans launched surprise attacks on Japanese merchant shipping, and this strategy quickly became the order of the day. As this proved to be very effective, the US submarines became ever bolder, attacking closer to the surface, rather than from the depths of the ocean, without a periscope in sight.

This was only possible because a year earlier, American codebreakers had succeeded in deciphering the Japanese naval codes and were now forwarding critical information to submarine captains with information on possible targets on the surface.

Consequently, US submarines were equipped with radar to detect vessels in the vicinity, while patrolling planes were used to spot enemy submarines below the surface.

The strike rate against Japanese vessels rose dramatically through 1943, as the Americans targeted both military and merchant shipping, even fishing fleets. Slowly but surely, the Allies were gaining the upper hand in the stormy waters of the Pacific, and with General Douglas MacArthur at the helm as Supreme Commander of Allied Forces in the Southwest Pacific Area, the Japanese were now facing a formidable enemy, at sea, in the air and on land.

Taking control in the skies had continued to be a preoccupation in the South Pacific, where American and Australian forces were gradually making inroads along the southernmost perimeter of Japanese-held territory. At the beginning of June, the American Admiral William Halsey gave orders for the invasion of New Georgia, the largest island in the western province of the Solomon Islands chain that lay immediately north of Guadalcanal.

The Americans were alarmed to learn that the Japanese had built an airfield at Munda, the largest settlement on New Georgia, and sporadic Japanese attempts to attack American positions on Guadalcanal soon became a problem.

The Japanese feared that if the Allies managed to hold Guadalcanal undisturbed, it would be the starting point for an operation of gradual island hopping up to the northern Solomon's.

This would put the strategically crucial Japanese base at Rabaul, on the island of New Britain, under real threat from the Americans, and anything Japan could do to halt the US forces in their tracks was considered worthwhile.

Even though the Japanese attacks on Guadalcanal were unlikely to shake the occupying troops from their positions, it was a hindrance, although the American advance towards Rabaul still gathered momentum.

US marines landed on the undefended southern tip of New Georgia and started an overland advance to the island's Viru Harbor. Without waiting to evict the Japanese garrison of more than 10,000 troops who were occupying the rest of the island, they began building an airfield where they had landed. Within just a fortnight Allied planes based at this new airfield were providing invaluable air support for the battle to take control of the whole of New Georgia. And as well as securing this island, when the Japanese airbase at Munda point fell into Allied hands just a few weeks later, the American troops at Guadalcanal were left in peace.

The Japanese attempts to bomb American positions on Guadalcanal from their base on New Georgia had been an indication of the kind of problem that the Allies could expect if Japan was allowed time to consolidate the perimeter defenses of its newly conquered empire. The Japanese culture of "no surrender" meant that every square mile of territory in the Pacific, whether on land or at sea would have to be fought for, to the death, if necessary.

. . .

The Allies had an unimaginably difficult task ahead of them, and the cost in terms of human sacrifice was destined to be immense, but the tide was without doubt now running in their favor as they launched a determined drive to push forward into the central Pacific.

And it wasn't only in the Pacific that the Allies were realizing that winning the war and ridding the world of Adolf Hitler and the Axis powers was going to be a costly business. The war was also taking its toll on civilian populations everywhere, because in the Soviet Union and throughout Europe, the death tolls reached horrific proportions.

Britain continued to be subject to sporadic raids by the Luftwaffe, and in cities under the authoritarian rule of Hitler's war machine, people were living in constant fear. Stories of the atrocities were terrifying, but there was also a hardening of resolve uniting those facing such appalling conditions, as the Allies stood firm in their resolve to overcome fascism to create a world free of tyranny for generations to come.

Nevertheless, for the time being at least, the most immediate preoccupation for the Allied leaders was the invasion of Sicily. There were many questions still to be answered, especially concerning what was likely to happen on a political level once the Allies reached the Italian mainland.

Resistance to Adolf Hitler's plans for a Thousand Year Reich was now anything but futile, and even those who had been so far collaborating with the German Führer were about to reconsider their position, meaning that the fight for control of Italy was about to get very interesting indeed.

TENTATIVE STEPS

July – September 1943

| Panzer tank – The German warhorse

As World War II progressed towards its fifth year, the German war machine, which for Adolf Hitler had once seemed so assured of military supremacy, was well and truly faltering. Defeat at Stalingrad in February 1943 had cost the Nazis dear and the Allies were well placed to capitalize on their advantage. However, the Allied leaders were all too aware of the dangers still to be overcome, and they proceeded with the utmost caution, beginning to take tentative but very positive steps towards victory.

By July 1943, progress was very definitely evident. At sea, the Allies were winning the Battle of the Atlantic. Measures agreed by British Prime Minister Winston Churchill and US President Franklin D. Roosevelt at the Casablanca Conference seven months previously, to beat the U-Boat menace, were now yielding results.

For the Germans, with morale plummeting among the U-Boat crews, their commander, Grand Admiral Karl Doenitz had no choice but to order them to withdraw from the main convoy routes in the North Atlantic. But for the Allies it was just the boost that they needed; success against the U-Boats meant that the British and the Americans could proceed to build up forces for *Operation Overlord,* the invasion of Western Europe.

In the skies over Europe, *Operation Pointblank,* the code name given at the Casablanca Conference for a round-the-clock bombing campaign against Nazi Germany and Fascist Italy, was underway.

The American Army air force pounded targets all over Western Europe by day, while the Royal Air Force continued by night.

In the meantime, the campaign in North Africa had ended in a total Allied victory. By mid-May 1943, nearly a quarter of a million German and Italian soldiers in Tunisia had passed into Allied captivity.

For Nazi Germany, it was a bigger military disaster than Stalingrad had been.

British and American military planners were now busy preparing for the next stage in the war, agreeing on a "Hitler first" policy. In May 1943, Churchill, Roosevelt and their military staff met in Washington DC in a conference code-named Trident. With the whole of North Africa about to fall into their hands, the Allies agreed an invasion of Sicily, code-named *Operation Husky,* was the next logical step.

But over where to go after that, there was no consensus. The Americans wanted to invade northern France in order to secure a rapid end to the war. The British too wanted a cross-Channel invasion but only after Nazi Germany's powerful forces had been worn down elsewhere. They feared a bloodbath similar to the slaughter in the trenches of the First World War.

The British argued that toppling Benito Mussolini's Fascist regime, knocking Italy out of the war and making the enemy fight for southern France, the Balkans or Greece, would be the best way to guarantee success for Overlord. The Americans strongly disagreed, arguing that such a strategy would be a diversion of resources and effort. They were pushing for an early cross-Channel invasion, as it would take the pressure off the Red Army on the eastern front.

Because all the while, lurking at the back of their minds was the fear that if they didn't, the Russians might do a deal with Adolf Hitler, as had been the case in August 1939. Nazi Germany still possessed huge swathes of Soviet territory. And as the snow melted with the return of spring, Hitler's generals looked forward to avenging the disaster at Stalingrad.

. . .

So, as preparations for *Operation Husky* fell into place, with Hitler convinced that his enemies were targeting an attack on Sardinia, thanks to the efforts of Allied Intelligence, the battle to regain control of mainland Europe began in earnest. At the Trident Conference in Washington DC the previous month, the combined US and British Chiefs of Staff had actually set a date for *Operation Overlord* for May 1st, 1944.

Nevertheless, the British were keen to gain a foothold in Europe much, much sooner. Sicily was just the first step; the whole of Italy was the real prize, or so Churchill and his military advisers argued. But General George C Marshall, US Army Chief of Staff and the real driving force behind America's war effort, was under great pressure from General Douglas MacArthur, commander of Allied forces in the South-West Pacific, to give him more resources for the war against Imperial Japan.

Marshall was prepared only to commit US forces to an invasion of Sardinia and instructed General Dwight D. Eisenhower to only *"mount such operations in exploitation of the attack on Sicily as might be calculated to eliminate Italy from the war"*.

Once the Trident Conference was over, Churchill and his senior most military adviser, General Sir Alan Brooke, Chief of the Imperial General Staff, flew to North Africa to try and persuade Eisenhower that Marshall was being short-sighted, and to ask for his support for their call for an invasion of Italy.

Under pressure from Marshall, Eisenhower was forced to be cautious; he told the British leaders that if *Operation Husky* was successful, he would lend his support for moving on into Italy, but not before.

While the Allies remained tentative, for Hitler's Axis powers, a major political and strategic crisis was developing. Inside Italy there was now a real fear that the Allies would topple the Fascist dictator Benito Mussolini and Adolf Hitler looked on events in the Mediterranean with increasing anxiety.

As a result of the huge burden placed on German forces by the fighting in Russia, and the loss of eight Axis divisions in Tunisia earlier in the year, the cupboard in the Mediterranean, so to speak, was practically bare.

The big strategic question now facing the Führer was where would the Allies strike next? His Mediterranean theatre commander, Field Marshal Kesselring, and Italian Army chiefs all believed that an invasion of Sicily was imminent.

But Hitler wasn't so sure. Blinded by the complete lack of reliable intelligence, he believed that the Allies would land in Sardinia. From there, they would logically take Corsica, which would be a stepping-stone for southern France or Italy. Alternatively, the Allies might invade Greece.

Hitler based his thinking on information gleaned from top-secret documents found on a Royal Marine officer whose body had been washed up on a beach in southern Spain back in April 1943. The Spanish authorities who found the body believed that the Royal Marine had drowned in an aircraft crash in the Mediterranean.

Copies of the original documents passed onto German Intelligence by a pro-Nazi Spanish naval officer appeared to show that Sardinia and Greece were next on the Allies' list. Hitler therefore ordered the dispatch of a panzer division to Greece, another motorized infantry division to Sardinia and two elite parachute divisions to southern France to be ready for any invasion.

In fact, the whole affair was the product of a remarkable British Intelligence operation as the Royal Marine in question had actually died of pneumonia back in Britain. His body had been dropped into the sea very close to the Spanish coast by a Royal Navy submarine, and all the documents and letters planted on him were of course fake.

Thanks to this clever deception, the half million strong Anglo-American army assigned to *Operation Husky* would outnumber the Axis troops left to defend Sicily by nearly two to one. The Germans in fact had only two under-strength formations with which to repel the onslaught.

No less than eight British, American and Canadian divisions were set to attack on the first day of *Operation Husky*, making it the biggest military operation undertaken by the Allies to date in the war.

In fact, more men would land on Sicily in the first twenty-four hours of this invasion than would land on the Normandy Beaches in a comparable period on D-Day, almost a year later. And what's more, two further divisions, one British and one American, would then reinforce the Allied beachhead on Sicily, once it was secure.

As the sun rose on July 5th 1943, five invasion fleets under the overall command of Admiral Sir Andrew Cunningham steamed towards Sicily from opposite ends of the Mediterranean. Off the fortress island of Malta less than twenty-four hours before the actual landings, the fleets formed two groups. The first was the Eastern Task Force under Royal Navy Vice Admiral Bertram Ramsey made up of almost 1,700 warships, troop transports and landing craft, complete with four British and Canadian divisions under the command of General Sir Bernard Montgomery.

The second group was the Western Task Force under US Navy Vice Admiral Kent Hewitt with another 1,700 vessels and four American divisions led by Lieutenant-General George S Patton.

. . .

The planners of *Operation Husky* had one other surprise ready for the Axis troops on the island, namely parachute and glider troops ready to land behind the invasion beaches from the 1st British Airborne and the US 82nd Airborne Divisions.

Following the successful but costly German airborne landings in Crete in May of 41, the Allies had raised several divisions of parachute and glider troops, and *Operation Husky* was set to be their baptism of fire.

Eisenhower, as ever the consummate professional, selected his deputy, General Sir Harold Alexander, widely known for his charm and coolness under fire, to take charge of *Operation Husky.*

And if charm and a cool head were ever needed, it was now, because serving under Alexander, as his principal battlefield commanders, were General Sir Bernard Montgomery, famous for his victory at El Alamein, and General George S Patton Junior, well known for his swash-buckling, aggressive leadership style.

Husky was the first operation in which both ambitious and notoriously egocentric battlefield commanders would find themselves serving alongside each other, and from the outset, if ever two personalities were destined to clash, it was Montgomery and Patton.

The Allied invasion of Sicily kicked off in the early hours of July 10th 1943. Patton's 7th Army would land on a forty-mile front on the island's south coast, while Montgomery's 8th Army would come ashore on a forty-mile-wide front on either side of Sicily's south eastern corner.

In the early stages of the planning for Husky, it had been intended that

Patton's primary objective was to be the port of Palermo on Sicily's north-western coast. But Allied military strategists were concerned that American troops lacked the combat experience necessary for such a bold operation. Instead, the 7th US Army was given the job of protecting Montgomery's left flank as it advanced towards Messina to block an Axis retreat.

For the American General, widely known as "Blood n' Guts" Patton, this can only be described as a red rag to a bull, and he was determined to prove the doubters wrong about the operational value of the men under his command. As Husky gathered momentum Patton soon got the chance to prove the point beyond any possible doubt.

Things couldn't have been better for the massive Anglo-American invasion fleet as it was able to approach Sicily virtually unopposed. Despite the fact that German U-Boats managed to sink six invasion transports and landing craft, there was no sign of enemy aircraft.

In the lead-up to *Operation Husky*, Allied bombers had wrecked all the airfields on Sicily, forcing the German Luftwaffe and the Italian Regia Aero-nautica to withdraw their remaining aircraft to mainland Italy. Against 4,000 Allied aircraft, they could only muster 1,500 machines. In fact, the main opposition to *Operation Husky* came from the weather. The day before the invasion, during the afternoon of the 9th, the wind whipped up a tremendous storm, which resulted in many of the men in the invasion fleet becoming horribly seasick.

Fortunately, the strong winds abated in the final hours before the first Allied troops stormed ashore, but in the skies above Sicily, there were strong air currents that played havoc with the formations of troop-carrying aircraft and gliders en-route to their drop and landing zones.

· · ·

The paratroopers and gliders were scattered all over the south of the island. Forty-seven out of 134 British gliders ended up in the sea; however, the sudden appearance of airborne troops who did reach their Sicilian destination, created mayhem behind the enemy-held beaches.

Canadian soldiers on the island of Sicily

At 2:45 in the morning on July 10th, under the cover of a shattering naval bombardment, the first Allied assault troops waded ashore.

Eisenhower's strategy had enabled the Allies to swiftly establish their first foothold on European soil, but although the invasion force knew full well that the enemy lay ahead of them, they had little idea of how much resistance they would be facing.

Interestingly in the British sector nearly all the defending Italian troops encountered by Monty's 8th Army surrendered with little or no attempt to put up a fight.

Not surprisingly most of the men serving in the six Italian coastal defense divisions on the island were Sicilian. They had little affection for Mussolini's Fascist regime and even less desire to see their homeland destroyed by the ravages of war. Within hours, Montgomery had four divisions ashore together with most of their heavy weapons, however, Patton and the Americans encountered much stronger opposition.

On the first day of the invasion, Italian and then German tanks appeared, but the Italians were quickly sent packing. Later in the day though a battle group from the Herman Goering Division succeeded in over-running an American infantry battalion.

The next day, July 11th, General Alfredo Guzzoni, the Italian commander-in-chief of all Axis troops on Sicily, ordered the Herman Goering Division, reinforced by the Italian Livorno Division, to drive the enemy back into the sea. What's more, German and Italian aircraft based on the Italian mainland joined in the attack and the US troops were soon under siege.

Patton's men fought desperately to keep the enemy at bay as panzers advanced to within two thousand yards of the invasion beaches. Eventually American ground and naval artillery broke up the Axis onslaught, and to the right of the 7th US Army's beachhead, a hastily assembled force of paratroopers and infantry stopped another German counterattack.

. . .

Patton's 7th Army suffered 2,300 casualties during the bloodiest twenty-four hours in the whole of the campaign for Sicily, and the Americans would suffer even more heavy losses before dawn broke on July12th. Aircraft and gliders carrying 2,000 men were ordered by Patton to reinforce the 82nd Airborne Division, and although 23 aircraft were shot down, killing a further two hundred US paratroopers, the threat in the American sector had passed.

With the beachheads secure, the Allies were swift to introduce two new American technological developments that would end up playing a huge part in defeating Adolf Hitler. The tank landing ship or LST, as it was officially known, and the amphibious two-and-a-half-ton supply truck, more confusingly known as the DUKW, proved invaluable in *Operation Husky*.

Needing to get men and munitions ashore at speed, the Allied invasion forces no longer had to depend upon the early capture of an enemy-held harbor, something that would be crucial when it came to *Operation Overlord*.

This planned invasion of Western Europe was already gathering momentum, and British engineers were busy developing an even more ambitious project to make sure that Allied troops and supplies could be put in place precisely where they were needed.

Mulberry was the code name for a prefabricated floating harbor capable of rising up and down with the tides off the coast of France, but a great deal more work was going to be needed to turn the daring concept into a reality.

Even so, having succeeded in getting hundreds of thousands of Allied troops safely ashore in Sicily, the cracks in the Allied high command were beginning to show. Canadian and British troops had quickly cleared the island's south east corner, but as they pushed northwards towards the port of Messina to trap all General Guzzoni's Axis forces, they met with stiff German resistance.

Panzer tanks, reinforced by elite paratrooper units flown in from southern France, now stood in the way.

The landscape also played its part too in making things more difficult because behind the panzers was the semi-active volcano, Mount Etna, rising ten thousand feet above the plain of Catania. To outflank German positions in the foothills of Etna, Montgomery got Alexander to shift the boundary between his 8th Army and Patton's 7th Army on July 13th. The boundary shift allowed the British to advance up Highway 124, the main road into the center of Sicily before turning north east at Enna towards Messina.

Patton was furious. Like many American generals, he detested Montgomery. By redrawing the inter-army boundary in Montgomery's favor, Alexander was consigning the 7th US Army to the role of flank shield for the 8th Army. Patton decided that the best way to get back at Montgomery was the capture of Palermo, Sicily's capital as well as a major port. With Palermo in US hands and his supply lines secure, he could then push east towards Messina and get there before his British rival.

To soften Alexander up, he got him to agree to a "reconnaissance" towards the town of Agrigento by his troops. Once Agrigento fell on July 15th, Patton persuaded Alexander to allow him to drive for Palermo. Brushing aside his British superior's second thoughts, 'Blood n' Guts' formed a special corps of three fast-moving divisions to seize Palermo. The Italian troops they encountered on the way did very little to stop them.

Palermo fell on July 22nd and forty-eight hours later, the whole of western Sicily and 53,000 Italian soldiers were in the 7th US Army's hands. In Italy, news of the capture of Palermo by Patton's troops was followeD-Days later by the collapse of the Fascist regime.

. . .

Although he had been dictator of Italy since 1922, Benito Mussolini had always shared power with the Italian monarch, King Victor Emmanuel III, and the Italian Army. The King and the Army had never liked Mussolini's alliance with Hitler. Now it threatened to bring them all down. The Allied invasion of Sicily was a warning to the anti-Fascist plotters that they were running out of time.

The final push was provided by a big US bombing raid on Rome on July 19th. The target had been the main railway marshaling yards, but many bombs fell wide, killing and wounding hundreds of Italian civilians. The mood in the city was now very hostile to the fascist regime. On July 24th, Mussolini summoned the Fascist Grand Council in Rome to head off the growing political crisis.

Much to Mussolini's surprise, his fellow Fascists informed him that they had lost confidence in him and his leadership and the following day, the King dismissed him from the post of prime minister and had him arrested. Without a shot being fired, Mussolini's fascist regime collapsed.

Marshal Pietro Badoglio, a former Italian Army chief, became prime minister and somewhat anxious not to antagonize the Germans, he announced that *"the war continues at the side of our Germanic all"*. News of Mussolini's downfall came at a critical moment in Hitler's campaign in the east.

Since July 5th, a titanic life-and-death struggle between the Wehrmacht and the Red Army had been fought in the baking heat of the Russian Steppes. But for the first time in the campaign on the eastern Front, Anglo-American military operations would play a crucial part in deciding its outcome. For most of the previous five months, there'd been stalemate on the Russian theatre.

An attempt by the Red Army to exploit their stunning victory at Stalingrad had been foiled by a brilliant counterattack of German forces scraped together by Field Marshal Erich von Manstein, one of Hitler's best battlefield commanders.

The city of Kharkov, captured by Soviet forces in February, was re-taken by a Waffen-SS panzer corps in March. But the Red Army had managed to hang on to a bulge of territory 120 miles wide and 90 miles deep between Orel in the north and Belgorod in the south. At its center was the town of Kursk. As warmer weather returned to the Russian front, Hitler and his generals considered what to do next.

On their maps, they could see that the frontline now ran from Leningrad in the north to Rostov-on-Don in the south. The bulge at Kursk and the Soviet armies crammed into it seemed ripe for the plucking. German Army Chief-of-Staff General Kurt Zeitzler wanted to slice it off in a powerful pincer movement. So too did two of Hitler's other key field Marshals, Erich von Manstein and Hans von Kluge. But the Führer was not yet willing to commit himself. After the capitulation of the last Axis forces in Italy on May 13th, he now feared an Anglo-American landing on mainland Europe.

Should the Wehrmacht try to wipe out the bulge at Kursk or should it wait for the Red Army to launch its main summer offensive? A big pre-emptive strike might upset Stalin's own plans but, if the Anglo-Americans landed in Sardinia, or Greece, or Sicily at the same time, Hitler would have no reserves to spare for the Mediterranean theatre.

For once, the Führer couldn't make up his mind. His Inspector of Panzer Troops, the famous panzer commander General Heinz Guderian, was firmly against the proposals.

He asked Hitler *"Is it really necessary to attack Kursk, and indeed in the east this year at all? Do you think anyone even knows where Kursk is? The entire world doesn't care if we capture Kursk or not."* The Führer replied *"I know. The thought of it turns my stomach."* Code-named *Operation Citadel,* the Kursk offensive, originally planned for May 4th, was repeatedly postponed.

In the meantime, information passed on to the Soviet High Command by British Intelligence through the dummy Lucy spy ring based in Switzerland and the Red Army's own sources gave Stalin plenty of warning of German plans.

By the summer of 1943, the Wehrmacht and the Red Army could field roughly 6 million soldiers each. But Nazi Germany was losing the arms race to the Soviet Union. Day by day, the balance of forces on the Russian front was tilting away from Hitler towards Stalin.

For the attack, the Wehrmacht was gathering no less than fifty divisions, including seventeen panzer divisions and providing the attack with extra punch were the new Tiger tanks, Panther tanks and massive Ferdinand self-propelled 88mm guns.

Altogether, the Germans fielded 900,000 men, 3,000 tanks and nearly 2,800 aircraft earmarked for *Operation Citadel.* But the delay in starting the offensive gave the Red Army time to construct an elaborate system of minefields, anti-tank ditches and anti-tank gun positions to protect the whole of the Kursk bulge up to a depth of ninety-five miles.

To prevent any breakthrough by the enemy, Stalin had committed no less than 1.3 million troops, 3,600 tanks, 20,000 cannon and nearly 2,800 aircraft. So, in addition to having lost the advantage of surprise, the Wehrmacht was outnumbered.

. . .

Nevertheless, on July 3rd, with no sign of any major Allied move in the Mediterranean, the Führer finally gave *Operation Citadel* the go ahead. Twenty-four hours later, German troops launched probing attacks on the Red Army's outer defensive perimeter. The next day, the main offensive began. On Army Group Center's front, the 9th Army under General Walther Model forming the northern pincer of *Operation Citadel;* tanks battled to crack open the Soviet defenses on a thirty-mile wide front. But after four days, the attack stalled.

In the south, 4th Panzer Army and Army Detachment Kempf, punched a hole twenty miles wide. By July 12th, they were on the verge of breaking through the Soviet defenses. On that day, the world's biggest tank battle to date occurred when two German and Soviet tank armies met to fight it out at Prokhorovka.

German soldiers surrender to Soviets

For eight hours, thousands of sweating, frightened men rode inside their heavily armored machines, hurling steel projectiles at each other in blinding heat and choking dust. Hundreds died, their bodies torn apart by shards of molten steel or incinerated by exploding fuel and ammunition. But even as the gigantic tank battle was raging, the Red Army launched an offensive against the Army Group Center. Model's 9th Army was forced onto the defensive.

. . .

The next day, July 13th, Hitler reviewed Citadel's progress. Some ground had been gained but German casualties had been heavy; 50,000 dead and wounded.

The Anglo-American invasion of Sicily three days earlier made the Führer a very worried man. Anxious to scrape together the reserves he needed to keep Italy in the war, he ordered a halt to the Kursk offensive. The decision marked the beginning of the end for the Germans in Russia. From now on, the initiative lay with the Red Army.

Within a fortnight, the Wehrmacht was forced to abandon the Kursk battlefields. On August 5th, 1943 Moscow celebrated the liberation of Orel and Belgorod with a huge firework display. Just under three weeks later, on August 24th, Soviet troops recaptured Kharkov for the second and last time. The Wehrmacht would fight on in the east, but all hope of victory had gone.

In the meantime, Hitler was busy trying to prop up his Italian ally, the Duce Benito Mussolini. On July 19th, Hitler flew to Italy to confer with Mussolini. At a heavily guarded villa in Feltre, the Führer talked non-stop for two hours to infuse his friend the Duce with fresh courage and resolve.

On the 24th Hitler's headquarters received the news of the Duce's resignation at the same time reports were coming in from Hamburg of a big air raid on the city. The raid was the first of three attacks on Hamburg in which RAF Bomber Command confused German radar defenses with hundreds of thousands of aluminum strips code-named Window.

With Luftwaffe night fighters and flak guns blinded, the British dropped incendiaries onto the old center of the city, setting it alight and creating a firestorm that sucked everything and everyone into its path.

· · ·

An estimated 30,000 men, women and children lost their lives and half a million people were made homeless.

In the final days of July 1943, rumors of the destruction and death toll in Hamburg spread a wave of fear through other German cities, so far, untouched by Allied bombing. And within the Nazi Party, people asked themselves for the first time, would popular discontent at the way the war was going cause the Hitler regime to collapse, like Mussolini's.

In the Allied camp, General Patton was determined to get to Messina first. He told one of his commanders, *"This is a horse race in which the prestige of the US Army is at stake. We must take Messina before the British."* The 7ᵗʰ US and 8ᵗʰ British Army found themselves pinned down in the foothills of Mount Etna and even when they succeeded in levering out the German and Italian troops from their hilltop positions, allied troops were held up by enemy minefields and bridge demolitions.

When the first American troops entered Messina early on the 17ᵗʰ, they found it to be deserted. Shortly after Patton had accepted its surrender, a small British motorized column entered the port. 'Blood 'n Guts' had won the race, but it was a hollow victory. In just six days and seven nights 40,000 Germans and more than 60,000 Italians had been evacuated across the Straits of Messina along with most of their vehicles, heavy weapons and stores.

Eisenhower and Patton (2nd from left)

With Sicily now in their hands, the British and the Americans could safely direct sea convoys through the Mediterranean instead of having to send them all the way around Africa to the Suez Canal.

Late on the 17th of August, the day *Operation Husky* ended, five hundred and seventy-one Halifax and Lancaster bombers took off from bases in Lincolnshire and East Anglia to attack the top secret German experimental weapons center at Peenemunde on the Baltic.

In the preceding months, RAF photo reconnaissance missions over Peenemunde had uncovered the existence of the A4 long-range rocket and the FG-76 flying bomb, which Adolf Hitler hoped to use against London before the end of 1943.

During the RAF attack, 1,600 tons of bombs and 231 tons of incendiaries were dropped, destroying much of the site and killing more than 730 people including two key German scientists. The following day, General Hans Jeschonnek, Chief of the Luftwaffe Air Staff, blew his brains out over his failure to prevent the bombing of Peenemunde.

The British hoped that this air raid would deal a fatal blow to the Nazis' secret weapon program. But as the year drew to a close, it was clear that the Germans were continuing with rocket and flying bomb trials in testing centers beyond the range of Allied bombers.

Also, on August 17th, Churchill and Roosevelt and their military and diplomatic advisers met for the second time in three months, this time on Canadian soil at Quebec.

The conference was code-named Quadrant. On the agenda: *Operation Overlord,* the Mediterranean theatre, the Far East and "Tube Alloys", the codename for the joint Anglo-American project to produce an atom bomb.

For months, the British leader had been advocating landings on mainland Italy because from there, the Allies could strike at the Balkans or open the sea route to the Soviet Union via the Aegean, if Turkey could be persuaded to abandon her neutrality.

Roosevelt met Churchill halfway. Once Allied troops were firmly established in Sicily, Eisenhower was ordered to begin planning an invasion of Italy.

Mussolini's overthrow made the project urgent but there was a time limit as many of the invasion craft provided by the Americans were due to be transferred to the Pacific.

However where should the Allies land? Churchill was all for landing as far up the Italian peninsula as possible, starting at Rome. *"Why should we crawl up the leg like a harvest bug, from the ankle upwards? Let us rather strike at the knee"* he growled.

Eisenhower's planners, unwilling to land anywhere beyond the range of Allied fighters, settled for what they believed was a safe compromise. *Operation Avalanche;* a landing of 190,000 British and American troops in the Gulf of Salerno, on the west coast of Italy. Once safely ashore, Allied troops would advance on Naples to secure their supply lines and then move forwards to the Adriatic to trap German forces still in southern Italy.

Hitler, informed by his intelligence agencies that the Italians wanted to defect, ordered the concentration of powerful reserves outside Rome and at other key locations throughout Italy.

Should Badoglio switch sides, the German high command drew up a plan, code-named Axis, to seize the King of Italy and the Italian government, disarm all Italian troops and occupy key installations.

But Hitler still hesitated, and in the meantime, he had not forgotten his friend Mussolini, who had been imprisoned by Badoglio's government since July 25th. SS paratroopers under the command of Major Otto Skorzeny were given the task of finding the Duce and bring him back to Germany.

On the fourth anniversary of Prime Minister Neville Chamberlain's declaration of war on Nazi Germany, British and Canadian troops belonging to Montgomery's 8th Army crossed the Straits of Messina in an operation code-named Baytown.

Under the cover of a heavy artillery barrage, they stormed ashore at Reggio di Calabria and encountered absolutely no resistance. By nightfall, they had taken prisoner three German stragglers and three thousand friendly Italians. For the first time since April 1941, British troops were back in force on mainland Europe.

But Montgomery had always doubted Baytown's value. In his view, a landing by the 8th Army at the toe of Italy would not help the main Allied landing at Salerno when it occurred, but he did what he was ordered. However, his troops, delayed only by small German rearguards, seemed to be in no hurry to advance northwards.

Over two days, from September 5th, American and British troops in the three divisions and the two commando brigades taking part in the assault phase of *Operation Avalanche,* embarked from ports in North Africa and Sicily.

They belonged to the 5th US Army under the command of General Mark Clarke. His army was due to land on a 35-mile front in the Gulf of Salerno between Amalfi on the Sorrento peninsula on the left and Agropoli on the right, with the town of Salerno roughly in the center.

Clarke hoped to surprise the enemy, so he dispensed with the usual preliminary aerial and naval bombardment. This was an unwise decision. Clarke was a courageous and charismatic officer but so far in this war he had not commanded troops in battle.

· · ·

As the invasion fleet headed towards Salerno, news of the signing of the armistice with Badoglio was broadcast on Allied radio. The announcement took most Italians by surprise, but it stirred the Germans into action. Troops under the command of Field Marshal Kesselring, Hitler's Mediterranean theatre commander, quickly implemented *Operation Axis*.

Most of the forces Badoglio hoped to bring over to the Allied side were either disarmed or overwhelmed. Fortunately for the US 82nd Airborne Division, its planned air drop on Rome had been cancelled at the last minute.

However, the main Italian battle fleet succeeded in putting to sea from its base at La Spezia. While it was steaming past Sardinia to meet the Royal Navy, the battleship Roma was blown apart by a new German anti-shipping weapon, the HS 293 glide bomb.

But the rest of the Italian fleet arrived safely in Malta. On September 11th, Admiral Sir Andrew Cunningham, Commander-in-Chief of the Royal Navy's Mediterranean Fleet, signaled the Admiralty in London *"Be pleased to inform their Lordships that the Italian Battle fleet now lies at anchor under the guns of the fortress of Malta".*

In the twelve hours before they landed in the Gulf of Salerno, the 80,000 Allied troops taking part in the assault phase of *Operation Avalanche* discovered to their dismay, that the enemy knew they were on their way as Luftwaffe bombers launched sporadic attacks on the invasion fleet.

Before dawn September 9th, the first waves of British and American troops boarded their landing craft and as they approached their invasion beaches, they came under fierce enemy fire. In the British sector, warships supporting the landing by the 46th and 56th Divisions bombarded enemy coast defenses.

· · ·

But in the American sector at Paestum, the commander of the 36th Texas Division, going into action for the first time, obeyed Clarke's order not to lay down a supporting artillery barrage on the shore. As a result, the Texans suffered heavy casualties.

Field Marshal Kesselring had guessed correctly the location of the Allies' main landing in Italy.

To defeat it, he had deployed six divisions under General Heinrich von Vietinghoff, commander of the 10th Army, in easy striking distance of Salerno.

But at first, the Allied landings went well. American Rangers and British Army Commandos quickly captured the town of Salerno and seized the mountain passes leading to Naples on the 5th US Army Corps' left flank. However, the three assault divisions soon had a hard fight on their hands as they pushed further inland.

The flaws in *Operation Avalanche* began to show themselves. The 5th US Army's beachhead was too wide for just three assault divisions and Von Vietinghoff's combat veterans moved quickly to exploit the gap between the British on the left, and the Americans on the right. The Rangers and Commandos defending the mountain passes found themselves dangerously exposed to probing enemy attacks.

On September 12th, the fighting at Salerno entered its most critical phase. The Germans were determined to eliminate the 5th US Army's beachhead before Montgomery's 8th Army had time to reinforce it from the south. In the next seventy-two hours, fierce counterattacks mounted by German battle groups almost succeeded in driving the Americans into the sea.

. . .

On the evening of September 13th, Mark Clarke even asked his naval commander to help evacuate 5th US Army headquarters from the beachhead.

But the enemy was driven off by the 5th US Army's own artillery and the guns of the Allied warships lying offshore. Allied reinforcements were rushed to Salerno and the moment of crisis passed. On September 16th, Montgomery's 8th Army finally linked up with Mark Clarke's 5th US. and on the same day, Von Vietinghoff ordered the German 10th Army to withdraw to the north. The 5th US Army's ordeal at Salerno was finally over.

As usual, the Germans fought a skillful withdrawal. It was not until late on October 1st 1943 that units of the British 7th Armored Division entered Naples which of course was *Operation Avalanche's* primary objective.

The operation was over. It had cost the Allies more than twelve thousand casualties, including 2,000 dead and 3,500 missing. But Von Vietinghoff's outnumbered and outgunned forces lived to fight another day.

So too had Adolf Hitler's friend and ally, Benito Mussolini. The Allies had taken their first tentative steps onto the European mainland. But the struggle for *"the underbelly of Europe"*, as Churchill was fond of calling Italy, was only just beginning.

17

NEW CHALLENGES

October – December 1943

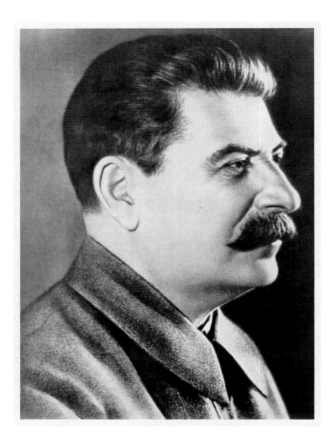

| Portrait of Stalin

W hen war broke out in 1939, as Nazi tanks stormed across the Polish border, it would have been virtually impossible to predict just how far reaching the consequences of Adolf Hitler's actions would be. By the winter of 1943 from the north, south, east and west the battle cries rang out across the globe, and the atrocities visited upon innocent civilians, particularly those of the Jewish faith, became ever more horrifically apparent. But as Hitler's Axis Powers crushed and subjugated entire populations, news of Nazi and Japanese crimes against humanity served to fuel Allied determination to win the war as quickly as possible.

. . .

The plight of those held in Concentration Camps was no longer hidden from view, and although it would still be some considerable time before surviving inmates would be liberated, there was now at least hope for some of them. What's more as October 1943 drew to a close, a formal Allied agreement to set up a United Nations' Commission on war crimes was put in place. Those responsible for atrocities would be called upon to account for their actions, and *"following orders"* would be no defense.

The months of October, November and December 1943 saw the culmination of many campaigns, and the foundations were laid for many more.

Events in the Pacific were rapidly gathering momentum, two years on from the surprise Japanese attack on the American Naval Fleet at Pearl. Without doubt the devastating efficiency of Japan's air force makes this one of the most well-known offensives of the entire Second World War, but through the course of this chapter you will discover that there were also many less well-known skirmishes in the Pacific that were equally fascinating.

As well as considering these events in the Pacific, we'll also be focusing on the Allied Campaign in Italy, following on from victory over Hitler's troops in North Africa. And all the while the conflict in Russia was becoming ever more significant, particularly as alliances shifted in the build up to the Cairo and Tehran Conferences, as the blueprint for the Allies' end game took shape.

So, beginning on October 1st 1943 new challenges take us to Italy when Allied forces entered the harbor city of Naples. The complex politics of Italy and the nation's position in World War II meant that the people of Naples had already revolted against the German Army of occupation before the Allies arrived. However, to get a true understanding of the events in Italy in 1943 we really need to back track to the end of the *First* World War.

. . .

Just as Adolf Hitler rose to prominence in Germany in the aftermath of WWI, in Italy, Benito Mussolini followed a very similar route to power. Born in 1883, the son of a blacksmith, Mussolini moved to Switzerland in 1902 in search of work and it was here that he became involved in Socialist politics.

When he returned to Italy in 1904, it was to become a journalist with a Socialist publication, but he broke away from the Socialists when they opposed Italy's entry into WWI, and when he was drafted in 1915, Mussolini took up arms for his country.

In all, Mussolini saw about nine months active service, but in the years after the war he returned to the political arena, this time not as a Socialist, but by forming the Fascist Party early in 1919. Like Adolf Hitler in Germany, Mussolini believed he would be his nation's savior, and where discontent was rife he found his supporters.

Many unemployed war veterans followed where Mussolini led, and were organized into squads of Black Shirts who terrorized their political opponents. It was the beginning of a dark age of oppression for the Italian people, and when the Fascists were invited to join a coalition government in 1921, things went from bad to worse when the Black Shirts marched on Rome.

Even the King of Italy, Victor Emmanuel III, turned to Mussolini, inviting the self-styled "Il Duce" to form a government with disastrous consequences as by 1925 democracy had been dismantled. Italy found itself in the grip of a dictator every bit as unpredictable as Adolf Hitler was becoming in Germany.

After the Wall Street Crash of 1929 saw the world fall into an economic depression, the 1930s found both Hitler and Mussolini empire building at an alarming rate. In Mussolini's case, Abyssinia, today better known as Ethiopia, was the main target.

As well as gaining inroads into Africa, Mussolini also supported General Franco in the Spanish Civil War, and more importantly, co-operated with Hitler and Nazi Germany to such a degree that it culminated in May 1939 in their "Pact of Steel", as World War II loomed large.

Italy formally entered World War II on the 10th of June 1940, officially signing up to the Tripartite Pact with Germany and Japan on the 27th September of that same year, in Berlin. Under Mussolini's leadership however, Italy was far from being a strong military nation, and as early as 1941 had suffered multiple defeats in Greece and at the hands of the British in North Africa.

Ironically, without German intervention Mussolini and the Italian army would have faced a catastrophic military collapse, and for the people of Italy, confidence in Il Duce was shaken if not stirred.

Despite Mussolini's pre-World War II activity in Africa, the Italians were defeated in the desert along with the Germans under the command of Erwin Rommel. And naturally, once soldiers of the caliber of the British General, Bernard Montgomery, had secured North Africa, the Allies looked towards Italy as the next logical stepping-stone back into mainland Europe.

The Allies successful campaign to take Sicily, code named *Operation Husky* began in July, and came as quite a shock to the Italians. Their position was truly precarious as not only did they have the battle hardened British, Canadian and American troops from North Africa to worry about, but their so called "allies", the Nazis, were equally menacing.

. . .

If the Italians surrendered, they would come under immediate German attack, and anger against Mussolini for putting Italy in such a predicament grew. With Sicily under heavy assault, early in July 1943 Mussolini was removed from power and put under arrest. The King of Italy himself took control, and with Marshal Badoglio taking charge of the government, Hitler feared an imminent Italian surrender to the Allies and ordered plans be put in place immediately to liberate Mussolini.

Having been humiliated on the eastern Front with the loss of Stalingrad, Hitler was determined that the dramatic turn of events in Italy, and all around the Mediterranean, would not be permitted to undermine his power even further. Consequently, when the Italians did surrender, unconditionally, to the Allies early in September, the Germans were swift to react.

Firstly, they liberated Mussolini and restored him as a puppet dictator, then they set to work, salvaging whatever they could as they attempted to halt the Allies in their tracks. What was about to unfold in Italy would change the course of the war, and the American President, Franklin D. Roosevelt, astutely commented in one of his famous fireside chat broadcasts that *"The first crack in the Axis has come. The criminal, corrupt fascist regime in Italy is going to pieces"*. The question now was who would pick up the fallen pieces first, the Allies or the Germans?

In the last days of September 1943, the Allies were making good progress in the south of Italy. While the King and Marshal Badoglio met the American General, Dwight D. Eisenhower, aboard HMS Nelson to sign a full armistice, to the north Hitler had annexed the German speaking regions of northern Italy.

What had seemed to the Allies an "easy" advance to Rome was now becoming very much more complicated as the lines between who was friend and who was foe became increasingly blurred.

. . .

By October 1st when the Allies marched into Naples, the Germans had been fighting a revolt by the citizens of the city. Matters had exploded into conflict when German soldiers began to loot a shop. At least amongst the devastation of Naples the Allies were assured the support of their new brother in arms.

Meanwhile on the Adriatic side of Italy as October began, the Allies had also captured Foggia, and with it the most important airport in the region.

Hitler's propaganda minister Joseph Goebbels was quick to assess the situation and realized that even his considerable talents would be stretched in putting a positive spin on this event.

The Allies now had the potential to launch air attacks on Nazi held strongholds in the Balkans as well as giving them a springboard to attack southern Germany. This was of little consolation though to the thousands of Italian soldiers who were now facing the full brunt of Hitler's wrath.

Even those who had surrendered to the Germans, including 5,000 on the Greek Island of Cephalonia, were brutally massacred by the Nazis, and with the pressures mounting, it wasn't only military personnel that faced the backlash of German retaliation.

On October 3rd the Gestapo ordered all the Jews in Athens to register and Greece quickly became an important focal point for the Allies, with Italy being so close by, but the Germans were equally determined to secure as much territory in the area as possible. Within 24 hours the British protectors of the Island of Kos had been beaten soundly by Hitler's Axis Powers, despite the "cracks" spotted in their armor by Roosevelt.

. . .

And as the Greek Jews were targeted, the Italian Jews were also about to discover the sting of Nazi persecution. On October 9th a hundred Italian Jews from Trieste were rounded up and sent to Auschwitz, and not one of them survived. This was the Day of Atonement in the Jewish Calendar, the ancient festival of Yom Kippur, one of the holiest of all Jewish holidays.

At Auschwitz, this day did not go unmarked as the Nazis picked out 1,000 inmates they claimed were too weak to work and executed them. Without the protection of being part of Hitler's Axis of Evil, the Jews of Italy were now SS targets.

There were nonetheless some advantages to be enjoyed because Eisenhower announced that there would be no more Allied bombing raids on Italy, and all efforts were made to prevent the ships of the Italian navy falling into German hands. But Hitler's retaliation was unrelenting, and as the Luftwaffe were ordered to attack the escaping ships as they headed for Malta, he also drafted in more ground troops from the Russian Front.

With the Nazis in full occupation of Rome, General Erwin Rommel was charged with commanding operations in Northern Italy, while General Kesselring had the daunting task of stemming the tide of the Allied advance in the south and protecting the Italian capital.

Although Kesselring could do little about Naples, the Führer would have been delighted at the devastation his General left behind for the Allies to deal with. The reprisals were appalling, as all communication, transport, water and power systems were destroyed, while the city's buildings burnt, bridges were bombed, railway tracks were torn up and the harbor was a mass of sunken ships.

The workload for the Allies was huge, and Kesselring would have been well aware that in excess of 800,000 civilians would now be reliant upon the Allies for their survival. Instead of speedily moving north to consolidate their advantage, the Allies were stalled as they dealt with the aftermath of Naples, but to their credit the port was restored, reopened and functioning within a week.

With the Allied Commanders' sights now set on Rome, there was no time to lose, and the German defensive line at the Volturno River, twenty miles north west of Naples, came under attack. The Volturno Line ran from the town of Termoli along the Biferno River, through the Apennine Mountains to the Volturno River. As early as October 6th Canadian tanks had forced the German troops of occupation to withdraw from Termoli and by the 12th of the month the American 5th Army had crossed the river to breach the German defensive line and in so doing push the Nazis back yet further.

The very next day the King and the Italian Government declared war on Germany as the battles raged on.

There were heavy civilian casualties as well as military losses with what happened at places like Campobasso being typical. Resonant with ancient history, even the city hall with all the archives was destroyed as the 1st Canadian Corps eventually took the city from the Germans.

By October 16th the Allies were just ninety miles from Rome, but on the very same day, in the capital, German SS officers seized more than 1,000 Italian Jews. However, with more than four thousand Jews given refuge in private homes, monasteries and convents, not to mention almost 500 hidden inside the Vatican, the Nazis once again found themselves thwarted by their former allies.

| Map of Central Europe and Italy

The Allied war effort was now really gathering pace as from the snow-clad mountains of Italy to the sweltering jungles of the Pacific, the dream that victory could be theirs, was steadily becoming a reality. The positive influence of Roosevelt, Eisenhower and the Americans were making a colossal difference and with them came propaganda every bit as effective as that manipulated by Joseph Goebbels and the Nazis.

Hollywood film stars rallied to entertain the troops, and from the glamorous Carole Landis to the comical Joe Brown, many entertainers were happy to play their part, no matter what the dangers to their own personal safety. And in this positive atmosphere, plans for the Allied invasion of France were also gathering momentum.

. . .

In the south of England exercises were taking place with tank landing craft, and by the middle of October the code name *"Mulberry"* had been selected for the hugely daring artificial harbors made of concrete that would be such an essential part of the D-Day landing plan.

Nevertheless, the principal Allied nations, the USA, Great Britain and Russia were far from feeling at ease with each other, especially as Russia had been so closely linked with Hitler in the early stages of the war. It was Winston Churchill, the British Prime Minister, who had speedily moved to recruit Joseph Stalin to the Allied cause after Hitler's *Operation Barbarossa,* when the Germans had invaded Russia.

Ever since, despite Hitler's confident prediction that the Soviets would crumble before him, the Russians had been a constant thorn in his side. But Churchill of all people, a man who in his long political life had changed his allegiances on more than one occasion, was all too aware of the disastrous consequences if Russia were to defect back to the Axis Powers.

Consequently, on October 18th in Moscow the American, British and Russian foreign ministers agreed that they would not consider any separate peace negotiations with Germany, while the very next day, in Washington, the Americans agreed to supply millions of tons of aid to the Soviets.

As October 1943 drew to its conclusion with the Allies maneuvering into position to sustain their assault on the Axis Powers, the cost in human suffering was escalating. On the 25th the Japanese completed the Burma-Thailand Railway, with the forced labor of 46,000 Allied Prisoners of War. More than 16,000 of them had died of starvation, brutality and disease, alongside many thousands more Burmese citizens caught up in a war not of their making, in which they too were forced labor for Imperial Japan.

. . .

Just as events in Southern Europe were now moving at a rapid pace, the same was equally true in the Pacific.

On the very first day of November US soldiers of the 3rd Marine Division landed in Empress Augusta Bay on the Solomon Island of Bougainville. Backed up by an impressive US Naval Task Force of four Light Cruisers and eight destroyers and commanded by the brilliant Rear Admiral Aaron S "Tip" Merrill, the Americans quickly consolidated their position.

The Japanese were equally quick to respond, launching air attacks from Rabaul, as well as dispatching their own powerful Task Force of cruisers and destroyers. Merrill was the first American Rear Admiral to use RADAR and, in this battle, it gave him a major advantage. Without RADAR the Japanese commander failed to assess the outcome of the battle accurately when Merrill retreated under cover of smoke.

Returning to Rabaul the Japanese believed they had been victorious and prepared to re-attack the Allied landing forces at Bougainville, without realizing Merrill's task force was still very much intact.

Two US aircraft carriers raided Rabaul on November 5th and having underestimated their enemy, the Japanese fleet sustained heavy losses, which meant that any danger to the now well-established US marines from Japan's Imperial Navy, had for the time being at least, passed.

Success in the Solomon Islands had been crucial to the Allies because it was from here that the Japanese had planned to expand into New Guinea, Papua and most worryingly of all, Australia. To re-cap a little, the campaign for the Solomon Islands had started back in February 1943 with General MacArthur leading a sustained American strategic offensive. By June, islands that people had never heard of in the west were suddenly on the map.

. . .

In *Operation Toenails* the Americans overcame Japanese resistance as they landed on the island of Rendova, with the crucial airfield at Munda within attack range from there. While American and Japanese ships battled for dominance in the waters of the Kula and Vella Gulfs, although there was no outright victory for the Allies, the Japanese were prevented from backing up their ground troops.

When Munda airfield fell to the Americans on August 5th, phase one of their campaign was complete, but there was still a great deal of work to be done clearing Japanese troops from New Georgia and the surrounding islands of Arundel, Baanga, Gizo, Kolombangara and Vella Lavella. The Japanese were a most tenacious enemy, honor bound never to contemplate surrender, always fighting to the death. In the build up to the Battle of Empress Augusta Bay in November 1943, *Operation Toenails* had been vital, and what lay ahead was destined to be equally challenging.

Interestingly the Japanese suffered much heavier losses of ships and planes than the Americans, but while the USA could manufacture replacements, by this stage in the war the Japanese could not. Nevertheless, the Japanese determination in battle, and policy of no surrender continued undaunted, serving notice to the Allies that whatever the outcome of the war against Hitler in Europe, victory over the Japanese was going to be a separate issue.

With the end of 1943 just weeks away Adolf Hitler was finding the troops available to him were becoming ever more thinly spread. Having to occupy Italy, as well as cope with another bitter cold winter on the Russian Front was bad enough, but the Germans were now in no doubt that an invasion of Western Europe sometime in 1944 was imminent.

In fact, on November 3rd Adolf Hitler issued Directive 51 warning of the anticipated Allied Landings, and his propaganda minister, Goebbels once again had a difficult task ahead of him convincing the German nation that their Führer was still invincible.

Goebbels' personal diaries offer a fascinating insight, and on the day before Hitler issued Directive 51, Goebbels made an entry regarding the fact that more than 9,000 German soldiers had been killed on the eastern Front in just nine days. He said *"We cannot sustain such a drain for long, we are in danger of slowly bleeding to death in the east".*

Whatever the public face of Nazi propaganda, Goebbels like many of his fellow high-ranking officials was fully aware of the all too real danger of Germany being defeated. Without doubt the Nazi propaganda machine was being stretched to the full by the events in Western Europe and Russia.

However, the Japanese Government was even more determined that the people of Japan should believe that their brave Imperial warriors were victorious, in every campaign of the Pacific offensive. There were of course plenty of occasions when they did score direct hits against the Allies, particularly out at sea, and on November 19th the Japanese Navy sunk the USS Sculpin, a Sargo class submarine.

Appropriately named after a remarkably stealthy fish that can survive out of water as well as in it, and capable of inflicting a painful sting, the sinking of the Sculpin was a major blow to the American Navy.

Yet the Japanese missed a golden opportunity to gain intelligence regarding the devastating attack the Allies were planning for the very next day on the three Atolls in the Gilbert Islands; Makin, Tarawa and Abemama. Aboard the Sculpin was Captain John P Cromwell who had been fully briefed on the offensive to take the Gilbert Islands, code-named *Operation Galvanic.*

. . .

When the submarine was first struck, the vessel's commander surfaced to give his crew the chance of survival, but a direct hit to the conning tower meant that he, along with many of his men, were killed outright. Cromwell was not amongst them but realized if he was taken prisoner by the Japanese he might reveal the secret plans under torture.

Bravely he went down with the sinking submarine rather than risk jeopardizing the operation and was posthumously awarded the Medal of Honor for devotion to his country.

To date the Americans had been given little chance to go on the offensive with the Japanese because after the shock of Pearl Harbor they had constantly been taking a defensive position. Interestingly the Battle of Tarawa was only the second time they had done this, the first being the Guadalcanal Campaign, where their amphibious landing force had met little resistance. But things were about to change dramatically.

Strategically the Gilbert Islands were of vital importance as the Allies increased their operations from the mid-Pacific to the Philippines and prepared to advance on Japan. Taking the Mariana Islands from the Japanese would be crucial if the US Navy stood any chance of succeeding in this objective, but naturally Imperial Japan was all too aware of this.

Because the Marianas, including the all-important island of Guam, had become a major target, Japanese reinforcements had been drafted in, with fortifications consolidated, to make the entire area as secure as possible.

The Americans knew that they would have to advance island group by island group, because before they could even reach the Marianas, they would need to wrestle the nearby Marshall Islands from Japanese control. But before they could do that, the enemy garrison on the Tarawa Atoll needed to be neutralized.

By now the Americans had enough experience of the Japanese to come prepared, and as *Operation Galvanic* began November 20th, over 6,000 US troops landed on Makin. On paper the occupying army made up of 300 Japanese soldiers and 500 Korean laborers, should have been easily defeated, but the battle was bitterly contested, and American casualties were high. It was a costly operation in other respects too as the US escort carrier, Liscome Bay, was torpedoed, killing 644 of the 900 crew.

Then an accident aboard the USS Battleship, Mississippi, during the pre-landing bombardment of Makin, when the turret exploded, resulted in a further 43 American deaths. The people of Makin were nevertheless delighted to greet their US liberators, offering coconuts as a token of their gratitude.

It was an experience the Allies were going to encounter many times in the coming months, as the freedom they were fighting so hard for, was returned to those so long oppressed by the Axis of Evil. With Makin secure, American troops began their assault on Tarawa Atoll, again about 6,000 of them, but there were 5,000 Japanese soldiers lying in wait for them.

A bloody battle ensued, lasting some seventy-six hours, with more than 1,000 of the Americans killed, and the Japanese statistics certainly make for some fascinating reading. Of the vast defending force only one Japanese officer and sixteen of his men survived, alongside 129 of the conscripted Korean laborers who had also made up the numbers.

For the American people, who had so far been protected by heavy censorship, the now unrestricted news reports were hugely shocking. Many condemned

Washington for allowing the offensive to go ahead, after seeing photographs of Americas' brave young men floating dead in the water. The realization that the Japanese were going to put up a long and terrible fight, really did hit home.

With their experiences on Makin and Tarawa, the Americans changed their tactics when they reached Abemama. Despite the much smaller Japanese garrison, one marine was killed within minutes during an attempted landing, so it was to settle for using Navy gunfire only to clear the army of occupation.

It was certainly effective, but not in terms of direct hits, because of the 25 Japanese defenders only 14 had been killed by gunfire, the rest had committed suicide.

The loss of the Gilbert Islands to the Americans was far from being good news for the Japanese Government back in Tokyo, but they did have the satisfaction of knowing the victorious US troops had suffered significant casualties in achieving their goal.

American B-17 bomber ready for action

But the bad news was not yet over for the Japanese as on November 25th American bombers attacked a crucial airbase on Formosa, or as we know it today, Taiwan.

The Japanese Navy operated heavily out of Formosa, which had been snatched from the Chinese, and the Americans destroying 42 of their aircraft in this mission was a huge blow. Air cover afforded the Japanese battleships extra protection and to lose so many planes was very costly indeed.

And it wasn't only the Americans giving the Japanese problems late in 1943, as on the same day in New Guinea, Australian forces captured vital territory.

Suddenly, despite their fierce fighting and "to the death" attitude, the Japanese were not looking quite as invincible as they had liked to appear.

Meanwhile as the final days of November dawned the pressure on Adolf Hitler in the west was increasing. On the 22nd the British carried out a night raid on the German capital, dispatching 764 bombers to attack Berlin. With direct hits on the Government section of the city including the Admiralty and Air Ministry, Hitler was incensed. He was safely resting at his Wolf's Lair Military Headquarters at Rastenburg in East Prussia, when even the Chancellery and his train in a Berlin railway siding suffered heavy damage.

The civilians of Berlin were not as fortunate as their leader however, as a hundred of them were crushed simply trying to get to safety in an underground shelter. Just as it had been for the civilians of London in the blitz, the number of innocent casualties escalated with 1,737 Berliners killed.

Goebbels once again committed his personal feelings to his diary noting that *"Hell itself seems to have broken loose over us"*.

The British lost 167 aircrew in the raid, but the very next night air command ordered a further raid on Berlin. This time 127 aircrew were lost, but the effect on the German capital was again devastating. With no heat, no light, and no water, and fellow Berliners dying all around, there was little even Goebbels could do to improve the morale of the German people.

For the Allies, there was work to be done wherever they turned and in Italy the push towards Rome continued. On November 20th the British 8th Army crossed the Sangro River for the first time, while Kesselring was appointed commander in chief of all German forces in Italy, as Rommel's services were now in great demand organizing the defense of the Atlantic Wall.

. . .

There were many major offensives like the bombing of Berlin and the continuing Italian campaign, but the little events were beginning to play a huge part too. In France the Resistance was undermining the German occupation at every turn, and with help from British Agents, the preparations for the long-awaited invasion of the coast of Northern France, were piece by piece, being slotted into place.

Pulling all the various elements of the Allied push for victory together was far from being an easy task. Meetings between the Allied leaders were incredibly difficult to orchestrate.

A prime example of this was the Cairo Conference held between the 22nd and the 26th of November. Winston Churchill, the British Prime Minister, and America's President Roosevelt met with China's Chiang Kai-Shek to discuss the Allied position against the Japanese.

Russia's Joseph Stalin refused to attend as he believed with the Chinese present it would be viewed by the Japanese as provocation on the part of the Soviets. On November 27th the Cairo declaration was nevertheless signed by the three leaders present, stating that the Allies would continue to employ military force until Japan's unconditional surrender.

It was also decided that when that happened all the islands of the Pacific, seized by the Japanese since the First World War, would be taken back, all territories Japan had seized from China would also be restored, and last but by no means least, Korea would become independent.

With the Cairo Conference complete, Churchill and Roosevelt looked towards further discussions on the Allies' plans to invade France. While Stalin's absence from Cairo had been manageable, it was time for "the big three" as they were so often dubbed, to meet, as the Tehran Conference began. Stalin had not travelled outside Russia since the Bolshevik Revolution of 1917, but the three unlikely allies arrived in Tehran amid the tightest security to agree the plan for an Anglo-American cross-channel invasion, planned for spring or summer 1944.

In the discussions on November 29th Churchill outlined to Stalin the conditions that needed to be met if *Operation Overlord* had any chance of succeeding. Firstly, there had to be a "satisfactory reduction" in the German fighter forces in northwest Europe.

Secondly, German reserves in France and the Low Countries had to be minimized on the day of the assault and thirdly, the Allies had to make sure the Germans could not transfer significant reinforcements from other fronts for the first sixty days of the operation.

Stalin was skeptical as to whether this was possible, but Churchill, as ever, found the right words to express what was required when he said *"It will be our stern duty to hurl across the Channel against the Germans every sinew of our strength"*.

But amidst discussions outlining the plans for *Operation Overlord,* Stalin also had quite an agenda of his own. He made it clear that the moment Germany was defeated, the Soviets would embark upon a war with the Japanese. Churchill described Stalin's declaration as a *"momentous decision"* that had to be kept absolutely top secret, in fact it wasn't even noted in the "secret" records of the Tehran talks.

There were also other matters on the table for discussion, but one in particular was ironically kept top secret from the Russians. Roosevelt and Churchill chose not to disclose to Stalin that scientists in America working on the atomic bomb were making massive progress, and that B-29 bombers were now being modified to carry and drop the deadly devices.

Hitler on a now rare public inspection clasping his left arm

The fear of new weaponry and scientific advances was huge for the Allies and the Axis alike, and in Britain concern over Hitler's designs for his unmanned rocket bombs continued to increase. Although it would still be many months before his V one rockets would be operational, a rare visit by Hitler to a flying bomb test site was scrutinized in the minutest detail.

Hitler at this time was always reluctant to leave his Wolf's Lair HQ due to growing fears that he would be assassinated, as his health, both mentally and physically deteriorated. It has been suggested that he was suffering from

Parkinson's Disease, but this has never been substantiated. In the light of this, British Intelligence knew that such a visit must have been important, and it was even speculated that the rocket bombs could weigh up to seven tons.

Consequently, Churchill's Government put in place plans to make millions of hospital beds available for those who might be injured by such a weapon. Prevention would nevertheless be better than a cure, so *Operation Crossbow* was also instigated to systematically bomb any site in Northern France that looked suspicious from reconnaissance photographs.

With the arrival of December, as the world waited for the end of another year at war, the major players continued to maneuver themselves into position. On December 7th the American President, Franklin D. Roosevelt appointed General Dwight D. Eisenhower to the much-coveted command of *Operation Overlord*.

Calm and levelheaded, with Eisenhower as Supreme Commander of the Allied Expeditionary Forces, Overlord was in a very safe pair of hands indeed.

And Eisenhower was not alone as the British General, Bernard Montgomery was also about to be called to rally for the Overlord cause.

He had been fully occupied in Italy since his rise to prominence with the British 8th Army in North Africa, but things were moving very slowly now in the Italian Campaign, as the Germans tightened their grip on Rome and other significant strongholds.

By the end of December Montgomery returned to England to command the 21st Army Group, while Oliver Leese took over Monty's role in Italy. Always outspoken, Montgomery with a characteristic lack of tact, announced that he was glad to be leaving what he described as the *"dog's breakfast"* of the Allied Campaign in Italy.

Ironically, there were dissenting voices, most notably from the American camp, claiming that "Monty" had actually played a part in creating the *"dog's breakfast"* and things did not exactly bode well for future relations between the opinionated Englishman and certain US Generals.

By the very nature of the Anglo-American offensive these strong-minded personalities were going to have to forget their differences and work together, and it would take all of Eisenhower's immense talent as a diplomat to ensure the very men needed to win the war did not end up fighting amongst themselves.

Even so, as more and more attention was now being focused on *Overlord,* the Allies still continued to push on towards Rome. For the Canadian, British and American troops fighting in Italy it was now evident that the battles ahead were going to be long, drawn out and costly. What had appeared to be a straightforward campaign was now going to become a war of attrition throughout 1944.

The Germans at the front of Cassino as 1943 drew to a close could not be dislodged, despite the best efforts of the Allies. The winter weather was making the task even more difficult, and any hope of matters in Italy being completely concluded before *Operation Overlord* commenced were fading fast. As Christmas appeared on the horizon, events in the Pacific also continued to hit the headlines.

On December 15th American troops landed on the Arawe Peninsula at the western end of New Britain in the Solomon Islands. It was a strategically important advance, with the capital of New Britain, Rabaul, still operating as a formidable Japanese stronghold.

With people everywhere praying for peace at Christmas time, World War II relentlessly marched ever onwards. On Christmas Eve the British once again bombed Berlin and on Christmas Day, American planes knocked out twenty-four of the flying bomb sites that had been spotted in Northern France.

In Washington President Roosevelt made his traditional broadcast to the nation. There was little comfort to be had from his wise words, which was totally appropriate after the recent events in the Pacific, and the horrific casualties inflicted upon the Americans by the Japanese. For the sake of those US marines and their families, the bitter pill could have no sugar coating.

Roosevelt pulled America together with a timely warning of what the year ahead was likely to bring, asking for one and all to find the strength and fortitude that would be required if the Allies were going to be victorious.

He said:

"The war is now reaching the stage when we shall have to look forward to large casualty-lists – dead, wounded and missing. War entails just that. There is no easy road to victory. And the end is not yet in sight".

It was evidently just what was required of the American President, as a day later US troops launched *Operation Backhander,* a landing on Cape Gloucester, on the extreme tip of New Britain. There was no festive holiday out in the Pacific and within a week the Americans had secured a vital airfield, giving them the perfect location to launch attacks on the yet unconquered half of New Guinea. This was a positive note for the year to end on for the Allies, but the Japanese fought back as fiercely as ever, and there was little doubt that the first months of 1944 would come complete with ever more conflict for the World at War.

The grand conferences had been attended, the now famous Allied leaders had been pictured chatting together at Cairo and Tehran and despite the major policy rift on human rights that existed between the Western Allies and the Russians, for the time being at least, they were presenting a united front. What would happen to the strained allegiances once the war was over was going to be extremely complicated, and on a global scale the ramifications were immense.

Yet from the sleepy seaside towns of southern England through to the ancient streets of historic London, it was this determined island nation that was about to take center stage.

For Adolf Hitler, his earlier inability to break the people's spirit and invade Britain would return to haunt him, as *Operation Overlord* now had the most stable of platforms to be launched from.

The people of Britain would once more be asked to stand firm and resolute, playing host to the many thousands of Allied troops and supplies required to cross the Channel and invade France.

Preparations were now almost complete to force the German army of occupation to retreat back across its own borders, in a prelude to Hitler's last stand. The Blueprint for victory was at long last about to be written.

18

BLUEPRINT FOR VICTORY

January – March 1944

| Eisenhower addresses the troops

W hen the clock struck midnight, marking the final moments of 1943, and the New Year of 1944 began, World War II continued at a rapidly accelerating pace. All eyes turned to London as the preparations for *Operation Overlord,* the long-awaited Allied Invasion of Northern France, were finalized.

In Germany Adolf Hitler and his high-ranking officials knew all too well that the invasion forces would soon be on their way, but where they would land, and perhaps more importantly, when they would cross the Channel, was yet to be revealed.

. . .

427

Hitler's public appearances were now very rare, and the Führer struggled to come to terms with the reality of the German situation. On all sides his position was becoming daily more untenable, with the Allies making good progress in both the European and Pacific Theaters of War.

With his henchmen all around him, Joseph Goebbels, Heinrich Himmler and Herman Goering to name but a few, Hitler grew increasingly withdrawn and was often irrational in his decision making. Even those closest to him finally began to realize that their leader was no longer the great savior of Germany that they had once believed him to be.

When war had broken out back in 1939 it had seemed that Adolf Hitler was invincible, as he offered a real solution to the problems of poverty faced by Germany in the aftermath of the First World War. Crippled by debts after paying reparations for being the aggressors, the Germans had been stripped of national pride and with his incredible oratory skills Hitler used this to his advantage, finding a ready audience for even his more extreme Nazi doctrines. Storming across Europe as other heads of state did all they could to appease him, the German people and the rest of the world could only watch and wait to see what he would do next.

Poland fell to the Nazis, quickly followed by Norway, Denmark, the Low Countries and France, as Hitler's stranglehold on Europe tightened. In the west the British fought on alone, but with a new Prime Minister, Winston Churchill, came real hope. Within weeks of him taking office Churchill courageously dispatched a massive flotilla of small boats to France to rescue more than 300,000 Allied Servicemen stranded on the beaches of Dunkirk.

It was a "miracle of deliverance" and morale all across the United Kingdom soared. This was a vital boost to those on the Home Front, especially as Hitler was about to launch the Battle for Britain as he prepared to invade the Island nation.

. . .

The one thing that Hitler hadn't accounted for though was the spirit of the British people, now they had an inspirational leader in Winston Churchill. When the Luftwaffe failed to crush the RAF in the air and Hitler changed tactics, targeting London in the blitz as well as other towns and cities, the British remained united in their determination to stand firm against the enemy.

It should have been a stark warning to Hitler that the world was not going to simply fall at his feet, but unheeding, he turned to the east and attacked the mighty Russians, his former ally, in what he decreed would be a quick and decisive victory.

Of course Hitler was not the only aggressor on the field of battle. His tripartite pact with the Japanese and the Italians meant that the Axis powers reached far and wide across the globe. With their own agenda and ongoing disputes with the Americans, the Japanese bombed Pearl Harbor in December 1941 and changed the face of the war dramatically, bringing the full might of the USA into the conflict.

Within the course of a year Hitler had gone from facing an Allied enemy held together by the spirit of the British people and the sheer determination of Winston Churchill, to an onslaught on all fronts. The economic power of the Americans combined with the colossal manpower of the Russians meant that the British had the breathing space they needed to recover and return to fighting strength.

It was nonetheless never going to be a heartfelt and comfortable alliance between the British, the Americans and the Russians not least since Hitler had made a non-aggression pact with the Soviets at the beginning of the war. Joseph Stalin, the Russian leader, every bit the dictator that Adolf Hitler was, ruthlessly carved up Poland with the German Führer, as the Red Army treated the besieged Poles with as much brutality as the Nazis had done.

For Churchill and the American President, Franklin D. Roosevelt, Stalin, even as an ally, was not to be trusted. However, in the immediate aftermath of *Operation Barbarossa*, when the Germans had stormed into Russia, Churchill held out an Olive branch to Stalin, calculating that the advantages to be gained from having the Soviets onside far outweighed the operational difficulties of working with them.

At first Stalin had questioned the importance placed by his fellow Allies on the North African campaign, wanting them to open a second front in Europe to take the pressure off his troops, but when Churchill visited Moscow for talks he was able to explain the long-term strategy. By securing North Africa the Allies would be able to launch an attack on Italy and get a foothold in Europe from the south, which would co-ordinate with the crucial invasion planned for Northern France.

It's quite often overlooked, but as we progress to consider the Blueprint for Victory, and the build up to *Operation Overlord,* there was a much smaller scale Allied invasion of France back in 1942.

On August 19th a joint British and Canadian commando raid was made on the French port of Dieppe, as 5,000 troops plus 50 American Rangers and half as many again Free French soldiers took part in *Operation Jubilee.*

Although unsuccessful, it did give the Allies vital information to help them plan a future assault on the French coast, that would eventually take shape as the D-Day Landings.

. . .

The casualties at Dieppe were a disaster for the Allies, especially for the Canadians, while all equipment and vehicles were abandoned on the beaches. Interestingly on hearing the news Hitler mocked his enemy, saying, *"the British have had the courtesy to cross the sea to offer the enemy a complete sample of their weapons"*.

But later, when he briefed his commanders Hitler's tone was far more reflective, when he told them *"We must realize that we are not alone in learning from the lesson from Dieppe. The British have also learned. We must reckon with a totally different method of attack and at a different place"*.

Dieppe may have been a minor blip on the radar of this global war, but like so many operations that failed to achieve their objectives, it nonetheless made a major contribution to the bigger picture.

As Hitler turned his attention back to Russia and the bloody battle that lay ahead for Stalingrad, and the Japanese slogged it out with Americans on the islands of the Pacific, the Western Allies were making steady progress in North Africa.

After the British under the command of General Bernard Montgomery had been victorious at the Battle of El Alamein, Hitler's "Desert Fox" General Erwin Rommel and the German troops were forced into retreat.

Operation Torch, the first Anglo-American invasion of the war involving a huge amphibious force, pushed the Axis even further back in Tunisia, and eventually in May 1943, when the British finally entered the nation's capital, Tunis, Rommel had no other option but to accept defeat.

The fight for North Africa was over and the Allies quickly made the most of their advantage, putting plans to take the attack to southern Europe via Italy into action. *Operation Husky* was their first offensive, focused on the Island of Sicily, and after a swift victory the campaign for Italy seemed to be theirs for the taking.

Yet in war the tide can turn in the blink of an eye, and the fight for Italy was anything but a foregone conclusion. Hitler was unable to prevent the Italians from surrendering and therefore ordered a German invasion of his former comrade in arms, Benito Mussolini's nation. This made the push for control of Rome by British, American and Canadian troops a much tougher task than had ever been anticipated. Despite the difficulties faced by the Allies in Italy as 1943 came to a close, plans for the liberation of France in the spring or summer of 1944 were now unstoppable.

As the Russians continued to attack the Germans from the east and the Americans battled for supremacy in the Pacific, Great Britain prepared to play host to the mightiest invasion force the world had ever seen.

No matter how positive the news was of Allied progress around the globe, those that Hitler had condemned to the Concentration Camps, whether Jews, Poles or Gypsies, faced greater suffering than ever.

Yet another Concentration Camp opened in Poland on New Year's Day, having previously been a forced Labor Camp, tyrannized by its commandant, Amnon Goth. His sadistic treatment of inmates was highlighted in the poignant film "Schindler's List", warning a whole new generation of the true horrors of war.

Even so, there was a growing resistance to Axis oppression, with brave individuals often making a personal stand against those who preyed on innocent civilians simply caught up in the conflict. In the Philippines an American mining engineer by the name of Wendell Fertig had refused to surrender when the Japanese had taken the islands back in 1942.

A civilian himself, he went deep into the jungle and built up a force of several thousand Filipinos and together they constantly harassed the increasingly tyrannical Japanese army of occupation. Wendell Fertig only ceased his guerrilla activities in the jungles of the Philippines when the American General, Douglas MacArthur returned to take the islands back from the Japanese later in 1944, just as he had promised he would do.

In the meantime, the British Royal Air Force had been systematically bombing Berlin for some time, and they had planned a further air raid for the first night of the New Year. Bad weather forced a brief postponement but by January 2nd it was business as usual with Hitler's seat of power under siege yet again.

Just as it was business as usual for the British pilots, the Americans continued to advance their campaign for New Guinea and New Britain out in the Pacific. Japan was still a long way away, but for the Russians their target of reaching Germany was getting closer by the day.

On January 3rd the Red Army were within ten miles of what had been the Polish border back in 1939, leaving Adolf Hitler in no doubt whatsoever that a Russian breakthrough was not far off.

More pressing on Hitler's mind however was the Allies' Cross-Channel invasion. American and British aircraft began *Operation Carpetbagger* on the 4th, dropping arms and supplies to resistance groups in France, Holland, Belgium and Italy, as the Allies' carefully planned preparations were being slotted into place. It was also time for the Allies to start calling the main protagonists entrusted with leading *Operation Overlord* to London.

. . .

General Bernard Montgomery, now Sir Bernard having been knighted by King George the Sixth in recognition of his victory at El Alamein, had returned to England from Italy to take command of the British contingent of the Allied Expeditionary Force. To his men "Monty", as they fondly knew him, was a hero they would follow to the ends of the earth, but for those in command of him "Monty" could be something of a loose cannon.

He was extraordinarily valuable in the fight against Hitler, but it was commonly quoted that Montgomery was great to serve under, difficult to serve alongside, but hell to serve over. For whoever was in overall charge of *Operation Overlord* earning the respect of "Monty" was crucial if this brilliant but difficult General was going to fulfill his undoubted potential.

The decision regarding the appointment of a Commander in Chief of the Allied Invasion Force had been taken back in 1943, and in January 1944 it was time for the American General, Dwight D. Eisenhower to take up his position in London.

On Winston Churchill's home territory, working with the maverick British Prime Minister was always going to be a challenge, and with "Monty" already in situ too, it was going to require a very firm hand on the helm to keep the invasion plan on track.

Even now, in the 21st Century, when people are asked to name the heroes of the Second World War, it's rare for Dwight D. Eisenhower to come top of many lists. Yet without Eisenhower's calm attitude, steely determination, quiet politeness and brilliant military mind the outcome of World War II might have been very different indeed. So, before going any further we'll take a brief look at the man charged with the successful execution of *Operation Overlord,* who was also destined to become the 34th President of the USA.

| Eisenhower meeting US paratroopers at Newbury, England

Born David Dwight Eisenhower in Grayson County, Texas, on October 14th, 1890 his childhood nickname "Ike" stuck with him throughout his life. Remarkably both of his parents were pacifists, but this didn't prevent him from attending West Point Military Academy, as they believed it would provide him with the best possible education.

With the outbreak of the First World War while Eisenhower was at West Point, he inevitably took up a military career, but even when the Americans entered the conflict in 1917, Eisenhower's duties in the tank core kept him close to home.

After the armistice was signed in 1918 Eisenhower forged ahead with his military career during the 20s and 30s, working under the command of such powerful men as General Douglas MacArthur. When World War II broke out in 1939 Eisenhower had earned a first-class reputation as an administrator and he found himself serving with MacArthur in the Philippines.

Promotions came quickly and when Eisenhower returned to America to take up posts in Washington, California and Texas he rose from Lieutenant Colonel to Brigadier General, attached to the General Staff in Washington, by the close of 1941. Before long Eisenhower became Assistant Chief of Staff in the Operations Division and his obvious administrative abilities led to his appointment as Commanding General, European Theatre of Operations in London.

It was after this that he became Supreme Commander of the Allied Forces in North Africa, and as the battle moved to Italy after Rommel had been driven out of Tunis, Eisenhower went with the action. He might not have been a soldier on the battlefield locked in hand to hand combat, but the rare gifts that the mild-mannered Texan possessed were equally as valuable in the fight against Hitler. And it was time for Eisenhower to show the world that he was up to the task now being asked of him as he arrived in London to take command of *Operation Overlord.*

It was of vital importance, as Eisenhower and the top brass of military commanders settled down to refine the plans for the D-Day Landings, that the people of Britain did all that they could to help the war effort. On the Home Front the Government became ever more involved in the education of the population so that every individual could play their part.

. . .

From early instructions to "Dig for Victory" to encourage food production, measures had been taken to keep everyone eating healthily. By the beginning of 1944 rationing had been a way of life for years, and teaching families to make the most of their weekly allowances was considered a Government matter. The Ministry of Food had drafted in Home Economists to encourage healthy eating, as imaginative recipes were dreamt up to make tasty meals from whatever was available, and popular entertainers were often recruited to the cause.

As we know the first rationing in 1940 was of bacon, butter and sugar, quickly followed by meat, tea, jam, biscuits, breakfast cereals, cheese, eggs, milk, canned fruit and sweets. Some foods occasionally appeared off ration, such as whale meat, but even the Ministry's cleverest cooks struggled to find ways to make it palatable.

The whole idea of rationing was to ensure that whether to the rich or the poor, food and essential items were distributed fairly. It would be unrealistic to think that there wasn't a thriving black market however, because although most of the people of Britain were both law abiding and public spirited, there were still some for whom "money" talked, despite the Government's best efforts.

Interestingly, despite food in the shops being rationed, meals served in restaurants were not. By the end of 1944 it was estimated that 9% of all food was eaten outside the home, with establishments known as British Restaurants opening up all over the country. Typically charging less than a shilling for a three-course meal they provided plain wholesome food wherever a suitable building could be found.

Laws were brought in so that even the most exclusive London restaurants were not permitted to charge more than five shillings, and three courses were the maximum allowed.

. . .

It was also compulsory for factories, so vital to the war effort, to provide canteens as the Government made sure that the population was as well-fed and healthy as possible in order to work at full capacity. It wasn't only food that was rationed, over time clothing, petrol and even soap was controlled by coupons.

Fashion definitely had to take a back seat, with any clothes available having to conform to the Utility standard, which meant minimal fabric, no turn-ups and no frills. Nylon stockings were a thing of the past, as ladies painted their legs with whatever they could find, and gravy browning seamed with eyebrow pencil proved to be a popular choice. But when the GIs started to arrive in Britain in 1942, they actually brought with them such luxuries as nylon stockings, along with chocolate, chewing gum and cigarettes, which did make the American servicemen very popular indeed.

The term GI actually came about because all of the US soldiers' equipment was stamped with the words Government Issue, which was quickly abbreviated to GI.

Eisenhower's fellow countrymen were a glamorous addition to the very ordered, duty bound existence of the women on Britain's Home Front, and throughout 1944 their numbers rapidly increased. This didn't always bode well for Anglo-American relations though, not least because the men left on the Home Front tended to be viewed as second rate for not being in uniform.

The expression *"over-paid, over-sexed and over-here"* was often used by the British men to describe the GIs, but from the ladies they danced and romanced, there were noticeably fewer complaints.

. . .

Nevertheless, there were broken hearts a plenty, especially with an estimated one and a half million GIs stationed in Britain in the run-up to D-Day. In excess of 15,000 of them married girls from the UK in 1944 alone, with the GI Bride phenomenon meaning that many of these young women moved to America, either during or after the war. But it was rarely a case of happy ever after. They often married after a whirlwind romance of no more than days, and the stark reality of life in a different country, thousands of miles from their families, meant that quite a number of these marriages ended in divorce.

Also, many thousands of girls became pregnant by American soldiers, often causing devastation within British families that continued long after the GIs had gone home. It's therefore not surprising that the British men left on the Home Front were unhappy about the conduct of their "Allies", with whom they simply couldn't compete, especially as they were generally overlooked by the female population, being mostly elderly, in poor health, in less glamorous occupations that were exempt from the call up, or worst of all, draft dodgers. There was also a group known as Conscientious Objectors who were permitted to register not to fight if their religion or their beliefs prevented them from doing so.

Several of them were sent to work in Britain's coal mines, but this didn't stop them from being branded as cowards for not being in uniform.

Late in 1943 and moving into 1944 this had a surprisingly adverse effect on another group of miners, who found themselves digging for coal for a very different reason.

Known as the "Bevin Boys" they were often mistaken by the community at large for Conscientious Objectors and shunned for cowardice. This was indeed an injustice as they worked incredibly long hours in the most difficult of conditions, and without them the British nation and the entire war effort would have been brought to a complete standstill.

. . .

In Britain's wartime coalition under Churchill's leadership there were a number of specially designated Ministries, and alongside the Ministry of Food there was also a Ministry of Labor and National Service, overseen by Ernest Bevin. As early as May 1939, after Hitler's troops had marched into Czechoslovakia, the Military Training Act was passed giving the British Government the power to call up men between the ages of 20 and 22 for 6 months military training. After war was declared the National Service (Armed Forces) Act became Law and men aged between 18 and 40 were called up, although this was extended in 1941 to include men up to the age of 51.

There were some occupations exempt from the call up, such as engineering and coal mining, but men could still volunteer. Early in the war many coalminers did just this, before the Government really appreciated what a problem it would become as fewer and fewer men remained at the coalface. Legislation had been put in place to deal with such situations, courtesy of the Emergency Powers Act of 1940, followed by the Essential Works Order a year later, meaning that those left on the Home Front could be conscripted into essential industries.

However, most of the potential conscripts were women who could not be sent down the mines, and although Bevin put out an urgent plea for men to volunteer, understandably there were few prepared to step forward.

With a real threat of the coalminers who did remain taking industrial action, Bevin needed to act fast.

The Minister devised a system whereby a percentage of those conscripted for National Service would be allocated to the mines. Each week, some say from his own hat, Bevin would draw a number between 0 and 9. Any of the men

WORLD WAR 2: THE CALL OF DUTY

called up that week with a National Service number ending with that digit would be ordered to the mines rather than into the armed forces.

It was not a popular course of action, and it blighted Bevin's political career, but it was effective, and these hard-working miners got their name after a speech Bevin gave in an effort to inspire them:

"We need 720,000 men continuously employed in this industry. This is where you boys come in. Our fighting men will not be able to achieve their purpose unless we get an adequate supply of coal".

Bevin's Boys certainly played their part, but their service to King and country has only been properly recognized in more recent times, which is ironic, as unlike those conscripted into the armed forces they were not released from duty until many years after the war had ended.

While Britain faced the challenges of food and fuel shortages with resilience, the Cross-Channel Invasion was transformed from a distant dream into an actual reality and the propaganda machine in Germany went into overdrive to persuade civilians that the war was still going their way.

And it wasn't only their own people that they tried to influence.

German propaganda radio broadcasts were made in English to undermine the Allied position, directly targeting civilians throughout the English-speaking nations. In a program called "Germany Calling", a fictitious character called Lord Haw-Haw warned of treachery on the part of the Allied leaders. In

January 1944 he suggested they were all about to be handed over to the Russians, playing on the British and American fear of communism.

It was hoped that the British public in particular would pressurize Churchill into agreeing a peaceful settlement with Hitler, but such a broadcast only served to convince Allied Intelligence that the Nazis were now clutching at straws.

The most famous voice to play Lord Haw-Haw was the American born but Irish raised William Joyce, who left England for Germany at the beginning of the war. As a senior member of the British Union of Fascists he would have been interned, but instead he became a naturalized German citizen.

Joyce was captured in Germany by the British shortly before the end of the war and hanged for treason. Although not a British subject, it was argued that as Joyce had once lied to obtain a British Passport, it was therefore his nation of choice, making him guilty of treason, a capital offense.

Hitler too was now getting to a stage where he was clutching at straws almost daily. The Führer was convinced in the early weeks of 1944 that all he needed to do was develop the jet aircraft to fight back against the anticipated Allied landings. He declared that *"If I get a few hundred of them to the front line, it will exorcise the specter of invasion for all time"*. It was just another example of Hitler losing his ability for logical thinking and decision making.

Another problem faced by Berlin was how to explain the defeat of the Germans, and more particularly, Erwin Rommel in North Africa. They had boasted that Rommel was an unbeatable military genius, so what to do with him next was something of a problem. After a while he was sent to Italy but when the New Year began, just as Eisenhower was called by the Allies to London, Rommel was called to defend the Axis position in France.

. . .

There is no doubt that Rommel's military instincts were remarkable and although at this time his fellow Commander, Gerd von Rundstedt firmly believed the Allied attack would come from Dover to Calais, Rommel was convinced that Normandy would be the chosen destination. As a result, Hitler's once highly favored Desert Fox spent the months of January and February 1944 surveying the beaches and countryside of Normandy.

Rommel inspects his asparagus

Mines and traps were laid along the shoreline and any field that would have been a secure landing site for aircraft or paratroopers was either flooded or spiked with what became famous as Rommel's Asparagus. These were long poles driven into the ground that made it impossible for planes or military personnel to land.

. . .

Even though it would be months before he was destined to be proved correct, for the time being at least, all Rommel could do was back his hunch.

One place where German troops had managed to hold ground was in Italy. Despite the Allies enjoying a head start, the Germans were now well and truly dug in around Monte Cassino, and they would have to be driven out if the Allies were to stand any chance of reaching Rome. On January 12th the French Corps attempted to capture the town of Cassino, but to no avail; the Germans held firm, leaving the Allies no choice but to wait for another opportunity.

It was nonetheless only a brief moment of triumph for Hitler as elsewhere his troops were coming under attack on all sides. Across German occupied Europe partisans were rising up against their oppressors. In Yugoslavia the leader of the revolutionaries, General Tito was a constant thorn in the Nazi's side, and what's more by this time, he was receiving considerable aid from the air, courtesy of the British and the Americans. And of course Russia continued to be a dangerous drain on Hitler's resources.

On January 15th the Red Army finally broke through the German defenses around Leningrad. The fight was so fierce that the Russians took few prisoners, with more than sixty thousand German soldiers killed, as the Red Army cleared the entire Leningrad Province.

Back in Italy the British had now joined the French in the Battle for Cassino, but once again the German's repelled their advances. North of Cassino as the Americans advanced towards Italy's Rapido River, they were also planning a daring landing from the sea at Anzio, just to the south of Rome. While Eisenhower met with his commanders in London to discuss *Operation Overlord* on January 21st, British and American troops, escorted by twenty-eight warships, sailed from Naples in *Operation Shingle,* the code name for the landings at Anzio. Just minutes after midnight the troops went ashore.

The 227 Germans based there were caught completely by surprise and offered little resistance. In twenty-four hours, 36,000 Allied servicemen had safely landed, with the loss of only 13 lives. Hitler had instructed his men to hold Italy at all costs, and within days the Allies realized that despite their early success, Anzio was far from being secure. German aircraft struck on January 23rd, sinking British support ships, preventing tanks and heavy artillery being brought ashore. The American Commander at Anzio hesitated, with disastrous consequences, giving the Germans the opportunity to rush in reinforcements.

As the Germans learned to their cost at Anzio, military intelligence was of vital importance, as knowing that the Allies were on their way would have made all the difference. At Bletchley Park, an elegant mansion at the heart of the British countryside, coded Axis messages were intercepted and deciphered. Not only were the Allies able to track what the Germans were planning, they were also able to ensure that the false intelligence they were feeding the enemy was getting through. With *Operation Overlord* imminent this was crucial as every effort was made to take all German attention away from Normandy.

As part of *Operation Fortitude,* a sophisticated and elaborate campaign to deceive the Germans over the proposed landing beaches of *Operation Overlord,* for every reconnaissance flight over Normandy, two were dispatched over the Pas de Calais. The First United States Army Group, commanded by the notorious American, General "Blood and Guts" Patton, was in fact a total fabrication, but the decoded messages from the Germans told the Allies that Hitler was moving troops from Russia in preparation to counter Patton and his imaginary men at Calais.

The Twelfth British Army made up of the 15th British Motorized Division, the

34th British Infantry Division, the 8th British Armored Division and the 7th Polish Infantry Division, likewise only ever existed on paper, and apart from Rommel's gut feeling about Normandy, the disinformation campaign was working perfectly. However, for those fighting in Italy, Russia and out in the Pacific the battles were anything but imaginary.

The Americans had been making good progress in the Pacific since 1943 gradually advancing towards the Mariana Islands, which would give them a strategically important base from which to launch attacks on Japan. But before they could reach the Marianas, they would need to take the Marshall Islands.

On February 1st a huge American landing operation overwhelmed the Japanese armies of occupation, but despite this, the defenders of the three islands under attack chose to fight to the death rather than surrender. For Japan the casualties were high, out of 8,000 of them on one island, 7,870 were killed, with the Americans losing less than four hundred men.

Even so, a full assault on Tokyo was still a very long way off, and the war in Europe would need to be concluded before the question of how to defeat the Japanese could be addressed.

In London Eisenhower was totally absorbed with plans for *Operation Overlord*, as he and his senior commanders realized just what a huge planning commitment they had taken on. Scientists, technical experts and a formidable intelligence operation would be crucial, and for the few people with the security clearance to be aware of the details, it seemed an impossible task.

At Buckingham Palace George VI was kept informed of Overlord's progress, and noting his thoughts in his diary for February 1944, he gives us a rare insight into the apprehension felt by those responsible for leading the daring operation. The King wrote *The more one goes into it, the more alarming it becomes".*

King George VI inspects the troops in Italy

Another operation that was rapidly taking on alarming proportions was the battle the Allies were having in Italy, attempting to hold their position on the beachhead at Anzio. The landing that had started with such promise for the Allies was being held off by the determined attacks of the Germans, and just a short distance away at Cassino, Hitler's troops were doing an equally good job of keeping the Allies at bay. As February wore on the battle for Cassino urgently needed to be resolved if the Allies were going to be able to take Rome before the start of *Operation Overlord.*

. . .

Leaflets were dropped addressed to "Italian Friends" telling them to leave the ancient monastery of Monte Cassino, as an Allied attack was imminent.

It was a timely warning just prior to four hundred tons of bombs being dropped on the magnificent early medieval shrine, killing the bishop and 250 civilian refugees sheltering there.

Alongside the Americans, Canadians and the British, Maori, Indian and Gurkha troops fought hand to hand against the German defenders amongst the ruins, and still the Allies failed to dislodge them from their vantage point.

In the skies over Europe the Allies continued to bomb Berlin, while the Germans in retaliation bombed London. With alarming accuracy four people were killed in an air raid virtually on the doorstep of the Prime Minister's home at number 10 Downing Street, but fortunately for Churchill he was away from home at the time.

For the RAF the bombing raids on Germany were very costly in terms of planes lost and men killed, but Churchill as ever was quick to defend his actions. With all thoughts focused on the liberation of France he said: "*the air offensive constitutes the foundation upon which our plans for overseas invasion stand*".

At the same time as the major cities of Britain and Germany were being bombed, the Americans were equally busy bombing the Japanese in the Pacific, sinking warships, merchant ships and aircraft, as well as taking another of the Marshall Islands. However, the Japanese were successful in scoring direct hits on American warships off the coast of Iwo Jima. As was now expected any survivors were slaughtered by the Japanese, and there were British warships that suffered a similar fate in the Indian Ocean.

· · ·

A new tactic emerged, because as soon as Japan's submarines had sunk the enemy ships, they surfaced in order to machine gun the survivors clinging to the life-rafts. There was little respect for a prisoner of war's human rights from the Japanese, and in the Concentration Camps the Germans behaved with equal contempt for their fellow man. In Dachau though, where so many atrocities had been committed, it's interesting to note that a clerk at the camp took a brave step.

On February 22nd, 31 Soviet Prisoners of War were dragged out of barracks and executed, and the clerk simply recorded their names, each and every one of them. Of the millions killed in Concentration Camps the majority were nameless victims of the Holocaust, but this particular clerk gave the dead men their dignity, creating a list that would one day provide evidence against those responsible for committing such barbaric crimes.

Spring was now upon the Allies, as February gave way to March, and with the time for the invasion drawing ever closer, Allied Military Intelligence worked tirelessly to pull all elements of the deception plans for *Operation Overlord* into place.

In Moscow the Soviets gave their blessing to the Anglo-American disinformation campaigns, and added an interesting one of their own, creating a spurious landing off the coast of Norway.

There were still setbacks, as a further Allied attack on Monte Cassino still failed to secure the location, and German troops marched into Hungary. Yet Hitler's stranglehold on power was slipping away from him, as some of his own officers were beginning to question his authority.

From his early days as Germany's Chancellor, Hitler had always feared the possibility of assassination, he had after all made many enemies along the way, but the fact that plots were now being discussed amongst his own men made everyone around him a danger. Without a doubt the Führer's days were numbered, but the damage he was still capable of inflicting upon the Allies was a very real danger to the success of *Operation Overlord,* which was gathering momentum by the hour.

In London there were endless rounds of top-secret briefings, as those Eisenhower had charged with making sure that everything was ready for the invasion were working around the clock.

And all the while the British wartime spirit prevailed as the citizens of London went about their day-to-day business as cheerfully as they could. Whether working in shops, offices or factories, everyone was doing their bit for the war effort, and in the evenings, they would volunteer as Air Raid Wardens and Fire Watchers to keep the city as safe as possible, whatever Hitler threw their way.

The fate of the free world lay in the hands of the experts hidden away in the lofty war offices of London, planning the largest and most audacious invasion force yet known to man. If it failed Hitler would have a chance of turning the war back in his favor, and with an operation of such epic proportions, the Allies would have little left to attack again.

The air-raid warnings continued to scream out and the bombs still fell on the streets of London, but as Hitler had learned to his cost, here was a people that refused to be crushed. Life went on, and people made the best of whatever pleasures they could find.

The West-End Theatres might struggle to put on a show in the evenings, but the lunchtime concert became a popular wartime phenomenon. The venues were unusual, the National Gallery was a great favorite popularized by the classical pianist Dame Myra Hess, and Londoners from all walks of life took time out from their busy schedules to be soothed by the lyrical melodies of Beethoven, Brahms and Mozart. It was indeed the calm before the storm, out of the corridors of power in London the blueprint for victory had been written, and D-Day was literally just a heartbeat away.

19

D-DAY AT LAST

April - June 1944

US troops on their way to Normandy

It was surprisingly hard for me to conceive, when I walked the peaceful, picturesque beaches along the west coast of Northern France for the research of this book and the related documentaries, that they were the setting for the remarkable, never to be forgotten Normandy Landings. The beautiful sands are known as the "Cote de Nacre", which poetically translates as the "Mother of Pearl Coast", and the beaches are awash with poignantly moving memories of that auspicious and historic day, when thousands of Allied troops came ashore on June 6th 1944.

The events that took place there are celebrated as D-Day, and without doubt this daringly heroic and ultimately liberating invasion marked the beginning of the end of World War II.

Since September 1939 when war broke out, for the Allies, victory and the prospect of peace was a distant and often uncertain dream, somewhere in the future, as Adolf Hitler and his Axis of Evil stormed to power across Europe.

But by 1942 the mists of doubt had slowly started to lift and the vision of a world free from tyranny began to emerge, and although up until D-Day the war could still have swung in Hitler's favor, as preparations were made, fortune seemed to have been smiling on the Allies for some time, firstly in North Africa and then across the Mediterranean into Italy. *"Before Alamein we never had a victory, After Alamein we never had a defeat".*

Prime Minister Winston Churchill spoke these words after the British Eighth Army had triumphed against Erwin Rommel, in the second battle of El Alamein. The Allies were at last making progress and although months and years of conflict still lay ahead the tide was definitely turning their way.

Now although the events of North Africa have been covered in detail in earlier chapters, it's worth taking a moment for a brief look back, as the key players in the D-Day landings were already emerging. This gives us the opportunity to discover a little more about the backgrounds of the remarkable heroes of *Operation Overlord,* who played such key roles in the Normandy landings.

The first battle of El Alamein had been far from conclusive. The Allied forces did battle with the Germans from the 1st to the 27th of July 1942, with the outcome being a stalemate at a cost of some 13,000 Allied casualties.

Even though this was far from ideal, the British still managed to take 7,000 prisoners and damage Hitler's North African campaign. Rommel's plans to advance to Alexandria and then Cairo were stalled, and this impasse also put a stop to Germany gaining control of the Suez Canal and many Middle Eastern oil fields, which would have had grave consequences for the Allies.

Lieutenant-General Bernard Montgomery took over the British Eighth Army in August 1942, and it was his insight and initiative that proved to be the downfall of the Nazis in the second battle at El Alamein. Using his experience of fighting in the First World War, Montgomery could anticipate and almost predict what was going to happen and managed his campaign accordingly.

Fortunately for Montgomery the air support he received was outstanding when compared with the German Luftwaffe and Italy's Regia Aeronautica, who instead of supporting their ground troops became embroiled in air-to-air combat. Overall Allied casualties were less than a half of those suffered by the Germans, which were 30% of Rommel's men, and he had no other option but to retreat, moving the remainder of his army to Tunisia where better defensive action could be taken.

Winston Churchill famously described the 14-day battle at El Alamein that ran from October 23rd to November 5th 1942 as not being the end, not even the beginning of the end, but perhaps, the end of the beginning, and it was certainly the point at which the Allies started on the road to victory, with the colorful characters of Rommel, Churchill and Montgomery all gaining valuable experience.

With the battle for North Africa over, the Allies could springboard into Europe across the Mediterranean, and the Island of Sicily was the next target. The Allied invasion, codenamed *Operation Husky,* was a mix of amphibious and airborne warfare with the aim of removing both the Sicilian air force and navy, giving the Allies access to the whole Mediterranean.

· · ·

German Intelligence had no knowledge of the invasion plans thanks to a decoy of documents planted on the corpse of a British Officer, stating that the Allies had no interest in Sicily. The papers claimed the next invasion target was to be Greece, so most of the German defenses were relocated. Paratroopers were the first to invade, just after midnight on July 9th, 1943 but due to very strong winds many landed miles off-course and in the wrong order, but the confusion actually proved to be very positive.

When the beach landings began the Allies faced very little opposition, but by July 13th resistance had grown, and the losses and casualties began to escalate. The remarkable American General, George Patton, who was the commander of U.S 7th Army, and equally as outspoken as Montgomery, captured the capital, Palermo, which proved to both the Italians and the Germans that Sicily had fallen, and they promptly retreated.

Hitler's forces managed to evacuate the whole garrison in Messina and because the Allies were at this point superior in the air and at sea, Germany's swift evacuation came as something of a blow, as they had failed to make the most of the situation.

Now, the individual charged with controlling Montgomery and Patton was General Dwight D. Eisenhower, and his task was far from easy. As progress through Italy was slow the tensions between Montgomery, Patton and another American, General Omar Bradley escalated, and it took all Eisenhower's diplomatic skill to prevent a war breaking out between his Generals, before the fight against Hitler and the final push for victory could begin. The invasion of Sicily heralded the Italian Campaign, but there had been some disagreement between the Americans and the British about strategies for ending the war, with President Roosevelt and the USA determined to liberate France first and foremost.

However, Winston Churchill believed Italy needed to be dealt with and taken out of the war as quickly as possible. As the Allies slowly battled on in Italy as 1943 wore on, the plans for a full-scale invasion of Nazi occupied Europe gathered momentum. The Russians, who were holding firm against Hitler in the east, attended the Tehran Conference along with the British and the Americans, bringing together Joseph Stalin, Winston Churchill and Franklin D. Roosevelt for the first time since the Soviets had become part of the Allied operation.

The time had come to put the final strategy to defeat Adolf Hitler in place, beginning with the invasion of France, codenamed *Operation Overlord,* and Dwight D. Eisenhower was once more the man selected to take charge as Supreme Commander. He would need to draw on the experience of the likes of Montgomery and Patton if the mission was to succeed, pulling together the various personalities, and as the Normandy beaches were selected as where the D-Day landings would take pace, there was a great deal to be done in a short space of time.

Early in 1944 Anglo-American Relations became tense when Montgomery insisted that in order for there to be success in Normandy the original plans of three Allied divisions must be increased to five. This would certainly curtail the American plans for *Operation Anvil* to play a major role in the invasion. Eisenhower was keen to create a diversion with an army from the Mediterranean landing on the Cote d'Azur in the south of France. But Churchill and the British were strongly against this and felt if resources were concentrated in Italy, Rome would fall to the Allies sooner.

Churchill even wrote to President Roosevelt asking that many of the landing ship tanks, better known as LSTs, be transferred from *Operation Anvil* to *Operation Overlord.* This dispute continued for some time until events in late April 1944 took the issue out of the Allies' hands, as our story of D-Day begins in earnest.

. . .

Preparation would be key if the Invasion of Normandy was going to be successful, and the fifty-mile-long landing beach zone would have to be split up into sections if a beachhead with adequate ports was to be established at speed, allowing the Allies swift access to the heart of occupied France. It was decided that the American army divisions would land closest to Cherbourg on beaches codenamed Utah and Omaha, while the British and Canadians would land on Gold, Juno and Sword beaches along the stretch of coastline leading to Caen.

Rehearsing for the invasion was vital and the Americans, who were due to land on Utah Beach, were involved in a practice mission codenamed Exercise Tiger. A similar stretch of Devon coastline was selected at Slapton Sands, as thirty thousand troops were put through their paces, but then disaster struck.

German E-boats from Cherbourg attacked and torpedoed five landing ship tanks, which dealt a bitter blow both to *Operation Overlord* and *Operation Anvil.*

At the beginning of the war Churchill had requested that great ships be built that could cast upon a beach large numbers of the heaviest tanks in any weather, and the LSTs certainly did just that. But the losses at Slapton meant the postponement of *Operation Anvil* in order to give as much support to D-Day as possible, and with 700 men lost the disastrous rehearsal was also a human tragedy.

Even so, as D-Day came ever closer, exercises like Tiger were still a necessity, despite the dangers. Because of the sheer size of the operation there was a great disparity in the experience and level of training between the various soldiers, sailors and airmen called upon for D-Day. Apart from those who had fought in the North African and Italian campaigns, many of the American divisions were being sent straight from the USA and would only be able to take part in a few weeks of intensive training on British soil.

· · ·

Without doubt the air force, navy and assault regiments would have to practice effectively and co-operatively in order for there to be a successful outcome to D-Day. If the troops were to be as prepared as possible, terrain had to be found that resembled the five Normandy landing beaches, and along with Slapton Sands, the Gower Peninsula, the Tarbat Peninsula, Culbin Sands and Burghead Bay were also selected.

Because these sites were used for military training purposes all the villages, farms and rural communities needed to be evacuated, and quickly.

Hundreds of people from each location had to leave their homes as more Allied troops from all over the world gathered in Britain, ready to invade France. Before long the south coast became a huge training and embarkation zone, with every eventuality planned for during April and May.

As well as men, vast quantities of ordnance and military vehicles were required, but most important of all, every move that was made needed to be kept secret. Hitler and his Generals knew full well that an attack was imminent, but one of the most astounding things about D-Day was the way in which Allied counterintelligence managed to keep the details of the invasion such a secret.

This was crucial to the success of *Operation Overlord,* and as much careful planning went into this part of the proceedings as into orchestrating the actual landings. A far-reaching system called "Bigot" was introduced to keep a check on who held complete information about Operation Overlord, and the amount of "Bigot" officers was kept to an absolute minimum to prevent any information whatsoever leaking out.

· · ·

Naturally, as time went on and the operation drew ever closer, the different forces needed to be briefed on the types of area they would be going to, but the fear of this information spreading was so great that anyone who knew the planned locations was kept under strict supervision, and in some cases kept behind the kind of barbed wire fences you would expect to find in a concentration camp.

At the Supreme Headquarters of the Allied Expeditionary Force, otherwise known as SHAEF, the disastrous events at Slapton Sands had given them unexpected cause for concern as ten 'Bigot' officers were among the 700 men who lost their lives along the Devon coast. A large-scale grueling mission was ordered to find all ten of the officers, because there was every possibility that they could have been carrying 'Bigot' paperwork, or worse still been captured and interrogated by the Germans. Eventually all ten bodies were found, and SHAEF could continue with *Operation Overlord,* safe in the knowledge that their secrets had not been compromised.

But this was far from being the only scare they had to deal with. One U.S Major-General was enjoying drinks at a London Hotel and without thinking complained that he couldn't get any supplies through until about June 15th, after the invasion. Needless to say, he was returned to the United States very quickly indeed. In another incident a young British soldier told his parents about *Operation Overlord* while home on leave. They felt it their duty to inform the military authorities, no doubt realizing the importance of what they had been told.

Senior officers USS Augusta

And it wasn't just careless talk that SHAEF had to worry about, in the lead-up to D-Day; a sudden gust of wind blew 12 copies of 'Bigot' documents out of a Whitehall office and security officers had to risk all to dodge the traffic so that each one was collected. Then, as if the weather hadn't been enough to contend with, a worrying coincidence seemed to arise in the 33 days leading up to D-Day. Words connected with the operation were answers to crossword clues in the 'Daily Telegraph' newspaper.

The names of the landing beaches Utah and Omaha cropped up, as did Neptune, which was the codename for all the naval operations involved, along with Mulberry, the artificial harbors that were planned for the beaches of Normandy, but most worrying of all was the clue "Big Wig" the answer to which was Overlord.

Immediately the retired schoolteacher who had set the clues was brought in for questioning, as he was suspected of being a Nazi spy who was tipping off the Germans. However, he convinced MI5 of his innocence, and this has gone down in history as one of the most bizarre coincidences of World War II.

SHAEF were right to be so cautious, the entire outcome of the war and many thousands of lives depended upon secrecy and when a railway employee at Exeter found a complete set of Overlord plans in a briefcase abandoned in a train compartment, it proved without doubt that ensuring information did not pass into the wrong hands was a major undertaking.

However, keeping the invasion plans secret was only a part of the process. There was a great deal of effort put into feeding the Germans incorrect information, and it worked very well indeed. For a start the most logical route for an Allied invasion would have been between Dover and Calais, and SHAEF did everything possible to make sure that this is what the Germans were expecting.

For every reconnaissance flight over Normandy, two were flown over the Pas de Calais, as well as floating dummy landing crafts in the Thames estuary and the Channel ports to add to the deception.

These diversions became so complex that the project of disinformation was even recognized officially as *Operation Fortitude*.

It proved to be totally believable and Rommel, who Hitler had put in charge of defending France from any Allied invasion was certainly convinced, keeping his troops concentrated around Calais, leaving Normandy open to attack.

As D-Day fast approached it was also essential that the French Resistance be told that the invasion force was on its way. They had worked tirelessly since the fall of their nation back in 1940 to obstruct the German occupying army in any way that they could. Consequently, two coded messages were broadcast by the BBC on the 1st and then the 5th of June, *"the long sobs of the violins of autumn"* followed by *"wound my heart with a monotonous languor"*. Far from being secret, the Chief of German Intelligence had been warned of the significance of these bizarre words, but when Rommel was told he believed it preposterous that the allies would announce their operation plans over the radio and dismissed this as being a part of the elaborate disinformation strategy.

A great deal of thought had gone into planning the perfect date for *Operation Overlord* and as Commander in Chief of the Allied Expeditionary Force, Eisenhower had considered everything from weather and tides, to phases of the moon. A full moon would be essential for light, along with a spring tide, and initially June 5th was settled on. Nevertheless, when the weather turned unseasonably stormy, the Allies faced an incredibly difficult decision.

Eisenhower knew that if he postponed for longer than a day the operation would have to wait a whole fortnight for conditions to be right again. Already there had been so many close calls, and who could say whether it would be possible to keep their plans secret from the Germans for a further two weeks?

| Troops and equipment prepare to board for D-Day

Plus there was now the issue of the thousands of men already aboard their ships, prepared for their mission, and not only would it be difficult for them to disembark without it being noticed, but they'd also have to be accommodated until the invasion could go ahead as planned. Eisenhower did however have the option of postponing until the following day when the weather forecast, even though still dreadful, was slightly more promising.

It was a very risky decision but to everyone involved it was definitely a chance worth taking, even though the sea crossing would be far from pleasant for the troops. To help with seasickness the soldiers had been advised to chew gum, but with the appalling weather that came with the dawn of June 6th, it was of little help. The only plus point was the fact that the weather was so bad the Germans had ruled out any chance of an invasion. Rommel had been so confident that he'd left France and returned home to Germany to celebrate his wife's birthday.

Operation Overlord began in two phases, the first being an air assault, while the second was the amphibious landing of allied infantry. The second phase was hugely dependent on the success of the first, as the airborne bombardment and influx of troops would build up a support force ready to ensure a swift breakout from the beachhead.

The air assault landings of British and American troops happened shortly after midnight, in the first few hours of D-Day. This was not only to secure the rear of the beachheads but also to neutralize as much opposition along the shoreline as possible.

It was strategically vital to capture two bridges North of the city of Caen, at the British and Canadian end of the landing beaches, as they provided the Germans with an opportunity to attack from inland. Also the bridges needed to be secured intact, as they were necessary if there was to be a smooth breakout from the beachhead.

The most famous of the crossings was originally called the Benouville Bridge, which was over the Caen Canal, but is known today as Pegasus Bridge because it's where the British 6th Airborne Division lead by Major John Howard had the first success of D-Day, after landing their wooden Horsa gliders perfectly on target. The name change came because Pegasus, the proud flying horse, was the insignia of the 6th Airborne Division, who were responsible for liberating the first of the French towns at Benouville shortly after winning the battle for Pegasus Bridge.

· · ·

The Allied airborne attack continued as planes from the US air force set off from the south of England to secure the North Western Perimeter and prevent any German counterattack towards the Cherbourg end of the landing beaches.

But the American 82nd and 101st Airborne Divisions did not fare quite so well as Major John Howard's men, because the terrible storms and heavy winds forced the paratroopers to land as much as 25 miles off course.

As part of the German defenses Rommel had flooded as many areas as possible that could have been suitable for parachute landings and had also scattered hundreds of mines that were famously known as "Rommel Asparagus". Quite often those who were lucky enough to avoid the dreaded asparagus often drowned under the weight of their heavy kit bags in the thick swamps that Rommel had created.

For months the D-Day planners had to struggle to find the best landing beaches in Normandy, and the invasion was due to begin at the most westerly stretch of shoreline, Utah, running for some 3 miles and located between Pouppeville and La Madeleine. As the Allied troop ships began to gather the weather that had made the journey so uncomfortable for the troops, proved extremely fortuitous, as the German E-Boats, sent out from Cherbourg, had to turn back to port. This gave the 30,000 American troops and 3,500 vehicles that were in position at 2am and ready to fight at the first light of day, almost a clear path into the area.

The airborne forces, despite so many of them landing off course had also played their part, and one of the best-known films about the Normandy landings, *"The Longest Day"* from the 1960s, features these early events, and one story in particular.

. . .

Just a short distance from Utah beach lies the charming town of Saint Mere-Eglise. In the early hours of D-Day 13,000 paratroopers dropped from the skies, one of them being a Private John Steele, who has gone down in history as a result of his most unfortunate landing. Steele's parachute became entangled with the fine steeple of the imposing church, leaving him to dangle helplessly.

For two hours he managed to limply hang on, pretending to be dead, but the Germans eventually spotted movement and he was taken prisoner. A dummy paratrooper still hangs from the steeple to this day, as a reminder of the incredible bravery of so many Allied servicemen as they gave their all to liberate France.

But some of the troops involved in the fight to gain control of Utah beach were a great deal more fortunate than Private Steele. Another contributor to the D-Day history books was Brigadier General Theodore Roosevelt, the eldest son of the former President of the USA. Despite being 57 years of age, as division commander he requested he be allowed to lead his men ashore in person, and although advised against such action, he was granted permission and landed on the beach with his troops.

However, because of the strong current and massive amount of smoke caused by the initial assault, Roosevelt's infantry landed a mile off course, to face only a handful of German soldiers who could do little to defend against this unexpected Allied advance.

Roosevelt is famously quoted, when told of the error, as having said *"we'll start the war from here"*, which he promptly did, leading the advance inland. Ironically the part of the beach where the troops were supposed to have landed was heavily defended and many more lives would have been lost had things gone to plan. Roosevelt certainly took full advantage of the situation, and his quick thinking and strategic intellect earned him the Medal of Honor.

. . .

The successful landing at Utah was better than Eisenhower could have possibly hoped for, especially as there were only 197 allied causalities and only 4 out of the 32 tanks sent ashore were lost. These figures were a credit to the skill and courage of all those involved in the landings, with the added advantage of luck very definitely playing its part. Nevertheless, the airborne forces paid a much higher price, with the real cost of gaining control of Utah beach being born by the many paratroopers who were killed or captured.

They were clearing the exits for five hours prior to the Utah landings and causing sufficient confusion to prevent a German counterattack. Unfortunately, by the end of the offensive the 101st Airborne division had lost 40% of its fighting force, which coupled with the men also lost in the Slapton Sands tragedy meant that the Americans suffered a great deal more at Utah than the casualty figures at first suggest. Today, the invasion at Utah is remembered for the very positive start it gave to D-Day, heralding the liberation of France.

There are many proud monuments along this most significant stretch of beach, and the popular Utah Beach Landing Museum is a wonderful place to visit, especially for those who want to know more about the incredible events of that June morning back in 1944 in person.

But the relatively straightforward triumph at Utah could not have been more different than the disastrous and very "bloody battle" that took place at the neighboring beach of Omaha. The objective was for American troops to secure a 5 mile stretch of coastline that would eventually link with the British force's landings at Gold Beach, but just as all went in favor of those landing at Utah the exact opposite happened to those destined for Omaha.

For a start, navigational difficulties due to the weather, worked against the invasion force, putting them directly in the line of fire of the very experienced

German 352nd division who just happened to be on a training exercise in the district. By this late stage in the war, with so many of Hitler's troops engaged on the eastern front fighting with the Russians, many of the troops defending the French coast would otherwise have been schoolboy conscripts.

| Troops giving first aid after landing

As well as the misfortune of a strongly defended position, an error of disembarkation had further disastrous consequences when 29 tanks were released from their landing craft too early, causing 27 of these essential support vehicles, and their crews, to sink, leaving the men clamoring ashore even more vulnerable to enemy fire.

· · ·

It's difficult to comprehend what it must have been like, particularly if you look at the quiet beach today, but this vivid account from an eyewitness certainly leaves us in no doubt as to how horrific the scene must have quickly become.

"Within 10 minutes of the ramps being lowered, "A" Company had become inert, leaderless and almost incapable of action. Every Officer and Sergeant had been killed or wounded… it had become a struggle for survival and rescue. The men in the water pushed wounded men ashore ahead of them, and those who had reached the sands crawled back into the water pulling others to land to save them from drowning, in many cases only to see the rescued men wounded again or to be hit themselves. Within 20 minutes of striking the beach "A" Company had ceased to be an assault company and had become a forlorn little rescue party bent upon survival and the saving of lives".

Even so the fighting spirit of those brave Americans shone through, and as companies who had become separated re-grouped, while the lower ranks stepped forward to replace their commanders who had fallen, advances were slowly but surely made.

It was a real team effort with the engineers clearing pathways across the beach and up the steep hill, working under intense fire, which frequently set off the explosives they were attempting to defuse, and the casualty rate was high. American losses were horrendous, but the Germans also took casualties of about 1200, which accounted for about 20 percent of the 352nd division. For the French, as they enjoyed the prospect of liberation, they also had to face the dilemma of how to deal with the fallen, whether friend or foe.

. . .

Needless to say having been oppressed by the Germans since 1940 it took some time for there to be a spirit of peace and reconciliation, but if you visit the graveyards along the coast of Normandy today you'll see how a dignified solution was eventually found for this problem.

At La Cambe, the German Cemetery, more than twenty-one thousand soldiers lie beneath the ground, the majority of which fell between D-Day and August 20th 1944. Each small square commemorates up to four men, some of them no more than boys, and the sheer volume of somber black stone crosses stand testament to the tragic loss of life experienced on all sides throughout World War II.

The cemetery is managed today by the German War Graves Commission and was completed in 1961, but since this time any German remains found from the conflict are brought here to La Cambe to rest in peace. It's interesting to note that across this rural landscape this is still quite a common occurrence, where so many lost their lives during the invasion of Normandy.

While the casualties of the aggressive German army are buried without pomp and circumstance, the contrast at the American National Cemetery and Memorial, appropriately located high on the cliffs above Omaha beach where so many US troops were killed, couldn't be more marked.

The brightly gleaming cemetery contains the remains of 9,286 soldiers in over 70 acres of land. There are thirty pairs of brothers buried together here, including Brigadier General Theodore Roosevelt, of Utah Beach fame, who died of a heart attack just over two months after the invasion on July 12th, alongside his brother Quentin, who had been killed in France during the First World War.

The 22ft bronze statue at the heart of the cemetery is entitled "The spirit of

American youth rising from the waves" and along with neat rows of bright, shining white gravestones is as thought provoking as the Teutonic somberness of La Cambe.

As well as being charged with taking the beaches at Utah and Omaha, the Americans were also given the task of attacking Pointe du Hoc, a strategic headland under German control. It was believed that a large gun battery was located at the summit with the potential to be a significant threat to the landing forces as they came ashore.

The plan was for the 2nd Ranger Battalion to land at the base of the 100ft cliff-face and climb to the top where they would then destroy the gun battery that had the beaches of Omaha and Utah within firing range.

Under the command of Colonel James E Rudder the brave Rangers battled hard under fierce attack to reach the top, while the Germans from their high vantage point had the distinct advantage. Out of the 225 men who took on this perilous operation 135 were killed, injured or listed as missing in action, making for a 60% casualty rate.

Then to add insult to injury, the surviving Rangers who made it to the top found that the anticipated big guns were nowhere to be seen. The guns were finally found some distance away in an unguarded apple orchard and immediately destroyed.

Moving ever onwards and into the British and Canadian sector, the next landing beach along from Omaha was codenamed Gold. The objectives for the troops here, along with those landing on Juno beach was to liberate the town of Bayeux, secure the Caen-Bayeux road and occupy the port of Arromanches.

. . .

The bombardment from the battleships at sea began at 5:45am and the landings took place 5 minutes earlier than scheduled at 7:25. Just as had happened at Omaha there were difficulties getting the allocated tanks ashore because of the weather conditions, and they had to be launched early due to the heavy seas, resulting in a dozen of them sinking before they reached the shore.

Even though the troops experienced some heavy resistance in the early hours, they managed to break through the German lines only sustaining casualties of around 400 men, compared to the thousands of lives lost at Omaha.

After securing Gold the British troops managed to join up with the Canadians who had landed on neighboring Juno beach, next along the coast, but were unable to complete their primary objective of reaching and securing the Caen-Bayeux road.

Today Gold beach is an idyllic holiday location and as people enjoy the seafront hotels, cafes and restaurants thoughts of D-Day may be far from their minds. However, looking out to sea there are plenty of reminders of those auspicious events. Arromanches is a charming town, but on June 6th 1944 it was of vital importance as a port, and from here you get a superb view of the remains of the Mulberry Harbors that the Allies constructed soon after the landings.

When planning *Operation Overlord*, the Allies quickly realized that both the American and British sectors would need harbors to ship in supplies once the beaches had been secured. Port en Bessin lay between the two sectors, but it simply wasn't large enough to handle all the equipment that would be needed at great speed. So the idea of constructing floating harbors was conceived, made up of component parts that could be towed across the English Channel in the wake of the invasion force.

. . .

The two harbors were constructed at the far end of Omaha beach and at Arromanches, codenamed respectively Mulberry "A" and Mulberry "B", and they were surprisingly large, being similar in size to the harbor at Dover. Each of these temporary constructions required 600,000 tons of concrete along with about 10 miles of floating roadways to cope with the flow of traffic. Unfortunately, the American Mulberry "A" was smashed to smithereens by more unseasonable weather in a powerful storm on June 19th, and this proved to be a major setback.

Luckily Mulberry "B" at Arromanches remained intact despite the terrible conditions, and it is the remains of this amazing construction that can still be seen along the shoreline today. Mulberry "B" proved to be incredibly efficient and was used to land over 2.5 million men, 500,000 vehicles and 4 million tons of absolutely crucial supplies and bearing the title Port Winston it was as steadfast and dependable as the British Prime Minister it was named after.

Returning to the invasion beaches our next port of call is Juno, and this is where some of the most incredible footage from June 6th, 1944 was actually shot. Interestingly there were around fifty camera crews recording all the landings on D-Day, which is a staggering figure, especially as they faced the exact same dangers as the troops they were filming.

At Juno the soldiers of the Canadian 3rd Division had been selected to advance into one of the most heavily defended stretches of the Normandy coastline. The earlier bombardment of this area was of little help to the troops, as the air force had failed to cause significant damage and the advanced naval attack that ran for an hour and a half only destroyed a small percentage of German bunkers. Nevertheless, about an hour after landing the Canadians had cleared the German sea line, but had sustained heavy casualties, however by evening they had still pushed several miles inland and secured the town of Saint-Aubin-sur-Mer.

. . .

The final Allied assault was on Sword beach, following on from Juno. Sword was the furthest east of all the beaches and only a matter of miles from Caen, and securing this key town was a primary objective for the collaboration of the British 3rd Infantry Division and the 27th Armored Brigade who landed here. Unlike Omaha and Gold beach, although heavily mined, the resistance on the beach was minimal, but the relatively small, concentrated landing area combined with the swift incoming tide meant that the operation became very hazardous as the thousands of men and equipment came ashore.

As the troops advanced inland, the resistance grew stronger and it wasn't long before the German's 21st Panzer Division was sent to Sword from Caen, and it took the Allies until evening to neutralize them. However, this escalating conflict meant that Caen could not be reached as planned, and the two groups of Allied infantry were stalled on the outskirts of the city.

This may not have been the most straightforward of landings, but the indomitable spirit of the advancing Allies was unmistakable, as each and every one of them played their part in the liberation of France.

One of the most incredible stories told of the events at Sword beach is that of Piper Bill Millin of Lord Lovat's 1st Special Service. As he stepped out, waist deep, into the water from the landing craft he started piping his own rendition of Highland Laddie. As the beach became littered with the bodies of the fallen, amongst all the smoke and confusion, Piper Millin continued to play. In fact it's said that he piped all the way from Sword beach to Pegasus Bridge, where Lord Lovat's men joined the British troops that had been the first to land in France on D-Day.

There were many tales of incredible heroism as the days of June 1944 saw *Operation Overland* forge further ahead, towards the very heart of France, as it was being liberated from Hitler's tyranny. Against all the odds by the end of D-Day 130,000 Allied troops had occupied the stretch of coastline between

Cherbourg and Caen, before Hitler's Generals had even realized what was happening.

The casualties had been significant for the Allies, on Omaha beach alone 3,000 brave Americans had lost their lives, yet the end of the war was now very definitely in sight. Hitler was far from finished, but the chances of a German victory were disappearing fast as June 1944 drew to a close. For the Allies morale was at an all-time high and as the success of D-Day was built upon, the dream of restoring peace to a free world was just that little bit closer to becoming a reality.

20

LIBERTY, EQUALITY AND FRATERNITY

July – September 1944

| Bringing the wounded and seasick ashore

W ith the promise of summer, the Second World War entered a very positive phase for the Allies in 1944. After success in North Africa in the latter part of 1942, and the Allied invasion of Sicily and the landings at Salerno in 1943, followed by the Anzio attack in January 1944, the German forces were losing their Italian stronghold. The Russians were becoming more powerful in the east, pushing ever closer towards Germany since the surrender of Hitler's troops at Stalingrad early in 1943.

Even in South East Asia the Allied battle against the Japanese, part of Adolf Hitler's Axis of Evil, was gaining momentum daily.

• • •

And of course, the daring *Operation Overlord*, which had culminated in the D- Day landings of June 6th, along the coastline of Normandy, had been a triumph beyond even the wildest dreams of the Commander in Chief, General Dwight D. Eisenhower.

Remarkably, Eisenhower had never actually seen active service, but he was nevertheless a superb administrator who was greatly admired by all the men he commanded, not least because of his pleasant and affable character. The respect and trust of the troops was of vital importance to Eisenhower, because he knew that once *Operation Overlord* began, every soldier, sailor and airman, regardless of rank or experience, would be key if the battle for Normandy was to be won. The Allies could have taken a shorter route to France across the English Channel, from Dover to Calais, but they deliberately chose a different route.

In fact, this is precisely what Hitler and his Generals were anticipating, and the Allies did all they could to convince the enemy that this was indeed the case. Secrecy had been paramount, because the element of surprise was vital if *Operation Overlord* stood any chance of succeeding.

A concerted campaign, *Operation Fortitude,* was instigated to keep the Germans believing that the invasion would target Calais and events soon proved that it had served its purpose. Adolf Hitler was fully aware that an attack on the western front, through France, was imminent, but early in 1944 the Soviet Red Army in Southern Russia was giving him a great deal more cause for concern. The Nazis attempted to stem the Russian tide by building large fortifications, but Hitler's fears of being forced into a retreat by the Allies, on all fronts, were being proved well founded.

Also, the Americans were now dominant in the Pacific against the ever-tenacious Japanese. Because of the sheer size of the US Navy, the Japanese were finding it difficult to secure the islands that they had previously seized.

However, for the Americans containment was the watchword during these crucial months of 1944, because until Europe was liberated, they would have to fight on without any Allied reinforcements, while the European theatre of war became the primary focus as *Operation Overlord* progressed.

In the weeks following D-Day the Allied Invasion force steadily made progress, liberating the people of France literally village by village. The excitement was rising and after so many years of Nazi oppression the Allies received the warmest of welcomes from those, they set free.

Back in Great Britain news of the triumphant landings certainly boosted morale, but for Adolf Hitler as the realization dawned that the battle for Normandy was being lost, it was time to retaliate. Hitler had always promised the German people that he had a secret weapon, and with news of the events in France traveling fast, he needed to boost morale and re-affirm the Nazi position of strength. The weapon in question was the V1 bomb, taking its name from a German word meaning "weapon of vengeance" and it most certainly was. The effectiveness of these bombs came from the fact that they were un-piloted, basically an early Cruise Missile, that could be launched from mainland Europe across the channel to target Britain. After being launched the precise autopilot technology would accurately track the target area where it was due to detonate, and the damage the bombs could do was horrific.

Powered by a combination of petrol and compressed air, the V1 could travel at great speed. They made a very loud buzzing sound from the jet engine that pulsated 50 times a second and this buzz gave the V1s many nicknames including the 'buzz bomb' and the 'doodlebug' after a loud Australian insect. The sound was terrifying enough, but when it went silent it was dangerous, with there being about 15 seconds before the huge explosion.

However, for Hitler and the German developers of the V1 there was one major disadvantage. There was no way they could be sure whether the bombs had reached their designated sites or not. As London was targeted relentlessly, there was a wall of silence, as none of the devastating hits or the casualty figures were reported by the press and great care was taken to ensure that news of the V1's success didn't reach Germany.

What's more the indomitable spirit of the British, typified by the people of London, had been a major problem for Hitler throughout the conflict, most notably during the blitz, and once again the Great British public stood firm in their resolve to see Hitler defeated. Extra barrage balloons were deployed and planes like the Spitfire were used to attack the V1s in the air and almost 2,500 of them were shot down. It was quickly evident that Hitler's secret weapon was not going to win Germany the war, and it also proved extremely counter-productive as the Allies became more determined than ever to do all in their power to see the Nazi reign of terror brought to a swift end.

For the British soldiers fighting in France, fear for their loved ones back at home made them push all the harder to breakout from the beaches and having had all the advantage of surprising the Germans, it was now imperative that they consolidated their position. Ironically Hitler's Generals still believed that the main attack would still come via Calais, with the Normandy invasion being a decoy, but the Germans soon realized they had a fight for survival on their hands.

General Bernard Montgomery, who had been instrumental earlier on in the war, leading British troops to victory in the second Battle of El Alamein before taking a significant role in the fight for Europe, certainly found heavy Nazi opposition at the eastern end of the D-Day landing beaches. His troops suffered many losses, and Montgomery was forced to retreat to rethink his tactics.

Boosting the German resistance in this area was crucial because if Caen fell to the Allies it would leave the road to Paris wide open. However, the occupying army were far from strong, despite increased numbers, and it appeared that they were operating without coordinated artillery support, suggesting a break-down in communication, which was enough to allow the Allies to continue their advance.

Since over a million Allied troops had landed in Normandy by mid-July, Montgomery could keep the Germans busy fighting in the North-East of France, which gave the Americans the opportunity to advance further south, and when Caen was eventually liberated on July 19th the Allies were in a very strong position indeed.

With a strategic pincer movement, the Allies steadily surrounded the Germans and the Nazis could do very little to hold onto their occupied French territory, and as more Allied troops were brought in, the Germans quickly became outnumbered and retreat was the only viable option open to Hitler and his Generals.

To make matters worse for Hitler, the situation on the eastern front was getting tougher by the day for the Germans as *Operation Bagration* gathered momentum.

Bagration was the codename for the Belorussian strategic offensive operation, which aimed to clear all German forces from Belarus in northern Russia to Poland, which had started on June 22nd and continued through until the 19th of August. There were four armies in place to take on this task, which consisted of the 1st Baltic Front and the 1st, 2nd and 3rd Belorussian Front. This mission, which was later described as *"the most calamitous defeat of all the German armed forces in World War II"*, resulted in the complete destruction of the three major components of the German Army Group in occupation, namely the Fourth Army, the Third Panzer Army and the Ninth Army.

· · ·

The speed the operation advanced at was remarkable, and by July 7th The Red Army had marched into Lithuania in Southern Russia and had managed to secure it by the 13th. By the end of *Operation Bagration* the German losses were so great that even forced conscription couldn't begin to replace the men that had been killed. The Axis lost about 20 divisions in all, and 50,000 Germans were captured and taken prisoner from the city of Minsk, which was the last big German base on Soviet soil, liberated on July 3rd.

When the Red Army saw the devastation of the villages, where vast numbers of the population had either been killed or deported under the brutal control of the Nazis, they marched the German captives through the center of Moscow, before thundering into Poland.

The statistics from *Bagration* are staggering. Overall German casualties, including those killed, injured or captured have been estimated at 670,000, with more than 59,000 vehicles destroyed. The Soviets nonetheless paid a very high price with as many as 60,000 men killed, but the Russians were by this time unstoppable as the Red Army thundered into Poland.

However, with the Polish Home Army already fighting the Germans in the Warsaw Uprising they waited rather than storm into the nation's capital. When Germany had advanced into Poland, triggering the start of the war back in 1939, the Nazis had been secure in the knowledge that the Russians would not attack them because of the non-aggression pact Hitler had made with Joseph Stalin.

In return Hitler had agreed that the Russians would split Poland with Germany, so consequently the Polish nationals were keen to take charge of their own affairs. The Warsaw Uprising began on August 1st 1944 just days before the advancing Red Army were due to arrive, with the Poles eager to triumph over their German oppressors. Sadly, they simply did not have the strength and the Germans fought hard to maintain their position.

. . .

When the Soviets arrived, they did not as expected, join the battle lines against the Germans, and literally came to a standstill within a matter of miles of the city.

| Price to pay for the Warsaw uprising

The Uprising continued for 63 days, and the sudden halt of the Red Army is a controversial issue that historians are still disputing to this day. It's been suggested that the Soviet advance from Russia had left the Red Army exhausted and lacking the power to take on the Germans, while others argue that this was not the case at all. Stalin may have called a halt so that the Polish Home Front would be defeated, as they would undoubtedly be opposed to the Soviet regime after the war. The Soviets claimed that it was lack of fuel after *Operation Bagration* that left them stopping short of Warsaw, but it's unlikely anyone will ever know for sure.

As September ended so did the Uprising and on October 2nd the Poles surrendered to the Germans, having lost 18,000 soldiers, while between 120,000 and 200,000 Polish civilians had died, most of them murdered by the German troops. After they surrendered the Nazis burned the ancient city to the ground, leaving nothing but ruins for the Russians to take control of when they finally reached Warsaw.

With the mighty Russian Allies advancing from the east, and American, British and Canadian troops gaining momentum in Western Europe, the German Generals knew that they were in a very dangerous position. Hitler's behavior was ever more irrational, and his symptoms of Parkinson's disease seemed on the increase. The Allies were slowly but surely winning the war, but it wasn't only his enemies that Hitler had to fear because on July 20th 1944 an assassination attempt came from within the ranks of his army, and what's more it very nearly succeeded.

For some time now, Hitler had made few public appearances and he was actually attending a meeting at his Wolf's Lair Headquarters in East Prussia, discussing the deterioration of the military situation on the Russian Front, when a bomb exploded killing four officers and severely wounding many others. Hitler survived, sustaining only minor injuries.

But it wasn't the work of one disaffected German; there were many more involved, although the main driving force was Colonel Claus Von Stauffenberg, one of Hitler's most trusted men who had close access to the Führer. It's interesting to note that there was a German Resistance movement dating back to Hitler's rise to power and it's worth just looking a little more closely at Von Stauffenberg's background to discover how this extraordinary event came about in the aftermath of D-Day.

. . .

Von Stauffenberg came from a high-ranking Roman Catholic family, his father being a significant figure in the German court, while his mother was a Countess. He was the eldest of three brothers and started out studying literature but eventually turned to the military for a career. Before the outbreak of the Second World War, Von Stauffenberg was commissioned as a lieutenant and studied weapons and transportation but was part of the German First Light Division that stormed into Poland in 1939. Von Stauffenberg was a supporter of Hitler at this point, and considered joining the Nazi party, especially as the Führer had signed a pact with the Catholic Church.

However, like so many of Hitler's treaties it wasn't long before there were serious infringements, and the Catholic Church began to condemn the Nazi's ideology.

The suppression of religion began to escalate within the Nazi regime, but it was the people of the Jewish faith who quickly became Hitler's targets. It was the Nazi's barbaric treatment of the Jews that first caused Von Stauffenberg to question his loyalty to Hitler, especially after an event that took place between the 9th and 10th of November 1938. Known in history as Kristallnacht, which literally translates as Crystal Night, this attack on the Jews was a warning to the world of what was to come. By the morning of November 10th, the Nazis had murdered 91 Jews, deported some 30,000 of them to concentration camps and destroyed over 2000 Synagogues.

Anti-Semitism was now an inherent part of Nazi ideology fueled by Hitler's fanatical hatred of the Jews who he blamed for Germany's economic decline since losing the First World War. Von Stauffenberg knew this was wrong, and when the violence extended further to include anyone involved with the Bolshevik movement his alarm bells were already ringing. Hitler gave written orders that anyone displaying any active representation of Bolshevik ideology was to be killed immediately and many right-minded Germans, including Von Stauffenberg, appealed against this.

As the war progressed Von Stauffenberg's opinion of Nazi conduct and policies deteriorated and he became convinced that Hitler was corrupting the German Empire by taking innocent lives, and by 1942 Von Stauffenberg knew in his heart that Hitler and his Nazi henchmen had to be stopped. In 1943, shortly after being promoted to Lieutenant Colonel of the 10th panzer Division, Von Stauffenberg's vehicle was bombed by the British during the Tunisia Campaign in North Africa.

He was fortunate to survive and was hospitalized for three months before being sent home to recover further. Von Stauffenberg's injuries were severe, he'd lost his left eye, right hand and most of the fingers on the other hand, but he was determined to continue as a soldier. However, it was during his rehabilitation that Henning von Tresckow, a serving officer but a conspirator in the German Resistance approached him. Aware of Von Stauffenberg's organizational skills and dislike of the Nazi movement, Von Tresckow offered him a job as a Staff Officer at the headquarters of the German Home Army in Berlin to assist when necessary in the fight to remove Hitler from power. Fully aware that his injuries meant he would never be able to assassinate Hitler without help, Von Stauffenberg agreed to take the position.

Von Tresckow was convinced that only the death of Adolf Hitler would stop Nazi tyranny, and as the Allies played their part, advancing towards Germany, the Resistance prepared to do their duty.

"The assassination must be attempted at all costs. What matters now is no longer the practical purpose of the coup, but to prove to the world and for the records of history that the men of the resistance movement dared to take the decisive step."

When Von Stauffenberg joined the movement, various plans were in place to kill Hitler and his highest-ranking officials, but somehow something always seemed to go wrong. Eventually Von Stauffenberg realized that despite his injuries he was able to get close to Hitler without arousing suspicion, so he put himself forward to carry out the assassination.

By this time the D-Day landings had been a great success for the Allies and the support for Von Tresckow and the German Resistance had increased as plans were put in place to rid the world of Hitler and the Nazis for good. On July 11th Von Stauffenberg attended a conference at the Berghof, Hitler's country retreat in the Bavarian Alps near Berchtesgaden, carrying a bomb in a briefcase. A colleague waited nervously in a getaway car for Von Stauffenberg to complete the assassination of Hitler, along with Henrich Himmler and Herman Goering, but again, it was not to be.

When Von Stauffenberg arrived, he realized that Himmler and Goering were not present, and after a telephone call to his co-conspirators, the decision was made to abort the mission and Von Stauffenberg returned to Berlin to try again another day. The conspirators wasted no time in re-scheduling and by the 15th Von Stauffenberg was ready with his bomb once again at Hitler's Headquarters in East Prussia. Fortune yet again failed to smile on Von Stauffenberg, as Himmler was absent from the meeting, and another assassination attempt was aborted.

Getting all three men together in one place, at the same time, was proving very tricky indeed, and the Nazis were certainly becoming very suspicious. Arrests were being made and the conspirators selected July 20th, knowing that speed was vital, and this would very possibly be their last window of opportunity. On the morning of the 20th Von Stauffenberg travelled from Berlin to Hitler's Wolf's Lair headquarters in East Prussia, armed with two bombs in a briefcase, where he entered the meeting room as planned, before the Führer's arrival.

Excusing himself to change his shirt, he found a small room in which to activate the pencil detonators using small pliers.

Having no right hand and only three fingers on his left this fiddly job was far from easy, and by the time a guard knocked at the door to hurry him back into the meeting he had only managed to activate one of the bombs. There was nothing for it, Von Stauffenberg could only hope that this one bomb would do the trick.

At just after half past twelve Von Stauffenberg placed the briefcase under the table in front of him, and as soon as he was able, with Hitler in position, he left the room using the excuse of an urgent phone call and waited for the explosion. But a latecomer to the meeting took the seat Von Stauffenberg had just vacated, and casually kicked the briefcase a vital few inches forward, out of the way.

When the bomb exploded at 12.42pm the unfortunate latecomer and three others were killed, but Hitler once again escaped death and was one of the least hurt in the blast because of the protection the large solid oak conference table had provided. Von Stauffenberg, who was observing the explosion, was certain that no one could have survived the enormous blast and headed back to Berlin convinced that Hitler was dead. Elated, Von Stauffenberg met with his fellow conspirators ready to take over power in Germany.

| Aftermath of assassination attempt

However, at seven o'clock that evening joy turned to despair as Hitler made a radio broadcast stating *"A very small clique of ambitious, unscrupulous and at the same time criminally stupid officers made a plot to remove me."* The German News Agency added *"The German people must consider the failure of the attempt on Hitler's life as a sign that Hitler will complete his tasks under the protection of a divine power".*

The *"very small clique"* that Hitler spoke of was actually a lot bigger than he could have imagined and when he sent the orders for Von Stauffenberg to be shot immediately, the officer charged with the task was himself a fellow conspirator and the orders were not undertaken or passed on. But capture was inevitable and before the day was over Von Stauffenberg and three of his fellow conspirators were found. At 1am on July 21st 1944 lit by the headlights of a truck, 36-year-old Von Stauffenberg uttered his last words, which translated were *'long live our holy Germany'* before being shot.

Von Stauffenberg's brother Berthold, along with over two hundred other conspirators were tried before a judge and sentenced to execution. Eight of these sentences, including Berthold's, allegedly were death by strangulation using piano wire hanging from meat hooks. These horrific killings were supposedly filmed and shown to senior members of the German armed forces, to discourage any further assassination attempts, as Hitler became more paranoid and dangerous with the prospect of Germany losing the war becoming a question of when rather than if.

While the battle for Normandy had raged on through June and the Russians pushed ever closer to Germany, out in the Pacific the Americans had been busy making waves. The target was the Mariana Islands and the first of these was Saipan. Japanese planes were shot down in their hundreds, and US submarines caused a significant amount of damage as they torpedoed Japanese carriers.

The Allies were victorious, and Saipan fell on July 9th 1944 followed by the resignation of the Japanese Prime Minister Tojo just nine days later.

He had attempted to conceal the events at Saipan, trying to convince his people that the Japanese had been victorious, but when the news leaked out Tojo had lost all credibility. The Americans were relentless following their victory at Saipan with a campaign to take the Islands of Tinian and Guam, which they achieved in August 1944. After the humiliation suffered at the hands of the Japanese at Pearl Harbor, the Americans were now poised to take the war to the Japanese mainland.

. . .

And as the summer of 1944 continued, back on the European Front the Americans were also being kept extremely busy as the breakout from the beach head gathered pace after the liberation of Caen. It was time for the Allies to work closely together now, and Montgomery had expected Eisenhower to appoint him Commander of the Ground Forces in Europe.

But with the American Generals Omar Bradley and George S Patton being key to the liberation of France as well as Montgomery, this was probably going to be unworkable. There had been antagonism between the American Generals and Montgomery since the Allied advance into Sicily, and Eisenhower knew only too well that his countrymen would never accept "Monty" in command of them.

Also, there were now a proportionally high number of US troops fighting in Normandy, so logically an American with overall leadership responsibilities would make the most sense. The obvious solution was for Eisenhower to take on the role himself, and to appease Montgomery, Prime Minister Winston Churchill promoted him to the rank of Field Marshal.

For Montgomery the next task was codenamed *Operation Goodwood*, launched on July 18th and its aim was to minimize German resistance to *Operation Cobra*, which would see the bulk of the American forces breakout from the beachhead and encircle the Germans, creating the Falaise Pocket. Cobra should have begun on the 18th as well but bad weather, something of a characteristic of the summer of 1944, meant that it was postponed until the 25th.

| Working further East through France

A further operation, codenamed *Atlantic* was given the go ahead to secure the Verrieres Ridge, which was a significant sector of high ground to the south of Caen. Taking this area would not only give a great defensive position but would also open up the path to the town of Falaise, which was proving very difficult to get to with the heavy German occupation of this strategic ridge.

When *Operation Atlantic* failed to achieve its aims, *Operation Spring* was launched with the Canadian General, Guy Simonds, given the job by Montgomery to devise a battle plan to take the ridge and Phase One began on July 24th. The North Nova Scotia Highlanders made the initial attack on the town of Tilly La Champagne in the early hours of the morning. Simonds had devised a way of bouncing light off the clouds to improve visibility, so the Allies could see the enemy positions. Unfortunately, this also meant that the ridge's German defenders could see the Canadians too, and this resulted in a hard and bitter fight.

In Phase Two the Calgary Highlanders targeted towns and a further ridge, and although they also faced tough German resistance the area was eventually secured.

The German counterattacks for both Phase One and Two were swift with Panzer tanks advancing against the North Nova Scotia and the Calgary Highlanders, forcing the Allies to retreat from their newly secured areas. The Black Watch then embarked on the Third Phase, targeting the town of St Martin before moving on to take the Verrieres Ridge.

During D-Day and the weeks after, the bad weather had worked in the Allies favor convincing Hitler's Generals that the invasion would not be until conditions improved, but this was not the case when it came to *Operation Spring*. The Germans moved their 9th SS Panzer Division into the area as soon as news of *Operation Spring* reached them. A postponement due to bad weather gave the German army time to reinforce the ridge with another 4 battalions of men. The Canadians suffered terrible losses, in this phase few soldiers survived to tell the tale, proving that despite the success of D-Day the battle for France was still far from being a forgone conclusion.

It would take until early August for this area around Caen to eventually be secured. Nevertheless, although the breakout was happening slowly, the Allies were making progress and on August 15th, *Operation Dragoon* was set in motion as the Allies prepared to make an amphibious landing between the southern French towns of Toulon and Cannes.

Dragoon had first been planned as Anvil, alongside *Operation Overlord* with troops attacking from the south at the same time as the Normandy landings. Co-operation between the Americans and the British had been crucial but not always harmonious throughout 1944 and Anvil had caused something of a rift.

Winston Churchill was convinced that the war in Italy needed to be concluded at speed, with pressure maintained until the capture of Rome, but the decision to start invasion plans for France was taken and *Operation Overlord* selected.

But while the beaches of Normandy were targeted the Americans were also due to land in Southern France, putting *Operation Anvil* into action. Both missions required landing ship tanks (LSTs) and Churchill asked President Roosevelt to transfer these crucial vehicles from *Operation Anvil* to *Operation Overlord,* but the Americans were not keen to do so.

This row continued for some time, until a rehearsal for loading men and machinery onto British beaches, like the five chosen for the Normandy landings, proved disastrous. As we know Americans training for Utah beach at Slapton Sands in Devon were attacked by German E-boats from Cherbourg, scoring direct hits on five landing ship tanks and killing more than 700 men. The Landing Ship Tanks were impossible to replace so close to D-Day and *Operation Anvil* was postponed.

Ironically, even after the success of D-Day Churchill was still opposed to Anvil arguing that resources would be put to better use in Eastern European countries, where he felt it was dangerous for their Russian Allies and Joseph Stalin to gain too much power. This is where it's suggested the name change for the Operation came from, with Churchill dragooned into accepting it by the Americans. After all Rome had fallen to the Allies in early June, so Churchill no longer had that argument, and after the success of *Operation Cobra,* which was due in no small part to American strength, the British

Prime Minister had no choice but to agree and Dragoon was set to commence on August 15th.

Calling on as many as 200,000 American, Canadian, Free French and British troops, the landings took place in seven different areas along the beachhead and were a great success. By the seconD-Day over 94,000 troops had come ashore and as so many German troops had been sent to fight in northern France, *Operation Dragoon* met little opposition. The invasion was carried out with speed and efficiency and in just 24 hours advances were made 20 miles inland.

For the French Resistance this was exceptionally good news and for those fighting on the streets of the nation's capital, hopes for a speedy liberation of Paris gained momentum. The French Resistance had been born when the Vichy Regime had been put in place after Hitler stormed into France in 1940, and it steadily grew and became more organized as the German occupation progressed.

Governing France during the occupation, between 1940 and 1944, and presided over by Marshal Phillippe Petain, the Vichy Regime was controlled by Hitler's Nazi henchmen. For the French this just added insult to injury and a Resistance movement quickly grew. Even so it was extremely difficult for the Resistance to mobilize as there were strict curfews in place, with censorship and propaganda also used by the Vichy government to keep control of the enraged French citizens.

Also, anyone even suspected of being a part of the Resistance was treated with viscous brutally, and in 1943 the Millice was set up, which was the Vichy Government's equivalent of the Nazi Gestapo. The Millice were responsible for killing thousands of their fellow Frenchmen during Hitler's reign of terror.

. . .

There were collective punishments and bloody massacres and even as late as June 1944, with liberation in sight, the killings continued. At one village, where the presence of the Resistance was suspected a German SS division murdered all 642 inhabitants, from babies to those in their nineties. The men were rounded up and mowed down with machine guns, while the women and children were burnt to death in the village church.

But by the time June 6th dawned the French Resistance could boast an army of about 100,000 and they were ready, willing and more than able to prepare the way and assist the allies in *Operation Overlord*. The military intelligence they could provide was invaluable and when it came to performing acts of sabotage on German power, transport and communications links they were extremely efficient.

Not surprisingly the Resistance wanted Paris liberated as soon as possible and an uprising began on August 19th. Even though Eisenhower, as the Allied commander, thought it too early to move into the city he was given an ultimatum that forced him to change his tactics.

Charles de Gaulle leading the Free French with the 2nd Armored Division threatened to send his army in, single-handed if needs be, to assist, and when the Russians failed to intervene in the Warsaw Uprising, Eisenhower agreed that the Allies would support him.

The Free French fought fiercely in their battle for Paris, and by August 16th the police, the workers on the Paris Metro and the postal service had all gone on strike. By the 20th the uprising was in full swing with barricades and trenches appearing everywhere.

Men, women and children were helping to carry materials on wooden carts for the Resistance, and a spirit of patriotism was growing.

. . .

After a short ceasefire both sides attempted to evaluate the situation. The Germans lacked any depth in numbers, while the Resistance lacked the weapons of war, which the Nazis still had an abundance of.

By August 22nd the battle for Paris was back in full swing and the Resistance managed to force many of the German army of occupation into retreat.

Enraged by this Hitler demanded that maximum damage was done to the city, and Dietrich von Choltitz, the man commanding the German army in Paris, gave the order for the bombing of the Grand Palais. Two days later the Free French 2nd Armored Division moved into the center of Paris forging ever onward and General Pierre Billotte, commander of the First French Armored Brigade appealed to von Choltitz's sense of decency with a simply worded observation *"I estimate that, from a strictly military point of view, the resistance of German troops in charge of defending Paris cannot be efficient anymore. To prevent any useless bloodshed, it belongs to you to put an end to all resistance immediately"*.

Hitler gave repeated orders not to surrender under any circumstances and is quoted as saying that the French capital *"must not fall into the enemy's hands except lying in complete debris"*. Von Choltitz made the hugely difficult and brave decision to disobey these threatening orders and allowed Paris to be taken back by the Free French intact.

Triumphantly Charles de Gaulle made a moving and extremely patriotic speech to the newly liberated people of France, letting the whole world know that *"We, who have lived the greatest hours of our History, have nothing else to wish than to show ourselves, up to the end, worthy of France. Long live France!"* De Gaulle was appointed President of the Provisional Government of the French Republic, which immediately came to power.

. . .

The liberation of Paris was a key event in the Allies' journey to victory in the Second World War, and as the road to Germany lay before them, the race for Berlin was now on.

The months of July, August and September 1944 were crucial for the Allies. After the build up to D-Day and the daring and courageous attacks on the German strongholds along the Normandy coastline, the true enormity of the task that had been undertaken was fully evident. After the relief of the events of June 6th, the Allies now had to face a long hard push through France to reach Germany.

For Adolf Hitler, despite events suggesting that he would never be able to win the war, the determination to fight on was as strong as ever. But the Führer's capacity to make rational decisions was deteriorating and his own high-ranking officials, including Herman Goering, Heinrich Himmler and Joseph Goebbels, were having serious doubts about Hitler's ability to lead them for much longer.

To consolidate their position in France the Allies would face many dangers yet, and as the Russians pushed for Berlin from the east, the Western Allies would have political issues to sort out with their Soviet counterparts, as they too had Berlin firmly in their sights.

With the end of the war coming into view the challenges for the free world were as great as they had been back in 1939, but at last it seemed that the hopes and dreams of a new age, free from the tyranny of Adolf Hitler, were about to be realized.

21

ONWARDS, EVER ONWARDS

October – December 1944

Briefing the officers on next target

E ven the formidable Nazi propaganda machine could do little to make Germany's position appear anything but compromised by the beginning of October 1944. For the early part of the war, after Nazi tanks had first stormed into Poland, it appeared that Adolf Hitler was invincible, and as time went on this was something that the German Führer not only believed, but also took for granted. But ever since the Americans had entered the war to fight for the Allies after the Japanese bombing of the US Naval fleet at Pearl Harbor, Hitler and his Axis of Evil had been put under increasing pressure on a global scale.

So, to recap a lot of history to absorb, lets look again at the key points. In North Africa by late 1942 the Germans had been defeated at the Second Battle of El Alamein as General Bernard Montgomery and the British Eighth Army had taken on Hitler's "Desert Fox", General Erwin Rommel and won. Montgomery's determination was equal to anything shown by the Germans to date, as typified on the eve of an earlier battle when he had destroyed all contingency plans for withdrawal, telling his officers *"If we are attacked, then there will be no retreat. If we cannot stay here alive, then we will stay here dead"*.

It was this remarkable fighting spirit that was beginning to shine through for the Allies, whether fighting in the European or Pacific Theatre of War, that was making all the difference. The tide was fast turning against Hitler.

Taking on the might of the Soviet Red Army back in 1941 had also resulted in Adolf Hitler getting more of a fight than he'd bargained for. His plans to defeat Russia quickly and decisively through the summer months before the onset of the bitter Soviet winter were dashed as the invading Germans faced fierce resistance.

By February 1943 the German 6th Army had been destroyed after the Battle of Stalingrad, and at the Battle of Kursk later in the year, for the first time the Nazi's devastating blitzkrieg tactics failed. Elsewhere, after the Allies triumphant progress in North Africa, *Operation Husky* targeted Sicily, before pushing on to make a bid for mainland Italy, but by this stage in the war Adolf Hitler's health was deteriorating, along with his military judgement. However, Hitler's position and that of his Axis compatriots was about to face the biggest threat to date, as an Allied Invasion force set out from the South Coast of England to liberate France and start the push for Berlin.

D-Day, June 6th 1944 was a major turning point, and had things not gone in the Allies' favor the outcome of World War II might still have resulted in a Nazi victory. Even so the Allies met pockets of German resistance and despite the success of D-Day, Hitler was not going to give up without a fight and as the summer of 1944 one of the most unseasonable on record, gave way to autumn, the Allies were all too aware that they still had a long, bitter and very dangerous fight ahead of them.

Meanwhile in the east the Russians were also playing their part, ruthlessly putting the operation, codenamed *Bagration*, into action. The aim of *Bagration* was to push all the German forces from what the Republic of Belarus is today back into Poland, and the results were brutal. Historians have described this operation as one of the bloodiest known to man, but more importantly for the Allies, it has also been described as *"the most calamitous defeat of all the German armed forces in World War II".*

The Red Army made rapid progress and soon reached Poland decimating German army units as they went, inflicting casualties that went beyond 670,000, and with Hitler's forces fully stretched after D-Day, there was no chance of bringing in reinforcements. Such devastating German losses to the east in *Operation Bagration* combined with those to the west during D-Day and the months after, quickly became a major cause for concern for the German people, and morale dropped to an all-time low.

• • •

Hitler needed to do something, and fast, to prove that the Nazis were still in control, and he unveiled his secret weapon. The V1 had been in production since the beginning of the war, but it was only now that Hitler unleashed the powerful missile on his enemy. Hitler focused the V1s on London where immense damage was caused. The devastation led to the immediate evacuation of all the children in London, but the British were very quick to deflect these attacks and out of the 2,452 that were launched, the RAF managed to shoot down over a third. However, a reporting blackout by the British press meant that the Germans had no idea how successful the attacks had been, and although deadly, Hitler's secret weapon had come too late to win him the war.

Back in France, a diminishing fuel situation was causing a problem for the Allies, and this stemmed from the lack of deep-water ports to ship in supplies. Montgomery, now enjoying the rank of Field Marshal, was busy in the north planning an advance into Germany from Belgium, but Eisenhower advised him to turn his attention to the port of Antwerp in order to open up a useful shipping harbor, which would improve the Allies' overall position. Montgomery, always difficult to command went ahead with the advance he had planned, using the excuse that Eisenhower's strategy needed a combat supply, which was at the time, unfeasible.

Codenamed *Operation Market Garden*, Montgomery had pushed forward in late September, with short sharp concentrated thrusts across the River Rhine. The Rhine was one of the biggest natural barriers that stood between the Allies and Germany, so Market Garden's biggest goal was to secure the bridges intact, which would allow for a fast advance towards Berlin.

The Market part of the mission referred to the large-scale airborne attack, which was vital for positioning, and the Garden part referred to the ground troops. For the operation to be a success these two forces needed to work together in perfect unison, but due to the lack of planning, problems began to arise. Previous operations as large as this took months to strategize and rehearse, but the preparations for Market Garden had been completed in just one week with no rehearsal and almost no tactical training.

Other commanders were concerned about the unpredictable operation, but Montgomery stubbornly stuck to his guns, even when shown photographic evidence of menacing lines of tanks very close to some of the landing areas, which he dismissed as being non-serviceable.

Operation Market Garden was unsuccessful in part because the fuel situation due to the Allies' failure to secure a port meant that the Germans had enough time to bring in reinforcements and consolidate their position. There were some 20,000 Allied casualties by the time Montgomery was forced to withdraw, and precious time had been lost.

It was now vital that a solution was found for the fuel problem, because without a steady supply route the western Allies' push for Berlin would be seriously thwarted. Just as Eisenhower had wanted in the first place, the Belgium port of Antwerp was the Allies next target, but as the bitterly hard-fought Battle of the Scheldt got underway, it was far from being an easy task for the Allies. The battle began on October 2nd along the Scheldt River, and even though the Germans put up fierce resistance to defend the port, it was eventually secured and immediately brought into service for Allied shipping.

The opening of Antwerp combined with the successful capture of the major port of Marseilles in the south of France, finally put an end to the crippling supply shortage that was threatening the Allies' ever improving position. The beginning of October also saw the end of the Warsaw Uprising, which is as controversial today as it ever was.

The Uprising saw Polish nationals fighting to liberate their capital city from the

Germans. It was a major part of the Polish Home Army's *Operation Tempest,* which aimed to free Poland from the Nazis before the Soviets could take control. It was soon clear however that Warsaw was too heavily guarded for the Poles fighting alone, giving the Russians the perfect opportunity to settle old scores.

After *Bagration*, the Red Army were less than 10km away from the struggling Polish Home Army, when they were ordered to come to an abrupt halt. The Soviets looked on as the Poles continued to fight a bloody battle for 64 days, before finally waving the white flag of surrender. At the heart of the controversy is speculation as to the reasoning behind the Russian leader, Joseph Stalin, failing to come to the aid of the Polish Home Army.

That the Soviets were busy during October is undeniable, and on the 6th they began the Debrecen Offensive in eastern Hungary. If the Russians could secure the area, it would give them a wide-open gateway into Germany from the south. The ferocious attack began with the 2nd Ukrainian Front storming past the Hungarian Third Army.

But then progress slowed, and the Germans were able to build up a strong defensive line. The Soviets treated the civilians of Hungary with utter contempt, committing atrocities that made the Hungarian troops fight even more determinedly and despite being outnumbered, along with the Germans, they managed to ensure that the Battle of Debrecen ended with the honors even. But the Axis could not hold the Russians at bay for long and on November 4th the Red Army managed to secure the Hungarian capital, Budapest, and the surrounding area.

October also saw the liberation of Athens. Greece had been invaded by the Italians in 1940 but managed to fight them off until Hitler reluctantly sent in his men in 1941, and from then until 1944 Greece was an occupied nation under Axis control. However, the exiled Greek government did manage to raise an army, which became very useful to the Allies in the North African and Italian campaigns.

At this point in 1944 the Russians were already advancing into Rumania and Yugoslavia and the German forces occupying Greece were strategically withdrawn, as they were in danger of being cut off by the Soviet advance, and when the western allies took control after liberating Athens, the Greek government in exile returned just over a week later.

However, losing occupied territory wasn't the only thing that Hitler now had to worry about. Paranoia and distrust of the people around him was also a growing issue. And this was not without foundation because there were several assassination attempts made on Hitler's life throughout 1944, but *Operation Valkyrie* on July 20th came the closest to succeeding. It was only a matter of hours before Von Stauffenberg was hunted down and executed, but the extensive investigation to find anyone who was involved was only just beginning. The brutality with which the accused were treated knew no bounds, and even some of Hitler's closest associates were implicated in the plot.

| Hitler's last meeting with Erwin Rommel

The most shocking name to appear was undoubtedly that of Erwin Rommel, Hitler's most trusted "Desert Fox", who had fought so hard for the Nazi cause in North Africa. Rommel had then been singled out for further distinction as it became obvious through late 1943 into 1944 that an Allied Invasion of France was becoming ever more likely, and he was given the task of defending the French coast.

On July 17th an air attack resulted in Rommel's car being bombed, and he was hospitalized with serious head injuries. During his military career Rommel had always been against some elements of the Nazi regime, especially the maltreatment of Jews, and when it came to the investigations after the July 20th assassination attempt, the "Desert Fox" came under suspicion.

· · ·

When documents from the coup's headquarters were located, Rommel's name was there, not only as a potential supporter but also as a possible leader if the assassination and subsequent take-over should prove successful. Even though there was no actual evidence of the conspirators communicating with Rommel, the Nazi inquisitors were on the injured man's case. Unfortunately, while Rommel had been recovering in hospital he had spoken out about his dissatisfaction with elements of Hitler's regime, and this was counted as positive evidence that he was a traitor to the cause.

Head of the Nazi Party Chancellery, Martin Bormann, was convinced that Rommel was guilty and pressed for the case to be put to the People's Court, but on October 14th 1944 Rommel received a visit from two Nazi officers who has a proposition for him to consider. Rommel was of course highly respected and a hero of the German people, which is why no doubt he was given a choice.

The officers informed him that he could either face Bormann and the People's Court, which would also mean the prosecution of his family and staff, or he could take his own life. The latter would mean Rommel received a state funeral and his family would be given a full pension and his death would be reported as that of a patriot.

Rommel bid his family farewell and left with the two officers who just hours later phoned his wife to say that her husband was dead. The German people were told that Rommel had died of a heart attack and as promised he was buried with full military honors, with Hitler sending Field Marshal von Rundstedt as his representative.

But as Rommel was laid to rest, the first major battle to take place on German soil was well underway at Aachen. The Battle of Aachen began on October 2nd, with the Germans fighting fiercely to defend their city, which was under attack by the Americans. Ironically during September, the German commander of the city of Aachen had seen his men were going to be seriously outnumbered, so had offered to surrender to the advancing Americans. Somehow instead of going to the Allies, the letter of surrender was delivered to Adolf Hitler, and the unfortunate commander was immediately arrested, and German reinforcements sent in.

Despite the brave fight put up by the Germans their efforts were in vain. With the Americans having almost 90,000 more soldiers than their enemy, the battle was going to be one sided to say the least. But because the Germans were on their own territory, they were able to hold their lines for a while, as well as managing to inflict heavy casualties on the Americans before their inevitable defeat.

By the time the battle was concluded as a decisive Allied victory on October 21st, the casualties for both sides were in the region of 5,000, but as the Germans also had 5,600 of their men captured it was a heavy price to pay in a battle that had been a foregone conclusion. October really was a key month and it wasn't only in Europe that there was heavy fighting.

In the Pacific the Americans were at last beginning to make headway against the Japanese and the battles fought between 1943 and 1944 were forcing them away from the relative security of their south and central island bases.

When the Japanese had taken control of the Philippines back in 1942, the American commander of the United States Forces in the Far East was General Douglas MacArthur, and President Roosevelt himself had ordered MacArthur to leave the Philippines, where he was based. MacArthur was reluctant to depart feeling the US army owed it to the people of the Philippines to stay and fight, and even considered resigning his commission to continue as a private soldier. However, in the end MacArthur followed orders and left for Australia, but not before he had vowed to return to see the Philippines liberated.

. . .

And on October 20th 1944 MacArthur and his staff waded knee deep through the water to march ashore on the Philippine Island of Leyte as the American General fulfilled his promise. The Battle of Leyte Gulf, a body of water to the east of the island, engaged the US and the Imperial Japanese Navies and raged between the 23rd and 26th of October.

General MacArthur returns to the Philippines

This was considered by many to have been the largest battle at sea of the Second World War, and in fact the whole of Naval history, but it can be segregated into four major battles.

. . .

Fleet Admiral William Halsey was in command for the Americans, and his in-depth planning combined with determined leadership meant that by the 26th the Allies had secured a decisive victory, despite being subject to the first ever organized Kamikaze bombings.

The troops now fighting for the island would be safe from a sea attack and although there was still some way to go, the tide in the Pacific was definitely flowing in favor of the USA.

Nevertheless, while the outcome in the Pacific was yet far from certain, the Western Allies were by this time beginning to believe that victory in Europe and the end of Hitler's reign of terror was in sight. As the Russian Red Army made swift and brutal progress, the Americans were discovering that fighting the Germans on their home territory was a dangerous business. A prime example was The Battle of Hurtgen Forest, an area that skirted the border between Belgium and Germany.

After the immediate shock of D-Day the Germans had managed to consolidate their positions and had built up their defenses, which was at last slowing down the Allied advance. As the Allies moved into Germany one of their major goals was to clear all of Hitler's troops from this heavily forested area, which would in turn prevent the Germans from reinforcing their front lines further North between Aachen and the River Ruhr.

The engagement began on September 19th and became the longest running battle on German ground in World War II. It was also destined to become the longest battle in US history, and as matters would not be concluded until February 1945, these really were the early stages.

For the Germans this was a vital piece of territory to hold, not least because Hitler was still planning a major come back with his "Ardennes Offensive", which would become better known as *The Battle of the Bulge*. It was to be an important staging area for the many troops, vehicles and armaments required to put the plan into action.

The Americans naturally had their own agenda, including taking control of River Ruhr's Dam, which could be opened to flood the entire area, something they might either want to do, or more importantly prevent the Germans from doing so. On October 5th in a first major phase the US 9th Infantry Division attacked the town of Schmidt, which was a significant link for the German's supply chain. The battle was fierce with both sides needing to hold their position, and it wasn't until October 16th that the struggling 9th Division was reinforced. In just 11 days 4,500 American troops were lost, serving notice that the Germans were far from beaten, and as a result the Allied reinforcements came thick and fast, capturing Schmidt by November 3rd.

As well as determined German resistance the terrain was also difficult with Hurtgen being an extremely dense conifer forest with hardly any roads, restricting vehicle access. In the few clearings the Germans had pre-set their guns to fire with deadly accuracy, and they had also been able to plant minefields that were covered by the winter snow of 1944. Equally the dense forest caused problems for Allied planes, as there could be little air support for the troops below.

The terrain became an even bigger problem in the second phase of the attack, as not only was the weather worse, but also tanks became essential in the battle. American engineers did manage to blast tank routes through the battle zone, but it was a perilous exercise. While the battle continued the weather and fighting conditions deteriorated and many lives were lost simply as a result of frostbite, trench foot and shear exhaustion.

A number of the Americans fighting here had also been involved in the Normandy Landings, and some who witnessed the bloody battle for Omaha beach, where over 3,000 troops were slaughtered, commented that by comparison to the Battle of Hurtgen Forest Omaha had been *"a walk in the park"*. Out of the 120,000 American troops involved at Hurtgen, some 33,000 were killed or incapacitated and although it resulted in an Allied victory, it was very costly, especially when you consider that German casualties were less than half those suffered by the Americans.

As time went on, although the capture of Antwerp and its large port had improved the supply situation, getting fuel through to the Allies was continuing to be problematic. The Nazis were still occupying the surrounding areas and Walcheren Island with its vantage point overlooking the Sheldt Estuary, was guarded by the German 15th Army.

Field Marshal Montgomery gave instructions that the Sheldt area was to be targeted and *Operation Infatuate* was put in place, with the task of removing the German threat to the Allied fuel supply route given to the First Canadian Army. The bombardment of the German defenders began at the end of October, but it wasn't until November 1st that the Canadians landed on Walcheren. But the Germans continued to put up a fierce fight until slowly but surely the Canadians cleared each section and the final phase began on November 8th.

After days of heavy fighting some 40,000 German troops from Walcheren Island and the surrounding area surrendered as the Canadian soldiers completed their mission. By the end of November, the port of Antwerp was fully functioning, and the Allies' fuel supplies were no longer in question.

Shortly after the Allies' amphibious landings at Walcheren, other ports were also captured, and as the numbers rose the stronger the Allied position became. The port of Zeebrugge in northwest Belgium had also been captured by the Allies in early November, marking the complete liberation of the Belgium nation.

. . .

It was certainly bad news for Hitler and his vision of a 1,000-year Reich, but the German Führer was still not ready to give up his dreams of world domination. Once more he turned his attention to attacking Great Britain as he unleashed the new improved V2 missile on London.

German Engineers had been set to work improving the V1, which had already dealt the people of Britain a bitter blow. However, the V1 had given a warning of its arrival due the loud buzzing sound it made and refining the V2 so that it was silent would improve its effectiveness dramatically. Speed and trajectory were also updated, which made it almost impossible for the V2 to be shot down by anti-aircraft guns.

The V2 was the single most expensive project of Hitler's Third Reich, and at 100,000 Reich Marks per rocket, the cost eventually became a problem, but not before Hitler, believing this to be a winning weapon, created 6,048 of these deadly rockets. There was also a tragic human price paid in the production of these weapons as they were manufactured in factories manned by inmates of the Mittelbau-Dora slave labor camp, and some 20,000 workers lost their lives before Hitler's new rocket was ready to launch.

The first V2s were fired in August 1944, but it wasn't until mid-November that they really got on target, hitting Britain about eight times a day. When attempts were made to shoot them out the sky the massive quantities of artillery shells raining down caused more damage than the rocket itself, and an alternative counter-offensive was needed.

| V2 Rocket launch site

It was evident that once the V2s had been launched, stopping them in their tracks was nigh on impossible, and the British knew that their only hope of destroying the rockets was to do so before they had even been fired. At first the RAF attempted to bomb the mobile V2 launch sites, but this proved to be prohibitively costly at a time when conserving valuable resources was of vital importance.

The next plan put into operation was to misinform the Germans about the directions in which to launch their weapons. British intelligence worked tirelessly so that false impact reports were sent back, and eventually they managed get the Germans directing the V2 rockets to targets in less populated rural areas.

· · ·

LIAM DALE

Far from solving the problem such measures just lessened the impact, and so late in the day, the most successful form of counterattack had to be the Allied advance towards Berlin, targeting the V2 launch sites as they went, pushing them out of range. But this was going to take some time, and as 1944 drew to a close, the V2s continued to be a very real threat to London and the surrounding areas.

Despite the colossal expense of the V2 project and the undeniable success of the attacks on London, Hitler's "miracle weapon" would make little difference to the outcome of the war.

The spirit of the people of London remained optimistic, although the V2s could hit at any time as they attempted to go about their daily business.

More than 150 shoppers and staff were killed in a single V2 explosion at a Woolworth's store, and in total the V2s claimed the lives of 2,754 British civilians, and injured a further six and a half thousand. As a device for punishing his enemies Hitler's V2s were certainly effective, but when it came to convince his supporters that the Axis powers could still win the war, despite hitting target after target, the V2s fell short of the mark. It was now obvious that the Third Reich was crumbling, and even Hitler's highest-ranking officers were beginning to realize that all hope was lost. But like a wounded animal the Nazi War Machine could still inflict terrible damage and destruction.

Hitler was determined to fight on and as the German position was carefully scrutinized, plans were put in place for one last stand. But it would be a huge undertaking for the remaining troops. They were short of manpower, the Luftwaffe by this stage had been pretty much neutralized by the RAF, and as the Allies' fuel supply improved, the Nazis' were left struggling after their Rumanian oil fields had been bombed.

. . .

516

Hitler knew that he needed to do something big. Even as he became daily more irrational, he would have realized that an outright victory was impossible, but he did believe that he could defend Germany in the long term if he neutralized the Western Front in the short term.

As had already been proven, the depleted German units were no match for the brutal Russian Red Army as their numbers were far too great, so Hitler turned his attention to a plan that would split the Allies, highlighting the difficulties they would face negotiating post-war agreements.

He especially wanted the Americans and the British to splinter away from the Soviets, and he also believed that the tensions between Montgomery and the American Generals could be exploited and used to his advantage. In his desperation Hitler believed that all he needed to do was buy enough time to produce bigger and more powerful weapons.

So, plans for a major offensive were drawn up. The military strategists offered many potential operations to Hitler, but only two were put forward for serious consideration. Both targeted the US army, as Hitler believed that the American public, who had been reluctant to back Roosevelt's plans to enter the war in the early days, would demand the withdrawal of their husbands and brothers from the European conflict, if they were to sustain heavy losses and be defeated in a major battle.

The first plan called for a two-pronged attack on the American troops in Aachen, with a further mission to encircle the US Ninth and Third armies as well. Eventually it was rejected, as there was little chance of it causing an Anglo-American spilt. The second plan however, had far more scope. Using their trademark blitzkrieg tactics, the Nazi objective was to split up the American and British lines and capture the port of Antwerp, which would not only cut Allied access to supplies, but also trap four complete armies behind German lines.

. . .

The operation was given the menacing title, *"The Watch on the Rhine,"* but it was destined to be recorded for posterity as *"The Battle of the Bulge"*.

In September 1944 the area of attack was discussed in detail. Hitler was insistent upon using the Ardennes as the staging area for the battle.

A success here in the Battle of France in 1940 had been crucial, and the Allies were unlikely to suspect a Nazi attack coming from this region as they focused on their own push towards Berlin. Many of Hitler's commanders were against *"The Watch on the Rhine"* for several different reasons.

Some felt that the mountainous terrain was simply too challenging. Others were concerned that if the weather was clear then the powerful Allied air presence would be able to target the German ground forces with incredible ease, and with the Luftwaffe not able to compete in the skies, the plan would stand little chance of success. Even the commanders put in charge of the operation also had doubts.

Field Marshals Walter Model and Gerd von Rundstedt believed that the additional task of capturing the port of Antwerp was too risky, and offered an alternative strategy to Hitler, but he insisted that the battle plans go ahead unaltered. The Watch on the Rhine called for 45 divisions with extra units to form a defensive line once battle had commenced. With the manpower shortage the German army was suffering, they could only muster up 30 divisions and this really was calling upon their last reserves.

Full divisions of war veterans and young recruits were grouped together that if matters hadn't been so desperate would have been dismissed as unfit for active service.

. . .

This really was Hitler's last chance to salvage anything from years of fighting, and he had no choice but to risk all.

The Nazi's diminishing fuel supplies was certainly a hindrance and even pushed back the commencement date from November 27th to December 16th.

But this was the very latest date possible if the attack on the Americans was to stand any chance of succeeding, Hitler could not afford for there to be any more delays.

German intelligence had calculated that the most likely date for a Soviet attack, to open the road to Berlin, would be December 20th. "The Watch on the Rhine" had to have started before this date, because Hitler was banking upon Stalin stalling his advance in order to see what the outcome would be if the Americans were attacked.

It had been some time since the fates had smiled upon the Germans and for this operation to go their way, luck would need to play its part. To begin with the thick fog that blanketed the war zone was very good news for the Germans as it meant that the Allies' air support could play little part in the battle. Also, the Germans managed to keep their plans highly secret and the element of surprise would give them a major advantage.

The Americans without doubt had superior manpower, so it was vital if the Germans were to stand any chance at all for the attack to come as a complete surprise.

Since Von Stauffenberg's assassination attempt on Hitler's life had nearly succeeded back in July security had been tightened, but matters concerning the Ardennes Offensive were tracked and controlled to prevent any information whatsoever being leaked to the enemy. Helpfully for the Germans, the French Resistance didn't stretch as far as the Ardennes, which meant that the Allies couldn't rely on their local knowledge to pick up what was going on, and German radio traffic was kept to an absolute minimum.

Instead telephones, telegraphs and teleprinters were used by commanders to organize maneuvers and communications, which meant that one of the Allies' most valuable assets to date, ULTRA, which usually intercepted all German operations, became almost useless. The Germans also employed similar tactics to those used by Eisenhower when he had been planning *Operation Overlord*, with all movements that were linked to the Ardennes Offensive carried out at night under a blanket of darkness.

However, despite the lengths that the commanders went to, word did reach Allied intelligence of a possible large-scale German offensive operation. But the Allies could not see how such a course of action would be possible for the almost vanquished Nazis, and the warnings were ignored as they pursued their own agenda, pushing ever closer to Berlin. As a consequence, there was little aerial reconnaissance undertaken by the Allies and Hitler's master plan quite literally went un-noticed.

Beginning at around 5am on December 16th, a devastating bombardment on unsuspecting US troops based in the Ardennes was launched. All the Nazi divisions scheduled to join the attack followed on and by 8am the battle was well underway.

The thick fog that had set in the night before really helped the Germans, making an Allied air response unfeasible, but as conditions worsened, the fog proved less advantageous, as the attacking troops were forced to go at a much slower pace than had been hoped for.

. . .

With the advantage of surprise, even with very limited troop numbers, the German divisions managed to encircle two American regiments in a pincer movement and forced them to surrender. All around the fighting intensified, and the violent battle continued as the weather got increasingly worse and the German advance slowed yet further.

Everything started to fall behind schedule, and as the Americans were now all too aware of what was happening, while retreating they blew up bridges and fuel dumps along the way, which slowed the Germans' progress even more. For the Germans, anger and frustration resulted in the captured Americans being treated with utter contempt. Bloody massacres became commonplace as Hitler issued orders for his troops to fight the battle with brutality in order to scare their opponent, and even though the end of the war was in sight, thousands of Americans would be slaughtered in the Ardennes.

Just a day after the operation commenced the Germans captured a US fuel station near the city of Malmedy, and as they moved off, they encountered a small group of American soldiers, who after a brief battle surrendered. These troops along with the POW's from the fuel station were herded into a field and shot, a cowardly and gratuitous act of violence with no advantage gained by the Germans whatsoever.

This futile act of brutality was eventually treated as a war crime, and the Malmedy Massacre, as it became known was tried on May 16th 1946 and the commander responsible for ordering the atrocity was sentenced to death by hanging along with 42 other members of his division.

What's more, the occurrence of the Malmedy and similar massacres in the last weeks of 1944 did have a negative impact on the perpetrators. As news reached the Americans fighting throughout the Ardennes, they became more determined than ever to withstand the German attack.

A case in point was when the Germans managed to encircle the Americans in Bastogne and Brigadier General McAuliffe the US troop's commander received a letter from the Germans demanding an immediate surrender.

McAuliffe's one-word reply, "*Nuts*" went down in history, and although the Battle of Bastogne raged on, Hitler's dream of a famous last stand that would at the very least salvage some Nazi pride began to fade.

The outcome of the Battle of the Bulge would not be decided in 1944, and as the fighting continued through Christmas and into the New Year the casualty figures for both sides continued to rise. 1945 was destined to bring peace to the world shattered by war, but as the push for Berlin and Hitler's ultimate defeat continued, the days of Roosevelt, Churchill and Stalin working together as Allies were beginning to draw to an inevitable close.

22

THE RACE FOR BERLIN

January – March 1945

Raising first flag on Iwo Jima

⋅ ⋅ ⋅

January 1945 was the beginning of the sixth year of the bloodiest and most destructive conflict in human history. In Europe, the heady mood of optimism of winning the war by Christmas, which the British and Americans had believed a distinct possibility in September 1944, had melted away in the face of fierce German resistance.

⋅ ⋅ ⋅

The progress of the armies commanded by General Dwight D. Eisenhower, Supreme Allied Commander in Europe, had been badly affected by supply difficulties and the onset of a bitter winter, and although the Allies had convinced themselves that a conclusive victory was now within their grasp, the race for Berlin would still take some winning.

As the Russian, British and American troops edged ever closer to the German capital, the opening months of 1945 would see some of the most brutal battles of the Second World War as the fight against the Axis powers intensified. This was equally true out in the Pacific too, as the struggle to overcome the Imperial Japanese Army continued. The Allied forces prepared for an attack on mainland Japan, and on a global scale there was a growing sense of hope that the war would soon be over.

But while the Nazi and Japanese troops refused to back down, battling fiercely even when staring defeat in the face, there were still months of fighting ahead, with many more lives destined to be lost, before victory could be celebrated.

Also, with thoughts turning towards to rebuilding Europe in the post war era, the cracks really began to show between the three major Allied powers as the democratic principles of America and Great Britain were at direct odds with Russia and the brutal communist regime of Joseph Stalin.

The Race for Berlin was now not only about defeating Adolf Hitler, but also key to the division of territory in the aftermath of the conflict. But for now, there was still a lot of ground to be covered before the war could be won.

As the New Year of 1945 dawned, in Europe all eyes were focused on the Battle of the Bulge that was still raging. Two weeks before on December 16th, a quiet, thinly held sector of the American front line on the Belgian-German frontier had suddenly been torn apart by a massive Nazi offensive.

. . .

The hills and woods of the Ardennes, the scene of Germany's great blitzkrieg offensive of May 1940, once more reverberated to the crash of artillery and the squeal of panzer tracks as Adolf Hitler's last desperate gamble in the west began. As the Germans pushed into Belgium, Hitler's immediate objective was the River Meuse, but the real strategic prize was the port of Antwerp, which lay another eighty miles away.

The loss of this vital supply center would have spelt catastrophe for Eisenhower's armies but there was also a more sinister edge to the campaign as Hitler aimed to encircle the US troops and destroy them. With only three American infantry divisions standing in the way of half a million German troops, supported by nearly one thousand tanks and assault guns, the surprise attack was a staggering success.

Despite US troops fiercely resisting the Nazi onslaught, after seven days of fighting, Operation *"Watch on the Rhine"*, quite literally punched a bulge in the American front line, which was fifty miles wide and forty miles deep.

Therefore "The Battle of the Bulge" was so named, but as the days past and Allied reinforcements poured in to defend the area, Hitler soon discovered that despite taking an early advantage, he had underestimated the strength of the enemy.

Before long the commanders of the 5th and 6th SS Panzer Armies realized that their troops were simply not strong enough to reach Antwerp or even the Meuse. With fuel running low and Allied bombers pounding their supply routes the advance of the 6th SS Panzer Army was stalled, and by Christmas Day the offensive in the Ardennes had run out of steam.

. . .

Meanwhile on the other side of the globe, Hitler's Axis partners, the Japanese were continuing to struggle against the Allied advance and by the end of 1944 Japan's Empire was rapidly shrinking as the pressure mounted. In northern Burma, a British-Imperial army led by General Bill Slim, supported by American air power, had instigated an offensive to recover the entire country. And further east, powerful American amphibious forces based in the Mariana Islands and New Guinea had invaded Leyte in the thousand-mile-long Philippines island chain.

The US Navy also had a few scores of their own to settle, and in the Battle of Leyte Gulf that followed, they managed to wipe out most of the Japanese navy, including all its remaining aircraft carriers. To the satisfaction of US commanders, the victory saw the attack on Pearl Harbor finally avenged.

By November 1944 mainland Japan was also beginning to feel the Americans' wrath at first hand. From airfields in the Mariana Islands 1,400 miles away, giant long-range B-29 Super Fortress bombers launched their first raids on Tokyo and other Japanese cities. The next stage in the Pacific campaign was underway and planning now began for a full assault on the Japanese mainland, as preparations were made to invade the islands of Iwo Jima and Okinawa.

And while the Americans were pleased with their progress in the Pacific, far away in Moscow, Soviet dictator Josef Stalin was also feeling very satisfied with the way the war was going. While the British and the Americans were battling to keep Hitler's panzers at bay in the Ardennes, the Red Army was busy building up its reserves for a massive new offensive in central Poland.

The Soviets' main objective was to target the coal mines and steel mills of Upper Silesia, Germany's easternmost industrial region. However, sensing final victory in the air, Stalin had his sights set on Berlin, and the way things were going, the Red Army would get there months ahead of the British and the Americans.

On January 1st New Year's Day 1945, on a dozen battlefields scattered across the globe it was just another day of death and destruction. In Western Europe the battle continued in the Ardennes. The Nazi bid for Antwerp in the North had failed miserably, but the 5th Panzer Army that had stormed through the central Ardennes was still battling on for control of Bastogne. This was one of the few Belgian towns where the road network of the Ardennes converged and if captured it would clear the way to the Meuse.

Unfortunately for the Nazis, the Americans defending the town belonged to the 101st Airborne Division, who were very possibly the finest soldiers in the entire United States army. In late December they had been joined by three divisions of the US 3rd Army sent by Lieutenant-General George 'Blood n' Guts' Patton. Spurred on by their flamboyant Army commander who ordered them to *"Drive like Hell!"* tanks and motorized infantry succeeded in breaking through the 5th Panzer Army's lines and between Christmas and New Year Bastogne had been wrestled from the Germans.

However, the Battle of the Bulge was far from being over, because the bloodiest battles of the winter war in the Ardennes were still to come. Refusing to give up the fight by January 1945 the 5th Panzer Army launched fresh assaults on American forces, now six divisions strong.

| Snow covered troops at the *Battle of the Bulge*

Hitler also had further plans that he hoped would shatter the Allied defenses, and at mid-morning on New Year's Day hundreds of Luftwaffe fighter bombers roared low over Belgium and the southern Netherlands. Luftwaffe chief Hermann Goering's contribution to the ground offensive in the Ardennes, *Operation Baseplate,* was underway at last.

Streaking low over the countryside, the attackers sprayed airfields with gunfire and bombs and within hours; four hundred and sixty-five British and American aircraft had been destroyed or badly damaged. However, the cost to Goering's airmen had been extremely high. Two hundred and seventy-seven German planes had been shot down and while the Allied air forces could easily replace the aircraft they had lost, the Luftwaffe would find it virtually impossible to replace its dead fighter pilots.

It was without doubt a busy New Year's Day for the Nazis, because fierce fighting also erupted along the Allied frontline between the River Saar and Switzerland as *Operation Northwind,* Hitler's latest, and in fact his last offensive in the west, began. Timed to exploit the difficulties faced by Eisenhower in the Ardennes, troops from two German army groups hurled themselves at positions manned by American and French troops on a seventy-mile front in Alsace-Lorraine.

However, unlike the surprise Ardennes Offensive, this time the Allies were prepared, and although the Germans succeeded in gaining some ground, they did not achieve their objective. Having failed to divert Allied troops from the Ardennes to the front further south in Alsace-Lorraine, by January 6th the Germans had abandoned all hope of capturing Bastogne, and this gave Eisenhower the opportunity to assemble his forces on both flanks of "the Bulge".

In the north, American and British troops were under the command of Field Marshal Sir Bernard Montgomery with the 21st Army Group, and in the South, the 3rd US Army was under Patton's command. Ordered by Eisenhower to launch a converging attack on the Germans in the Bulge, their immediate objective was the crossroads town of Houffalize. Only twenty-five miles separated Montgomery and Patton's troops but as temperatures plunged below zero and the bitter winter weather set in, progress was soon reduced to just a mile a day.

Frozen roads slowed up tank and motorized units, engine oil froze up and infantrymen discovered that their rifles and machine guns wouldn't work.

· · ·

There was also the added risk of land mines planted in the snow which were becoming another serious menace

Whereas Allied infantry were unused to advancing through deep snow drifts and frozen roads, the Germans had already experienced extreme winter weather fighting in Russia and were much better prepared for the icy conditions. Even so, despite the problems the bitter weather posed for the Allies even Hitler soon realized that the game in the Ardennes was up.

On January 8th, he gave his frontline commanders permission to abandon the Bulge west of Houffalize, and seven badly battered panzer divisions pulled back through the town as Allied artillery pounded their lines of retreat.

As the troops under Montgomery and Patton kept up their dogged pursuit of the retreating German forces, by January 16th, they recaptured Houffalize and by the end of the month the Allied frontline was back exactly where it had been six weeks earlier.

Hitler's gamble in the Ardennes had failed and "The Watch on the Rhine" had resulted in a devastating loss of life on both sides. The Germans had suffered 91,000 casualties and although the Allies had won the offensive, they had fared little better. Amongst the American forces, casualties were shockingly high reaching 89,000, with 19,000 of those being fatalities.

As the bodies were counted the *Battle of the Bulge* emerged as the costliest American campaign of the Second World War.

What's more the engagement not only took its toll in humanitarian terms, because for the Anglo-American high command it opened several old grievances that had been festering for some considerable time.

Just four days after the Ardennes offensive had started back in 1944, Eisenhower had ordered Montgomery to take temporary command of all British and American forces on the northern side of the Bulge. Militarily, the decision made perfect sense because the German offensive had upset the existing American command structure, but not everyone was happy with the arrangement.

US General, Omar Bradley, who was renowned for getting on well with everyone, disliked Montgomery intensely, having had difficulties working with him in the past, protested fiercely, and although Montgomery quickly brought stability to the northern side of the Bulge, his self-promoting attitude upset and annoyed the Americans.

After telling the US Generals that their broad-front strategy was to blame for the current crisis, he went on to infuriate them even further at a press conference on January 7th by giving the impression that he alone had rescued them from disaster. Livid with rage, Bradley and Patton threatened to resign unless Montgomery was removed from command of the northern Bulge.

To keep the peace Montgomery eventually apologized for his tactless remarks, which kept his position secure, but the bad feeling continued as the focus switched to the strategic direction of the campaign.

The British, including Montgomery, with the backing of Churchill and his military advisers, continued to argue in favor of a quick, narrow thrust aimed at the German capital Berlin.

. . .

Eisenhower however was not prepared to implement such a strategy, being very aware of the vast numbers of men that would be lost in the process, especially as the American troops now outnumbered the British in North West Europe by more than three to one.

Meanwhile in the Soviet Camp Josef Stalin had his own agenda. Since August 1944, powerful German forces had kept the Soviets pinned down in central Poland five hundred miles to the east of Berlin. Therefore, instead of pushing on towards the Nazi capital, Stalin had elected to invade the Balkan states in southeast Europe. Brushing aside less powerful German forces, Soviet troops poured into Hungary, Rumania and Bulgaria, overrunning the Ploesti oil fields vital to the Nazi war economy and triggering the collapse of the pro-Nazi regimes in Bucharest and Sofia.

By November, Belgrade, the Yugoslav capital had fallen to the Red Army and local communist partisans, but in the following month Soviet forces advancing across the Hungarian plains were prevented from taking the capital Budapest as the Hungarian army supported by strong German reinforcements fought back furiously.

But all the while German high command had been watching the Red Army pour reinforcements behind its front on the River Vistula in central Poland with growing anxiety. Army Group A, the German soldiers responsible for defending this sector could only muster 400,000 men and little more than a thousand tanks.

It was a desperate situation and by late December, Army Chief of Staff Colonel-General Heinz Guderian pleaded with Hitler to halt the Ardennes offensive and send more reinforcements to the eastern front.

Hitler and Eva Braun dine together

The Nazi Führer ignored the request and was more cut off from the reality of the deteriorating situation than ever. When early in the New Year he was given a report by German military intelligence identifying no less than 225 infantry divisions and 22 armored corps in the Red Army's order of battle on the eastern front, he had exclaimed *"Who is responsible for producing all this rubbish? Whoever he is, he should be sent to a lunatic asylum!"*

In fact, the Red Army outnumbered the 400,000 German troops of Army Group A by five to one and on January 12th, the long-awaited Soviet offensive began.

As a fierce artillery barrage shattered the calm, over the next seventy-two hours, three Soviet army groups made up of some three million troops, 10,000 tanks, 20,000 artillery pieces and 7,000 aircraft burst out of their bridgeheads on the Vistula.

. . .

Their main objective was the coalfield and steel plants of Upper Silesia, the one German industrial area that had largely escaped Allied bombing, but Stalin and his closest military advisers also had a much greater prize in mind; they were determined to get to Berlin before the British and the Americans.

Three notorious Soviet commanders had been given the task of leading the Red Army towards the German capital and fulfilling Stalin's hopes and dreams. Marshal Konev, Marshal Rokossovsky and the Soviet Army's most famous battlefield commander Marshal Zhukov. Together they would storm westwards across the war-torn Polish landscape, edging closer to Berlin by the day.

By January 17th the ruined Polish capital, Warsaw, had been seized from the Nazis, and as the Red Army continued to advance soon German civilians from all around the Reich's eastern provinces began to flee. While more territory fell, Nazi guards running labor and concentration camps also began joining the exodus to the west and with them came hundreds of thousands of Jewish slave laborers. Starving and wracked by illness tragically thousands would die as they marched westwards through the snow.

Many of these bedraggled figures came from the notorious camp of Auschwitz, which was soon to be liberated by the Soviets.

Only a few thousand prisoners remained when the Russian soldiers arrived on January 27th 1945 and as the ruins of gas chambers and crematoria were uncovered the true extent of the unimaginable atrocities committed by the Nazis was revealed.

At least one and a half million people had died at Auschwitz and for those liberating the camp it was undoubtedly a chilling and disturbing experience to walk within its walls.

. . .

As the remorseless advance of the Soviets continued however, Hitler's reign of terror was clearly ending.

As the Red Army continued their march west, to the horror and dismay of the Nazis, the Russians quickly crossed what had been the pre-war German/Polish border. On January 31st, Zhukov's spearhead reached the River Oder at Kostryn, and on February 13th, Konev's 1st Ukrainian Front caught up with them and dug in to create a fifty-mile-wide front along the River Neisse. In just four weeks, the Red Army had advanced four hundred and fifty miles and Soviet troops were now just fifty miles from Berlin.

With practically the whole of Eastern Europe under Soviet control, Stalin was in a confident mood and in a very powerful position. There was no doubt that Germany faced imminent defeat, and while Britain and America still held their ground to the west, Churchill and Roosevelt were keen to discuss the final phase of the conflict and how to restore order in post-war Europe.

At the beginning of February Stalin persuaded Churchill and Roosevelt to travel to the Soviet Union to meet him at the Black Sea coastal resort of Yalta in the Crimea.

The American president was keen to nurture and consolidate relations with the Soviet Leader, but beneath his cheerful exterior, as Winston Churchill arrived at the airfield, he harbored a deep mistrust of Stalin's intentions.

Nevertheless, there were agreements to be made and setting aside personal opinions, on February 4th the big three and their senior military and diplomatic advisers sat down at the Livadia Palace to an intense round of negotiations that would last a full eight days. Ironically, first and foremost on the agenda was Poland, the nation Hitler had stormed into way back in 1939, forcing Britain and France to declare war on Germany.

Churchill was insisting upon free and fair elections for the Poles, in fact both he and the American President agreed that all liberated European and former Axis countries should be given the right to democratic elections. Also, of utmost importance to Roosevelt was ensuring Stalin joined the New World Order, the United Nations, and to secure his assistance in the war against Japan.

The Soviet leader agreed to participate in the war against Imperial Japan three months after Germany had been defeated as well as agreeing to join the United Nations. However, he asked a high price in return for his assistance in the Pacific War.

For a start Stalin wanted the recognition of Soviet interests in Mongolia and Manchuria, which were nominally part of China. He also wanted access to Port Arthur in Korea and possession of the Kurile Islands then occupied by the Japanese. Roosevelt's military chiefs had many reservations about agreeing to such demands, but even so their President agreed to each request.

By the time the Yalta conference ended Stalin had got exactly what he wanted, but only after the war's conclusion would Britain and America realize that a democratic and liberal world was the last thing on the Soviet leader's mind. Under his control, Eastern Europe would be swiftly engulfed into the Communist regime.

However, entering the final phase of the war, and considering the future of Germany, the Big Three were all of one accord; they would accept nothing short of an unconditional surrender.

· · ·

With the Red Army ready to attack Berlin from the east, Stalin asked that the British and Americans provide practical help for his troops. Heavy Allied bombing raids on railway centers in eastern Germany would interrupt the flow of Nazi reinforcements to the front to face Zhukov and Konev's army groups.

As thousands of bombers were available for front line service in England and Italy, it was a request that the British and Americans could easily accommodate, and as military teams present at Yalta agreed to the Soviet request for assistance, one target loomed large on the maps of the Allied bomber chiefs.

It was the German city of Dresden, famous for its many architectural splendors, including several magnificent palaces, and was much admired as the Baroque Jewel on the River Elbe. But as well as being renowned for its beauty, Dresden was also a hub for industry, producing many commodities for the German war effort, with the benefit of an important regional railway center.

So far it had escaped heavy Allied bombing because of its distance from RAF bases, but soon after the Yalta Conference all this would change. Over the course of the 13th and 14th of February 700 RAF heavy bombers took off and were soon swarming above the city. Before long thousands of incendiaries and high explosive bombs were being released onto Dresden's elegant streets and avenues and a terrifying firestorm took hold.

By the time the bombardment ended the city was reduced to rubble and ruins and thousands of people had lost their lives.

According to official figures, anything from 21,000 to 35,000 people had been killed, but the railway, which the raid had aimed to cripple, was left undamaged. However, the destruction of Dresden did little to affect the outcome of the war and the huge death toll presented Nazi propaganda chief

Josef Goebbels with a unique opportunity to embarrass RAF Bomber Command, and its chief Air Marshal, Sir Arthur Harris.

As the news of the loss of the city's magnificent palaces and cathedral along with rumors of 200,000 dead, all cleverly exaggerated by Goebbels, was circulated in neutral Swedish and Swiss newspapers, the British Foreign Office became suitably alarmed.

But the devastation caused by Allied bombing raids was not confined to Europe, because far away in the Pacific, US Major General Curtis LeMay was coordinating attacks on Imperial Japan that would prove just as horrifying as the attack on Dresden.

Giant Boeing B-29 Super Fortresses had been raiding Tokyo and other Japanese cities from bases in the Mariana Islands since November 1944, but when the attacks didn't prove as effective as LeMay had hoped, by January 1945 he had decided to make drastic changes to his strategy.

The majority of Japan's town and city dwellers lived in houses made of wood and paper, so LeMay realized that incendiaries would cause the greatest possible devastation. He therefore decided that low-altitude night attacks would prove far more effective than high-altitude daylight raids.

On February 24th, eleven days after the annihilation of Dresden, the Americans launched their first night raid on Tokyo with one hundred and seventy B-29s carrying only incendiaries in their bomb bays. The resulting fires destroyed one square mile of the city, and this raid was just the beginning.

Two weeks later, on the night of March 9th LeMay organized a much bigger attack on the Japanese capital, dispatching three hundred and twenty-five B-

29s. Crammed into their bays were bombs filled with highly flammable magnesium, phosphorous and napalm, while their defensive guns were removed to increase the range and payload.

As the aircraft took off the weather conditions were perfect for the attack, the air was dry and strong winds were blowing, which would ensure the fires spread swiftly around the city. Flying in streams ranging from five to nine thousand feet above the target to confuse artillery fire, the American bombers were soon looming above the city.

The sky quickly lit up as nearly 1,700 tons of incendiaries were dropped in three hours. As fierce winds whipped up the flames, the fire began to rapidly scythe its way through the streets lined with wooden huts. As tens of thousands of people tried to escape, their routes were blocked by vast walls of fire and they had little hope of survival. Sixteen square miles of the city were consumed by flames and by daybreak, the bodies, reduced to ashes, were simply scattering like sand.

More than 100,000 souls had perished in the flames; it was the deadliest air raid in the whole of the Second World War and had cost US bomber command only fourteen B-29s.

Between March 1945 and August 15th when the Japanese finally surrendered, Curtis LeMay's bomber crews would wreck sixty-four Japanese cities, cripple the nations war industries and reduce 2.5 million buildings to rubble.

Cockpit of a Lancaster Bomber

The Japanese put the civilian death toll at more than one million people. Seven decades later, the controversy generated by the fire raids on Dresden and Tokyo still haunts the world. Nevertheless, at the time, advocates of area bombing like Air Marshal "Bomber" Harris and Major General LeMay justified the tactic claiming it helped to win the war.

Even so by 1945 Japan still showed no sign of surrendering and although the Allies had been steadily winning back territory from the grip of the Empire of the Rising Sun, there were still many bitter battles ahead.

While American troops continued the fight to reclaim land they'd lost to Imperial Japan at the outbreak of the Pacific War, by January 1945 General

Douglas MacArthur was preparing for the next step in the recapture of the Philippines.

With Leyte and Mindoro secure, the next step in the campaign to avenge the American defeat of 1942, was the invasion of Luzon, the largest island in the Philippines chain.

On January 9th, 175,000 American troops belonging to Lieutenant-General Walter Krueger's 6th Army landed on the south shore of Lingayen Gulf on Luzon. Defending the territory on the ground Japan's General Yamashita understood American forces had the upper hand in firepower and mobility.

As a result, he ordered his 170,000 Japanese soldiers to retreat deep into the jungle, from where he hoped they would have a better opportunity to over-come the opposition. But while the struggle continued throughout January, by the end of the month, Krueger's army was closing in on the Philippines capital, Manila, and the Japanese realized that their grip on the island was slipping.

Meanwhile secondary landings by more US amphibious forces and para-troopers had come to support Krueger's army, and by February 3rd the first American troops had reached Manila. Three years earlier defeated American soldiers had walked through the streets, with their General, Jonathon M. Wainwright, subdued and bedraggled as the Japanese looked on in triumph.

Those that had survived the ordeals of the last few years were still being held prisoner along with many civilians and it was Krueger's first objective to liberate the thousands of people who were still suffering in the Japanese prison camps.

. . .

As the 1st and 8th US Cavalry Divisions and Filipino guerrillas advanced into the northern outskirts of the city, 6,000 civilian Filipino, American and British Commonwealth citizens were discovered interned at the University of Santo Tomas as well as 1,000 American prisoners of war at Bilibid Prison. Meanwhile two commando raids organized by American special forces liberated hundreds of starving disease-ridden captives in camps at Cabanatuan and Los Banos.

While fighting erupted all over the city, the prisoners were soon set free and evacuated to safety, as every effort was made to regain control of Manila. Ironically, just like MacArthur back in December 1941, Yamashita had wanted to spare the beautiful capital of the Philippines from destruction and had ordered his troops out of the city.

However, 16,000 Japanese naval troops and nearly 4,000 soldiers led by Rear Admiral Sanji Iwabuchi disobeyed his orders and re-occupied the city, as fighting quickly escalated into what has been recorded in the history books as the worst urban battle of the Pacific Theatre of war.

Manila's civilian population found themselves caught up in the deadly crossfire, and many people were killed, with thousands shot or bayoneted as Iwabuchi's men ran amok.

Filipino women and girls were hunted down, raped and murdered by the score and as the Americans continued to bombard the city with aerial raids and tank attacks even more lives were lost. The fighting didn't end until March 3rd when the Japanese garrison had been entirely wiped out, by which time civilian deaths had risen to staggering proportions.

But for the Americans and Filipinos alike, victory had come at a high price. There were 6,000 US casualties, with more than 1,000 fatalities, and while the city lay in ruins, the civilian death toll rose to an estimated 100,000. These were terrible times for the people of Manila, and while the Americans attempted to restore order as civilians tried to piece their shattered lives back together, the Allied plans to invade Japan continued at an even more determined pace.

In fact, as the battle for Manila had been raging, a huge American amphibious invasion force made up of the aircraft carriers, battleships, cruisers and destroyers of the 5th US Fleet, was steaming towards the island of Iwo Jima, eight hundred miles south of mainland Japan. Normally uninhabited, Iwo Jima was barely four miles long and a little over two miles at its widest point. Dominating its southern end was Mount Suribachi, an extinct volcano five hundred and forty-six feet high.

The plan was to convert this pile of rock and volcanic ash into one big airstrip for General Curtis LeMay's B-29 Super Fortresses and P-51 Mustang fighter escorts. This would bring LeMay's bombers one step closer to Tokyo and assist in terrorizing Japan's cities.

The attack on Iwo Jima started with ten weeks of heavy bombing and three day's naval bombardment, to break down Japanese defenses.

Then at 2am on February 19th, *Operation Detachment,* the invasion of Iwo Jima began. As a storm of high explosives and steel lashed the island, 70,000 US Marines braced themselves for an assault landing and just before 9am, the first waves of US Marines hit the beach. Much to their surprise, they found no sign of the enemy and for a moment, they thought that the weeks of bombing and shelling had destroyed the Japanese defenses.

However, the reality of the situation was quite the opposite, and the massive American bombardment had left Iwo Jima's 23,000 strong garrison virtually unharmed, hidden away in an extensive complex of tunnels, bunkers, weapons pits and gun emplacements.

Suddenly the air was filled with the thunder of the heaviest mortar and artillery fire that many of the American troops had ever seen, much of it from gun emplacements on Mount Suribachi.

As the US marines pushed inland through the arid landscape, unable to dig foxholes in the volcanic sand they had no option but to move towards the barrage of bullets. As more and more men were scythed down by machine gunfire from cleverly concealed bunkers, by sundown there were already 2,500 casualties.

The scene was described by one reporter as "a nightmare from hell", nevertheless, despite the growing number of casualties the American forces slowly edged closer towards the base of Mount Suribachi. This resulted in the containment of the Japanese troops defending the mountain, and on the fifth day of the invasion, February 23rd 1945 a marine patrol managed to reach the summit and unfurl the Stars and Stripes.

A short time later five US marines and a US Navy medic raised a second and much larger American flag over Mount Suribachi, and the dramatic photograph taken of the event was soon circulating around the world. It came to symbolize the raw courage of the US Marine Corps, but the battle for Iwo Jima was far from over. Three of the men in Joe Rosenthal's stirring photograph were killed shortly afterwards as the 4th and 5th Marine Divisions, reinforced by the 3rd US Marine Division, proceeded to clear the rest of the island. The marines suffered extremely heavy casualties as they fought for Iwo Jima, quite literally, yard by yard.

Fighter-bombers and warships offshore provided much needed additional firepower, but grenades, demolition charges and flamethrowers were the only effective means of blasting the Japanese out of their hiding places.

Over the course of a month's bitter fighting, the Japanese on Iwo Jima were gradually dragged from their underground hideouts, but it cost the lives of many Americans. On March 16th Iwo Jima was declared officially 'secure' but another five days passed before the Japanese command post on the north west side of the island was located and destroyed. Finally, on March 26th 1945 after 35 days of the bitterest fighting, the battle was over.

Of the island's 23,000 strong Japanese garrison, barely one thousand had survived as prisoners of war. Meanwhile the Americans had lost almost thirty percent of their entire attacking force with 28,000 casualties, and almost seven thousand deaths. In fact, overall, the Americans had suffered more casualties than the Japanese.

Although the Allies now had a base one step closer to Japan from where Curtis Le May could launch his terror bombing, the fighting on Iwo Jima was a grim foretaste of the ordeal that lay in store for the sailors, soldiers and marines assigned to the Americans' next big operation in the Pacific.

In the battle against Japan, this was to be the invasion of Okinawa, and while the Marines prepared themselves for yet another battle, back in North West Europe the Allied armies commanded by General Dwight D. Eisenhower were ready for the endgame. Their aim was to eliminate all German forces west of the River Rhine, and in so doing set the stage for the final drive into the heart of Nazi Germany.

Field Marshal Montgomery's troops began the attack with *Operation Veritable* as British and Canadian troops targeted German positions over a narrow stretch of territory between the Maas and the Lower Rhine on February 8th, backed up by a barrage of one thousand guns that lasted five and a half hours. Support was expected from the American 9th Army as they launched *Operation Grenade* to cross the River Rur, further south, but in response German engineers blew up the dams that controlled the rivers in the target area, causing extensive flooding.

It was clear that *Operation Grenade* would have to be postponed until the water level dropped, leaving the British Second and Canadian First army to fight on their own. With weather conditions deteriorating and the ground beneath their feet turning to mud, they struggled on using amphibious vehicles and sheer determination.

In the meantime, plans had been made for a huge Allied aerial offensive aimed at destroying German lines of communication to prepare the way for *Operation Grenade,* which had been rescheduled. Roads, railways, bridges and canals all over Western Germany were successfully targeted, and civilian casualties were heavy.

Finally, on February 23rd *Operation Grenade* got underway as the 9th US Army began its assault across the River Rur, while General Omar Bradley's 12th US Army Group launched its own race for the River Rhine in O*peration Lumberjack.*

On March 7th, soldiers belonging to the 9th US Armored Division seized the Ludendorff Bridge at Remagen before its astounded German defenders had time to set the demolition charges properly.

With lightning speed, General Bradley ordered the 1st US Army to rush as many troops as possible across the bridge. General Patton was also active, and by March 21st under his command the 3rd US Army had surrounded the German divisions in his sector. Twenty-four hours later, Patton's men had crossed the Rhine between Mainz and Mannheim and their bridgehead was secure.

In six weeks, the Germans had lost 290,000 troops west of the Rhine. With the Allies across the last natural major obstacle in the west, there was little the Nazis could do to prevent the British and Americans advancing all the way to Berlin.

As the British Prime Minister arrived on March 24th, he crossed the Rhine and set foot on its eastern bank, in a truly symbolic moment.

Churchill was now eager to press on towards Berlin, but with so many Allied servicemen already lost in bitter battles, on March 28th 1945 Eisenhower took decisive action to begin the final stage of the campaign for North West Europe.

Much to Churchill's dismay, Eisenhower, who was intent on keeping Allied casualties to a minimum, declared that Berlin was no longer a major military objective, leaving the task of securing Hitler's last stronghold to the Russians.

Scarcely believing the news, to the east Stalin ordered Marshal Zhukov and Marshal Konev to the Kremlin to plan the Red Army's final offensive against Nazi Germany.

Soon the Soviets would begin their advance, and in just two months the European war would be over, but for now the final countdown for Berlin had only just begun, and the most important battle of all was about to be played out.

23

CHURCHILL'S FINEST HOUR

April – June 1945

| Lancaster crew pre-flight

I n April 1945 the Second World War was nearing its conclusion. In Europe, Allied armies were driving ever further into Nazi Germany from east and west and victory was, quite literally, within their sights. For Adolf Hitler, once the triumphant master of an empire that stretched from the Pyrenees to the Volga, the writing was on the wall.

Now a Berlin recluse in his underground bunker, surrounded by only his most loyal supporters, the Führer's every word still meant life or death for the German people and the millions of foreign slave laborers and concentration camp inmates in Nazi captivity. Before the guns would be finally silenced, hundreds of thousands of innocent souls would perish in the flames and rubble of the dying Third Reich.

On the opposite side of the world, Hitler's Axis partner, Imperial Japan had been left reeling by the Americans fighting out in the Pacific Theatre of War. Sustained by the world's greatest economy, the reach and shear power of the USA was by now simply staggering. Huge amphibious armies protected by massive naval forces were leapfrogging across the Pacific ever closer to Japan and giant B-29 bombers were raining fire and high explosives onto its cities.

In the waters around Japan, American submarines had almost run out of ships to sink and in the meantime the Japanese population, some 90 million strong, faced economic collapse and starvation.

In the Far East British troops had recaptured Burma from the Japanese, who had been in occupation since 1942, and back in London, Prime Minister, Winston Churchill, was receiving equally encouraging news from the fighting on all fronts.

Even so, after five years of steering the nation through the stormy waters of war, Churchill was weary and anxious about the future. The old warrior was concerned that the British Empire, exhausted and financially drained by such lengthy fighting, would be sidelined as the endgame came into view by its more powerful American and Russian Allies.

Winston Churchill had undeniably given his all for King and country and an Allied victory promised to be his finest hour, but he was wise to be cautious, and quite incredibly his own future as the nation's Prime Minister was far from assured.

As April 1st 1945 dawned, three weeks had passed since the first American troops had seized the Ludendorff Bridge over the River Rhine at Remagen before the Germans had been able to demolish it. The rest of the 46 road and rail bridges that had spanned the Rhine had all been blown up and ironically the Ludendorff Bridge collapsed under the shock of constant near misses by German artillery fire and air attacks just ten days after the 1st US Army had used it to secure a bridgehead on the east bank of the Rhine.

The Rhine was the only major natural obstacle between the armies led by General Dwight D. Eisenhower, the Allied Supreme Commander in Europe, and the rest of Germany. Once the Rhine had been crossed the rest of the German nation would be accessible, and Eisenhower's troops might well have reached Berlin before the Red Army, who had been held up at the River Oder, ninety miles beyond the city, since the end of January.

When Eisenhower had assumed total command of ground operations in September 1944, his land campaign in North-West Europe had its critics, one of the most vociferous being Field Marshal Sir Bernard Law Montgomery. "Monty" led the 21st Army Group as the Allies really started to make progress in Germany through March and into April 1945.

. . .

Charged with putting *Operation Plunder* into action Montgomery's 21st Army Group saw Canadian, British and American troops cross the Rhine near Wesel. Montgomery's men captured all their objectives, sustaining only minor losses within hours. However, *Operation Varsity,* in which two Allied airborne divisions were dropped beyond the east bank of the Rhine did not fare so well, suffering heavy casualties.

Watching the drama unfold in the skies from the relative safety of the west bank of the Rhine was none other than Winston Churchill himself. Always keen to visit the front whenever he could, Churchill had travelled to General Eisenhower's tactical headquarters overlooking the river. As ever Churchill was determined to throw himself into the center of the action, and much to Eisenhower's dismay, the British Prime Minister, now in his 70s, leapt into an American landing craft and crossed the Rhine.

But Churchill had more to contemplate than Eisenhower worrying about his personal safety with the looming division of Europe into two rival ideological and military blocs.

Churchill believed that the now ailing American President, Franklin D. Roosevelt, seriously underestimated the danger posed by Joseph Stalin and the Russians. The British Prime Minister wanted Eisenhower and the Western Allies to advance all the way to Berlin, before the Soviets could get there, but Eisenhower regarded the destruction of German military power as his primary mission.

Berlin was not his main priority. But for the time being with German artillery spotters and snipers still active on the east bank of the Rhine, Eisenhower's immediate task was to persuade Churchill to return to the comparative safety of the west bank before he got hurt.

· · ·

While the delicate negotiations were taking place to retrieve Churchill, 150 miles further upstream the 3rd US Army's 5th Infantry Division had strategically and without any of Montgomery's pomp and circumstance, crossed the Rhine at Oppenheim. With little love lost between the 3rd US Army's commander, the flamboyant American General, George "Blood n' Guts" Patton and Montgomery, and with old scores to settle Patton would have been delighted to get across the Rhine before Monty's 21st Army Group.

In fact, Patton managed to lead five divisions across the Rhine at Oppenheim, where there was little opposition, ensuring that the road to Berlin and victory in Europe was now wide open.

But German resistance to the Allied advance was weakening daily, with a home guard made up of old men and young boys who were as afraid of what would happen as the beleaguered civilian population.

And worse was to come for them, because from the safety of his bunker beneath the Reich Chancellery building in Berlin, Hitler demanded that *"the battle should be conducted without consideration for our own population"*.

Ordering the destruction of all industrial plants, the main electricity works, water works, gas works together with all food and clothing stores to create a desert for the advancing Allies, Germany's Führer declared *"If the war is lost, the German nation will also perish... there is no need to consider what the people require for continued existence."*

April 1st, 1945 was actually Easter Sunday a traditional day of celebration for the Christian Church, and for the Allies there was increasing cause for celebration. As Montgomery's 21st Army Group advanced, they were flanked, by the American 9th Army, forming the northern pincer of a giant encircling maneuver around the Ruhr, Germany's industrial heartland, while the 1st US Army formed the southern pincer.

Units from the two American armies met near Lippstadt, and seventy-two hours later the encirclement of the 'Ruhr Pocket' was complete. Within this slowly shrinking perimeter were the remnants of twenty-one divisions totaling 430,000 German soldiers of Army Group B together with millions of tired, hungry and frightened German civilians and foreign slave laborers, all trapped and at the mercy of the Allies.

There were also considerable advances being made in the Pacific, with the Americans preparing for *Operation Iceberg*. The target was Okinawa, only 340 miles from southern Japan, and the largest in the Ryukyu chain of islands. If an amphibious landing was successful Okinawa would provide the Americans with a springboard for the final invasion of mainland Japan. Less than a week earlier, Iwo Jima, the first island in the Japanese archipelago to be invaded by the Americans, had finally been declared secure after six weeks of bitter fighting.

Immortalized by photographs and film showing US Marines and a US Navy medic raising the Stars and Stripes on top of Mount Suribachi five days after the first landings on February 19th, the Iwo Jima fighting had cost the lives of 6,825 American and 21,703 Japanese soldiers.

Although an Allied victory the Battle of Iwo Jima was a chilling prelude to *Operation Iceberg*. For the invasion of Okinawa, the Americans assembled a force of 102,000 soldiers, 88,000 marines and 18,000 navy personnel under Lieutenant-General Simon Bolivar Buckner Jr., commander of the 10th US Army. Supporting Buckner's troops was a massive fleet of 1,600 ships, including forty aircraft carriers, eighteen battleships, thirty-two cruisers and two hundred destroyers. The warships lying offshore, and the carrier-borne aircraft were at battle stations, ready to blast Okinawa into submission.

. . .

At 6 am, the bombardment of the beaches at Hagushi began and after three hours, the intense naval barrage ceased and troops of the Third Amphibious Corps and 24th Army Corps stormed ashore.

Much to the Americans' surprise however, the assault waves encountered no opposition at all. Follow-up troops rapidly headed inland and by noon they had taken their immediate objectives, the airfields at Kadena and Yomitan.

By nightfall the 10th Army had more than 60,000 men ashore and the beachhead was now nine miles wide. But the Japanese were nowhere in sight. In fact, Okinawa's Japanese garrison had positioned itself well inland to avoid American naval gunfire, many concealed in the caves of the island's rocky landscape.

The Japanese 32nd Army defending the island was 120,000 strong, with 70,000 of them being regular army troops. They were good, battle-experienced men but the remaining 50,000 were a mix of naval troops and locally conscripted islanders who were poorly trained and inadequately equipped. Even so the Japanese had plenty of artillery and the terrain without a doubt favored a defensive position. At sixty miles long and being an average eight miles wide, much of Okinawa was made up of hills covered with pine forests and thick undergrowth.

Renowned for constructing strong and well-concealed defensive positions, the Japanese were ready and waiting for the enemy as the Battle for Okinawa commenced, but by April 3rd, the Americans had reached the eastern shore, effectively splitting the Japanese forces on Okinawa in two.

General Buckner quickly initiated Phase II of his plan the objective of which was to take the northern half of the island.

· · ·

The 6th Marine Division advanced towards the Motobu peninsula on the western side of the island, where they encountered Japanese troops defending a natural fortress of wooded ridges and ravines, but by the 18th of April the Marines had cleared the Motobu peninsula. Most of the northern half of Okinawa was now in American hands.

In the meantime, the Allied invasion fleet off Okinawa had come under a ferocious assault from the air. The Japanese High Command had assembled more than 2,000 aircraft on airfields in southern Japan and Formosa, today known as Taiwan, to disrupt the invasion of Okinawa, and despite bombing raids on their bases by American B-29s and carrier-borne aircraft in the weeks before *Operation Iceberg,* many were still ready for action.

Leading the Japanese air onslaught were aircraft packed with bombs and aviation fuel flown by young pilots on a one-way suicide mission. They were the Kamikaze, which in Japanese means Divine Wind.

| American troops on Okinawa

In the thirteenth century, typhoons scattered and sank two Chinese fleets on their way to invade Japan. The Japanese called these storms the Divine Wind. Now the Japanese High Command hoped that another Divine Wind would scatter the American fleet off Okinawa. On April 6ᵗʰ 1945 the Japanese *Operation Chrysanthemum* began with massed Kamikaze attacks on the Allied invasion fleet.

Although fired up with fanatical devotion to their Emperor, most of the Kamikaze pilots were novices and Allied fighters managed to shoot dozens of them down well before they had the chance to do any damage.

. . .

But there were plenty of Kamikaze who did succeed in breaking through and for two days, anti-aircraft gunners on board Allied warships fought desperately to knock them out of the sky.

An incredible thirteen American destroyers were badly damaged or sunk and it was a threat the Allies needed to take very seriously indeed. In the next three months, hundreds more Kamikaze pilots hurled their aircraft and themselves at Allied warships and practically all of them, just as they intended, lost their lives.

By the time the fighting on Okinawa came to an end, the Kamikazes had sunk thirty-six Allied vessels and badly damaged another 368. Most of the 4,907 American sailors killed and the 4,874 wounded during the invasion of Okinawa perished during Kamikaze attacks. For the US Navy, these were grim statistics, while on Okinawa, the land battle was just beginning.

The highest concentration of Japanese forces was to the south of the island and on April 4th General Buckner ordered the 24th Army Corps to advance in a southerly direction from the American beachhead. As the 7th and 96th Infantry Divisions pushed on towards Shuri, Okinawa's ancient capital, they met fierce resistance from Japanese troops defending a position the Americans had christened 'Cactus Ridge'.

There was a bitter hand-to-hand struggle for "Cactus Ridge", but by April 9th, the Japanese had been toppled from their vantage point, but at a high price with 1,500 American casualties. But the way to Shuri was still barred by Japanese defenders along the Kakuzu Ridge and the fierce fighting continued until superior American firepower forced the island's defenders to call off further attacks.

· · ·

Even so, Buckner's advance had stalled and the fight for Okinawa was anything but over.

Meanwhile back in Europe the British, Canadian and American armies were driving ever deeper into Germany after successfully crossing the Rhine in late March 1945. In contrast to the bloodletting in the Pacific, their casualties were light. Most German troops they encountered were keener to give up rather than fight. But during their advance, the western Allies were uncovering the ghastly evidence of the Nazis' crimes against humanity.

On April 4th 1945 troops belonging to Patton's Third US Army overran the Ohrdruf labour camp near the town of Gotha. In the camp, they discovered piles of corpses, some covered with lime, and others partially incinerated.

These unfortunate souls had been prisoners that the fleeing SS guards considered too ill to walk, and they had been shot before the camp was evacuated.

News of the horrors at Ohrdruf quickly spread, and on April 12th, General Dwight D. Eisenhower, Supreme Commander of Allied Forces in Europe, visited the camp with General Patton and General Omar Bradley, commander of the 12th US Army Group, to see for themselves what they had been fighting for.

But worse was still to come, and as advance units of the 3rd US Army entered another much larger camp outside the city of Weimar at Buchenwald, despite the horror of the situation they were at least able to liberate 21,000 sick and starving inmates.

The British and Americans knew about Nazi concentration camps, but little had prepared them for the reality.

. . .

After inspecting Ohrdruf, Eisenhower informed General George C Marshall, the head of the US Joint Chiefs of Staff in Washington DC, that what he had seen beggared description, as he let the world know the truth about what Hitler and the Nazis had done.

On April 12th the famous CBS radio correspondent, Edward R Murrow visited Buchenwald, and he too reported his findings, but over the airwaves to all who would listen. Buchenwald was not an extermination camp but for the 238,000 prisoners from all over Europe and the Soviet Union who passed through its gates from July 1938 to April 1945, it was a place of terror and death. 56,000 inmates are believed to have perished in the camp.

Eisenhower did all that he could to publicize the dreadful conditions inside Ohrdruf and Buchenwald, and being of German ancestry himself, he was determined to confront the German people with their collective responsibility for these appalling crimes. The Americans forced inhabitants from the district surrounding the camp to come and witness the atrocities committed in their name and walk past the piles of emaciated bodies awaiting cremation at the camp furnace.

On Buchenwald's parade ground the German civilians were also shown an appalling and truly bizarre collection of trophies collected by the SS. These included human organs in jars of formaldehyde, shrunken heads, and lamp-shades and book bindings made with skin from prisoners specially selected for their colorful tattoos.

The horrors of the concentration camps continued to be revealed, but the liberation had come too late for so many inmates, and in the weeks that followed thousands died as a result of their terrible suffering at the hands of their captors.

Buchenwald slave survivors

However, while this human tragedy played itself out as the world looked on, the death of just one man was about to change the course of history. On April 12th, President Franklin Delano Roosevelt, known to millions simply as 'FDR', the man responsible for bringing the Americans into the war, had died. Paralyzed with polio since his late thirties, and under immense pressure as America's President since 1933, through the great depression and then the war, Roosevelt's health had been deteriorating for some time.

· · ·

At the Yalta Conference in the Crimea in February, Roosevelt had met Stalin and Churchill to discuss the post-war division of Germany, but his appearance had shocked everyone present, he was evidently a very sick man. On returning to the United States, the President addressed the US Congress, although too ill to stand, he spoke whilst seated. The main theme of his speech was his vision for the United Nations Organization. He said *"The Crimean Conference ought to spell the end of a system of unilateral action, the exclusive alliances, the spheres of influence, the balances of power, and all the other expedients that have been tried for centuries – and have always failed. We propose to substitute for all these, a universal organization in which all peace-loving nations will finally have a chance to join"*.

It was a remarkable legacy for Roosevelt to leave to the world, and although very unwell, he continued to lead the Americans in the fight against Adolf Hitler and his Axis of Evil.

At the end of March, Roosevelt travelled to Warm Springs, Georgia, to prepare for the international conference in San Francisco at which the United Nations Organization would be created, but during April the 12th he complained of a terrible headache.

Shortly after Roosevelt suffered a massive brain hemorrhage and died within hours; he was 63 years old and had missed seeing his dedication to the Allied cause rewarded with the fall of Berlin and Victory in Europe by only a matter of weeks.

In the United States and amongst the Allies, news of Roosevelt's death was met with disbelief and grief. FDR had been in the White House for longer than any other American president.

In 12 years, he had led the United States to economic prosperity and to the very threshold of victory over Nazi Germany and Imperial Japan.

All over the USA flags were lowered for thirty days of official mourning. Hundreds of thousands of grateful Americans made the pilgrimage to gather along the railway line between Warm Springs, Georgia and Washington DC to watch a funeral train bring Roosevelt's body back to the nation's capital.

Even more people gathered together in Washington to line the streets as FDR's coffin was taken to lie in state in the Capitol Building, and his state funeral was one of the most emotional occasions in Washington's entire history.

But there was still a war to be won, and America turned hopefully to the new President, sixty-year old ex-US Senator Harry S Truman, yet a relatively unknown figure on the international stage. Truman had taken on the mantle of the US Commander-in-Chief just as the Second World War was about to enter its final and most dramatic stage.

In Germany, the British 2nd Army was making rapid progress towards the Danish frontier and the Baltic, while the 12th US Army Group were busy completing operations around the 'Ruhr Pocket'. By April 21st the fighting was over and 325,000 German soldiers filed patiently into American captivity. Overwhelmed by the huge number of men surrendering that required food and shelter, the Americans created makeshift prisons along the Rhine.

But sadly, during the next days and weeks, due to the sheer enormity of the task, many hundreds of these men died as a result of their already poor state of health, before their captors had a chance to care for them properly. What's more tensions were now beginning to appear within the Allied camp.

. . .

Winston Churchill and the British were in favor of pushing ahead to take Berlin before the Russians could get there, but Eisenhower and the Americans favored a policy of crushing all further German armed resistance first. Rumors were abounding of a powerful Nazi defensive position that had been established in the German and Austrian Alps manned by fanatical SS troops, and Eisenhower diverted a great deal of the American military effort southwards to neutralize this threat.

On April 11th, leading units of the US 9th Army that had reached the River Elbe, the last major natural obstacle before Berlin, were ordered to halt. But the Russians were still forging ever onwards displaying ruthless efficiency, with the Red Army thrusting aside the large number of German forces sent by Hitler to defend Hungary, and by April 13th the Soviets had captured Vienna.

In Berlin, where Hitler's chief of Nazi propaganda, Josef Goebbels was still celebrating news of Roosevelt's death with his Führer, hopes were beginning to grow that the alliance between the British, the Americans and the Soviets would now crumble. However, despite differences of opinion about what should happen after the war all three of these major players were ready to end Hitler's reign of terror, once and for all. On April 16th, Stalin's long-awaited offensive on the Oder-Neisse River line, ninety miles east of Berlin, began in earnest.

The Russian Red Army had three main objectives, the first was to capture Berlin, the second was to seize any material and any remaining scientific personnel connected with the Nazi atom bomb program and last but not least to snatch as much German territory as possible in the process. The assault began with a shattering artillery bombardment as two and a half million Russians moved into position for the final offensive against Hitler and his Berlin hierarchy.

One and a half million of these soldiers were under the orders of the Red

Army's most experienced battlefield commanders, Marshal Zhukov and Marshal Konev, who were given the task of storming Hitler's center of operations.

They outnumbered German ground forces by nearly three to one, the artillery by four to one and tanks and other armored fighting vehicles by nearly six to one.

Joseph Stalin was well aware that there was fierce competition between the two Marshals to get to Berlin first, and he had actually given Zhukov's 1st Belorussian Front on the Oder Line a head start, much to the annoyance of Konev whose 1st Ukrainian Front on the River Neisse was some distance further away from the Nazi capital.

But Zhukov did not have things all his own way, as directly in front of his troops were the Seelow Heights, the most heavily defended sector of the German frontline that lay ten miles beyond the River Oder. After four days of extremely fierce and bloody fighting the Heights were finally cleared, while by April 19th, Konev's 1st Ukrainian Front had managed to break free of the Neisse Line, finding themselves advancing quickly through open country.

As April 20th dawned, Adolf Hitler's 56th birthday, there was little for the Führer to celebrate. Zhukov and his men had made a rapid advance from the Seelow Heights and were already shelling the center of Berlin with long range artillery. As the day progressed the Soviet forces enveloped the Nazi capital to the north and south, and over the next forty-eight hours began to steadily tighten their grip on the city. The Russians were now taking charge and during the night of April 21st the Royal Air Force Mosquito bombers made a final raid on Berlin.

At precisely 8:30am the very next day the Soviet commanders gave the order *"open fire at the capital of Fascist Germany"*, and by April 23rd, Berlin had in effect been isolated by the Russians. For Adolf Hitler, now trapped in his Führerbunker there was no possible escape and realizing that Berlin was doomed he declared his intention to remain there and take his own life.

Nevertheless, the fighting for Berlin was far from over and Soviet casualties were continuing to mount despite the inevitability of the battle's outcome. There were some 45,000 troops defending the city and despite being badly equipped and disorganized there was still a sting in the tail.

Some belonged to the Waffen-SS, the combat arm of the SS only open to those classed by Hitler's racial purity regime as being true Aryans, while others were French volunteers from the 'Charlemagne' Division. Their ranks were reinforced by thousands of poorly armed members of the Volkssturm, conscripted males between the ages of 16 and 60 who were not already serving in the German Home Guard, as well as members and Hitler Youth volunteers.

A separate detachment of 2,000 Waffen-SS soldiers had been put in charge of defending the Führerbunker and the rest of the government district, but there was little even they could do against the Russian onslaught.

As well as being outnumbered the German defenders faced a massive artillery attack. The Russians were well equipped with Katyusha rockets, which were self-propelled from mobile launchers.

These rockets, named after a popular Russian wartime song about a girl called Katyusha, could be devastating and the Soviets troops were quickly blasting their way into the center of Berlin.

· · ·

Their main target was the old German parliament building, the Reichstag, but across the entire city there was fierce house-to-house and hand-to-hand fighting. The fighting ebbed and flowed with each Red Army attack and German counter-offensive, however in the heat and fury of combat, nobody was taking any prisoners, on either side.

The action was not only confined to Berlin. Eighty miles to the south west of the city, at the ancient town of Torgau on the River Elbe, the eastern and western Allies had an historic meeting. The first contact was made between troops of the 9th US Army's 69th Division and the 58th Guards Division in Konev's 1st Ukrainian Front on April 25th, which has gone down in history as Elbe Day.

This was a perfect photo opportunity for a small army of American and Soviet journalists and cameramen, who were brought together the next day to record the official meeting between the American and Russian soldiers as they shared a moment of celebration, friendship and exchanged gifts.

However, despite the outward appearance of unity the tensions between the Allies were growing. Immediately after the photos had been taken, the Americans returned to their side of the Elbe and stayed there. This was much against the wishes of General Bill Simpson, the 9th US Army commander who wanted to continue the push towards Berlin, but Eisenhower had already rejected this, electing to leave the way clear for the Russians.

This was because when Roosevelt, Churchill and Stalin had agreed the plans for restructuring post war Europe at the Crimean Conference, Berlin would be located deep within the Soviet zone.

There was literally nothing to be gained and keeping US casualties to a minimum was obviously a major consideration, especially after the American's terrible losses at the Battle of the Bulge. Also, the risk of incurring casualties as a result of Soviet 'friendly fire' in the chaos of the battle torn streets of Berlin was simply not worth taking, so the Red Army continued its remorseless progress.

By April 29th the Russians were within a mile of the Führerbunker, and as the news reached Hitler, he was also told that the Italian fascist dictator Benito Mussolini was dead. After attempting to escape to Switzerland with his mistress, Clara Petacci, Mussolini had been captured and the pair were executed, and their mutilated bodies put on display before the vengeful crowds.

For Hitler there was no escape and rather than face the same fate as Mussolini the Führer took control of his ultimate destiny.

He put his affairs in order, signed his Last Will and Testament and married his mistress Eva Braun. Hitler's dream of a Thousand Year Reich was over, and on April 30th with the Russians getting ever closer, the newlyweds committed suicide, and afterwards their bodies were taken out of the Führerbunker and burnt by SS bodyguards in the garden of the Reich Chancellery.

As 10,000 desperate German troops continued defending Berlin's battered government district to the last, on May 1st, the Reichstag, the most traditional symbol of German power, finally fell to the Soviets. While the Russian soldiers flew the Red flag from its battered roof, Hitler's heir apparent Josef Goebbels took drastic and tragic action, killing each of his six children before he and his wife committed suicide.

Hitler had ordered Goebbels to flee if Berlin was captured, but for the first time the Führer's most loyal supporter disobeyed the man he had devoted his life to serving. Things were by this time moving at a dramatic pace and on

May 2nd the commander of the Berlin garrison, General Helmuth Weidling, capitulated to the Russians, and within hours, all the guns in the city had fallen silent.

The Soviets took nearly half a million German prisoners, but there are no accurate figures for the many thousands of soldiers and civilians who perished. However, Eisenhower's determination to keep US troops out of the battle for Berlin proved to be well founded as the Red Army counted the cost. At least 81,000 Soviet soldiers were killed during the fighting in and around Berlin, while sustaining another 280,000 casualties.

Civilians try to cope in a bombed Berlin

With the fighting over, the Russians also had the daunting task of organizing food supplies for the surviving civilian population and making the city habitable again. But paradoxically, while this was happening many ordinary Soviet soldiers, motivated by revenge and often fired up by alcohol, rampaged through Berlin, committing atrocities equally as appalling as those associated with the Nazi regime.

And while the promise of peace was imminent in Europe, and the war still raged on in the Pacific, news that the Japanese were at last being brought to a standstill reached the west. As the Germans capitulated to the Russians on May 2nd, British and Indian troops completed their advance through central Burma and captured the capital Rangoon, with just a matter of hours to spare before the monsoon rains began.

As the world would see in the months ahead, the Japanese refusal to contemplate surrender slowed Allied progress considerably. However, despite the fighting continuing in Burma for another three months, the campaign was effectively over with the fall of Rangoon.

The Japanese mainland was also being attacked with little opposition and in the Philippines, American troops led by General Douglas MacArthur had managed to contain more than two hundred thousand Japanese soldiers on the islands of Mindanao and Luzon. Again, resistance was fierce as the Japanese fought bitterly to hang onto their mountain strongholds, but on June 26th MacArthur was finally able to declare that the Philippines Campaign was over.

Ironically, it was also late June 22nd to be precise, that the Okinawa Campaign was also declared at an end.

It had lasted a grueling 87 days, and more than 100,000 Japanese soldiers had perished in the fighting with at least another 7,000, mostly local conscripts, taken prisoner. A further 100,000 Okinawan civilians are also thought to have died during the fighting. Although victorious, the Americans paid a huge price, suffering more than 50,000 casualties, with at least 12,000 fatalities.

The Japanese had served notice that concluding the fighting in the Pacific, despite events in Europe, was going to take all the Allies' resolve to see through. It was a chilling prospect for the American military planners considering an amphibious assault on Japan, as they began to calculate what the losses were likely to be.

Based on the 30% casualties experienced by the US 10th Army on Okinawa, a conservative estimate would suggest that a staggering 300,000 Americans would be killed or injured. Finding a way forward would demand a new approach to warfare, but as we return to the European theatre of war, the early days of May 1945 certainly provided the Allies with much to celebrate.

With fighting in Italy and in Berlin all coming to an end on May 2nd events quickly gathered momentum. Just forty-eight hours later came the unconditional surrender of all German forces in North-West Europe, and it was given to British Field Marshal Bernard Montgomery in a tent on the Luneburg Heath.

It was a sombre occasion, with little ceremony, followed on May 5th by Admiral Karl Donitz, Commander-in-Chief of the German Navy and President of Germany, as directed by Hitler's Last Will and Testament, ordering the 350 U-Boats at sea to cease combat operations with immediate effect.

Everything was now in place for the War in Europe to be concluded and early on May 7th the Germans' representatives, General Jodl and Field Marshal Keitel, signed the instrument of final unconditional surrender at Eisenhower's headquarters at Rheims in France.

It was agreed that at 23:01 hours Central European Time, on May 8th, all forces under German control would stop fighting.

When Stalin heard the news of the capitulation at Rheims, he was furious that there was no senior Soviet commander at the signing, and insisted that Keitel, Jodl and their entourages fly to Berlin to surrender to a representative of his choice. Consequently, at Karlshorst, just outside Berlin, Keitel was forced to sign a further document of surrender presented by Marshal Zhukov, the Russian responsible for playing such a huge part in the fall of Berlin.

At last the news that the world had been waiting for since 1939 was ready to be announced, and plans were put in place for Victory in Europe Day to be celebrated on May 9th.

However, good news travels fast because by the 8th rumors of the imminent end to the fighting in Europe prompted celebrations in Great Britain, on the streets of London and throughout the nation.

Fueled by the tide of public excitement, at 3pm, Prime Minister Winston Churchill once more broadcast to the British people *"Hostilities will end officially at one minute after midnight to-night, but in the interests of saving lives the 'Cease fire' began yesterday to be sounded all along the front"*.

It was an incredible day, and the euphoria out on the streets was contagious. From nowhere celebratory teas were mustered as entire communities joined together and Winston Churchill went to Buckingham Palace to take his place alongside the Royal Family, who had come out onto the balcony to acknowledge the cheers of the sea of people gathered all around.

Almost five years to the day when Churchill had taken on the challenging role of Prime Minister back in 1940, this moment on the very first VE Day, has been described by many as having been Winston's finest hour.

However, it wasn't only Winston Churchill and the people of Britain celebrating the news of Hitler's demise and the fall of the Nazis. Across the Atlantic the Americans, despite continuing to fight a war of attrition with the Japanese, took time out to enjoy the occasion.

. . .

For Harry S Truman, May 8th and the victory it represented was dedicated to the memory of his predecessor Franklin D. Roosevelt, who had done so much to rid the world of tyranny. Still in mourning for their recently past President, America's flags remained at half-mast, but it was nonetheless a time for looking forward with hope to a new era, and ironically, it also happened to be President Truman's 61st birthday.

But while to this day Britain and America celebrate VE Day on May 8th, the Russians honor the 9th, the date that had originally been set aside by the Allies all those years ago.

For the Soviet people, VE Day is still both a celebration of great joy and intense sorrow. At least twenty million Russian citizens had perished since the 22nd of June 1941; the day that the Nazis had invaded the Soviet Union, laying waste to entire cities, towns and villages, which had been left in ruins, and the terrible losses have never been forgotten.

Across Europe nations were liberated, from the British Channel Islands to the Greek Islands in the Aegean Sea. Dunkirk, St Nazaire and La Rochelle all gained their freedom, as did Norway and Denmark.

Even the strip of territory stretching from the western Netherlands to Czecho-slovakia still under Nazi control was handed back, as German troops capitu-lated to local Allied forces, fleeing west wherever possible to avoid capture by the vengeful Soviets.

The final act in the destruction of Nazi Germany took place on the 23rd of May when British troops arrested Admiral Donitz at his Flensburg headquar-ters near the Danish border.

. . .

From this point onwards the major Allied powers, Great Britain, the United States, the Soviet Union and France ruled supreme over Hitler's now disbanded German Empire, but the question of what next, needed a definitive answer.

Always eloquent, in his VE Day broadcast, Churchill had expressed what the rest of the world was thinking *"We may allow ourselves a brief period of rejoicing but let us not forget for a moment the toil and efforts that lie ahead. Japan in all her treachery and greed remains unsubdued".*

Yet it was Harry S Truman who had the technology within his grasp to force the Japanese to surrender, and after just weeks in office the responsibility for launching a nuclear attack on Japan rested very firmly on the new President's shoulders.

24

BRAVE NEW WORLD

July – September 1945

Churchill V for victory

A s the western world celebrated peace in Europe and the overthrow of Adolf Hitler's regime, the war continued to rage in the Pacific, and there was still no end in sight for the battles of the Far East. For the Japanese, to surrender was a fate worse than death, and driven by ancient traditions they were determined to fight to the very last man.

As allied casualties continued to rise, and the United States prepared for their invasion of the Japanese home islands there were soon grave decisions to be made, and in the final stage of the global conflict steps would be taken to defeat the eastern enemy, which would transform the face of war forever.

This last chapter brings us to the conclusion of a conflict which would prove to be the most destructive in the history of mankind and the events of July to September 1945 would not only mark the end of the Second World War, but the beginning of a brave and dangerous new world.

On July 17th 1945 the leaders of the victorious nations met in Potsdam, just a few miles west of Berlin, to discuss the future of post war Germany.

Among those attending was the British Prime Minister, Winston Churchill whose future in office as I previously mentioned was by now far from assured. Not long after VE day the British wartime coalition had broken up and a general election would soon decide whether Churchill was re-elected as Prime Minister or replaced by the Labor leader Clement Atlee.

The Soviet dictator, Joseph Stalin also attended the Potsdam Conference and was by now reaping the rewards of Germany's defeat as he laid claim to territory in central Europe. And there was also a new face in the political arena; Harry S. Truman. Truman had taken the place of the American President

Franklin D. Roosevelt after his death in April and would prove to be considerably less sympathetic towards the communists than his predecessor.

With political turmoil looming on the horizon these three men had much to contemplate, but despite their differences, they still shared a common goal; to ensure that Germany should never wage war again. With this in mind during the Potsdam Conference it was agreed that Germany should be split into four occupation zones.

What eventually became known as West Germany would be divided between Britain, America and France whereas East Germany would be occupied by the Soviets. The capital Berlin, which was within the Eastern Soviet sector, would also be divided between the allies, with the United States and Great Britain controlling the west and the Russians controlling the East.

The Soviet soldiers had set about occupying Berlin after their victory in May, but by July they were joined by the first American, British and French occupation troops as they moved into the western sectors of the city. Those who observed Berlin in the aftermath of the war were taken aback by the state of the capital where they found much of the population suffering from starvation and attempting to live amongst the rubble of devastated buildings.

Almost all transport in and out of Berlin was now inoperative and adding to the problem of food shortages, bombed-out sewers had contaminated the city's water supplies. The allied aerial attacks of the past few years had clearly taken their toll and combined with the large artillery pounding from the soviets during the Battle of Berlin, up to a third of the city had been destroyed.

In early July Churchill was among those who witnessed the damage to the city firsthand. As he walked through the devastated streets, passing the wrecked government buildings, Churchill was clearly moved by what he saw and later said that his hate for the Germans had died along with their surrender. But despite any sympathy Churchill may have had for the German population, the allied leaders were eager to deal justice to those responsible for the Nazi regime and its crimes.

Hitler's war of aggression had led to an immense loss of life, with over twenty million dead in the Soviet Union alone. Tragically the greater proportion of war casualties in Russia and most European nations had been civilian rather than military, and as the end of the war approached, the allies began to discover the true horror of how so many people had died.

During the advance on Berlin, American and Soviet commanders had discovered concentration camps filled with victims from all over Europe and Russia. In some camps none of the inmates had been left alive and only piles of bodies remained; in others those who had survived the horrors of their internment were severely malnourished and in a desperate state.

It was soon evident, that not thousands, but millions of people had been systematically murdered by the Nazis, including soviet civilians and soldiers, ethnic poles, gypsies and those who had opposed the Nazi regime. Above all, the Nazis had targeted the Jews, and around two thirds of Europe's Jewish population had been killed in what would later be called the holocaust.

As the war crimes mounted, at Potsdam it was decided that an International Military Tribunal on behalf of the American, British, Russian and French governments should be formed. This body would conduct the most famous of all war crime trials at Nuremberg, a town renowned for hosting Nazi rallies and considered the ceremonial birthplace of the party. It was felt that this was a fitting place to mark the Nazi's symbolic demise, and the trial to punish the major war criminals of the European Axis countries would at least see some justice served for the horrors of Hitler's unforgiving regime.

. . .

Among the highest-ranking Nazi officials sentenced at Nuremberg was Hermann Goering, the commander of the Luftwaffe, and second in command to Adolf Hitler. He was sentenced to death for being a leading political and military aggressor in the war and for his role in the extermination of the Jews. But Goering would thwart the Nuremberg judges when he committed suicide the night before his public hanging.

Others to be sentenced at Nuremberg were Rudolph Hess, who had been Hitler's deputy before he was captured in Britain in 1941. Hess was given a life sentence and would remain in Spandau prison, Berlin for the remainder of his days, dying allegedly by suicide August 1987.

Karl Donitz, the initiator of the U-boat campaign, and President of Nazi Germany in the days after Hitler's suicide was given a ten-year sentence; and Wilhelm Keitel the head of the Wehrmacht was sentenced to death by hanging.

Many of the doctors who had performed medical experiments in Nazi concentration camps were also sentenced at Nuremberg. But as justice was dealt out to the Nazis, the allies understood the Second World War was far from over, and although Nazi Germany was now defeated, their allies, the Japanese were still at large.

The so-called Empire of the Rising Sun had begun the war with the west back in December 1941, when they bombed the American Naval base at the now legendary Pearl Harbor and their conquests across South East Asia and the islands of the Pacific had been as every bit as successful as the German advance across Western Europe.

. . .

But as American naval forces recovered their strength, bit by bit the allies had begun to oust the enemy from their conquered terrain.

From New Guinea to the Philippines the Japanese were soon fighting defensive battles and by the summer of 1944 the island-hopping campaign of Admiral Chester Nimitz, Commander in Chief of the US Pacific Fleet, had brought allied forces to the Mariana Islands and closer than ever to Japanese home territory.

Throughout the spring of 1945 the drive towards enemy home territory continued and American Joint chiefs of staff began to discuss the final invasion plans for Japan, code-named *Operation Downfall.*

Japan was an archipelago made up of thousands of mountainous and volcanic islands, which made its invasion a daunting prospect.

Of the four main islands, Honshu, Hokkaido, Kyushu and Shikoku there were few areas suitable for invasion. Only the beaches on the Kanto plain of Honshu, southwest and southeast of Tokyo and the beaches of Kyushu presented suitable attack zones. The allies decided that a two-stage invasion should be launched the first of which code-named *Operation Olympic* would attack southern Kyushu. After building airbases here, cover would then be provided for the next step, *Operation Coronet,* which was the attack on Tokyo Bay on Honshu.

Operation Olympic was scheduled for November 1st, and the combined naval armada would be the largest ever assembled in the history of warfare. Fourteen US divisions were scheduled to take part in the initial landings and once the invasion of Honshu was underway, 25 divisions would be involved.

· · ·

The main concern for the Americans was the potential for huge casualty rates. The Japanese had demonstrated that they were willing to fight to the death if necessary, and there were also fears of biological warfare, which the Japanese had used during their war with China. It was estimated that there could be over a million US casualties during the attack and in April 1945 the extremes to which the Japanese would go to protect their homeland had taken an even more sinister turn.

The heavily fortified island of Okinawa which lay 340 miles from Japan was to be used as a staging post in the invasion of Honshu, and on April 1st British and American ships delivered marine and army divisions to its shores. But as the marines struggled to root out the enemy the allied invasion force was to encounter Japan's most lethal weapon.

The Japanese had turned to the ancient myth of the Kamikaze to save their empire and had set in motion their last great attack: *Operation Chrysanthemum.*

Wave after wave of pilots plunged towards the allied ships and to their deaths. In the next three months 36 allied vessels were sunk, and hundreds more were damaged while the battle to wrestle Okinawa from the enemy continued.

Although the allies finally prevailed and won the bitter struggle, by the time the campaign was over on June 22nd there were more than 50,000 American casualties with at least 12,000 fatalities; even the mission's commander General Buckner had been killed.

In the first six months of 1945 U.S. casualties in the Pacific had exceeded those suffered during the previous three years put together and put allied commanders in no doubt that any attempt at invading the home islands would indeed lead to not thousands but possibly millions of casualties.

. . .

But despite allied convictions that Japanese military and civilians alike would fight to the bitter end to defend their homeland by the summer of 1945 many people in Japan were desperate for peace.

Since February over 60 cities around the country had been bombarded by LeMay's terror attacks and Tokyo was in ruins. The Diet building, where the Japanese government gathered was soon one of the few structures left standing. As the death toll rose, and industries vital to the Japanese war effort were destroyed, the situation in the country became desperate. Millions of people began to flee from the cities and those that stayed faced a dismal existence.

In addition to the bomb attacks General Le May had also launched *Operation Starvation,* in which vital water routes and ports were mined to disrupt enemy shipping. Before long there were desperate fuel and food shortages and while life deteriorated in the home islands, for the first time Japanese civilians began to turn against the military.

Across the country people called for peace, desperate to end the war as the American bombers continued to destroy everything in their path. Changes in Japanese leadership also began to reflect the country's hopes for peace. The war mongering Prime Minister Tojo, who had led Japan into war in 1941, had been forced to resign after the fall of Saipan in the summer of 1944. His replacement Kuniaki Koiso was in office for less than 9 months and after his fall from government in April 1945 Baron Kantaro Suzuki had been elected to govern the country.

Prime Minister Suzuki was a retired admiral and an aged hero of the Russo-Japanese war and unlike the more militant members of the government he did not believe that his country should go down fighting.

. . .

His presence in government was a clear indication that the peace party was prevailing in Japan and by now even the Japanese Emperor Hirohito began to press for concrete plans to end the war, realizing that his empire had no hope of surviving against the American onslaught.

As the conflict in Europe drew to a close in May 1945, the call for peace became more urgent than ever, as the full weight of American forces were now focused on the Pacific. The aim of Prime Minister Suzuki's cabinet was to secure any peace terms short of unconditional surrender and to do this, Suzuki turned to an unlikely ally.

Way back in April 1941, Japan had signed a neutrality pact with Russia and although the Japanese were also bound to Nazi Germany after signing the Tripartite pact, they had made the decision not to join Hitler when he began his war on the Soviets in June 1941.

With the agreement with Russia still standing in 1945 the Japanese cabinet hoped that the soviets could act as mediators for a negotiated surrender with the allies. Suzuki and his officials decided to send Prince Fumimaro Konoe, to Moscow to head the peace delegation. Konoe had tried desperately to prevent Japan from going to war with America in the first place and it was hoped that he could now somehow secure a peaceful future for his country.

However, the Japanese had no idea that Stalin had already made an agreement with the British and Americans concerning the future of Japan.

During the Yalta conference in February 1945, with little consideration of the treaty made with the Japanese four years earlier, the Soviet leader, agreed to participate in the war against Imperial Japan three months after the defeat of Nazi Germany. In return he was promised attractive territorial concessions; including Japanese occupied Manchuria, the Kurile Islands and

Port Arthur in Korea, which were all beneath the Japanese sphere of influence.

It's hardly surprising therefore that when Suzuki's delegates contacted the Soviets to negotiate peace they were met with silence from Moscow, and soon fears began to grow that the soviets could pose as much of a threat as the Americans.

On the day the Potsdam Conference commenced on July 17th US and British warships fired 200,000 tons of shells into the coastal area north east of Tokyo, as the build up to invasion continued. Soon after, the Soviet Union recalled all embassy staff and families from Japan, hinting that they also intended to attack. The future was looking decidedly bleak for the land of the rising sun.

But there was soon another unexpected twist in the tangled intricacies of world politics, as Truman and Churchill became increasingly concerned with what appeared to be aggressive expansionism on the part of the Soviets. By July the Red Army controlled the Baltic states, Poland, Czechoslovakia, Hungary, Bulgaria and Rumania and refugees fearing a communist take-over, were fleeing in their millions.

Contrary to agreements that had been made at Yalta in February, Stalin had also set up a communist government in Poland against the wishes of most Poles.

The Soviet Leader defended his actions insisting his control of Eastern Europe was a defensive measure against possible future attack, but as communist influence grew in Europe, America and Great Britain were beginning to fear that the Japanese were the least of their worries. Truman harbored deep suspicions of the communists, and was anxious that in East Asia as elsewhere, Russia should make as little headway as possible.

.   .   .

As far as the American President was concerned the less the Soviet Union was involved in the last stages of the war, the better, and it was with great relief that he received news that there might be an alternative to Russia's involvement.

This ray of hope was The Manhattan Project, a secret US scheme to develop Albert Einstein's research in nuclear fission. Scientists had been quietly developing Einstein's theories at Chicago University and on July 16th a breakthrough was made. In New Mexico scientists successfully tested the deadliest and most powerful weapon on earth, the atom bomb and with this weapon at their fingertips the Americans realized they could shorten the war and reduce American casualties without the aid of the communists.

| Harry S. Truman signs the order

As Truman began to make all attempts to exclude the Soviet Union as an invading force, the race for Japan was on. At 20th Air Force headquarters in the Marianas, Curtis LeMay and his staff worked around the clock to devise a plan for the use of the new top-secret weapon against the enemy.

The Soviets in the meantime were gathering forces on the border with Manchuria in South East China, in preparation for their agreed invasion of

Japanese territory scheduled for August 8th, exactly three months after the surrender of Nazi Germany.

As tensions mounted back in Potsdam, there were sudden changes in the political arena. Winston Churchill had left the conference on July 25th to hear the outcome of the British election, but he had not been re-elected. Clement Atlee now returned to Germany in his place as the new British Prime Minister, and to join Truman and Stalin in the final decision making of the war.

| German U-Boat surrender in London

Together they made a final plea for Japan to surrender in the Potsdam Declaration on July 26th. Allied terms were that those responsible for the policies that had led to war were to be forever eliminated, the war criminals should be punished, and Japan occupied.

Back in Japan Suzuki still waiting and hoping for a response from the Soviet Union to their pleas for a peace agreement gave a seemingly inscrutable reply, perhaps due in some part to the ambiguities of the Japanese language.

For the Allies this was a final gesture of defiance and on August 6th 1945 the history of warfare was changed forever. Truman ordered the atom bomb to be loaded onto a B-29 plane named after the pilot's mother, Enola Gay.

It took off from the runway on the island of Tinian and set off for its target; an important military center called Hiroshima, with a civilian population of over three hundred thousand.

It was a calm sunny Monday morning and the city was bustling with activity when at 8:15am the bomb was dropped.

The devastation spread over four square miles, killing 30 percent of the population instantly. Humans and buildings alike disintegrated in the explosion and the firestorm that ensued claimed many more lives. All that was left of Hiroshima by the time the smoke had cleared was a wasteland of flattened streets, many of its inhabitants now nothing but literally shadows, burnt into crumbling walls by the blast of white light.

For hours after the attack the Japanese government didn't know what had happened and were only given some indication when a plane was dispatched to survey the city. A huge cloud of smoke was still rising above Hiroshima, but the true horror of the situation was only just beginning. The Japanese soon realized that the death toll was rising as survivors began dying from radiation sickness.

| Hiroshima aftermath

While Japan reeled from the attack, President Truman made the announcement that the "atomic bomb" had been dropped on Hiroshima, and sternly warned if the Japanese *do not now accept our terms they may expect a rain of ruin from the air the like of which has never been seen on Earth*.

Two days after the attack on Hiroshima, the Soviets began to storm across the border into Manchuria on August 8th, ending all hopes the Americans had of keeping the Soviets out of the Pacific theatre. But Tokyo still failed to respond to the call for an unconditional surrender, and on August 9th, Truman carried out his threat by dropping yet another bomb on Japan, this time on the city of Nagasaki.

. . .

As another city crumbled into ruin, the Japanese government and the emperor realized they no longer commanded the fate of their country.

Faced with further nuclear attacks Emperor Hirohito, was forced to put aside any hopes of an honorable end to the war. *"The unendurable must be endured"*, he announced and finally at midday on August 15th 1945, Japan accepted the Potsdam declaration and agreed to unconditional surrender.

One day later President Truman made the speech that the world had been waiting for. When the news of surrender arrived a surge of relief swept across the American forces, who had been battling against Japan for almost four years. The bloodshed was finally at an end and the Pacific War was over.

On August 30th US troops of the 6th marine division landed on a beach south of Tokyo marking the beginning of America's occupation of Japan, and as US command was firmly established the stars and stripes were triumphantly raised over the Japanese homeland. Later that same day the commander of US forces in the South West Pacific Theatre, General Douglas MacArthur flew into Atsugi airfield in Tokyo, and prepared to take control over the conquered Empire.

On the morning of September 2nd, the Japanese delegation boarded the US battleship Missouri in Tokyo Bay to make the unconditional surrender official. MacArthur who was to take on the role of new supreme commander of allied forces in Japan, directed the ceremony which marked the end of the Pacific conflict, and his speech to the onlookers reflected the hopes of millions of people around the world, that finally peace would be restored.

Representing Emperor Hirohito, the Japanese foreign minister, Shigemitsu, formally surrendered for his country, and committed Japan to the complete disarmament and surrender of all military forces; and when all the nations that had taken part in the Pacific battles had signed the document, MacArthur drew the war to a poignant close by saying *"Let us pray that peace be now restored to the world".*

The Second World War officially came to an end at 8 minutes past 9 on September 2nd 1945.

Across the Pacific and South East Asia, the Japanese now laid down their arms. On September 4th imperial forces surrendered on Wake Island, three years and four months after the Americans had been driven from its shores. In Malaya and throughout South East Asia Command, British Commonwealth forces accepted the surrender of the Japanese troops, and soon the Union Jack was flying proudly over the British colonial city of Singapore once more, almost four years after its invasion.

In the Philippines the once known Tiger of Malaya, General Yamashita surrendered the remainder of his army to General Jonathon Wainwright, who had led the battle to defend the island nation back in 1942. The general had been held in prison camps since surrendering to the enemy 40 months earlier, and the moment to deal justice to the man responsible for so many American and Filipino deaths had come not a moment too soon for Wainwright.

Just as the Nuremberg trials had judged those in Nazi Germany, those deemed responsible for the war in the Far East would be punished for their part in the bloodshed. Along with Yamashita, the wartime premiere General Tojo, who had been so eager to lead his country into battle against the west, would be given a harsh judgement and sentenced to death for his crimes.

Meanwhile as all dreams of empire building gradually disappeared, the Japanese would learn to live alongside the Americans as the occupation of their country began. Japan would now evolve into a new nation, where foreigners infiltrated every walk of life, and ancient laws and customs were adapted to suit a very different existence.

Although many years of struggle lay ahead, as the horrors of war slowly started to fade away, Japan like Germany would emerge transformed from the ruins of conflict. The Second World War had raged for six bitter years and claimed millions of lives from Europe to Asia and beyond, but as it ended humanity could finally hope for a better future, as the dawn of a new era in world history was about to begin.

| American troops in Paris celebrate Japanese surrender

Would you please consider leaving a review? Even just a few words would help others decide if the book is right for them.

I've made it super simple: just visit **LiamDale.net/WW2review** and you'll travel to the Amazon review page for this book where you can leave your review.

Best regards and thank you in advance,

Liam

EPILOGUE

Nuremberg Trials

The Nuremberg Trials (named after the location where they were held) was the process by which prosecution of culpable protagonists were held to account for their parts specifically in the atrocities of WW2. The primary target was Herman Goering the highest-ranking Nazi officer captured although a total of 24 participants were accused of participating in war crimes and crimes against humanity as the most significant offenses.

Of the 24, 12 were sentenced to death by hanging. However, the primary guilty offender, Goering committed suicide the day before sentence could be carried out. The last surviving member of the 24 was Rudolf Hess who died by suicide in Spandau Prison in 1987.

Below are some rare photos taken during the trials, including Goering on the stand.

Goering detained

Nuremberg Trials

| Goering on the stand

| Nuremberg Trials

ABOUT THE AUTHOR

Liam Dale is a unique character in the world of books, film and television, who has the ability to write, produce, present and direct at the highest level. Whatever the subject matter, Liam's honest, down to earth, creative journalistic vision brings an extra dimension to any story, making even the most traditionally academic or limited special interest topics accessible to a far wider audience. From Jane Austen to ancient steam trains, ghosts and witches to giant fish species, Liam Dale's style is synonymous with quality entertainment, enlightening, delighting and amusing to equal measure.

OTHER WW2 BOOKS BY LIAM DALE

WORLD WAR II SERIES

D-Day: The Normandy Invasion

America in World War II

Battle of Dunkirk: Operation Dynamo

The Hitler Conspiracies

Wartime Britain

80TH ANNIVERSARY OF WW2 SERIES

The World War II History Journals

1939

1940

1941

1942

1943

1944

1945

Made in United States
North Haven, CT
17 January 2023

31187004R00333